GROWTH, POVERTY AND EQUITY

Story of India's Economic Development

GROWTH, POVERTY AND EQUITY

Story of India's Economic Development

RUDDAR DATT

DEEP & DEEP PUBLICATIONS PVT. LTD.
F-159, Rajouri Garden, New Delhi - 110 027

GROWTH, POVERTY AND EQUITY
Story of India's Economic Development

ISBN 978-81-8450-088-2

Typeset by RAHUL COMPOSERS
358, Pocket-B, Phase-II, Sector-16B, Dwarka, New Delhi - 110 075

Printed in India at MAYUR ENTERPRISES
WZ Plot No. 3, Gujjar Market, Tihar Village, New Delhi - 110 018

Published by DEEP & DEEP PUBLICATIONS PVT. LTD.,
F-159, Rajouri Garden, New Delhi - 110 027 • Phone : 25435369, 25440916
E-mail : ddpubs@gmail.com • ddpbooks@yahoo.co.in
Showroom :
2/13, Ansari Road, Daryaganj, New Delhi - 110 002 • Telefax : 23245122

Contents

PART II

SOCIAL ISSUES

Preface

Long-term objectives or the goals of economic development in India were stated very clearly in the First Five Year Plan as follows: "Maximum production and full employment, the attainment of economic equality or social justice which constitute the accepted objectives of planning under present day conditions are not really so many different ideas but a series of related aims which the country must work for. None of these objectives can be pursued to the exclusion of others, a plan of development must place balanced emphasis on all of these".

India has completed a period of development for nearly 57 years which is a sufficiently long period to attain these objectives substantially. We can broadly classify this period into two broad phases. During the first forty years, India followed the model of state-sponsored industrialization. After 1991, India shifted to the LPG model of development and pushed forth a process of development based on Liberalisation, Privatisation and Globalisation. In other words, it depended on market forces to accelerate growth, employment and poverty reduction.

The motivation for this volume on *Growth, Poverty and Equity* is to make an assessment of the state of development of our economy to fulfil the long-term goals of economic development. In the first phase of our development, it was necessary to overcome the inertia, set-up institutions and develop a pattern of production which should give us a feeling of self-reliance. It was also necessary to promote human development and develop a cadre of technical and managerial personnel so as to manage newly developed industries. By and large, we succeeded in our endeavour. As a consequence, average GDP growth which was around 3.5 percent during 1960-61 to 1980-81 was pushed up further to a level of 5.5 percent during 1980-81 to 1990-91. After the new economic reforms initiated in 1991, the average GDP growth further moved up to 5.8 percent during 1990-91 to 2000-01 and to 7.0 percent during 2000-01 to 2006-07. India was able to push its growth rate to 9 percent in 2005-06 and is likely to achieve 9.2 percent growth in 2006-07. During the 11th Plan (2007 to 2012), we aim at moving to the average growth rate of 9 percent.

India is considered as one of the fastest developing economies of the world and the perception about India is that it is likely to become an economic superpower in the next two decades along with China. This hype about the new trajectory of development forced us to examine whether the development process has been able to make the desired impact on poverty reduction and attainment of full employment.

The purpose of our study is to examine the myth and reality of India as an economic superpower. The study has revealed two very perceptive observations. A normal expectation is that higher rate of growth would accelerate the process of reduction of poverty and also to take us nearer to the goal of full employment. But facts speak otherwise.

Poverty estimates show that percent of population below the poverty line declined from 36 percent in 1993-94 to 27.5 percent in 2004-05. The rate of poverty reduction slowed down to 0.74 percent per annum during the post-reform period (1993-94 to 2004-05) and the total number of poor increased to 300 million in 2004-05, as against 260 million estimated in 1999-00. The point to note is that in a period of higher GDP growth, the rate of decline in poverty was less than observed during 1973-74 and 1986-87, when the average GDP growth was around 5 percent.

A debate has been going on in the country that there is a need to redefine the poverty line on the basis of 'basic needs approach', rather than by merely using the calorie norm of 2,400 calories for the rural areas and 2,100 calories for the urban areas which is only a 'starvation line'. National Commission for Enterprises in the Unorganised Sector in its report submitted in 2007 prepared an estimate and stated that 77 percent of the total population, totaling 836 million were roughly below an expenditure class of Rs. 20 per capita per day. This accords roughly with $2 (purchasing power parity level), used at the international level for estimating people in poverty, using basic needs approach. According to World Development Report (2007), population of India below poverty using $1 per day in 1999-00 was 34.7%, but rises to 79.9% when the criterion of $2 per day was used. It does not usher well for a country aspiring to be an economic superpower to carry the stigma of having 77 percent of its population living in poverty.

For the removal of poverty, it is vitally necessary that unemployment be reduced to the minimum possible extent. Along with this, the quality of employment should improve so that the people are enabled to cross the poverty line. But facts on the ground level reveal that although in the post-reform period, GDP growth has improved, but the rate of unemployment on CDS basis increased from about 6 percent in 1993-94 to 7.32 percent in 1999-00 and further to 8.3 percent in 2004-05. Moreover, the planners have no hope that organised sector would be able to generate more jobs even during the 11th Plan (2007-2012). Obviously, increase in jobs to the extent of 65 million has to come either from an improvement in the growth rate of agriculture or from the enlargement of the job potential of the unorganised sector.

This requires a strategy to step up the growth rate of unorganised sector. This necessitates an improvement in the productivity and job quality of the unorganised sector, as suggested by Special Group headed by Dr. S.P. Gupta, the then member of the Planning Commission in 2002. There is, therefore, a need to study the problems faced by the different constituents of the unorganised sector and suggest remedies to resolve those problems. It is heartening to note that the UPA Government appointed the National Commission for Enterprises in the Unorganised Sector in 2004. Since the Commission has submitted its report in 2007, there is a need to implement the measures suggested by the National Commission so that the unorganised sector is strengthened so as to improve its productivity and job quality and employment generating capacity.

Even Prime Minister Manmohan Singh is skeptic about the direction of reforms. He has raised the question: Are we encouraging crony capitalism? Is this a necessary phase in the development of capitalism in India? The fact of the matter is that the government has failed to provide a level playing field for small and medium enterprises, as against providing a large number of concessions and incentives for the large scale sector. Undue concessions and tax benefits for Special Economic Zones (SEZs) is another glaring example of promoting iniquitous growth. This has created problems of displacement and rehabilitation of owners of land and sharecroppers whose livelihood has been put in jeopardy. Even the so-called Left Government of West Bengal pushed SEZ development in a ruthless manner. The strong backlash by the people supported by the opposition Trinmool Congress and some of the left coalition partners like CPI and Forward Block was witnessed. As a consequence, there was a thaw in the unrelentless push to establish SEZs.

Similarly, opening retail sector to Foreign Direct Investment (FDI) and even to big business in India threatened the employment of 40 million persons in retail. In Uttar Pradesh, there were violent protests against Reliance Fresh. Mayawati Government took a very bold stand to close down Reliance Fresh stores and thus signalled a new policy towards retail sector. This is bound to have repercussions in other states. Even Commerce Minister Kamal Nath who was earlier a strong votary of opening retail to big business and FDI is having second thoughts on this question. But the distressing fact is that the Government, instead of listening to reason and have course correction, only understands the language of violent agitations and protests.

In view of the disillusionment with the reform process to reduce poverty at a rapid pace and promote the rate of growth of employment as the best means to win the confidence of *Aam Admi* (Common man), the levers of policy are now sought to be changed and the Eleventh Plan intends to follow the path of "*Towards faster and more inclusive growth*" as its key objective. A detailed X-ray of the 11th Plan approach has been presented.

Besides, the economic issues, Part-II of the book is concerned with two principal social issues: Sachar Committee Report on economic and educational status of the Muslim Community in India and the issue of Reservations and Social justice. A close perusal of Sachar Committee Report only convinces one that the Report overbends to present the Muslim Community as a weak and oppressed community in India. However, to paint all Muslims belong to weaker sections is as fallacious as assuming all Hindus as more developed. There is no doubt that certain grievances of Muslims towards Urdu language, linking Madarsas to mainstream education, etc. should be immediately addressed. The recommendation of the Sachar Committee to constitute an Equal Opportunities Commission needs urgent attention so that the weaker sections among all socio-religious groups are taken care of. High quality Government schools are needed by the poor in all communities, because the richer classes are able to send their children to unaided high cost private schools, which operate under the pseudo name of public schools. The weaker sections of the Indian society, Hindu, Muslim, Sikh, Jain or Buddhist cry for help and ways and means should be found so that their social status is improved, rather than exclusively budgeting for Muslim community. It is, therefore, essential to sift the grain from the chaff of the Sachar Committee Report. In a secular democracy, the thinking in terms of Muslims, Hindus, Sikhs and Christians should give way to a better approach of thinking as Indians. This is what the national leaders during the struggle for independence and even after independence taught us and practiced. But the unfortunate aspect of the present polity is the rise of regional parties which are main drivers of the ruling party.

The other major social issue discussed is Reservations and Social Justice. The issue has been dealt with in detail. However, it may be stated that reservations based on caste divide society and if the ultimate goal is to develop a casteless and classless society, as suggested by the framers of the Indian Constitution, then it would be more desirable to develop models of justice which take into account gender, caste, class, schooling, region (rural/urban) and not limit reservations only on the basis of OBCs or non-OBCs. There may be political consensus on caste-based reservations due to compulsions of vote-bank politics, but there is no social consensus. From the point of view of social justice, it would be necessary to develop a multi-dimensional model.

It is really surprising that the Supreme Court is raising issues in a more rational manner than the political class in India. For instance, the stand of the Government that the principle of reservations is applicable only to employment and not education, is wholly unwarranted. The Government has now yielded and shown its willingness to exclude the creamy layer to the Supreme Court. The Supreme Court has raised the question. Some castes have gained from reservations for over five decades and can no longer be treated as OBCs. It has asked the Government to provide a list of castes included among OBCs which have been the beneficiary of reservation under OBC quota, and have been excluded from the list. The principle followed by the Government, once an OBC, always and OBC, is basically wrong.

However, there is a caveat. All efforts at building superstructure without strengthening the foundations of school education will not succeed in the long-run. The Supreme Court observed on 27th September 2007: "First give foundation and then apply snowcem. You cannot reach first and second floor without making a ground floor." Moreover, a measure conceived for a period of 10 years in the Constitution has been extended for nearly six decades. It appears that there is a need to fix a time-frame for reservations so that ultimately, reservations have to be brought to an end.

To what extent, we have been able to successfully dwell on the issue of Growth, Poverty and Equity, readers alone will judge. Our purpose is to move towards the attainment of higher goals set out in the Indian Constitution, rather that get bogged down with narrow, short-term interests of political parties.

I must take this opportunity to thank Professor K.D. Gangrade, former Pro-Vice-Chancellor, University of Delhi for carefully going through the various chapters and offering valuable comments.

My thanks are also due to Mr. A.N. Tiwari for constant secretarial assistance.

RUDDAR DATT

Abbreviations

AIIMS	All India Institute of Medical Sciences
ASI	Annual Survey of Industries
ASSOCHAM	Associated Chamber of Commerce and Industry
BPO	Business Process Outsourcing
CDS	Current Daily Status
CEO	Chief Executive Officer
CGF	Credit Guarantee Fund
CII	Confederation of Indian Industry
CPI	Consumer Price Index
CPIAL	Consumer Price Index for Agricultural Labourers
CPIIW	Consumer Price Index for Industrial Workers
CPINM	Consumer Price Index for Non-manual Employees
CSO	Central Statistical Organisation
CW	Casual Worker
CWS	Current Weekly Status
DE	Directory Enterprises
DGET	Director General of Employment and Training
DTA	Domestic Tariff Area
EOC	Equal Opportunity Commission
EOUs	Export Oriented Units
EPZ	Export Processing Zones
FB	Forward Block
FDI	Foreign Direct Investment
FICCI	Federation of Indian Chamber of Commerce and Industry
FTWZ	Free Trade and Warehousing Zone
GAR	Graduate Attainment Rate
GDP	Gross Domestic Product
GNI	Gross National Income

GRO	Grievance Redressal Officer
HCR	Head Count Ratio
HDI	Human Development Index
HRD	Human Resource Development
ICMR	Indian Council of Medical Research
ILO	International Labour Organisation
IMF	International Monetary Fund
IMR	Infant Mortality Rate
IT	Information Technology
LPG Model	Liberalization, Privatization and Globalization Model
MBCs	Most Backward Castes/Classes
MNCs	Multi-national Corporations
MPCE	Monthly Per Capita Expenditure
MRTP	Monopolies and Restrictive Trade Practices
NABARD	National Bank for Agriculture and Rural Development
NAFUS	National Fund for Unorganised Sector
NAS	National Accounts Statistics
NBA	Narbada Bachao Andolan (Save Narbada Movement)
NCAER	National Council of Applied Economic Research
NCEUS	National Commission for Enterprises in the Unorganised Sector
NCRL	National Commission for Rural Labour
NDA	National Democratic Alliance
NDE	Non-directory Enterprises
NFHS	National Family Health Survey
NIN	National Institute for Nutrition
NREGA	National Rural Employment Guarantee Act
NRI	Non-Resident Indian
NSDP	Net State Domestic Product
NSS	National Sample Survey
NSSO	National Sample Survey Organisation
O/L	Output Employment Ratio
OAE	Own Account Enterprises
OBC	Other Backward Caste
PG	Poverty Gap
PGI	Poverty Gap Index
PPP Basis	Purchasing Power Parity Basis
PSEs	Public Sector Enterprises

PSU	Public Sector Undertaking
RBI	Reserve Bank of India
RDA	Regular Daily Allowance
RSP	Revolutionary Socialist Party
RW	Regular Worker
SC	Scheduled Caste
SDI	Skill Development Initiative
SE	Self-employed
SEZ	Special Economic Zone
SHGs	Self-help Groups
SMEs	Small and Medium Enterprises
SNA	System of National Accounts
SPG	Squared Poverty Gap
SRC	Socio-religious Categories
ST	Scheduled Tribe
TFR	Total Fertility Rate
TISS	Tata Institute of Social Sciences
UGC	University Grants Commission
UNDP	United Nations Development Programme
UPA	United Progressive Alliance
UPS	Usual Principal Status
UPSC	Union Public Service Commission
UPSS	Usual Principal and Subsidiary Status
URP	Uniform Recall Period
WPR	Work Participation Rate

PART I

ECONOMIC ISSUES

"We have definitely accepted the democratic process. Why have we accepted it? . . . . Because we think that, in the final analysis, it promotes the growth of human beings and of society; because, as we have said in our Constitution, we attach great value to the individual spirit of man to grow. . . . We do want high standards of living, but not at the cost of man's creative spirit, his creative energy, his spirit of adventure . . . of all those fine things of life which have ennobled man throughout the ages. Democracy is not merely a question of elections."

—*Jawaharlal Nehru*

CHAPTER

1

Democracy, Growth and Equity in India

India, soon after attaining independence in 1947, started the process of planning in 1950-51. A long period of 57 years under the impact of planning has accelerated the process of growth. The strategy of planning can be broadly divided into two periods—A period of 40 years from 1950-51 to 1990-91 in which we were broadly guided by the Nehru-Mahalanobis model of the development of heavy and basic industries along with achieving the goal of socialist pattern of society. The second period started in 1991 with the introduction of New Economic Reforms. This model envisaged a dismantling of the system of controls and licenses, and freed private enterprise to undertake investment. The role of the public sector was sought to be reduced to providing social and economic infrastructure. The number of industries reserved for the public sector were reduced from 17 to 8 and the private sector was assigned a bigger role. The restrictions imposed under the Monopolies and Restrictive Trade Practices (MRTP) Act requiring prior approval for investment were totally removed. Besides this, restrictions on the inflow of foreign investments by multinationals were also eliminated. The watchwords of the policy of reforms were *Liberalization, Privatisation and Globalisation*. This is referred to, in popular parlance as the LPG model of development.

But the basic question is: Did the growth process under New Economic Reforms lead to improving the living conditions of the masses? Or has it helped only the upper classes—the rich and the neo-rich?

World is pursuing the simultaneous achievement of three goals—Democracy, growth and equity. It is, therefore, imperative to study whether India has achieved sufficient success in attaining these goals.

1. GROWTH OF DEMOCRACY

India has developed a vibrant democracy. But for the period 1975-77, when emergency was imposed, India has a regular system of elections to the Parliament and the state legislatures. The democratic tradition has got embedded in the Indian psyche, and people have rejected governments which did not fulfil the aspirations of the people, both at the level of the Centre and the States. This has made the elected representations very cautious in taking decisions. They have to keep in mind the likely reaction of the people to any particular policy. Although sometimes, the party-in-power feels that they would be able to divert the attention of the masses by raising issues of caste, language, conflict between north and south, but people have shown their robust wisdom in judging political parties on the touchstone of people's welfare. This democratic tradition has to be strengthened.

But political democracy is meaningless without economic democracy. It is in this context that the objectives of growth and equity assume importance.

2. ACCELERATING GROWTH

Growth implies an expansion of the production of goods and services by the people. Without increasing production, it is not possible to provide a better standard of living to the people.

A review of the growth of Gross Domestic Product (GDP) would be important in this context.

TABLE 1.1
GDP Growth at 1993-94 Prices

	GDP Growth Rate (at 1993-94 prices)
1960-61 to 1970-71	3.6
1970-71 to 1980-81	3.2
1980-81 to 1990-91	5.5
1990-91 to 2000-01	5.8
2000-01 to 2004-05	6.4

Source : Computed from CSO, *National Accounts Statistics* (2006).

Table 1.1 provides data about GDP growth at 1993-94 prices. During 1960-61 to 1970-71, GDP growth rate was on the average 3.6 percent; it declined to 3.2 percent during 1970-71 to 1980-81, but picked upto 5.5 percent during 1980-81 to 1990-91 and further moved upto 5.8 percent during 1990-91 to 2000-01. During 2000-01 to 2004-05, GDP growth rate averaged 6.4 percent.

The data reveal that even in the pre-reform period, GDP growth rate picked up to 5.5 percent during 1980-81 to 1990-91. After the introduction of the reforms, GDP growth even rose further to 6.4% during 2000-01 to 2004-05. There is a continuous tendency built in the Indian economy to step up growth of GDP.

However, the CSO has discontinued the 1993-94 base year series and replaced it with 1999-00 prices as the base year in the New Series.

On the basis of the New Series (1999-00 prices as base year), the annual average growth GDP during the 5-year period (2000-01 to 2006-07) works out to be 7.0 percent. This indicates that Indian economy has moved up to a new trajectory of GDP growth during 2000-01 to 2005-06. The Eleventh Plan target of average GDP growth to rise to 9 percent per annum, therefore, appears to be feasible. Obviously, credit for high GDP growth rate after 1991 has legitimately to go to economic reforms.

TABLE 1.2

GDP at 1999-2000 Prices

	Rs. Crores	*Growth over the previous year*
1999-2000	86,525	
2000-01	18,64,773	4.4
2001-02	19,72,912	5.8
2002-03	20,47,733	3.8
2003-04	22,22,591	8.5
2004-05*	23,89,660	7.4
2005-06**	26,04,532	9.0
2006-07***	28,44,000	9.2
Annual Average Growth Rate		
2000-01 to 2006-07		7.0

* Provisional ** Quick estimates *** Advance estimates.

Source : Central Statistical Organization and Economic Survey (2006-07).

High Rate of Saving and Investment

Data provided in Table 1.3 indicates that the Indian economy started with a very low rate of savings in the 1950s at 10 percent of GDP and has moved up to 23.2 percent in 1990s. During, 2000-01 to 2004-05, the average rate of saving further went upto 26.3 percent.

TABLE 1.3
Decadal Trends in Saving Rates

	1950s	*1960s*	*1970s*	*1980s*	*1990s*	*2000-01 to 2004-05*	*2004-05*
Gross Domestic Saving	10.0	12.6	17.5	19.4	23.2	26.3	29.1
1. Private Corporate Sector	1.0	1.5	1.6	1.8	3.7	4.2	4.8
2. Public Sector	1.8	2.8	3.7	3.0	1.0	-0.2	2.2
3. Household Sector	7.2	8.4	12.2	14.6	18.5	22.4	22.0

Source : *Reserve Bank of India Bulletin*, May 2007, p. 882.

It may also be noted that the Indian economy has reached a saving rate of 29.1% in 2004-05, which is considered very high by international standards. As a consequence, rate of investment reached a record level of 30.1 percent in 2004-05. The gap between the investment and saving rate is only 1 percent and this measures the inflow of foreign savings. This implies that the dependence of the Indian economy on foreign savings was only marginal. About 96.7 percent of total investment was funded by gross domestic savings.

3. INDIA EMERGES AS AN ECONOMIC SUPERPOWER

During the last decade, a perception is growing in the world that China and India are becoming two major economic superpowers in the world. Consequently, business firms, more especially multi-national corporations, are moving towards India and China so as to take advantage of the prevalent and fast growing market in these two countries. Accompanied with this phenomenon is rise of business tycoons in India. According to *Forbes List 2007*, India added to its list 14 new billionaires taking its total to 36. The combined net worth of these 36 billionaires was of the order of $191 billion—equal to one-fourth of India's GDP. Simultaneously, there is the growth of the Indian middle class which is, according to a study by the National Council of Applied Economic Research (NCAER), around 28.4 million households by 2009-10. The income range of the middle class has been defined as Rs. 2 lakhs to Rs. 10 lakhs per annum. This implies that by 2009-10, about 153 million persons will be covered in the middle class. Along with this, 3.8 million households comprising a population of 20 million are estimated to be rich, i.e. an income level of over Rs. 10 lakhs per annum.

All these developments have created an impression in the world that India is growing as an economic superpower and so the mad rush towards India by big business all over the world.

To understand the situation, it would be worthwhile to examine the Gross National Income on Purchasing Power Parity basis (PPP) of the world's economies with a total GNI (PPP) above $1,000 billion. Table 1.4 provides information for 13 economies which fall in this range. GNI (PPP) has been used since it provides us an idea about the size of the market in the country.

Although GNI (PPP) per capita of India in 2005 was only $ 3,460, but on account of the large size of its population of the order of 1,095 million, GNI (PPP) was of the order of $3,787 billion and thus, India was ranked at No. 4 in the world. USA was ranked at No. 1, followed by China and Japan. But even though India was fourth in the world in total GNI, in terms of per capita GNI, USA was 12 times that of India, Japan 9 times that of India and China 1.9 times that of India.

TABLE 1.4

GNI and Per Capita of Gross National Income of Select Countries in 2005

Country	*Population (Million)*	*GNI*		*GNI PPP*	
		$ Billion	*$ Per Capita*	*$ Billion*	*$ Per Capita*
1. USA	296	12,970	43,740	12,438	41,950
2. China	1,305	2,264	1,740	8,610	6,600
3. Japan	128	4,988	38,980	4,019	31,410
4. India	**1,095**	**793**	**720**	**3,787**	**3,460**
5. Germany	82	2,852	34,580	2,409	29,210
6. UK	60	2,264	37,600	1,968	32,690
7. France	61	2,178	34,810	1,855	30,540
8. Italy	57	1,725	30,010	1,657	28,840
9. Russian Fed.	143	639	4,460	1,523	10,640
10. Spain	43	1,100	25,360	1,120	25,820
11. Korean Republic	48	765	15,830	1,055	21,850
12. Canada	32	1,052	32,600	1,040	32,220
13. Mexico	103	753	7,310	1,034	10,030

Note : Countries have been arranged in the descending order on the basis of GNI (PPP).
Source : World Bank, *World Development Report* (2007).

Table 1.5 reveals that the Indian economy experienced an average annual growth of GDP the order of 6 percent during 1990-2000 and it further improved to 6.9 percent during 2000-05. Along with this, the population growth rate during 2000-05 came down to 1.5 percent per annum.

Obviously, India can be ranked at No. 2 in GDP growth during 1990-2005, only next to China which experienced a growth rate of a little over 10 percent in GDP during 1990-2005. GDP growth in India has been further rising and has been reckoned at 9.2 percent during 2006-07. Consequently,

India can take pride along with China for being reckoned among the fastest growing economies of the world. With population growth rate declining to 1.5% during 2000-05, the per capita GDP growth will also get accelerated and if this trend continues for over the next two decades, the gap between the per capita GDP of India as compared with the high income economies of the world will further narrow down.

TABLE 1.5

Growth Rates of GDP in Selected Economies

Country	*Average Annual GDP Growth*		*Average Annual Population Rate (%)*	
	*1990-2000**	*2000-05*	*1990-05**	*2000-05+*
1. USA	3.5	2.6	1.1	1.0
2. China	10.6	9.6	0.9	0.6
3. Japan	1.1	1.4	0.2	0.2
4. India	**6.0**	**7.0**	**1.7**	**1.5**
5. Germany	1.8	0.7	0.3	0.1
6. UK	2.7	2.4	0.3	0.2
7. France	1.9	1.5	0.5	0.6
8. Italy	1.5	0.6	0.2	-0.1
9. Russian Fed.	-4.7	6.2	-0.2	-0.4
10. Spain	2.7	3.1	0.7	1.4
11. Korean Republic	5.8	4.6	0.8	0.5
12. Canada	3.1	2.5	1.0	1.0
13. Mexico	3.1	1.9	1.4	1.0

Source : *World Bank, *World Development Indicators* (2007).

4. RISE OF BIG BUSINESS TYCOONS IN INDIA

In the sixties and the seventies, there was a big debate in India regarding the growth of monopolies and all this led to the passage of the Monopolies and Restrictive Trade Practices Act (1970). All proposals of new investment or expansion of investment were referred to the MRTP Commission for clearance. But the Industrial Policy of 1991 dismantled all these restrictions and freed big business to undertake heavy investments.

This led to the emergence of a large number of billionaires in India. Forbes (2007) has included 36 billionaires from India with a total networth of $191 billion (Rs. 8,60,000 crores). In the world, according to *Forbes 2007*, there are 946 billionaires, out of which India has a share of 36 (3.8 percent of total). It may be noted that India has surpassed Japan with only 24 billionaires with a networth of $64 billion. Even China had 24 billionaires in 2007.

The new billionaires have amassed wealth from media to computer software, from real estate to liquor. Among them, the prominent names in computer software are Azim Premji of WIPRO, N. Narayana Murthy of INFOSYS, Nandan Nilekani, G. Gopalakrishnan and Shiv Nadar of HCL.

A good number of developers or builders have also found a place in the billionaires list. The notable among them are Kushal Pal Singh of DLF, Ramesh Chandra of Unitech, Grandhi Rao of GMK, Jaiprakash Gaur for JP Associates, Vikas Oberoi for Oberoi Construction and Pradeep Jain of Parsvanath developers.

The Billionaire Club spearheads the corporate sector in India. Out of them, the top 8 account for a total networth of $ 123 billion. This accounts for 64.3 percent of total networth of all the 36 Indian billionaires. This indicates the growth of monopoly capital in India in which top 8 billionaires are in possession of nearly two-third wealth of all the billionaires.

5. GROWTH OF THE INDIAN MIDDLE CLASS

Another development of great significance is the growth of the Indian Middle Class. A common perception was the Indian middle class was of the order of 200-250 million. During the last five decades, Indian middle class has been growing in numbers as a reflection of the process of development. But no attempt was seriously made to estimates its size and economic strength. The existence of a huge middle class had a very strong impact on increasing the demand for consumer durables viz., refrigerators, washing machines, coolers, air conditioners, mopeds, scooters, motor cycles, cars, etc. This prompted the industrialists to make a systematic study of the size of the middle class. National Council of Applied Economic Research (NCAER) made a study entitled "*The Great Indian Middle Class*." Since the middle class has, of course been defined in many ways, mainly cultural, sometimes in terms of education or lifestyles, most of these variables were not quantifiable. NCAER has made an attempt to study the numbers falling in various income categories and then defined the middle class in terms of annual income ranging between a Rs. 2-10 lakhs. Its publication "*The Great Indian Middle Class*" has made the following findings:

1. The Middle Class, defined as households earning Rs. 2-10 lakh annually increased over 15 percent per annum. Between 1995-96 and 2001-02, the total middle class households increased from 4.5 million to 10.7 million—an increase by 138 percent. By 2009-10, They are expected to grow to 28.4 million accounting for a total population of 153 million.
2. At the bottom of the middle class tier is the category defined as 'seekers' who have just moved into the middle class bracket with income Rs. 2-5 lakhs. These people have grown by a little over 15% annually between 1995-96 and 2001-02. This group of nearly 9

million households are the primary buyers of most durable goods and services, such as entry-level cars, colour television and refrigerators. However, their AC penetration is low (13% only).

3. There is the category referred to as 'strivers' numbering 1.7 million households with an annual income Rs. 5-10 lakhs. They have a distinct profile as compared with their lesser cousins. They are growing at the fast rate of 18 percent annually. A large majority of them (50 percent of such households own better quality cars, larger apartments and better quality refrigerators, washing machines and ACs).
4. Rich class with annual income over Rs. 10 lakhs accounted for only 0.8 million households in 2001-02, but is expected to rise to 3.8 million by 2009-10, indicating an annual increase of 21.4 percent. This class buys high class durable goods—such as luxury cars, big bungalows, totally airconditioned residences and offices as well as guzzling soft drinks and costly liquors.
5. As a result of economic prosperity resulting from GDP growth of the order of 6.1 percent per annum and the distribution of income in favour of the middle class and rich households, the demographic pattern is undergoing a rapid change. Since the economy has grown during 2001-02 and 2005-06 at the rate of over 7 percent of GDP per annum, this process is being fuelled further. Consequently, the size of the middle class will rapidly increase from 10.7 million in 2001-02 to 28.4 million households by 2009-10—average growth rate 12.9 percent.
6. The distribution of households among various categories shows that the lowest income class (deprived) is expected to fall from 72% to 52%—a dramatic shift of nearly 20 percent. As against it, the aspirers tend to show a rise from about 6% to 13% during 2001-02 and 2009-10. Obviously, the growth process is fiercely promoting the middle class and the rich.
7. Metropolitan towns like Mumbai and Delhi witnessed a fast growth in the Indian middle class. For instance, the middle class in Delhi grew from 0.26 million in 1995-96 to 1.21 million in 2001-02, i.e. nearly a five times jump in a span of 6 years. There was a boom in small trading centres or B-Class cities like Nagpur, Vadodara, Ahmedabad, Surat and Vijayawada also.

To sum up: It may be mentioned that the growth process is leading to a rapid increase of the Indian middle class, confined more to the cities and metros. In that sense, it does not adequately promote inclusive growth, but it leads to greater concentration of income in the urban areas *vis-a-vis* rural areas.

6. INDIAN MNCS : MERGERS AND ACQUISITIONS

Business confidence among bigger Indian companies has been growing. Several of them have grown so strong that they have acquired several companies in developed countries and acquired the status of Multi-national Corporations. The phenomenon became so powerful that *The Economist* described it as an "Indian invasion." A few mergers and acquisitions which evinced world-wide attention may be mentioned in this connection.

Lakshmi Mittal has become the biggest steel producer in the world through a series of take-overs and has his eye on Arcelor, Europe's largest steel company.

Tata Steel has emerged as the world's fifth largest steel company after acquiring Corus for $12 billion.

Aditya Birla Group of Hindalco has acquired an important place among global aluminum giants, taking over Novelis for $6 billion.

Anil Aggarwal of Vedanta/Sterlite has taken over Konkola, Zambia's biggest coppermine from Anglo American.

Jindal Steel and Power Ltd (JSPL) won a contract to mine Bolivia's huge El Mutun Iron ore deposit, and convert part of it into steel.

Dr. Reddy's Labs and Suzlon Energy are some other important companies which have shelled out over a billion dollars in taking over foreign companies.

Bharat Forge has become the largest producer of forgings in the world after having taken over six plants abroad.

Tata Group has acquired stake in a number of ventures abroad.

Not only that, some of the major targets of Indian companies are:

Hindujas intend to buy Telecom Italia for $ 12 billion, Reliance Industries Limited want to takeover GE Plastics for $10 billion and Scottish Woods Group for $ 4 billion. Appollo has a target of acquiring UK Hospital for $ 2.34 billion. OVL has set its eyes on Sakhalin (Russia) for $ 8 billion.

Recently in May 2005, Vijay Mallaya of UB (United Breweries) Group has acquired 100 percent equity in Whyte and Mackay for £795 million (Rs. 4,783 crores).

Thus, there is the rise of Indian MNCs. They are acquiring high level of confidence to bid major companies over the globe. A number of other bids are emerging. As a consequence of globalization, Indian MNCs are spreading over the globe and sharing economic power in the world. This implies that there is an outflow of Indian capital to various parts of the world.

Thus, the major achievements of post-reform period are:

1. Accelerating the growth of GDP to more than 8% per annum, thus making it possible for the economy to grow at 9-10% in the next 5 to 10 years.

TABLE 1.6
Overseas Forays by the Tata Group

Year	*Tata Company*	*Acquired company*	*Country*	*Stake acquired*	*Consideration*
(1)	*(2)*	*(3)*	*(4)*	*(5)*	*(6)*
February 2000	Tata Tea	Tetly group	UK	100 percent	£ 271 million
March 2004	Tata Motors	Daewoo Commercial	Korea	100 percent	$ 102 million
February 2005	Tata Steel	NatSteel Asia	Singapore	100 percent	$ 468 million
December 2005	Tata Chemicals	Brunner Mond	UK	63 percent	Rs. 798 crores
April 2006	Tata Steel	Millenium Steel	Thailand	67 percent	$ 167 million
June 2006	Tata Coffee	Eight' O Clock Coffee	US	100 percent	$ 220 million
October 2006	Tata Tea	Energy Brands	US	30 percent	$ 677 million

2. The emergence of India as an economic superpower and occupying the 4th place in the world in terms of GDP on Purchasing Power Parity basis.
3. Emergence of big business tycoons in India and according to Forbes (2007), India had 36 billionaires with a total net worth of $ 191 billion (Rs. 8,60,000 crores), surpassing Japan and China.
4. India has a growing middle class (persons in the income range of Rs. 2-10 lakh per annum) which is likely to be of the order of 153 million in 2009-10. The middle class is growing at the rate of 15% per annum, but more confined to the cities and metros. In that sense, it does not adequately promote inclusive growth.
5. The emergence of Indian MNCs has started the process of acquisition and mergers of foreign firms which has attracted world-wide attention.

Looking at all these developments, Prime Minister Manmohan Singh on May 1, 2007 expressing his disappointments with these developments said:

> "I was struck by a comment in the media that most of the billionnaires among India's top business leaders operate in oligopolist markets, and in sectors where the government has conferred special privileges on a few. This sounds like crony capitalism. Are we encouraging crony capitalism? Is this necessary phase in the development of modern capitalism in our country? Are we doing enough to protect consumers and small businesses from the consequences of modern capitalism in our country?"
>
> "We cannot depend on a few large industrial houses and capitalists for driving our industrial process. The employment intensive nature and the greater regional spread of small and medium enterprises makes them an attractive option for our industrial growth process."

7. THE NEGLECT OF THE COMMON MAN

More and more evidence of the growth process in the post-reform period reveals that the benefits of growth accrue to the top 150 million in the Indian society and the remaining 900 million are denied a share in the benefits of growth. It would be appropriate to present pressing evidence in this regard:

I. Slowing Down of Poverty Reduction with Increasing Rate of GDP

NSSO results on the basis of large sample survey data on household consumer expenditure (NSS 61st Round) for 2004-05 are the basis of poverty estimates. They reveal:

Poverty estimates based on URP (Uniform recall period) indicate 28.3% of rural population and 25.7% of the urban population was below the poverty line. For the country as a whole, 27.5% of total population was below the poverty line in 2004-05.

The Planning Commission in its *Approach to the 11th Five Year Plan* (December, 2006) states: "the percentage of population below the poverty line is provisionally estimated at 27.8% in 2004-05. Thus the average decline in percentage of population below the poverty line over the period 1993 to 2004 is 0.74 percentage points per year, much less than implied by the official 1999-2000 data. Because of the slower pace of reduction in the percentage of the poor, the estimated number of poor is now estimated be approximately 300 million in 2004-05, larger than the official estimate of 1999-2000."[1]

It may be recalled that the official estimate for poverty in 1999-2000 was 26.1% for the country as a whole and 260 million were estimated as poor.

"To conclude, the extent of decline in the post-reform period in poverty is not higher compared to the pre-reform period in spite of overall growth. Apart from other factors, an increase in inequality seems to have slowed down the rate of reduction in the post-reform period. . . . However, there are two unambiguous conclusions. One is that there is no evidence of a higher rate of decline in poverty in the post-reform period as a whole compared to the pre-reform period. Secondly, inequality increased significantly in the post-reform period as compared to the earlier decade. Higher inclusive growth that increases agriculture and non-farm growth, and a reduction in regional, rural-urban and social disparities are important for a faster reduction in poverty. Human development is equally important for poverty alleviation. Therefore, policies that increase growth and equity have to be followed simultaneously. . . . There is also a need for focused intervention on the 115 million hard core poor."[2]

2. Increasing Unemployment Despite Sharp Increase of GDP

Economists measure unemployment on Usual Principal Status (UPS) and Current Daily Status (CDS). The UPS expresses open unemployment whereas CDS expresses a more comprehensive measure of unemployment which besides open unemployment includes under-employment. In a developing economy like India, the poor cannot afford to remain unemployed and thus, the option before them is between a low paid job and no job, and they accept a low paid job even if it does not provide continuous regular employment. It implies that under-employment is a more serious and more pervasive problem prevalent in India.

Table 1.7 provides us a picture about the trend of unemployment during the last two decades:

TABLE 1.7

Unemployment Rates : Alternative Measures

	Usual Principal Status (UPS)	*Current Daily Status (CDS)*
Rural		
1983	1.91	7.94
1987-88	3.07	5.25
1993-94	1.80	5.63
1999-2000	1.96	7.21
2004-05	2.50	8.20
Urban		
1983	6.04	9.52
1987-88	6.56	9.36
1993-94	5.21	7.43
1999-2000	5.23	7.65
2004-05	5.30	8.30
All-India		
1983	2.77	8.28
1987-88	3.77	6.09
1993-94	2.56	6.03
1999-2000	2.81	7.32
2004-05	3.06	8.30

Source : Planning Commission (2001), *Report of Task force on Employment Opportunities* and NSS Report No. 515: *Employment and Unemployment Situation in India* (2004-05).

Data provided in Table 1.7 shows that current daily status unemployment rate had declined from 8.28% in 1983 to 6.03% in 1993-94, but rose to 7.32% in 1999-00 and then further increased to 8.3% in 2004-05. This fact has been acknowledged in the Approach to the Eleventh Plan as under: "Average daily status unemployment rate, which had increased from 6.1% in 1993-94 to 7.3% in 1999-00, increased further to 8.3% in 2004-05." (p. 72). It may be noted that Current Daily Status unemployment rates in both the rural and urban areas indicate nearly the same magnitude of CDS unemployment rates, viz., 8.3 percent. Thus the major problem of the Indian economy is not open unemployment but under-employment.

It may also be noted that agricultural employment has increased at less than 1% per annum, slower than the population growth and much slower than the growth in non-agricultural employment. As a consequence, there was a *sharp increase in unemployment from 9.5% in 1993-94 to 15.3% in 2004-05 among agricultural labour households which represent the poorest groups.*

Non-agricultural employment expanded at a high rate of 4.7% during 1999-2005, but the entire increase was in the unorganized sector and mainly in low productivity self-employment.

Declining Wage Share and Real Wages

"According to the Annual Survey of Industries, real wages stagnated or declined even for workers in the organized industry, although managerial and technical staff secured large increase."

"The wage share in our organized industrial sector has halved after the 1980's and *is now among the lowest in the world.* One reason for this is increasing capital intensity of the organized sector, another is outsourcing." (*An Approach to the 11th Five Year Plan,* p. 72.)

The Planning Commission has set the goal of inclusive growth. It notes the fact that despite sharp increase in productivity, real wages of labour have declined. ILO Report on *Labour and Social Trends in Asia and the Pacific (2006)* brings out the hard reality that between 1990 and 2002, there was a decline in real wages in manufacturing in India by 22 percent, despite an increase in manufacturing labour productivity of over 84 percent over the same period. Obviously, this implies that the fruits of economic reform are being pocketed by the corporate sector, while labour is denied its due. Ironically, the salaries of managerial and technical personal have been increasing at the rate of 15% per annum. The Planning Commission's 'inclusive growth' fails to provide any strategy for improving the share of labour in the surplus generated by faster growth. Critics have serious doubts about the sincerity with which the equity objective is sought to be achieved by the 11th Plan. Leaving the determination of wages to market forces and taking away even the modicum of protection by labour laws will give the organized sector business magnates unbridled power to freely exploit and pauperize labour.

Incentivization the Growth of Large Industry, Neglecting Small and Medium Enterprises

The Reform Process has provided all incentives to large industries. On the other hand, it continues the policies of de-reservation of small industries. The 11th Plan has recommended complete de-reservation of SSI products and withdrawal reservation from 326 items which are still reserved. It continues to harp on labour law reform, even after acknowledging that there is no hope from the organized sector to generate additional employment.

8. SEZ POLICY—A BLATANT EXAMPLE OF SUBSIDISING BUSINESS TYCOONS

The Government has recently been emphasizing the expansion of Special Economic Zones, as the new radiators of industrialization and export promotion.

The Government promised to acquire vast tracts of land from farmers and provide it to big industrial magnates and developers. This, by implication, meant taking away the livelihood of not only owners of land, but also those of sharecroppers and tenants.

Not only that, SEZs shall be exempt from a host of taxes and duties like customs duty, excise duty, service tax, value added tax, dividend tax etc.

SEZ would be exempt from the application of labour laws. They will be treated as 'foreign territory' for the purpose so that SEZs can attract entrepreneurs, meaning thereby, big industrial houses to set-up industrial units. Labour Commissioners will have no jurisdiction to inspect SEZs, even to implement safety and environmental norms in these units. All industrial units and other establishments in SEZ shall be declared 'public utility service' in which any strike shall be illegal. This implies that SEZ will not comply with the provisions of the Industrial Disputes Act, 1947. The employers will have the right to "hire and fire" and employ contract labour to any extent.

IMF Chief Economist estimated that the loss of revenue to the public exchequer from exemption of taxes and duties will be of the order of Rs. 1,75,000 crores. The Government has failed to convince the opponents and critics of SEZ that the spread effect on employment will be grater than its back wash effects in Special Economic Zones. Rather, facts stare us in the face that backwash effects in terms of employment are greater than the spread effects. Even judging on the touchstone of exports, SEZ projects in 2004-05 were able to provide exports barely to the tune of Rs. 17,730 crores (4.9% of total exports). The question which the nation has to decide is: Should it promote the SME sector which has much greater employment potential as well as export potential or should it encourage SEZ which has much less employment potential and do not justify on the basis of export potential?

SEZ Policy of the Government was so blatantly anti-people that it led to massive protests against the West Bengal Government. Ultimately, the Left Government had to suffer a retreat. This led to protests against SEZ in other states as well. The Central Government is considering a revision of SEZ policy in terms of size, the question of acquisition of land and compensation, not only for owners of land, but also others allied persons who were to be affected in terms of loss of livelihood.

Moreover, it has raised the question of parity between SEZs and Domestic Tariff Area. This logically inconsistent policy militates against the concept of 'inclusive growth' because it promotes 'exclusive growth' in terms of unbridled profits for a small section of big business, at the cost of millions of workers to suffer unbridled exploitation at their hands. It is a cruel joke on the nation that the trumpeters of competition are promoting a "totally protectionist" policy for promoting the interests of big business and developers.

9. WIDENING GAP BETWEEN THE LIVING CONDITIONS OF RURAL INDIA (BHARAT) AND URBAN INDIA

Census data on living conditions indicates that the rural-urban divide is widening. Regarding housing facilities, whereas urban areas have 79 percent permanent houses, this proportion in contrast is only 41 percent in rural areas. Moreover, temporary houses account for only 5 percent in urban areas, but their proportion is as high as 23 percent in rural areas. Drinking water within the premises was available to only 25 percent of rural population, while the figure of urban areas was 65 percent. In urban areas, 88 percent of households are electrified and only 12 percent use kerosene. In rural areas, only 43.5 percent of households are electrified and 55.6 percent depend on kerosene. Bathroom facility was available to 70 percent of urban households, but merely 23 percent rural households had this facility. Only 26 percent of urban households had no latrine, but as against it, 78 percent rural households did not have a latrine. In rural areas, only 4 percent of households had closed drainage, 30 percent open drainage and 64 percent had no drainage. In urban areas, 19 percent of households did not own any of the specified assets, such as radio, television, telephone, bicycle, scooter/motor cycle/moped, car/jeep/van, but in rural areas this percentage was 41 percent. Census of India (2001) has given a wake-up call to the Government that the development process has strengthened living conditions in urban India to a much greater extent than in rural-India. The situation in some of the poor and backward states in appalling. We should direct the development process to strengthen rural-India and bridge the rural-urban divide.

TABLE 1.8

Living Conditions in India as per Census Data (2001)

	Rural	*Urban*
Permanent Houses	41	79
Temporary Houses	23	5
Drinking water within premises	25	65
Electrified households	43.5	88
Households using kerosene	55.6	12
Bathroom facility	23	70
No latrine	78	26
None of the specified assets	41	19

Source : Compiled from *Census of India* (2001), *Series 1, Tables on Houses,* Household Amenities and Assets.

Dismal Performance with Regard to Reduction in Mal-nutrition

The National Family Health Survey (2005-06) has recorded that the progress regarding reduction of child malnutrition during the 7-year period between 1998-99 and 2005-06 has been very poor.

TABLE 1.9

Progress in Reducing Child Malnutrition

	NFHS-2 (1998-99)	*NFHS-3 (2005-06)*
Children under 3 yeas who are		
(a) Stunted	46	38
(b) Wasted	16	19
(c) Underweight	47	46

Source : *National Health Surveys* (Fact Sheets).

The data presented in Table 1.9 indicates that between 1998-99 and 2005-06, (a) the proportion of children who are stunted (too short for age) marginally declined from 46% to 38% and (b) those who are wasted (too thin for height) increased from 16% to 19%. Similarly, (c) the proportion of underweight children indicated merely 1 percent decline in 7 years and was still high at 46% in 2005-06.

Conclusion

The total picture that emerges after a review of the achievements and failures of the post-reform period is that the planners are able to push forth the growth objective of GDP rising to a level of over 9 percent in 2006-07 and along with it, the level of saving and investment has been raised to 32% and 34% respectively. These are creditable achievements for which the country can legitimately feel proud.

But the irony of the growth process is that it has failed to percolate the benefits of growth down the line among the poor and weaker sections of society, but has lined up the pockets of the better-off sections of society. Consequently, poverty is widerspread and around 300 million persons (27.5% of the population) were living below the poverty line. Out of them, 115 million are chronically poor and represent the hard core of poverty. Evidence also suggests that with a slowdown in poverty reduction, inequality has increased. If we enlarge the definition of poverty on the basis of basic needs approach, as it befits a country emerging as an economic superpower, then 69% of the population are below the poverty line. The present poverty line may be appropriately described as *starvation line*. The level of unemployment on CDS basis was as high as 8.3% in 2004-05. There is gross failure on the agricultural front and the actual average annual growth rate achieved in the 10th Plan was 1.7 percent as against the target of 4 percent. There is no reduction in regional disparities and five poor states account for 55 percent of total poor. The child population suffering form malnutrition was as high as 46% in 2005-06.

The question which the critics raise is: Growth for whom? Is it for *aam admi* (Common man) or for the millionaires and billionaires and the richer classes in general. Effective measures are needed to promote inclusive growth, rather than paying lip sympathy for the poor and downtrodden.

10. NEED FOR COURSE CORRECTION

Simultaneous movement in a positive direction to further the objectives of Democracy, Growth and Equity can be achieved, if there is a commitment on the part of the state and the community to push pro-poor growth, to provide a voice in decision-making to the poor and the Dalits so that they can act as a pressure groups on the Government to act and act decisively.

To ensure equity withy growth, which the Planning Commission now refers to as 'inclusive growth', there is a need to develop a report card of the Government on pursuing GDP growth objective along with the employment objective. After all poverty is just a reflection of either no employment or low level of employment. Simultaneous upward movement on the GDP Growth and Employment Growth should be the watch-word of the New Approach. All policies of the State should be judged by the touchstone of employment generation. This implies the decisions regarding investment priorities, state allocation of funds, etc. should be made after an analysis of the spread and backwash-effects on employment.

In this respect, the advice of Joseph Stiglitz, former Chief Economist of World Bank and Nobel Laureate (2001) is of great relevance: "Success means sustainable, equitable and democratic development that focuses on increasing living standards, not just on measured GDP." There are many examples in the world, when growth of GDP was accompanied by increase in poverty. For instance, in Latin America, from 1981 to 1993, while GDP went up by 25 percent, the proportion of population living on under $ 2.15 a day increased from 26.9% to 29.5%. Obviously, growth was not equitably shared among different sections of the society. Thus, the society seems to be successful in economic growth, but then development has failed: In contrast, East Asian Governments grasped the powerful lesson that success requires social and political stability which in turn depends upon both high levels of employment and limited inequality. To achieve these ends in view, the leaders of the society must have a conviction to move the social system accordingly.

In India, there appears to be a weak commitment to limited inequality along with high levels of employment growth. Prime Minister Manmohan Singh in his 10 point Charter to industry made two significant points: Resist excessive remuneration for promoters and senior executives. Avoid conspicuous consumption since such vulgar display of wasteful expenditure insults the poverty of the less privileged. It plants seeds of resentment in the minds of have-nots. In response to the reaction of the captains of industry, that CEOs remuneration cannot be legislated, the Prime Minister yielded after a couple of days by issuing a clarification that the Government does not intend to bring a legislation in this regard. Similar weakness was shown by the Prime Minister on the issue of excluding the creamy layer form the benefit of reservations in OBC quota. After issuing a statement that in his view, creamy layer should be excluded from the benefit of reservations in admission to higher education institutions, he succumbed to the pressure of alliance partners of RJD and DMK who bulldozed the Government to take a stand that the principle of creamy layer does not apply in education, but was limited to employment. Obviously, the stand was logically inconsistent when put on test of hard logic. The basic quality of the leader to take a principled stand is the hallmark of his commitment to the weaker sections of the society, otherwise people begin to feel that these are mere words. It would have raised his image if the Prime Minister had told industry to heed the advice and not force the Government to take strict measures in this regard. It may be mentioned, CEOs and promoters draw remuneration which is 667 to 3,333 times the salary of the lowest paid employee.

Like its predecessor NDA Government, the UPA Government also flaunts GDP growth rate as the index of its success of 'shining India', forgetting the 'suffering India' of over 900 million.

The country is witnessing a curious phenomenon. The prices of luxuries are falling and the prices of necessaries are sharply rising. This erodes the real purchasing power of the people. Consequently, real wages are indicating a decline. The question arises: Does a fall in real wages in the face of GDP growth rising to over 9 percent indicate movement towards inclusive growth?

In case, the country intends to attain the objectives of development, then it must focus on the people, since development is about transforming the lives of the people by enhancing their capabilities that education brings and thus providing individuals greater freedom to move up higher in the social ladder.

Keeping the social goal of inclusive growth, India should re-examine some of its policies which run counter to its avowed social goal.

Stimulating Agricultural Growth

Indian Government has been fixing the target of agricultural growth during the Ninth and the Tenth Plan at 4 percent per annum, but in practice realized 2.7% in the 9th Plan and only 1.7% in the Tenth Plan. To identify the causes of sluggish growth of agriculture, it appointed a high power Commission under the Chairmanship of Dr. M.S. Swaminathan, World renowned agricultural scientist. The National Commission on Farmers suggested the following 5-point action Plan:

1. Undertake *Soil health enhancement* through integrated measures in improving organic matter and macro-and-micro nutrient.
2. Promote water-harvesting, conservation and equitable use of by-empowering panchayats to become 'pani panchayats.' A sustainable water harvesting system should be established in rain-fed areas lacking assured irrigation.
3. Keeping in view, the decline in profitability and farmer's distress, the Government should reduce the rate of interest on crop loans to 4 percent.
4. Bridge the growing gap between scientific know-how and field-level do-how both in production and post-harvest phase of farming. This could be accomplished by training farmers through the agency of Krishi Vigyan Kendras (Agricultural Science Centers) in both production and post-harvest technologies.
5. The gap between what the rural producer gets and the urban consumer pays should be narrowed down, as has been done in the case of milk by Dr. V. Kurien.

Besides, the National Commission on Farmers placing the unfinished agenda in land reform first in its list of five factors central to the present agrarian crisis states, "The first and foremost task of the National Policy on Farmers should be in the area of land reform with particular reference to tenancy laws, distribution of ceiling surplus land, attention to common property and wasteland resources and consolidation of holdings. . . . Giving access to land and homesteads not only reduces poverty but is the bestway to bring dignity in the lives of today's excluded." (Quoted by the *Approach Paper of the 11th Five Year Plan*, p. 29).

But the greatest irony of the Indian polity is to include land reform as a part of agricultural strategy in every plan, but to conveniently forget it at the time of implementation, since neither the Central Governments nor the State Governments are keen to take up land reform as priority. Even consolidation of holdings programme has been abandoned. Neither there is any progress in the distribution of ceiling surplus land. But for the Left Front Government of West Bengal which implemented 'Operation Barga' in 1977, no other state government has taken up the issue of land reform with the much-needed urgency. West Bengal did benefit in the form of a big boost to agricultural productivity thereafter. With the new wave of economic reforms introduced after 1991, emphasizing liberalization, privatization and globalization, the State Governments have practically abandoned land reform in their agenda of agricultural policy. However, there is a need to pay attention to this issue. But alas! This requires strong political will which is conspicuous by its absence.

SEZ Policy for Future Industrialization should be Suitably Modified

Recently, the Government introduced the policy of creating *Special*

Economic Zones (SEZs) as the harbingers of future industrialization. In its over-enthusiasm, the Government announced that SEZs will be entitled to exemptions form all taxes, such as corporation tax, custom duties, service tax, value added tax, etc. Besides, they will be considered foreign territory for application of labour laws. The Government would acquire land for the SEZ projects and would transfer it industrial houses and developers. SEZ policy came under fire in West Bengal on the acquisition of land in Singur and Nandigram. People's resistance was so strong that the Government had to put this policy on hold. Even within the left front, CPI and Forward Block were opposed to this policy which aimed to put more profits in the pockets of industrial magnates and developers and take away the livelihood of owners and tenant-cultivators of land.

The Standing Committee of the Parliament has finalized its Report which will be tabled in the Parliament. The main recommendations of the Committee are:

1. No new special economic zones shall be approved till the existing SEZ Act and Rules are amended.
2. All projects should be set-up on waste and barren lands. The standing committee has also recommended a 5,000 hectare ceiling for multi-product units proposed on barren lands. The ceiling is 2000 hectares for a unit proposed on partly cultivable land.
3. Processing area should not be less than 50 percent of total area. It was initially 25 percent and then increased to 35 percent.
4. Land Acquisition Act should be changed.
5. Land should be given on lease.
6. One member of each displaced family should be given a job.
7. Current fiscal incentives, tax holidays given to SEZ should be reviewed.
8. Yardsticks should be laid down to evaluate the performance of a developer.

An effort has been made in the Report to reconcile the interests of all stakeholders.

There is a need to provide fiscal incentives only if the SEZ is located in a backward area. There is no justification for providing exemptions for taxes and duties, if SEZ units are set- up around the Metropoles or big cities where infrastructure is already developed. Besides this, every proposal should indicate the likely employment generation on the completion of a SEZ. This should be compared with loss of employment and displacement for the residents in rural areas.

Promoting the Growth of Small and Medium Enterprises (SMEs)

The large industries and those proposed under SEZ are capital-intensive and they will not generate enough jobs for our rapidly growing labour force. Prime Minister Manmohan Singh conceded this when he stated: "We cannot depend on a few large industrial houses and capitalists for driving our industrial process. The employment intensive nature and the greater regional spread of small and medium enterprises makes them an attractive option for our industrial growth process."

The Reform Process has been emphasizing investment by large industrial houses, but as facts reveal, there is no possibility that large enterprises will provide the much needed growth of employment. Thus, if the country has to simultaneously aim at higher GDP growth and more employment to absorb 65 million person who are expected to enter the labour force during the next 5 years (2007-08 and 2011-12), the country has no option but to strengthen and expand small and medium enterprises. The availability of credit for these enterprises has to be enlarged. The government should make credit at relatively low rates of interest so that credit does not result in a heavy burden pushing up the cost of production of SMEs. Besides this, assistance has to be given to improve the technology of these enterprises so that the productivity of labour improves. Government may design incentives linked with expansion of employment, rather than linking them to production only. A fast growing SME sector can contribute significantly to both production and employment. The country should shift the gears of policy so that SMEs are promoted in a mission mode.

Housing for the Poor and Weaker Sections

Housing is a labour intensive activity. There is a need to remove the shortage of permanent houses both in the rural and urban areas. Not only that, an effort has to be made that basic amenities of life such as drinking water, toilets and electricity are also provided. The country has to launch a massive programme to provide housing and basic civic amenities.

The situation in rural areas is much worse than in urban areas. There is a need to help the poor in the provision of shelter. The government should, therefore, take up the provision of housing and target that in a period of 10 years, the country will fulfil the goal of "Housing for all." This also generates massive employment and thus raise the income of the poor who will be drawn to build houses.

Changing the Principles of Allocating Funds for Education

At present, the system of grants for education provides higher per student assistance in metropoles and cities, while schools in rural areas languish. There is a need to reverse the system of grants so that schools in rural and remote areas are provided more funds. Strengthening infrastructure of these schools will make them more attractive. It is really very disappointing that rural schools do not have separate class rooms for each class. There are no separate toilets for girls. Many schools are single teacher or two teacher schools. It is high time that attention is devoted to strengthening the physical infrastructure of the schools as well as the human infrastructure in the form of adequate number of teachers. This alone shall help to reduce dropout rates among the poor. Moreover, it can also significantly enlarge employment.

Improving Skills to Meet the Demands of our Expanding Knowledge Economy

In view of the increasing use of computers and Information Technology in all walks of life, the demand for skilled labour is on the increase. Since this requires greater access to higher education and vocational training, only those who can afford costly education and vocational training, are able to benefit from the expanding opportunities of employment. Consequently, the poor are being priced out because they cannot afford expensive higher education and vocational training. Thus, the state should:

(a) Provide subsidized higher education and vocational training for the poor; and
(b) Institute a large number of merit-*cum*-means scholarships for the poor.

Such measures, if taken on an emergency basis as a national priority, can help the poor to rise in life.

Improving Health Facilities

There is wide-spread malnutrition among the poor, more especially children and women. The proportion of anaemic children the age group 6-35 months was 79.2 percent in 2005-06 and this proportion among ever-married women in the age group 15-49 years was 56.2 percent. Anaemia is the result of poor diet among poor and lower middle class families. The question, basically is to make a frontal attack on poverty. Besides this, there is a need for strengthening programmes for the care of children like ICDS and also for lactating mothers.

To sum up: Development process in India if it has to promote growth with equity, must look at the simultaneous growth of GDP and employment. This requires strengthening agricultural growth which has languished during the last decade, because agriculture still accounts for the livelihood of 58 percent of the population. There is a need to strengthen industry so that a significant proportion of population dependent on agriculture is transferred to industry for livelihood. However, the scope of large industry to generate employment is extremely limited, because, by its very nature, large industry is capital intensive. Thus, in order to provide livelihood to the migrants from rural areas, it would be vitally necessary to strengthen the growth of small and medium enterprises which are labour intensive.

To take advantage of the growing employment potential of the service sector, more especially, in the newly emerging areas, it is necessary to strengthen higher education and skill formation. The poor can benefit only if the base of elementary education is strengthened so that more and more poor children move up to higher education and vocational training. Besides this, it would be necessary to provide free and/or low fee level higher education to enable the poor to take advantage of the growing opportunities.

India has been carrying forward the process of industrialization since the Second Five Year Plan started in 1956. Big industrial units were set-up in steel, fertilizers, ship building, aircraft manufacture and several other basic and heavy industries related to infrastructure, and large tracts of land were acquired. But Government had established a relation of trust, and thus, the process moved on smoothly, because it was motivated by 'public purpose'. Moreover, for industrial units to be established in backward areas, Government provided incentives and tax concessions. Consequently, there was enthusiasm about the industrialization of the country. Private sector also got strengthened to set-up units, once basic infrastructure was made available.

The present Government has failed to create a sense of enthusiasm among the people about SEZs as the major vehicles of industrialization. Rather they are seen as promoting 'crony capitalism' in the country, as symbols of generating inequalities and totally inclined towards MNCs and Big Business Houses to earn huge profits. There is, therefore, a need for course correction. SEZs alone cannot be the answer for rapid growth. They can only be supplements in the process of growth. If this view is acceptable, there is a need to bring about a balance between SEZ and non-SEZ units and thus, rationalization of incentives and tax concessions has to be undertaken, rather than tilting the balance in favour of SEZ units. The basic difference between China and India is that whereas China operates under a single party rule, India has a vibrant multi-party democracy. In this political structure, the Government cannot ignore the perceptions of the people towards 'welfare' and 'public purpose'. Consequently, it would be prudent to develop a unique SEZ model within the socio-political framework of the country, rather than blindly imitating China.

References

1. Planning Commission, *Towards Faster and more Inclusive Growth, An Approach to the 11th Five Year Plan,* December 2006, p. 71.
2. Mahendra, Dev S. and Ravi (2007), Poverty and Inequality: All-India and States, 1983-2005, *Economic and Political Weekly,* February 10, 2007, pp. 519-20.

CHAPTER

2

Poverty, Employment and Growth

I. INTRODUCTION

Dr. Manmohan Singh, the Prime Minister of India, in his first broadcast to the nation on June 24, 2004 stated: "Growth is not an end in itself. It is a means to generate employment, banish poverty, hunger and homelessness and improve the standard of living of our people. It must also be environmentally sustainable."

"Equity and efficiency are complementary, not contradictory and we must move forward on both these while maintaining a high degree of fiscal and financial discipline and a robust external economic profile."[1]

Dr. Singh in a very succinct manner has summarised the findings of the research scholars on the theme of growth, poverty and employment and has also indicated the strategies that need to be developed to promote equity and efficiency, as complementary factors in the growth process.

Basically, two school of thought emerged in this context—One led by the economists of the World Bank-IMF who emphasized economic reforms and their primary instruments were liberalisation, privatisation and globalisation which could raise the rate of growth of GDP, and unemployment and poverty removal were treated as the corollaries of the growth process. [Ahluwalia, M.S. (2001); Bhagwati, Jagdish (1993); Srinivasan, T.N. (2000)].

On the other hand, quite a large number of eminent economists have been arguing that growth *per se* is not likely to result in a pro-poor growth to take care of the employment and poverty problem, but the content of growth with emphasis on policies which help the poor to become a part of the development process, rather than a residuary beneficiary was emphasized. A galaxy of economists have hammered through their research that there is a need to emphasize agricultural growth, development of rural infrastructure as also urban infrastructure, the boost required for the unorganised sector *vis-a-vis* the organised sector, to create and orient institutions of credit to help the deprived sections, as also to grant them ownership or tenancy rights on land, mines, fisheries and forests so that the poor, the tribals, the scheduled castes/scheduled tribes and other backward castes join the mainstream. Research was also focussed on rural *versus* urban growth and poverty and the need to understand the contradictions and complementarities of these two major sectors of the economy [S.P. Gupta (2000), Sheila Bhalla (1997), Eitenne Gilbert (1992), Mahendra Dev, S. (1997), Gaurav Datt and Martin Ravallion (1997, 1999, 2002), Radhakrishna, R. (2002), Sen, Abhijeet (1992), Bardhan, Pranab (1987), Krishnan, T.N. (1992)]. The Planning Commission has also contributed to this debate and the Ninth and Tenth Plan are specifically important in this respect.

2. PROFILE OF POVERTY

Ninth Plan besides giving the 'head-count' ratio as a measure of poverty also used the concept of 'poverty gap' (PG) developed by the World Bank to capture the depth of poverty. Poverty Gap, as a measure, "adjusts the poverty ratio with difference between the per capita consumption of the poor and the poverty line expressed as a percentage of poverty line . . . A more comprehensive measure of the severity of poverty is the squared poverty gap (SPG). The SPG is composed of not only the poverty ratio and poverty gap ratio, but it also captures the consumption distribution of the poor as measured by the co-efficient of variation."[2] On this basis, the Ninth Plan measured the intensity of poverty during the 20-year period (1973-74 to 1993-94).

Commenting on the rate of decline, the Ninth Plan observes: "It will be seen (Refer Table 2.1) that the annual average rate of decline of the poverty ratio during the period 1973-74 to 1993-94 has been 2.05 per cent both in rural and urban areas, and 2.09 per cent for the country as a whole. The poverty gap ratio during this period declined by 3.31 per cent per year in rural areas, 2.71 per cent per year in urban areas and 3.2 per cent per year for the country as a whole. The SPG declined even faster by 4.38 per cent, 3.07 per cent and 4.13 per cent in rural, urban and the country respectively."[3] From this, the Ninth Plan draws an optimistic policy conclusion: "The fact that the more distribution-sensitive measures of poverty have declined progressively faster during the last 20 years is a cause for optimism. It implies that the depth and severity of poverty has reduced faster than the incidence, and that over time, there has been a trend towards a greater degree of clustering of the poor around the poverty line leading to a situation where economic growth is likely to have a considerably larger impact on poverty reduction than before."[4]

TABLE 2.1
Incidence of Poverty

Year	Poverty Ratio			Poverty Gap Index			Squared Poverty Gap		
	Rural	Urban	Total	Rural	Urban	Total	Rural	Urban	Total
(1)	(2)	(3)	(4)	(5)	(6)	(7)	(8)	(9)	(10)
1973-74	56.4	49.0	54.9	16.56	13.64	15.95	6.81	5.26	6.48
1997-78	53.1	45.2	51.3	15.73	13.13	15.15	6.48	5.25	6.21
1983-84	45.7	40.8	44.5	12.32	10.67	11.96	4.78	4.07	4.61
1987-88	39.1	38.2	38.9	9.11	9.94	9.32	3.15	3.60	3.26
1993-94	37.3	32.4	36.0	8.45	7.88	8.30	2.78	2.82	2.79
Annual Average Decline	2.05	2.05	2.09	3.31	2.77	3.21	4.38	3.07	4.13

Source : Planning Commission (1998), *Ninth Five Year Plan (1997-2002)*, Vol. I, p. 30

However, Gaurav Datt[5] of the World Bank in his profile of poverty from 1973-74 to July 95-December 97, has shown that Head-count index of poverty for the rural areas declined from 55.72 per cent in 1973-74 to 35.37 per cent in June 1991—the pre-reform period, but in the post-reform period, it rather increased to 36.47 per cent during July 95-December 97. In the urban areas, it declined from 47.96 per cent in 1973-74 to 33.08 per cent in June 91—the pre-reform period and further registered a decline to 29.02 per cent in December 97. He has also studied the depth of poverty. The main conclusions of the study are:

1. While there is a marked declined in both rural and urban poverty rates between 1993-74 and 1986-87, there is no sign of anything comparable thereafter.
2. For the rural sector, for the period 1973-74 and 1990-91, head-count index of poverty declined at the annual rate of 2.7 per cent, the rate of decline since then (i.e. in the post-reform period), is not significantly different from zero.
3. For the urban sector, during 1973-74 and 1990-91, head-count index of poverty declined at the annual average rate of 2.2 per cent, the same trend is continued in the post-reform period (1990-91 to 1996-97) at the annual average rate of 2.2 per cent.
4. While the urban sector seems to have continued its march of poverty reduction in the process of growth, rural poverty reduction was choked off by lack of rural growth. (Refer Table 2.2)

Gaurav Datt has identified stagnation in rural growth as the principal cause for slow-down in the reduction of poverty. This certainly puts a question mark on the direction of reform process in emphasizing only the corporate sector as the engine of growth. The relatively lower importance given to agriculture and agro-based industries located in rural areas provides an explanation for the lack-lustre performance in poverty reduction in post-reform period.

NSSO 55th Round and Poverty Reduction Controversy

NSSO on the basis of its 55th Round which has a large sample covering the period July 1999 to June 2000, estimated a significant decline in poverty to 26.1 per cent based on 30 day recall and 23.3 per cent on 7 day recall methodology. This has made comparison with earlier estimates not possible. Moreover, economists have questioned the use of methodology by the NSSO.

Abhijit Sen criticizing the NSSO writes, "Moreover, the limited results now available from the 55th round show clearly that the answers to both one week and 30 day questions have been contaminated by the presence of the other. Quite possibly, exclusive reliance on the 365 day question in the case of clothing, etc. has also altered responses. As a result, consumption

TABLE 2.2

Poverty in India, 1973-97

NSS Round	Survey Period	Head-count Index		Poverty Gap Index		Squared Poverty Gap Index	
		Rural	Urban	Rural	Urban	Rural	Urban
(1)	(2)	(3)	(4)	(5)	(6)	(7)	(8)
28	Oct. 1973-Jun. 1974	55.72	47.96	17.175	13.602	7.128	5.219
32	Jul. 1977-Jun. 1978	50.60	40.50	15.025	11.687	6.057	4.526
38	Jan. 1983-Dec. 1983	45.31	35.65	12.549	9.517	4.841	3.557
42	Jul. 1986-Jun. 1987	38.81	34.29	10.013	9.100	3.700	3.395
43	Jul. 1987-Jun. 1988	39.23	36.20	9.275	9.121	2.982	3.056
44	Jul. 1988-Jun. 1989	39.06	36.60	9.504	9.537	3.291	3.293
45	Jul. 1989-Jun. 1990	34.30	33.40	7.799	8.505	2.575	3.038
46	Jul. 1990-Jun. 1991	36.43	32.76	8.644	8.509	2.926	3.121
Pre-reform	Jul. 1989-Jun. 1991	35.37	33.08	8.222	8.507	2.751	3.080
47	Jul. 1991-Dec. 1991	37.42	33.23	8.288	8.244	2.680	2.902
48	Jan. 1992-Dec. 1992	43.47	33.73	10.881	8.824	3.810	3.191
50	Jul. 1993-Jun. 1994	36.66	30.51	8.387	7.405	2.792	2.417
51	Jul. 1994-Jun. 1995	41.02	33.50	9.285	8.382	2.995	2.799
52	Jul. 1995-Jun. 1996	37.15	28.04	8.098	6.781	2.527	2.222
53	Jan. 1997-Dec. 1997	35.78	29.99	8.312	7.762	2.757	2.725
Post-reform	Jul. 1995-Dec. 1997	36.47	29.02	8.205	7.273	2.642	2.474

Source : Gaurav Datt, "Has Poverty Declined since Economic Reforms"? *Economic and Political Weekly*, December 11-17, 1999.

estimates from this round are not comparable to those from previous NSS rounds, and will probably be virtually useless for any assessment of changes in consumer demand."[6]

However, Pravin Visaria, the then Chairman of NSSO Governing Council prefers 'one week recall', although he agrees that this shall make these estimates not comparable with the earlier estimates. He opines: "Overstatement of the level of poverty has thus quite likely been a consequence of a long reference period for the collection of data on food consumption by our people."[7]

Abhijit Sen has gone so far as to demand that in order to maintain the integrity of the India's Statistical System, it would be necessary to conduct another large Consumer Expenditure Survey using 30-day recall as early as possible. This would restore the credibility and dignity of the NSSO.

The Government, however, did not agree to conduct another Consumer Expenditure Survey, but quietly adopted the results of the 30-day recall for its official use. The Tenth Plan, therefore, used the findings of the 55th Round of NSS for future planning on poverty reduction.

TABLE 2.3
Percentage of Population below Poverty Line—All-India

	Rural	*Urban*	*Combined*
1993-94	37.7	32.4	36.4
1999-2000	27.1	23.6	26.1
Annual Average Decline	-5.1	-5.1	-5.3

Source : Compiled and computed from Planning Commission, *Tenth Five Year Plan (2002-07)*, Vol. III, pp. 40-42.

From the data provided in the Tenth Plan, it could be inferred that there was a sharp decline in poverty during 1993-94 and 1999-2000 from 36.4 per cent in 1993-94 to 26.1 per cent in 1999-00. Average annual decline was of the order of 5.3 per cent for the country as a whole and 5.1 per cent in rural as well urban areas.

While most of the research studies for the decade of the nineties led to a general consensus that rural poverty at the all-India level did not show any perceptible declining trend, the results of NSS 55th round suddenly indicate a sharp reduction even in rural poverty from 37.3 per cent in 1993-94 to 27.1 per cent in 1999-2000 on the basis of 30-day recall period. Ironically, the reduction in rural poverty is greater than the reduction in urban poverty—a finding which is not in conformity with the research findings of the economists for the same period [Datt (1999), S.P. Gupta (2000)].

3. PROFILE OF EMPLOYMENT AND UNEMPLOYMENT

Economic liberalisation was introduced with a gusto in 1991 and the main argument given was that the regime of controls and licences has put fetters on the development process. Unless controls and licences regime is dismantled, the economy would not be able to expand. Investment was stifled, the regime had resulted in the growth of corruption and established a nexus between the politicians and the bureaucrats, which was acting as a shackle on the growth process. It was hoped that once the economy is freed from the regime of controls, quotas and licences, it shall result in a much higher growth rate of GDP and a significant expansion of employment. Economic liberalisation was hailed as a panacea in the same manner as socialism was considered to be the only method of achieving growth with social justice during the first four decades of development.

It would be of interest to understand as to what happened to the process of employment growth in the post-liberalisation period. Although the reform process resulted in an acceleration of GDP growth, it was not accompanied by a commensurate increase in employment. As facts stand today, public sector employment was halted because the public sector began to withdraw from several areas. Moreover, in its effort to shed extra fat, the public sector units started the process of downsizing by getting rid of redundant labour. It was expected that since organised private sector was expected to be the torchbearer of economic reforms, employment in the organised private sector would grow at a much faster rate. But this did not happen even in the private sector. Faced with the process of internal liberalisation and of globalisation, even in the private sector, industrial units started shedding excess labour and to compete with foreign players, new technology was increasingly introduced resulting in loss of jobs. Thus, the growth rate of employment in the economy, which was of the order of 2.0 per cent per year during the 10-year period 1983 to 1993-94 as per NSS data, sharply declined to less than 1 per cent in the period 1993-94 to 1999-2000. As a result, the critics of economic reforms described the process of economic liberalisation as that of 'jobless growth'.

It would be, therefore, appropriate to review the dimensions of the problem of unemployment and employment during the last two decades.

Changing Dimensions of Unemployment and Employment

From data provided in Table 2.4, certain disturbing trends in the unemployment rates become evident in the post-reform period. Although the reforms were introduced in 1991, yet the year 1991-92 was particularly a depressed year and the reform process really got a going by 1993-94. Thus, 1993-94 to 1999-2000—the 6-year period can be considered as the period of liberalisation. It may be noted that all the four categories of unemployment showed a declining trend during the period 1977-78 to 1993-94, but the trend got reversed during 1993-94 and 1999-2000. Open employment as measured by UPS criterion declined from 4.23 per cent in 1977-78 to 2.56 per cent in 1993-94, but indicated an increase to 2.81 per cent in 1999-2000.

TABLE 2.4
Unemployment Rates: Alternative Measures

(Percentage of Labour Force)

	Usual Principal Status (UPS)	*Usual Principal and Subsidiary Status (UPSS)*	*Current Weekly status (CWS)*	*Current Daily Status (CDS)*
(1)	*(2)*	*(3)*	*(4)*	*(5)*
Rural				
1977-78	3.26	1.54	3.74	7.70
1983	1.91	1.13	3.88	7.94
1987-88	3.07	1.98	4.19	5.25
1993-94	1.80	1.20	3.00	5.63
1999-2000	1.96	1.43	3.91	7.21
Urban				
1977-78	8.77	7.01	7.86	10.34
1983	6.04	5.02	6.81	9.52
1987-88	6.56	5.32	7.12	9.36
1993-94	5.21	4.52	5.83	7.43
1999-2000	5.23	4.63	5.89	7.65
All-India				
1977-78	4.23	2.47	4.48	8.18
1983	2.77	1.90	4.51	8.28
1987-88	3.77	2.62	4.80	6.09
1993-94	2.56	1.90	3.63	6.03
1999-2000	2.81	2.23	4.41	7.32

Note : These estimates are based on NSS data combined with Census data.
Source : Planning Commission, *(2001) Report of Task Force on Employment Opportunities*, Table 2.1.

The current weekly status (CWS) unemployment rate which was 4.48 per cent in 1977-78 declined to 3.63 per cent in 1993-94, but rose to 4.41 per cent in 1999-2000.

Even the most comprehensive measure of unemployment, viz., current daily status (CDS) unemployment rate declined from 8.18 per cent in 1977-78 to 6.03 per cent in 1993-94, but the declining trend reversed to 7.32 per cent in 1999-2000.

The same situation can be observed with respect to both urban and rural areas. However, it may be noted that whereas CDS rate for urban areas increased very slightly from 7.43 per cent in 1993-94 to 7.65 per cent in 1999-

2000, this very rate increased much faster from 5.63 per cent in 1993-94 in the rural areas to 7.21 per cent in 1999-00. The same phenomenon could be observed in all the four measures of unemployment both in the rural and the urban areas. This underlines the relative neglect of the rural economy in the first phase of economic reforms.

Usual Principal Status (UPS) measures open unemployment throughout the year, but current daily status (CDS) besides taking into account open unemployment also measures under-employment. From the data given in Table 2.4, it becomes obvious that whereas the UPS rates are modest, the CDS rates are quite high. In other words, *the major problem of the Indian economy is not open unemployment but under-employment.*

Growth Rates of Employment

The growth rates of employment and labour force derived from NSS data are given in Table 2.5. From this data, the following points emerge:

1. The growth rate of employment declined sharply from 2.04% per annum during the 10-year period 1983 to 1993-94 to barely 0.98 per annum during the period 1993-94 to 1999-2000. The Task Force on Employment Opportunities admitting deceleration in employment growth mentions: "This sharp deceleration in the growth of employment has naturally been the focus of much attention and comment, raising fears that economic growth in 1990s has been of a 'jobless' variety."[8] This implies that the growth rate in employment is less than the growth rate in labour force and this has resulted in an increase in the unemployment rate.
2. In agriculture, the growth rate of employment observed during 1983 to 1993-94 was 1.51 per cent, but during the period of liberalisation, the growth rate of employment became negative (–0.34 per cent) during 1993-94 and 1999-2000.
3. In the manufacturing sector, employment growth rate was 2.14 per cent during 1983 to 1993-94, but declined marginally to 2.05 per cent during 1993-94 to 1999-2000.
4. Construction sector witnessed an employment growth of 5.32 per cent during 1983 to 1993-94, and this growth rate further increased to 7.09 per cent during 1999-2000.
5. In trade, employment growth rate was of the order of 3.57 per cent during 1983 and 1993-94 and it improved further to 5.04 per cent during 1993-94 to 1999-2000.
6. In transport, storage and communications, employment growth rate increased sharply from 3.24 per cent during 1983 to 1993-94 to 6.04 per cent during 1993-94 and 1999-2000.
7. Financial services witnessed a marginal decline in growth rate from 7.18 per cent during 1983 to 1993-94 to 6.20 per cent during 1993-94 and 1999-2000, though the growth rate was sufficiently high.

TABLE 2.5
Growth of Employment by Sectors

Industry	*Employed workers (million)*			*Annual growth rate (%)*	
	1983	*1993-94*	*1999-2000*	*1983-94*	*1994-2000*
Primary	**208.99 (69.0)**	**245.16 (65.5)**	**239.83 (60.4)**	**1.6**	**-0.34**
1. Agriculture	207.23 (68.4)	242.46 (64.8)	237.56 (59.8)	1.51	-0.34
2. Mining and Quarrying	1.76 (0.6)	2.7 (0.7)	2.27 (0.6)	4.16	-2.85
Secondary	**41.66 (13.8)**	**55.53 (14.8)**	**66.91 (16.8)**	**2.9**	**3.14**
3. Manufacturing	34.03 (11.2)	42.5 (11.3)	48.01 (12.1)	2.14	2.05
4. Electricity, Gas and Water Supply	0.85 (0.3)	1.35 (0.4)	1.28 (0.3)	4.5	-0.88
5. Construction	6.78 (2.2)	11.68 (3.1)	17.62 (4.4)	5.32	7.09
Tertiary	**52.11 (17.2)**	**73.76 (19.7)**	**90.26 (22.7)**	**3.53**	**2.42**
6. Trade	19.22 (6.3)	27.78 (7.4)	37.32 (9.4)	3.57	5.04
7. Transport, Storage and Communications	7.39 (2.4)	10.33 (2.8)	14.69 (3.7)	3.24	6.04
8. Financial Services	1.7 (0.6)	3.52 (0.9)	5.08 (1.3)	7.18	6.2
9. Community, Social and Personal services	23.8 (7.9)	32.13 (8.6)	33.2 (8.4)	2.9	0.55
Total Employment	**302.76 (100.0)**	**374.45 (100.0)**	**397.00 (100.0)**	**2.04**	**0.98**

Notes : 1. Growth rates for the primary sector have been worked on the basis of data by the Task Force on Employment Opportunities.
2. Figures in parenthesis give the percentage of the sector in the total employment during the respective year.

Source : Compiled and computed from the data provided by the Planning Commission (2001), *Report of Task Force on Employment Opportunities*, Table 3.2.

8. Community, social and personal services witnessed a sharp deceleration in employment growth from 2.90 per cent during 1983 to 1993-94 to merely 0.55 per cent during 1993-94 and 1999-2000. This was largely the consequence of shedding the load of excess employment in the public sector by imposing a continuous ban on recruitment and not filling up even the positions vacated by retirement of public sector employees.

We have grouped the data into primary, secondary and tertiary sectors. In the primary sector, there is a deceleration of growth rate of employment during post-liberalisation period (1994-2000). In the secondary sector, the combined effect of manufacturing and construction resulted in a modest improvement in the growth rate from 2.90 per cent in the pre-liberalisation decade to 3.14 per cent in the post-liberalisation period. However, in the tertiary (or service) sector, there is a deceleration in growth rate of employment to 2.42 per cent in the post-liberalisation period as against 3.53 per cent in the pre-liberalisation decade. This was mainly the consequence of a sharp deceleration in employment growth in the community, social and personal services to 0.55 per cent in the post-liberalisation period as against 2.90 per cent in the pre-liberalisation decade.

From Table 2.6, two patterns in employment generation may be noticed—the first pattern pertains to the period 1983 to 1993-94. In this pattern, nearly 51 per cent of additional employment came from the

TABLE 2.6
Share of Different Sectors in Increase of Employment

(*million*)

Period I	***1983 (1)***	***1993-94 (2)***	***Increase during (1983-93)***	***Share in Increase (%)***
Primary	208.99	245.16	36.17	50.5
Secondary	41.66	55.53	13.87	19.3
Tertiary	52.11	73.76	21.65	30.2
Total	302.76	374.45	71.69	100.0
Period II	***1993-94***	***1999-2000***	***Increase during 1994-00***	***Share in Increase (%)***
Primary	245.16	239.83	-5.33	-23.6
Secondary	55.53	66.91	11.38	50.4
Tertiary	73.76	90.26	16.50	73.2
Total	374.45	397.00	22.55	100.0

Source: Compiled and computed from the data given in Table 5.

primary sector, 19 per cent from the secondary sector and 30 per cent from the tertiary sector. In the second pattern that developed during 1993-94 and 1999-2000, nearly 50 per cent of the additional employment was generated in the secondary sector and 73 per cent in the tertiary sector; however, in the agricultural sector, there was a fall in employment by nearly 23 per cent. The post-liberalisation period thus appears to be one, which neglected agriculture. The virtual stagnation of the agricultural sector in terms of output and deceleration in terms of employment appears to be the distinguishing feature of this pattern.

Unemployment Rates—Urban and Rural Differences

Data provided in Table 2.7 reveal that unemployment rates are traditionally higher in urban areas than in rural areas. As against an unemployment rate of 10.3 per cent in 1977-78 in urban areas, the rural unemployment rate was 7.7 per cent (CDS basis). There was a significant fall in the rural unemployment rate in 1987-88 to 5.3 per cent, but the urban unemployment rate was of the order of 9.4 per cent, significantly higher. After 1993-94, the period of liberalisation rural unemployment rate again increased to 7.2 per cent while urban unemployment also marginally increased to 7.7 per cent during 1993-94 to 1999-2000. Higher levels of unemployment in the urban areas could be explained by a larger proportion of organised sector unemployment which forces people to either remain employed or unemployed, since the chances for getting engaged in low productive activities are relatively fewer. As against this, the rural areas indicate higher levels of disguised unemployment. Gradual and continuous decline of urban unemployment rates till 1993-94 and even a very marginal increase in 1999-2000 may be due to greater attention being given to urban

TABLE 2.7
Unemployment among Urban and Rural Areas

(As percent of labour force)

Survey Period	*Rural Areas*			*Urban Areas*		
	Male	*Female*	*Persons*	*Male*	*Female*	*Persons*
1977-78	7.1	9.2	7.7	9.4	14.5	10.3
1983	7.5	9.0	7.9	9.2	11.0	9.5
1987-88	4.6	6.7	5.3	8.8	12.0	9.4
1993-94	5.6	5.6	5.6	6.7	10.5	7.4
1999-2000	7.2	7.3	7.2	7.2	9.8	7.7

* Unemployment rate on current daily status basis.
Source : National Sample Survey Organisation Surveys.

areas in the development process, but the increase in unemployment rates in rural areas may be due to the neglect of rural areas in the post-reform period. It may also be due to a shift in the composition of employment from self-employment to casual labour.

Male-Female Differences

Table 2.7 also brings out the stark reality that female unemployment rates are significantly higher in urban areas at 9.8 per cent as compared to male unemployment rate at 7.2 per cent in 1999-00. Over the last-two decades, however, female unemployment rates have come down from 14.5 per cent in 1977-78 to 9.8 per cent in 1999-2000, but the male unemployment rates declined from 9.4 per cent to 7.2 per cent during this period. This only underlines the fact that there is a greater absorption of female labour in urban areas and this trend needs to be strengthened so as to completely eliminate male-female differences in unemployment rates.

In the rural areas, male female unemployment rates showed divergence during 1977-78 and 1987-88, but thereafter the difference in male female unemployment rates seems to have narrowed down during 1993-94 and 1999-2000.

Unemployment Rate Across Household Monthly Per Capita Expenditure

Table 2.8 provides information according to Household Monthly Per Capita Expenditure (MPCE) Classes for the year 1999-2000 on the UPSS and CDS criteria basis separately. A close perusal of the data reveal that both in the rural and the urban areas, the lower consumption groups show much lower rates of unemployment on the basis of the UPSS criterion, but this pattern gets reversed on the basis of CDS criterion. But as the expenditure levels improve, there is an increase in unemployment rate on the basis of UPSS criterion and a fall on the basis of CDS criterion. In other words, the difference between UPSS and CDS rates indicates a decline with increase of MPCE of the class. This only highlights the stark reality that the poor cannot afford to remain unemployed since their waiting power is very weak and take up any work—low paid or high paid, full time or part time, continuous or intermittent to make both ends meet. The high degree of CDS unemployment rate is a reflection of the high degree of under-employment among the poor.

Unemployment Rates and Regional Differences

Data about 17 major states of the country pertaining to unemployment rates has been presented in Table 2.9. Although during 1999-2000, the All-India unemployment rate was 7.29 per cent, states show very wide

TABLE 2.8

Unemployment Rates by Household Monthly Per Capita Expenditure (MPCE) : 1999-2000

(As percent of labour force)

MPCE	*Rural*			*MPCE*	*Urban*		
	UPSS	*CDS*	*Difference*		*UPSS*	*CDS*	*Difference*
(1)	*(2)*	*(3)*	*(4)*	*(5)*	*(6)*	*(7)*	*(8)*
0-225	1.06	11.31	10.25	0-300	2.91	9.61	6.70
225-255	1.02	9.62	8.60	300-350	5.21	9.67	4.46
255-300	1.27	8.12	6.85	350-425	4.08	8.20	4.12
300-340	0.98	7.46	6.48	425-500	5.43	9.20	3.77
340-380	1.20	6.56	5.36	500-575	5.81	9.20	3.39
380-420	1.43	6.18	4.75	575-665	8.12	8.63	0.51
420-470	1.59	6.48	4.89	665-775	5.85	8.19	2.34
470-525	1.79	6.14	4.35	775-915	4.95	7.18	2.23
525-615	1.78	5.60	3.82	915-1120	5.08	6.65	1.57
615-775	2.21	6.06	3.85	1120-1500	4.21	5.68	1.47
775-950	2.44	5.57	3.13	1500-1925	3.49	4.67	1.18
950 and above	2.54	5.25	2.71	1925 & above	2.99	4.10	1.11
All	**1.43**	**7.21**	**5.78**	**All**	**4.63**	**7.65**	**3.02**

Source : NSSO Survey 55th round (1999-2000).

TABLE 2.9
Unemployment Rates* and Regional Differences

(Percent of labour force)

State	*Unemployment Rate*		
	1987-88	*1993-94*	*1999-2000*
1. Kerala	21.19	15.50	20.77
2. West Bengal	8.13	9.87	14.95
3. Tamil Nadu	10.36	11.44	12.05
4. Assam	50.9	7.96	8.00
5. Andhra Pradesh	7.35	6.67	7.94
6. Orissa	6.44	7.28	7.38
7. Bihar	4.04	6.25	7.35
8. Maharashtra	4.67	4.97	7.09
9. Haryana	7.59	6.59	4.67
10. Gujarat	5.79	5.73	4.63
11. Karnataka	5.06	1.80	4.01
12. Madhya Pradesh	2.86	3.42	4.60
13. Delhi	4.77	1.91	4.58
14. Uttar Pradesh	3.44	3.45	4.27
15. Punjab	5.07	3.08	4.15
16. Rajasthan	5.74	1.33	3.06
17. Himachal Pradesh	3.12	1.82	2.93
All-India	**6.09**	**6.03**	**7.29**

* Current Daily Status Basis.

Note : States have been arranged in the descending order of unemployment rates for 1999-2000.

Source : *National Sample Survey.*

variations from about 3 per cent in Himachal Pradesh and Rajasthan to about 12 per cent in Tamil Nadu, about 15 per cent in West Bengal and about 21 per cent in Kerala. It is rather intriguing that a state like Kerala, which has shown the sharpest decline in poverty, should also show the highest rate of unemployment. The Planning Commission Task Force suggests the following tentative hypothesis to explain variations: "States where wages are kept higher than the neighbouring regions either by strengthening the bargaining power of labour or by provision of social security (Kerala, West Bengal and Tamil Nadu) have a higher incidence of unemployment."[9] But the question which the Task Force does not answer is: Should these states weaken the bargaining power of labour or not take social security measures in view of the fact that neighbouring states do not realize their social responsibility? It would be more desirable to examine in depth the social and economic conditions in different states so as to understand more fully the inter-state variations.

4. STRUCTURE OF EMPLOYMENT IN INDIA

The structure of employment may be studied by recognising the following characteristics: (i) Distinction between organised and unorganised sector, and (ii) the relative share of self-employment, regular salaried employment and casual labour. It would be of interest to examine the structure from these two points of view.

Organised *v.* Unorganised Sector Employment

The organised sector usually refers to employment in the public sector and in private sector establishments employing 10 or more persons. It is commonly believed that wages in the organised sector are much higher than in the unorganised sector. Moreover, the organised sector being regulated also provides greater job security and other benefits. Within the organised sector, jobs in the public sector receive relatively higher wages and accompanying benefits than those in the private sector for similar skills. Besides this, public sector offers greater job security.

Data given in Table 2.10 reveal that the share of organised sector employment in total employment, which was of the order of 7.93 per cent in 1983 as well as 1988 declined to 7.08 per cent in 1999-2000. The organised sector employment, which was 24 million in 1983, increased to 27.37 million in 1994 indicating a growth rate of 1.20 per cent per annum during 1983-94. However, during the post-reform period (1994-2000), organised sectored employment crept up slowly from 27.37 million in 1994 to 28.22 million in 1999-2000, indicating a growth rate of merely 0.53 per cent per annum. This was largely the consequence of virtual stagnation of employment in the public sector during 1994-2000 and growth rate was (–) 0.03 per cent per annum, but the private sector employment grew from 7.93 million in 1994 to 8.70 million in 1999-2000 indicating a growth rate of 1.87 per cent per annum. But since the public sector accounted for over 69 per cent of total employment in the organised sector, enlargement of private sector employment was not able to effectively offset the deceleration experienced in the public sector employment.

It may be noted from Table 2.11 that in agriculture, organised sector employment is negligible. Even in a major sector like manufacturing, organised sector employment is only of the order of 14 per cent and as much as 86 per cent of employment is generated through the unorganised sector viz., handlooms and powerlooms and other village and small scale industries, i.e., tiny sector in the SSI sector. There is deceleration in organised sector employment in financial services, transport, storage and communications. There is virtual stagnation in organised sector employment in community, social and personal services. In trade, organised

TABLE 2.10

Total Employment and Organised Sector Employment

Sector	Employment (million)				Growth rate (% per annum)	
	1983	1988	1994	1999-2000	1983-94	1994-2000
(1)	(2)	(3)	(4)	(5)	(6)	(7)
1. Total population	718.21	790.00	895.05	1004.10	2.12	1.93
2. Total labour force	308.64	333.49	381.94	406.05	2.05	1.03
3. Total employment	302.75	324.29	374.45	397.00	2.04	0.98
4. Organised sector employment	24.01 (100.0)	25.71 (100.0)	27.37 (100.0)	28.11 (100.0)	1.20	0.53
5. Public sector	16.46 (68.6)	18.32 (71.3)	19.44 (71.0)	19.41 (69.1)	1.52	-0.03
6. Private sector	7.55 (31.4)	7.39 (28.7)	7.93 (29.0)	8.70 (30.9)	0.45	1.87
7. 4 as % of 3	7.93	7.93	7.30	7.08		
8. 2 as % of 1	43.0	42.2	42.7	40.4		

Notes : 1. Total employment figures are on Usual Status (UPSS) basis.

2. The organised sector employment figures are as reported in the Employment Market Information System of Ministry of Labour and pertain to 31st March of 1983, 1994 and 1999.

3. Figures in brackets indicate the percentage of employment in the public sector and private sector to total organised sector employment.

Source : Compiled and computed from Planning Commission (2001), *Report of the Task Force on Employment Opportunities*, p. 2.25.

TABLE 2.11
Organised Sector Employment by Industry

(*Employment in million*)

	1993-94		*1999-2000*		*Share of Organised Sector (per cent)*	
	Total[3]	*Organised Sector*[1]	*Total*[4]	*Organised Sector*[2]	*1993-94*	*1999-2000*
(1)	*(2)*	*(3)*	*(4)*	*(5)*	*(6)*	*(7)*
Agriculture	242.46	1.48	237.56	1.39	0.61	0.58
Mining and Quarrying	2.70	1.09	2.27	1.01	40.37	44.49
Manufacturing	42.50	6.40	48.01	6.75	15.05	14.06
Electricity, Gas and Water Supply	1.35	0.97	1.28	1.00	71.85	78.12
Construction	11.68	1.23	17.62	1.18	10.53	6.70
Trade	27.78	0.45	37.32	0.49	1.62	1.31
Transport, Storage and Communications	10,33	3.11	14.69	3.15	30.11	21.44
Financial services	3.52	1.53	5.05	1.65	43.46	32.67
Community, Social and Personal services	32.13	10.93	33.20	11.49	34.02	34.61
Total	**374.45**	**27.18**	**397.00**	**28.11**	**7.26**	**7.08**

1 & 2 as on 31.3.1993 and 31.3.1999.
3 & 4 as on 1.1.94 and 1.1.2000.

Sources: 1. DGET for employment in organised sector.
2. NSSO, *55th Round of Employment and Unemployment in India (1999-2000).*

sector employment is negligible at 1.31 per cent. Deceleration of growth in organised sector employment has led to the shift towards unorganised sector, which implies a shift from better quality and secure employment to inferior and insecure employment.

Self-employed, Regular Salaried and Casual Labour

Data on the basis of category of employment is given in Table 2.12 separately for rural and urban areas. In rural areas, in 1999-2000, 56 per cent of the workers were self-employed, about 7 per cent were regular salaried workers and 37 per cent were casual labourers. The proportion of self-employment in rural areas was around 63 per cent in 1977-78 and it has shown a decline over the last two decades. The share of regular salaried

TABLE 2.12
Distribution of Workers (Usual Status) by Category of Employment

(Percent of total workers)

Year	*Category of Employment*		
	Self-employment	*Regular salaried*	*Casual*
1. **Rural Areas**			
1977-78	62.6	7.7	29.7
1983	61.0	7.5	31.5
1987-88	59.4	7.7	32.9
1993-94	58.0	6.4	35.6
1999-2000	56.0	6.7	37.3
2. **Urban Areas**			
1977-78	42.4	41.8	15.8
1983	41.8	40.0	18.2
1987-88	42.8	40.3	16.9
1993-94	42.3	39.4	18.3
1999-2000	42.1	40.1	17.8
3. **Rural and Urban combined**			
1977-78	58.9	13.9	27.2
1983	57.4	13.9	28.7
1987-88	56.0	14.4	29.6
1993-94	54.8	13.2	32.0
1999-2000	52.9	13.9	33.2

Source : NSSO Surveys.

workers has slightly declined from 7.7 per cent in 1977-78 to 6.7 per cent in 1999-2000. But there has been an increase in casual labour from 29.7 per cent in 1977-78 to 37.3 per cent in 1999-2000. The increase in casual labour is a reflection of the conversion of marginal cultivators into agricultural labourers.

The situation is very different in urban areas. The share of self-employment, though significant, has remained more or less about 42 per cent during the entire period—1977-78 to 1999-2000. Similarly, the regular salaried workers have been around 40 per cent and only 18 per cent of urban workers are casual labourers. The scenario, by category of employment, was more or less stable in the urban areas during 1977-78 to 1999-2000.

Taking the country as a whole, whereas in 1977-78, about 59 per cent were self-employed, 14 per cent were regular salaried workers and 27 per cent were casual labour, the situation changed by the year 1999-2000 and 53 per cent were self-employed, 14 per cent were regular salaried workers and

33 per cent were casual labourers. In other words, the regular salaried workers' proportion has remained constant during the last two decades and the decline witnessed in self-employment was converted into higher proportion of casual labour. Since casual labour is not associated with job security and other associated benefits, increase in the proportion of casual labour is generally treated as an index of deterioration in the quality of employment.

5. EMPLOYMENT POLICIES AND THE UNORGANISED SECTOR

The *Task Force on Employment Opportunities* headed Dr. Montek Singh Ahluwalia submitted its report to the Planning Commission on 1st July 2001. The Report was sharply criticised by economists, sociologists, policy-makers, trade union leaders. The Task Force suggested measures like boosting private sector investment in agriculture, development of integrated agricultural complexes and food parks by the corporate sector, to give contracts to agro-companies to develop degraded and waste lands, to involve large industrial units, including MNCs to develop food processing industries, to involve large firms in construction, retail trade, road transport, etc. In other words, the total responsibility for employment generation was to be given to the corporate sector. To facilitate this process, the report suggested total dereservation of small industries in the next four years and reform of the labour laws by deleting Chapter VB of the Industrial Disputes Act so as to give the employers an unbridled right to hire and fire labour. It was felt by the policy-makers that such failed strategy, if followed, would create greater resistance because it was anti-labour and pinned exclusive faith on GDP growth via corporatisation of the economy. It was largely believed that most of the recommendations were employment restricting, rather than employment generating. It was also believed that with this strategy to achieve the goal of creating 10 million jobs per year as directed by the then Prime Minister, was well-nigh impossible.

Although the Planning Commission did not formally reject the Report of the Task Force, but it gave burial to this Report by appointing S.P. Gupta Special Group on Targeting 10 Million Employment Opportunities on 5th September 2001.

Estimate of Employment and Unemployment

The Special Group on the basis of the NSS data has estimated the number of unemployed to be of the order of 26.58 million in 1999-2000, as against 20.13 million in 1993-94 (current daily status basis). The growth rate of unemployed works out to be 4.74 per cent per annum for 1993-94 to 1999-00, as against a decline in the number of unemployed during 1983 to 1993-94. This only underlines the fact that unemployment rate which was 8.33 per cent in 1983 declined to 5.99 per cent by 1993-94, but increased to 7.32 per cent in 1999-2000. The Special Group Report mentions : "The present rising unemployment is primarily an outcome of a declining job creating capacity of growth, observed since 1993-94. The employment growth fell to 1.07 per cent per annum (between 1993-94 and 1999-2000) from 2.7 per cent per annum in the past (between 1983 and 1993-94) in spite of acceleration in GDP growth from 5.2 per cent between 1983 and 1993-94 to 6.7 per cent between 1993-94 and 1999-2000."[10] (Tefer Table 2.13) "Explaining the situation, the Special Group Report mentions: The employment elasticity of the 80s and early 90s of 0.52 went down to 0.16 in the late nineties. The organised sector's employment generating capacity (measured in terms of employment elasticity) came down to near zero and in the public sector has been negative in most cases. This is primarily because of :

(i) The present policy of shedding excess labour that this sector is carrying in order to meet the growing market competition, often known as rightsizing;
(ii) The trend towards increasing capital intensity per unit of output; and
(iii) The pattern of growth moving in favour of capital intensive sectors."[11]

Organised *v.* Unorganised Sector Employment and Unemployment Scenario

Employment in the organised sector has been hardly 8.34 per cent, of which public sector accounts for 5.77 per cent and private sector only 2.57 per cent in the total employment generated in 1999-2000.

The organised sector is dominated by public sector which contributed 70 per cent of the total employment in this sector. This is mainly in: (i) mining, (ii) electricity and water, and (iii) community and social services. These three constitute nearly 60 per cent of public sector employment and unfortunately, all of them are showing negative employment elasticity. This only underlines the fact that the public sector contributed to a very small extent in total employment generation during 1993-94 to 1999-2000. It implies that the public sector has shown almost a jobless growth, when its employment elasticity was 0.015. Further, in future a large part of this sector's potential may be negated by the impending downsizing policy (often called as right-sizing) of the government, which affects this sector significantly.

The main source of employment generation is the unorganised sector of economy including self-employment and small business where the present contribution is as high as 92 per cent of the total employed labour force. Its main employment generating activities are : (a) agriculture and allied, (b) trade, restaurants and hotels including tourism, (c) some of the social sectors like education and health, (d) small and medium enterprises

TABLE 2.13
Profile of Employment and Unemployment

	1983	1993-94	1999-2000	Employment Growth Rate (% per annum)	
	(Million persons)			1983 to 1993-94	1993-94 to 1999-2000
(1)	(2)	(3)	(4)	(5)	(6)
All India					
(1) Population	718.20	894.01	1003.97	2.0	1.95
(2) Labour force	261.33	335.97	363.33	2.43	1.31
(3) Workforce	239.57	315.84	336.75	2.7	1.07
(4) No. of unemployed (2-3)	21.76	20.13	26.58	-0.08	4.74
(5) Unemployment rate (%) (4÷2×100)	8.33	5.99	7.32		
Rural					
Population	546.61	658.83	727.50	1.79	1.67
Labour force	204.18	255.38	270.39	2.15	0.96
Workforce	187.92	241.04	250.89	2.40	0.67
No. of unemployed	16.26	14.34	19.50	-1.19	5.26
Unemployment rate (%)	7.96	5.61	7.21		
Urban					
Population	171.59	234.98	276.47	3.04	2.74
Labour force	57.15	80.60	92.95	3.33	2.40
Workforce	51.64	74.80	85.84	3.59	2.32
No. of unemployed	5.51	5.80	7.11	0.49	3.45
Unemployment rate (%)	9.64	7.19	7.65		

Source : Planning Commission (2002), *Report of Special Group on Targeting Ten Million Employment Opportunities per year.*

mainly in rural non-farm sector, (e) transport and construction. It may be noted that small and medium enterprises contribute to nearly 80 per cent of manufacturing employment and its employment elasticity is relatively 3.8 times more than that of the organised sector. Thus, to achieve a more favourable effect on employment, what is needed is a shift in the percentage composition of manufacturing in favour of small and medium enterprises (SMEs).

Agriculture is another source of employment generation as it accounts for 57 per cent of India's total employment in 1999-00. Between 1983 and 1993-94, its employment elasticity was as high as 0.70, but in the post-reform period (1993-94 to 1999-2000), its employment elasticity has declined to 0.01. "But given an appropriate policy, this sector can still be a gold mine for generating faster employment by changes in the sectoral composition of agriculture in favour of labour-intensive high value areas like horticulture, floriculture, agro-forestry, minor irrigation, watersheds, etc."[12]

The other employment generating areas in the unorganised sector that have been identified are trade, restaurants and tourism, and information technology (IT). They are all witnessing a high growth of above 9.0 per cent per annum and are having very high employment elasticities. The transport, construction and the other service sectors are also equally equipped for high growth and employment intensiveness.

The special Group Report concluded its analysis of employment situation in the following manner: "To sum up, with some changes in the inter and intra-sectoral composition and adopting appropriate labour-intensive technology, growth in the unorganised sector can be significantly raised. The appropriate organised sector, especially its public sector component, has a rather low employment generating potential, being handicapped by a negative employment elasticity with the exception of the financial sectors and potentiality in certain parts of social sector like education, health, etc. But these two have as a low weightage as 3.3 per cent to the total employment. The community and social services need a major change in the composition in favour of health, education, etc. and only then can it substantially contribute to the growth. Already a significant increase in the weightage of this sector in this group is in sight. It was 25.8 per cent in 1993-94 and 33.3 per cent now. These two sub-sectors together are showing a growth rate of around 4.5 per cent per annum compared to this sector's growth of 0.2 per cent per annum between 1993-94 and 1999-2000. Given the Tenth Plan target on education, literacy and health standard, the scope of its growth and potential employment generation is very high."[13]

"As the absorption capacity for high skill jobs has its own limit in the organised sector, the future plan for education and training should keep in mind the type of skills needed for many newly emerging activity sectors like IT, tourism, financial services and the vast unorganised SSI and services sector including the new areas in agriculture and the non-farm rural activities."[14]

Table 2.14
Present Employment Scenario in India (1983 to 1999-2000)

(Employment in Million Growth Rate per cent per annum)

	Current Daily Status			*Employment Growth Rate*		*GDP Growth Rate (% per annum)*		*Employment elasticity*	
	1983	*1993-94*	*1999-2000*	*1983 to 1993-94*	*1993-94 to 1999-2000*	*1983 to 1993-2000*	*1993-94 to 1999-2000*	*1983 to 1993-94*	*1993-94 to 1999-2000*
	1	*2*	*3*	*4*	*5*	*6*	*7*	*8=4/6*	*9=5/7*
1. Agriculture	151.35 (63.18)	190.72 (60.38)	190.94 (56.70)	2.03	0.02	2.9	3.1	0.7	0.01
2. Mining and Quarrying	1.74 (0.73)	2.54 (0.80)	2.26 (0.67)	3.66	-1.91	6.2	4.7	0.59	-0.41
3. Manufacturing	27.69 (11.56)	35 (11.08)	40.79 (12.11)	2.28	2.58	6	7.8	0.38	0.33
4. Electricity, Gas and Water Supply	0.83 (0.34)	1.43 (0.45)	1.15 (0.34)	5.29	-3.55	8.4	6.8	0.63	-0.52
5. Construction	7.17 (2.99)	11.02 (3.99)	14.95 (4.44)	4.21	5.21	4.9	6.3	0.86	0.82
6. Trade, Hotels and Restaurants	18.17 (7.58)	26.88 (8.51)	37.54 (11.15)	3.81	5.72	5.6	9.2	0.68	0.62
7. Transport, storage and communications	6.99 (2.92)	9.88 (3.13)	13.65 (4.05)	3.36	5.53	6.1	8.7	0.55	0.63
8. Finance, insurance, real estate and Business services	2.1 (0.88)	3.37 (1.07)	4.62 ((1.38)	4.54	5.4	10.1	8.4	0.45	0.64
9. Commity, Social and personal services	23.52 (9.82)	34.98 (11.08)	30.84 (9.16)	3.88	-2.08	5.7	8.4	0.68	-0.25
All	**239.57 (100.00)**	**315.84 (100.00)**	**336.75 (100.00)**	**2.7**	**1.07**	**5.2**	**6.7**	**0.52**	**0.16**

Note : Figures in brackets are percentages of total employment in respective column.
Source : Compiled and computed from the *Report of the Special Group* on *Targeting Ten Million Employment Opportunities per year (2002).*

TABLE 2.15

Employment Scenario (1999-2000) in India

	Total*	Organised Sector			% of organised sector to total sectoral employment	% of Public sector to total employment	% of Public sector to organised sector	% of private sector to total organised sector
		Public sector	Private sector	Total				
	1	2	3	(4) =(2+3)	5-4/1	6=2/1	7=2/4	8=3/4
1. Agriculture	190.94	0.52	0.87	1.39	0.73	0.27	37.16	62.84
2. Mining and Quarrying	2.26	0.93	0.09	1.02	44.69	41.15	91.41	8.59
3. Manufacturing	40.79	1.57	5.18	6.75	16.55	3.95	23.25	76.75
4. Electricity, gas and water supply	1.15	0.96	0.04	1.00	96.96	83.48	95.91	4.09
5. Construction	14.95	1.11	0.07	1.18	7.90	7.42	93.97	6.03
6. Trade, hotels and restaurants	37.54	0.16	0.32	0.49	1.31	0.43	23.54	66.46
7. Transport, storage and communications	13.65	3.08	0.07	3.15	23.08	22.56	97.81	2.19
8. Finance, insurance, real estate and business services	4.62	1.30	0.36	1.65	35.71	29.14	78.34	21.66
9. Community, social and personal services	30.84	9.79	1.70	11.49	37.26	31.74	85.21	14.79
Total	336.75	19.42	8.70	28.11	8.34	5.77	69.06	30.94

*On current daily status basis.

Source : Same as for Table 2.14.

The Future Strategy

On the basis of the data collected and analysed by the Special Group, it was found that in the unorganised sector, the employment elasticity was as high as 0.213 in 1999-2000 whereas in the organised sector, it was as low as 0.066, i.e. almost a jobless growth. Moreover, in the year 1999-2000, the total contribution to employment by the organised sector was only 8 per cent of which private sector segment's contribution was hardly 2.5 per cent. Rest 92 per cent came from the unorganised sector. The Special Group, therefore, opined: "On this basis, one can see even if the organised sector grows at 20 per cent per annum and the private organised sector at 30 per cent per annum, their contribution to total employment will increase hardly by 1.5 to 2 per cent of the total over the Tenth Plan. This proposition however remains hypothetical since given the capital intensity in this sector as of today (above 5.5), this high growth will not be sustainable because of the saving investment constraint of the economy. On the basis of this ground reality, the Group concluded that exclusively for generating the desirable high level of employment, we have to target the unorganised sector, including small and medium enterprises, which also cover a large part of the services sector of the economy."[15]

Data provided in Table 2.16 reveals that in 1999-2000, the unorganised sector contributed nearly 59 per cent to GDP, but its contribution to employment was of the order of 92 per cent. Besides this, it contribution to exports was also substantial. But of late, because of the opening up of the economy with deregulation and market orientation including withdrawal of several key subsidies, the unorganised sector in general and especially some of its components are meeting with growing sickness and slowing down of activities. During 1993-94 and 1999-2000, as a consequence of the policies of liberalisation, the flow of bank credit of scheduled commercial banks increased significantly towards the organised sector from 46.2 per cent in 1993-94 to 62.9 per cent in 1999-2000, whereas in the unorganised sector, it fell from 53.8 per cent in 1993-94 to 37.1 per cent in 1999-2000. This was despite the fact that the unorganised sector continued to provide employment to 92 per cent workforce in the economy. This affects the growth rate and efficiency of the unorganised sector. This trend has to be reversed. Special Group, therefore, recommended:

> "To sum up, the employment strategy for future, to meet the plan's employment goals is to encourage the use of labour intensive and capital saving technology, in general and to rejuvenate the growth of the unorganised sector in particular, which at present contributes 92 per cent to the country's employment and enjoys more than seven times labour intensity per unit of production, as compared to the organised sector. However, the unorganised sector needs to be made more productive to sustain itself against the domestic and international

> competition by proper choice of programmes and policies compatible with India's economic reforms and the WTO rules."[16]

Drawing lessons from international experience, the Special Group Report repudiates the view of some economists, more especially that of the chairman of the Taskforce of the Planning Commission on Employment Opportunities Dr. Montek Singh Ahluwalia that the organised sector with its better productivity and high job quality is going to replace unorganised small business totally to provide higher growth, better quality of life and employment in the economy. But facts, pertaining to most developed and newly industrialised economies, reveal that small business is providing major employment opportunities and also surviving alongside with the highly organised large sector. For example, in the US all firms under the small Business Act contribute nearly 50 per cent of the private workforce along with more than half of GDP. Similarly, in Japan, of the total 54.16 million people engaged nationwide (excluding those in primary industries), 42.27 million, i.e. 78 per cent employment is in small and medium enterprises and the total value in manufacturing from SMEs is 51 per cent, in wholesale trade 64 per cent and in retail 78 per cent. Similarly, in China, SMEs provide 75 per cent of urban job opportunities and their number of units exceeded 8 million, being 99 per cent of total enterprises in China. Therefore, the question of easing out the SMEs by large organised sector in India in foreseeable future is ruled out. The organised and unorganised sectors are to co-exist satisfying the different needs of development and growth, as has happened in most of the developed and newly industrialised economies.

The Special Group Report, therefore, categorically mentions:

> "The case for encouraging the growth of the organised sector is certainly supported by its capacity to invest in major infrastructure (in most cases, they are capital intensive) to give support systems to the rest of the economy, but for generation of employment, their growth cannot be regarded as the answer."[17]

The total employment generation by the private organised sector is barely of the order of 2.58 per cent of the total. On account of its low employment base and low employment elasticity, even if it grows at the rate of 30 per cent per annum over the Tenth Plan period, its contribution to total employment will increase from 2.58 per cent to 3.5 per cent of the total employment by end of the Tenth Plan.

It has been argued by the Task Force on Employment Opportunities that the present Industrial Disputes Act (1956) should be amended to enable the employers to have complete freedom to hire and fire. Such a change in legal conditions will make the organised sector more employment-friendly and the employment generation in this sector can be improved. The Special Group examined this question, but it held the view : "With considerable excess labour being carried by the public sector in the organised segment and a jobless nature of growth in the organised sector as a whole, the immediate effect may turn out to be net labour shedding. This should be assessed against the present high level of unemployment. In this context, one should also remember that the social security support in India is much below the standard provided in developed countries, because of which their tolerance level of unemployment is very high. . . . One should remember that the contribution of total employment by the organised private sector is hardly 3.5 per cent and, therefore the potential of generating sizeable employment in this sector, even by changing the law will be insignificant over the Tenth Plan period."[18] But given the fact that the organised sector (especially the public sector) is already carrying excess labour, the immediate effect will be more firing than hiring. The Special Group, thus, stated : "Therefore, purely on the ground of employment generation, the favourable effect of any change in this legislation is marginal, at least in the short-term. Gradual withdrawal of the Act could be considered, observing the net impact on employment at every phase. Along with it, the social security coverage may be increased and care should be taken of the retrenched labour."[19]

The Special Group did not deem it as a correct policy to seek the answer to the question of increasing productivity and job quality in the organised sector, as has been suggested by Ahluwalia Task Force on Employment Opportunity, but is of the strong view :

> "The only answer to this situation is to increase productivity and job quality of the unorganised sector. It means that all attempts should be made to implement those policies, which will release the basic growth constraints and by ensuring a level playing field for this sector. . . . In the attempt to increase the labour productivity, more emphasis should be on the growth of this sector rather than for substituting labour by capital. Further, to improve the job quality and its security, major changes in legislation will be needed regarding basic social security measures working conditions, minimum wages and protection of labour interests."[20]

To sum up, S.P Gupta Special Group Report on Employment was unique in many ways:

- It rejected the reform process as a panacea for all ills of economy, especially referring to unemployment.
- It rejected the thesis of the reformists that the organised sector, more especially the corporate sector, could usher an era of zero unemployment and removal of poverty in the near future.

TABLE 2.16

Output, Employment and Productivity of Organised and Unorganised Sectors of the Economy

	Organised Sector			*Unorganised Sector*	*Grand Total*
	Total	*Public Sector*	*Private Sector*		
	(1)	*(2)*	*(3)*	*(4)*	*5=1+4*
Value-added GDP (Rs. crores at 1993-94 prices)					
1993-94	256,849 (36.80)	1,80,843 (25.90)	76,006 (10.90)	4,41,143 (63.20)	6,97,992 (100.00)
1999-2000	4,18,920 (41.10)	2,66,519 (26.10)	1,52,401 (15.00)	6,00,425 (58.90)	1,019,345 (100.00)
Growth Rate (Per cent)	8.5	6.68	12.3	5.27	6.52
Bank Credit (Rs. 000 crores)					
1993-94	80.8 (46.00)	28.1 (16.00)	52.7 (30.00)	94.9 (54.00)	175.7 (100.00)
1999-2000	247.4 (62.90)	66.8 (17.00)	180.6 (45.90)	145.9 (37.10)	393.3 (100.00)
Growth Rate (per cent)	20.5	15.5	22.8	7.4	14.4
Employment (million)					
1993-94	27.18 (8.60)	19.3 (6.10)	7.88 (2.50)	288.66 (91.40)	315.84 (100.0
1999-2000	28.11 (8.35)	19.42 (5.77)	8.69 (2.58)	308.64 (61.65)	336.75 (100.00)
Growth Rate (Per cent)	0.56	0.1	1.64	1.12	1.07
Employment elasticity	0.066	0.015	0.133	0.213	0.165
Labour productivity growth (per cent per annum)	7.88	6.67	8.38	4.1	5.38
Relative Labour Intensity (Organised/Unorganised) 1999-2000	0.1345				

Notes : 1. Figures in brackets are percentages of grand total in the row.
2. Outstanding bank credit refers to all scheduled commercial banks.

Source : Compiled and computed from Planning Commission (2002), *Report of the Special Group on Targeting Ten Million Employment Opportunities per Year.*

- It focused attention on the unorganised sector, which provides employment to 92 per cent of labour force and has remained neglected so far.
- It repudiated the theory that amendment of the Industrial Disputes

Act to give power to the employers to hire and fire shall lead to enlargement of employment. Rather it would result in more firing than hiring.

- It underlined the need for improving productivity and job quality of the unorganised sector. For this purpose, it highlighted the need for major changes in legislation regarding basic social security measures, working conditions, minimum wages and protection of labour interests, rather than throwing the workers at the mercy of the market forces.
- It laid down a policy prescription for providing 50 million jobs during the Tenth Plan—30 million based on 8 per cent growth of GDP and 20 million based on Special programmes.
- It rejected the view that elasticity of employment in agriculture is zero. Rather it stressed the need to diversify and strengthen agriculture so that by 2011-12, about 51 per cent of employment is generated through agriculture.
- On the basis of international experience and the imperative need of our country, the Report brought out the fact that small and medium industries are not only to co-exist with large industries, but should also become the principal contributors to industrial growth and employment.
- The employment issue has to placed on a high priority and not treated as "business as usual". It, thus, sought active state intervention to resolve the issue.
- It underlined the need for a change in the credit policy of the banking system to stop the decline in the share of bank credit from 54 per cent to 37 per cent for the unorganised sector in the short-span of 6 years (1993-94 to 1999-2000).
- It highlighted the fact that the employment elasticity of the unorganised *vis-a-vis* the organised sector is 3.23 times and thus the State must protect and strengthen this sector.
- It warned the state that unless civil administration in the urban areas and the panchayats in the rural areas do not work hand in hand along with the state to reduce unemployment in the new environment, unemployment at the end of the Tenth Plan will reach 40 million i.e., nearly ten per cent of labour force—a very grim prospect indeed.

If one studies carefully many of the policy changes suggested in Common Minimum Program of the United Progressive Alliance (UPA) Government led by the Congress in 2004, the conclusion is inescapable that S.P. Gupta's Special Group recommendations could be considered as the precursors of the new policy, though it may be noted that the NDA government did not seriously implement them.

Unemployment during the Tenth Plan

Mid-Term Appraisal of the 10th Five Year Plan (2002-07) by the Planning Commission notes that the plan had targeted to create 10 million jobs per year and thus a total of 50 million jobs during the 5-year period. This was based on the assumption that the economy will grow at the rate of 8 percent per annum and that the normal growth process would generate 30 million jobs and the balance of 20 million jobs would be created by special programmes aimed at employment generation. These 50 million jobs were to be created against a total addition to the labour force by 35 million persons. This was intended to take care of the backlog of unemployment. The Mid-Term Appraisal confesses in a forthright manner: "However, in the first three years of the Plan (2002-05), the pace of creation of employment opportunities may not exceed the addition to the labour force."[21]

Pending the availability of the results of the 61st Round of the Nation Sample Survey (2004-05), estimates are based on GDP growth rate and the observed employment elasticities in the recent past. It may be noted that during the first three years of the Tenth Plan, GDP growth has averaged 6.5 percent per annum which is below the target of 8 percent per annum. The most depressing part of the situation is that in the agricultural sector which engages more than 55 percent of labour force, the average output growth was miserably low at 1.2 percent per annum on the average as against the target of 4.2 percent per annum.

From the data provided in Table 2.17, it becomes obvious that as against the growth of labour force by 1.8 percent during 2001-02 and 2004-05, employment growth averaged 1.7 percent per year—slightly lower than the labour force growth. Consequently, the backlog of unemployed which was 33.5 million in 2001-02 increased to 36.4 million by 2004-05—an increase by nearly 3 million.

TABLE 2.17
Estimates of Labour Force, Work Opportunities and Unemployment during 2002-05

	Unit	*2001-02*	*2002-03*	*2003-04*	*2004-05*
1. Labour Force	Million	378.21	385.02	391.95	399.00
2. Employment	Million	344.68	349.89	356.16	362.64
3. No. of unemployed (1-2)	Million	33.53	35.13	35.79	36.36
4. Unemployment rate	%	8.87	9.12	9.13	9.11

Notes : 1. Employment estimates are based on observed output elasticity of employment (1994-2000).
2. Labour force growth was assumed at 1.8 percent per annum in the Tenth Plan.
* Calculated on the basis of the data.

Source : Planning Commission, *Mid-Term Appraisal of the 10th Five Year Plan (2002-07)*, p. 264.

A very disheartening feature of the employment situation is that employment has decreased in the organized sector which is seen as the engine of economic reforms. Table 2.18 provides estimates of growth of employment during the first three years of the plan on CDS basis in the organised sector. It may be noted that between 2001 and 2003, both the public and the private sector have indicated a decrease of employment.

TABLE 2.18
Estimates of Employment in Organised Sector

(*Lakh persons as on March 31*)

Year	*Public Sector*	*Private Sector*	*Total*
2001	191.38	86.52	227.89
2002	187.73	84.32	272.06
2003	185.80	84.21	270.00

Source : Ministry of Labour and DGE&T.

The decline in the Public sector employment may be due to shedding the load of surplus workers, but decline in employment in the organised private sector can only be explained by the substitution of capital-intensive technology because it has been claimed that the corporate sector has been growing in terms of output at a much faster rate than the overall industrial sector including small and medium enterprises. However, during the 2-year period, the cumulative decline in employment of the public as well as the private sector was of the order 7.9 lakh jobs.

This only underlines the stark reality that whatever additional employment was generated in the first three years of the Tenth Plan, it was in the unorganized (or the informal) sector of the economy. Obviously there is a need to pay more attention to the unorganized sector to fulfill the employment objective—a conclusion drawn by the S.P. Gupta, Special Group.

6. RELATION BETWEEN EMPLOYMENT AND GROWTH

Bhaumik, S.K. (2000) has examined the relation between employment and growth. For this purpose, he uses the Employment and Unemployment Quinquennial Surveys of National Sample Survey Organisation (NSSO) for the years 1983 (NSS 38th Round), 1993-94 (NSS 50th Round) and 1999-00 (NSS 55th Round). In the study, the periods from 1983 to 1993-94 and 1993-94 to 1999-2000 represent the pre-reform and post-reform periods respectively. The study analysed the growth of unemployed in India and the states, using unemployment on CDS concept since this provides a far more comprehensive measure of unemployment *vis-a-vis* estimates based on other measures (US-adj and CWS). Information for the all-India as well as 15 major States for the years 1983, 1993-94 and 1999-00 has been used in the study. Besides the study uses NSDP (Net State Domestic Product) at constant prices for the purpose for All-India as well as 15 major states.

The issue addressed was: Does attainment of higher economic growth necessarily lead to reduction in the number of unemployed? A simple regression analysis was conducted of the growth rates of unemployed on the growth rates of NSDP (both total as well as sectoral) separately for the pre-reform and post-reform periods. The regression results are presented in Table 2.19.

"It is observed that the relationship between growth rates of total NSDP and the number of unemployed has been negative and statistically significant during the pre-economic reforms period in India. The same negative (and statistically significant in most cases) relationship is obtained even when we regress the growth rates of the unemployed on the sectoral NSDP. Further, the relationship between the growth rates of unemployed and per capita NSDP also appears to be negative and statistically significant. These results imply that during the pre-reforms period, the states that registered a significant decline in the growth of the unemployed were the ones that achieved higher growth of NSDP. It is also clear that higher NSDP growth rates in individual sectors (particularly in primary and secondary sectors) during the pre-reforms period helped in reducing growth rates of the unemployed. Clearly, the growth trajectories observed during the pre-reforms period were beneficial from the point of view of unemployment reduction in India."

"The situation changes drastically during the post-reforms period. During this period, the relationships between growth rates of unemployment and that of total NSDP are found to be positive. However, these relationships are found to be statistically insignificant. This implies that higher positive annual growth rates of NSDP do not necessarily mean lower unemployment growth rate. But if we examine the relationships between growth rates of the unemployed and those of sectoral NSDP, the same appear to be positive and statistically significant in the case of primary sector. The same positive, though statistically insignificant, relationship was observed when we considered growth rates of NSDP from secondary sector as an explanatory variable. It is also disturbing to note that, unlike the situation during pre-reforms period, the relationship between the growth rates of unemployed and per capita NSDP is positive (though statistically insignificant) during the post-reforms period. These results imply that in the post-reforms period the states that experienced higher growth rates of NSDP are not necessarily the ones that also recorded higher rates of decline in the number of unemployed. On the contrary, the positive relationships between the two in the post-reforms period, though not significant in some cases, imply that the higher rates of economic growth experienced by several states of India during the post-economic liberalisation period have failed to reduce the growth rates of unemployment."[22]

TABLE 2.19

Results of Regression of Growth Rate of Unemployed (CDS) on NSDP Growth Rates

Period	*Dependent variable*	*Independent variable*	*Intercept*	*Slope coefficient*	*t-statistic for slope*	R^2
(1)	*(2)*	*(3)*	*(4)*	*(5)*	*(6)*	*(7)*
Pre-reform (1983/1993-94)	Unemp. Gr. Rate	NSDP Gr. Rate – Primary	2.25	-0.73	-1.40**	0.13
	Unemp. Gr. Rate	NSDP Gr. Rate – Secondary	6.93	-1.21	-2.17*	0.27
	Unemp. Gr. Rate	NSDP Gr. Rate – Tertiary	2.89	-0.46	-0.56	0.02
	Unemp. Gr. Rate	NSDP Gr. Rate – Total	5.69	-1.18	-1.53**	0.15
	Unemp. Gr. Rate	Per Capita NSDP Gr. Rate	3.80	-1.34	-1.89*	0.22
Post-reforms (1993-94/1999-2000)	Unemp. Gr. Rate	NSDP Gr. Rate – Primary	1.74	1.26	1.58**	0.16
	Unemp. Gr. Rate	NSDP Gr. Rate – Secondary	1.67	0.45	0.80	0.05
	Unemp. Gr. Rate	NSDP Gr. Rate – Tertiary	6.42	-0.30	-0.44	0.01
	Unemp. Gr. Rate	NSDP Gr. Rate – Total	1.61	0.51	0.60	0.03
	Unemp. Gr. Rate	Per Capita NSDP Gr. Rate	3.08	0.33	0.38	0.01

Note : * and ** imply significance at 5 and 10 per cent levels respectively.

Source : Bhaumik, S.K. (2003), *Indian Journal of Labour Economics*, Vol. 46, No. 1, p. 87.

The study clearly shows that "there was significant increase in the number of unemployed in all-India in the post-economic reform period. While the number of the unemployed in the country actually declined during the period, 1983 to 1993-94 (from 21.61 million to 20.24 million), it increased to a level of 26.43 million in 1999-2000. The increase in the absolute number of unemployed in the post-reform period has been visible irrespective of regions (rural/urban) and sex of the labour force (male/female). However, the all-India picture reveals that the segments of the labour force representing rural areas suffered relatively more in terms of increasing unemployment during the post-reforms period in India."[23]

7. RELATION BETWEEN PATTERNS OF GROWTH AND POVERTY

Gaurav Datt and Martin Ravallion (2002) who have studied the relationship between patterns of growth and poverty observe:

> "It is also notable that agriculture as a whole has lagged the non agricultural sector in the 1990s; while India's aggregate GDP grew at a rate of 6.7 per cent per annum over 1993-94 to 1999-00, agriculture and allied services grew at only 3.2 per cent per annum. The importance of rural economic growth and agricultural growth in particular to poverty reduction in India has long been recognised."[24]

Growth in large states with high levels of poverty is what matters most for aggregate poverty reduction. Datt and Ravallion have drawn two major conclusions:

1. Non-agricultural growth has not been concentrated in the states where it would have had the greatest impact on poverty nationally. A more pro-poor geographic pattern of growth in India's non-agricultural economy would have required higher growth in states such as Bihar, Madhya Pradesh, Orissa and Uttar Pradesh. Nor has the geographic pattern of agricultural growth been particularly pro-poor. The states with higher growth in agricultural yields were not the key states with higher shares of India's poverty.
2. Non-agricultural growth was less effective in reducing poverty in states with "poor" initial conditions in terms of rural development (in both absolute terms and relative to urban areas) and human resources. Low farm productivity, low rural living standards relative to urban areas and poor basic education and health all inhibited the prospects of the poor participating in growth of non-agricultural sector . . . for example, more than half of the difference

TABLE 2.20

Poverty and Growth Indices for 14 Major States

State	*Head-count Index of Poverty for 1993-94*	*Share of National Poverty 1993-94 (Percentage)*	*Shared Weighted Elasticity*	*Percentage Increase in Non-agriculture Output per Capita 1993/94-1999/2000*	*Percentage Increase in Farm Output per Hectare 1993/94-1999/2000*
(1)	*(2)*	*(3)*	*(4)*	*(5)*	*(6)*
Bihar	60.3	16.7	-0.043	29.3	0.5
Assam	44.5	3.1	-0.023	13.2	27.8
Madhya Pradesh	44.0	9.2	-0.059	18.1	26.8
Rajasthan	43.3	6.1	-0.033	44.3	64.5
Maharashtra	43.2	10.8	-0.054	27.4	11.4
Orissa	40.3	4.0	-0.023	26.3	36.7
Uttar Pradesh	40.1	17.8	-0.120	37.3	26.1
Karnataka	37.4	5.3	-0.035	53.4	11.9
Tamil Nadu	34.9	6.0	-0.032	58.9	-6.4
Gujarat	33.7	4.4	-0.025	38.1	29.9
Andhra Pradesh	29.5	6.1	-0.017	43.2	21.9
Kerala	28.8	2.6	-0.034	73.5	64.0
West Bengal	25.9	5.5	-0.056	49.4	83.0
Punjab	21.4	2.5	-0.021	43.2	14.0

Notes : 1. The States have been arranged in the descending order on the basis of head-count index of poverty.

2. The shared weighted elasticity in column 3 is the product of the elasticity of poverty to non-agricultural output and the share of national poverty in column 2. Output measures in columns 4 and 5 are deflated by the consumer price index for agricultural labourers for consistency with other data in the model.

Source : Re-arranged from Gaurav Datt and Martin Ravallion (2002), "Is India's Economic Growth Leaving the Poor Behind?", *Journal of Economic Perspectives*, Vol. 16, No. 3, p. 103.

> between the elasticity of the head-count index of poverty and non-agricultural output for Bihar (the state with lowest absolute elasticity) and Kerala (the highest) is attributed to Kerala's substantially higher initial literacy rate. Women's literacy matters no less than men's; indeed women's literacy is a slightly more significant predictor of elasticity of poverty with respect to economic growth.

Datt and Ravillion (2002) give a key message for policy makers: "The revealed importance of human resource development as a precondition for pro-poor growth in India reinforces the concerns of Dreze and Sen (1995) and others that *rapid poverty reduction in India will require more than economic reform*. The key message emerging from recent research is that achieving a policy environment conductive to growth interacts multiplicatively with human resource development."[25] (Emphasis added).

However, Datt and Ravallion did not include in initial conditions the role of institutional changes introduced by Kerala and West Bengal Government by way of land reforms which helped them to increase farm output per acre by 64 per cent and 83 per cent respectively during 1993-94 and 1999-00—a short span of six years. As a consequence, these states were able to bring about a sharp increase in non-agricultural output per capita during 1993-94 and 1999-2000—in Kerala by 73.5 per cent and in West Bengal by 49.4 per cent. These states were, therefore, able to trigger the process of pro-poor growth during this period. This factor provides an explanation to the sharp reduction in poverty experienced by these states during the 6-year period—1993-94 to 1999-00 in a significant manner.

8. PRESENT STATE OF POVERTY AND UNEMPLOYMENT

A basic and long standing concern relates to whether the growth strategy will bypass the poor, excluding them from the benefits of growth. This is obvious from the fact that the much higher growth of non-agricultural GDP is not trickling down to the poor, because agriculture is now accounting for 22% of GDP, but is supporting 60% of the labour force. In view of this scenario, the rate of decline of poverty despite a sharp increase of GDP growth to over 7 percent has slowed or is at best, very modest.

Planning Commission's Estimate of Poverty on the basis of 61st Round of NSS-2004-05

NSSO results on the basis of large sample survey data on household consumer expenditure (NSS 61st Round) for 2004-05 are the basis of poverty estimates. The data were collected on uniform recall period (URP) using 30-days for all items. The data was also available using 365 days for 5 frequently purchased non-food items namely, clothing, footwear, durable goods, education and institutional medical expenses and 30-days recall period for the remaining items, known as mixed recall period (MRP), the Planning Commission, using the Expert Group methodology has estimated poverty in 2004-05 using both the distributions. The following results were obtained:

1. Poverty estimates based on URP indicate 28.3% of rural population and 25.7% of the urban population was below the poverty line. For the country as a whole, 27.5% of total population was below the poverty line in 2004-05.
2. The corresponding figures obtained from MRP indicate 21.8% in rural areas, 21.7% in urban areas and 21.8% for the country as a whole was in poverty in 2004-05.

The Planning Commission in its *Approach* to *the 11th Five Year Plan* (December, 2006) states: "Using the methodology of the Expert Group on Estimation of Proportion and Number of Poor 1993, the percentage of population below the poverty line is provisionally estimated at 27.8% in 2004-05. Thus the average decline in percentage of population below the poverty line over the period 1993 to 2004 is 0.74 percentage points per year, much less than implied by the official 1999-2000 data. Because of the slower pace of reduction in the percentage of the poor, the estimated number of poor is now estimated be approximately 300 million in 2004-05, larger than the official estimate of 1999-2000."[26]

It may be recalled that the official estimate for poverty in 1999-2000 was 26.1% for the country as a whole and 260 million were estimated as poor.

Table 2.21 provides state level data on poverty ratios during 2004-05. The lowest poverty ratio was 5.4% for Jammu and Kashmir and highest poverty ratio was for Orissa (46.4%). States with poverty ratio of less than 15% were Jammu & Kashmir, Punjab, Haryana, Himachal Pradesh, Delhi and Andhra Pradesh. As against them, states with poverty ratio above 30% were Maharashtra, Uttar Pradesh, Bihar, Jharkhand, Madhya Pradesh, Chhattisgarh, Uttarakhand and Orissa.

Five States, namely, Uttar Pradesh, Maharashtra, Bihar, West Bengal and Orissa accounted for 166 million poor (about 55% of the total poor estimated at 302 million). This shows the high concentration of poor in these 5 states.

TABLE 2.21

Number and Percentage of Population below Poverty Line (2004-05) based on URP Consumption

Sl. No.	State	Rural: % of Persons	Rural: No. of persons (in lakhs)	Urban: % of Persons	Urban: No. of persons (in lakhs)	Combined: % of Persons	Combined: No. of persons (in lakhs)
	(1)	(2)	(3)	(4)	(5)	(6)	(7)
1.	Jammu & Kashmir	4.6	3.7	7.9	2.2	5.4	5.9
2.	Punjab	9.1	15.1	7.1	6.5	8.4	21.6
3.	Himachal Pradesh	10.7	6.1	3.4	0.2	10.0	6.4
4.	Goa	5.4	0.4	21.3	1.6	13.8	2.0
5.	Haryana	13.6	21.5	15.1	10.6	14.0	32.1
6.	Delhi	6.9	0.6	15.2	22.3	14.7	22.9
7.	Kerala	13.2	32.4	20.2	17.2	15.0	49.6
8.	Andhra Pradesh	11.2	64.7	28.0	61.4	15.8	126.1
9.	Gujarat	19.1	63.5	13.0	27.2	16.8	90.7
10.	Assam	22.3	54.5	3.3	1.3	19.7	55.8
11.	Rajasthan	18.7	87.4	32.9	47.5	22.1	134.9
12.	Tamil Nadu	22.8	76.5	22.2	69.1	22.5	145.6
13.	West Bengal	28.6	173.2	14.8	35.1	24.7	208.3
14.	Karnataka	20.8	75.0	32.6	63.8	25.0	138.9
15.	**All-India**	**28.3**	**2209.2**	**25.7**	**808.0**	**27.5**	**3017.2**
16.	Maharashtra	29.6	171.1	32.2	146.3	30.7	317.4
17.	Uttar Pradesh	33.4	473.0	30.6	117.0	32.8	590.0
18.	Madhya Pradesh	36.9	175.7	42.1	74.0	38.3	249.7
19.	Uttarakhand	40.8	27.1	36.5	8.9	39.6	36.0
20.	Jharkhand	46.3	103.2	20.2	13.2	40.3	116.4
21.	Chhattisgarh	40.8	71.5	41.2	19.5	40.9	91.0
22.	Bihar	42.1	336.7	34.6	32.4	41.4	369.2
23.	Orissa	46.8	151.8	44.3	26.7	46.4	178.5

Note : States have been arranged in the ascending order on the basis of combined poverty ratio in 2004-05. Poverty line Rs. 356.0 in rural areas and Rs. 538.6 in urban areas (Per capita monthly expenditure).

Source : Planning Commission, Press Release, March 2007.

TABLE 2.22
Poverty Estimates based on URP

	1993-94	*2004-05*
Rural	37.3	28.3
Urban	32.4	25.7
Total	36.0	27.5

Source : Planning Commission, Press Release March, 2007.

Dev and Ravi's Study on Poverty

S. Mahendra Dev and C. Ravi have also analyzed indepth the data of the 61st round of NSS (2004-05) and compared it with the period 1983-93. Major finding of the study are:

1. The study reveals that over-all poverty in India in 2004-05 was 28.3%, slightly higher than the estimate of the Planning Commission, although the study uses the official poverty lines as updated for 2004-05, i.e. Rs. 356 for rural areas and Rs. 538.6 of per capita monthly expenditure for urban areas. Accordingly rural poverty ratio was 29.2% and for urban areas it was 26.0% for 2004-05.
2. The absolute number of poor declined to around 315.5 million in 2004-05 from around 324 million in 1993-94—indicating a decline of 9 million during the 11-year period.
3. The study has estimated the 'very poor' defined as those who are below 75 percent of poverty line. There was a decline in the proportion of the very poor from 15.5% in 1993-94 to 10.3% in 2004-05. This implies the very poor accounted for 115 million among the total poor reckoned at about 316 million. Obviously, the share of *hard core* or chronic poor is quite high, around 37 percent of the total poor.
4. Data provided in Table 2.23 and 2.24 reveals that poverty continued to decline from 44.9% in 1983 to 36.0% in 1993 and further to 28.3% in 2004-05. This phenomenon was also observed in both rural and urban areas. However, it was noted that total poverty declined at the rate of 0.85 percentage points in the pre-reform period (1983-93), while the corresponding figure for the post-reform period was 0.70 percentage points per annum. From this, it can be inferred that the rate of decline in total poverty was slower in the post-reform period than in the pre-reform period. The same pattern was observed in the rural as well as urban areas.

TABLE 2.23

Percentage and Poor and Very Poor in India (URP Basis)

	Poverty Ratios (in percent)			*Change in Poverty (%age points per annum)*	
	1983	*1993-94*	*2004-05*	*1983-94*	*1994-2005*
Rural					
Poor	45.8	37.3	29.2	-0.81	-0.73
Very Poor	25.5	15.4	9.6	-0.97	-0.52
Urban					
Poor	42.3	32.3	26.0	-0.92	-0.59
Very Poor	22.5	16.0	12.0	-0.61	-0.36
All-India					
Poor	44.9	36.0	28.3	-0.85	-0.70
Very Poor	24.8	16.5	10.3	0.80	0.40

Source : S. Mahendra Dev and C. Ravi, Poverty and Inequality—All-India and States, 1983-2005, *Economic and Political Weekly*, February 10, 2007.

TABLE 2.24

Absolute Number of Poor and Very Poor in India on the URP basis

	1983	*1993-94*	*2004-05*
Rural			
Poor	252.0	247.2	232.2
Very Poor	140.6 (55.8)	102.0 (41.3)	76.7 (33.1)
Urban			
Poor	72.3	77.4	83.3
Very Poor	38.4 (53.1)	38.0 (49.1)	38.4 (46.1)
All-India			
Poor	320.4	324.6	315.5
Very Poor	179.0 (55.2)	140.0 (43.2)	115.1 (36.5)

Note : Figures in brackets refer to percentage share of very poor to the total poor.
Source : Dev and Ravi (2007), *op. cit.*

This implies that though the GDP growth was higher in the post-reform period, yet it failed to impact poverty reduction rate significantly and a result, a higher rate of poverty reduction than observed in the pre-reform as normally expected, did not take place.

To understand slower rate of poverty reduction in the post-reform period, Dev and Ravi calculated Gini co-efficient for the urban and rural areas.

From the data provided in Table 2.25, it is evident that inequality of consumption represented by the Gini coefficient seems to have increased significantly for both rural and urban areas in the post-reform period—the rate of increase being much higher for the urban as compared to rural areas.

Mahendra Dev and Ravi from their study draw the following conclusion:

> The relationship of income and Gini elasticities with the levels of head-count poverty ratios "shows that the states which have low poverty ratios had high income and Gini elasticities. The policy implication is that growth alone would not be sufficient for reduction in poverty and policies that reduce inequality are also important in these states. On the other hand, states such as Bihar, Orissa, UP and MP which have high poverty ratios show low income and Gini elasticities. It shows that growth is more important in these states than distribution policies."

Table 2.25
Gini Co-efficient for Rural and Urban Areas

	Poverty and Inequality			*%age change per annum*	
	1983	*1993-94*	*2004-05*	*1983-94*	*1994-05*
Gini Co-efficient					
Rural	30.79	28.55	30.45	-0.21	0.17
Urban	34.06	34.31	37.51	0.02	0.29

Source : Dev and Ravi (2007), *op. cit.*

"To conclude, the extent of decline in the post-reform period in poverty is not higher compared to the pre-reform period in spite of overall growth. Apart from other factors, an increase in inequality seems to have slowed down the rate of reduction in the post-reform period. . . . However, there are two unambiguous conclusions. One is that there is no evidence of a higher rate of decline in poverty in the post-reform period as a whole compared to the pre-reform period. Secondly, inequality increased significantly in the post-reform period as compared to the earlier decade. Higher inclusive growth that increases agriculture and non-farm growth, and a reduction in regional, rural-urban and social disparities are important for a faster reduction in poverty. Human development is equally important for poverty alleviation. Therefore, policies that increase growth and equity have to be followed simultaneously. . . . There is also a need for focused intervention on the 115 million hard core poor."[27]

There is another problem raised by Mohan Guruswamy *et. al.* about the definition of poverty line. "While the definition of hunger in terms of calories can remain constant, the definition of poverty is relative to the present levels of general prosperity . . . the present official poverty line is based only on calories and hence accounts for little else but the satiation of one's hunger. *It would have been more accurate to define this as a starvation line, as that is exactly what it is.*"[28] (Emphasis added). The Planning Commission, thus, intends to reduce *starvation line* up to 10 percent by 2017. For providing a basic minimum, poverty line needs to be redefined in terms of basic needs approach. While India is aiming to become a super-economic power by 2020, it will only reduce starvation by that date. In the light of this, India should adopt the International Poverty Line of $2 per day as the basis of determining the percentage of people in poverty. As per the *Human Development Report (2005),* on the basis of $1 per day, for the year 1999-2000, people below the poverty line in India were of the order of 34.7% and if we use the norm of $2 per day, then 80 percent of the Indian population was below the poverty line. The present poverty line on the basis of calories does not even meet the rock bottom standard of poverty set at $1 per day, not to speak of reaching the standard of $2 per day basis on basic needs approach. The Planning Commission should, therefore, upgrade the poverty line to reach international standards as it intends to do in other sectors of manufacturing, services and yield of output in agriculture. It should not seek a false sense of satisfaction that it has been able to effectively reduce poverty.

Changes in Poverty over the period 1987-88 and 2004-05

Figures based on 30-days recall period are more reliable than those based on 365 days recall period. This only underlines the fact that as against the figure 26.1 percent of total population being poor in 1999-00 as indicated in the Tenth Plan, the proportion of poor in 2004-05 was higher at 27.5 percent in 2004-05. This casts a shadow on the implications of the reform process for poverty removal. It appears that the percolation of the benefits of high rate of GDP growth to the poor is abysmally low.

Table 2.26 provides information about changes in poverty incidence during the 17-year period (1987-88 to 2004-05) for urban and rural areas. For the first time, the data reveal that poverty in urban areas at the all-India level was 29 percent in 2004-05 as against 28 percent in rural areas. Higher HCR of poverty in urban areas as against rural areas is only a recent phenomenon.

Since rural areas account for about 72% of the total population, rural poverty is the major determinant of overall poverty in a state. Rural poverty data shows that rural poverty levels in 2004-05 continue to be very high in Orissa (47%), Chhattisgarh and Jharkhand (43%), Bihar (42%), Madhya Pradesh (37%), Uttar Pradesh (34%) and Maharashtra (32%). However, the States which have been successful in reducing rural poverty are: Jammu &

TABLE 2.26

Poverty Incidence in Major States Compared over 1987-88 to 2004-05

(Percentage of population)

	Urban			*Rural*		
	2004-05	*1993-94*	*1987-88*	*2004-05*	*1993-94*	*1987-88*
All India	**29**	**33**	**38**	**28**	**37**	**39**
West Bengal	24	23	33	28	41	46
Kerala	23	24	45	13	25	25
Uttar Pradesh	32	35	40	34	42	45
Bihar	42	34	53	42	58	58
Assam	7	8	17	23	45	35
Jammu & Kashmir	10	15	13	3	18	26
Jharkhand	22	—	—	43	—	—
Karnataka	33	40	49	24	30	31
Maharashtra	33	35	35	32	38	45
Andhra Pradesh	34	38	45	11	16	21
Gujarat	18	28	40	20	22	28
Rajasthan	27	31	36	18	26	31
Madhya Pradesh	48	48	43	37	41	46
Haryana	21	16	18	13	28	15
Tamil Nadu	28	40	42	24	33	42
Orissa	50	41	43	47	50	55
Himachal Pradesh	4	9	—	8	30	16
Chhattisgarh	46	—	—	43	—	—
Punjab	10	11	13	9	12	13

Source: National Sample Survey, *61st Round (2004-05).*

Kashmir (3%), Himachal Pradesh (8%), Punjab (9%), Andhra Pradesh (11%) and Haryana as well as Kerala (13%).

9. UNEMPLOYMENT RATES IN THE PRE AND POST-REFORM PERIOD

61st Round of the NSS has provided us information about the state of unemployment in 2004-05 and has also provided comparative analysis with the previous rounds. The following points emerge:

1. Compared to 1999-2000, during 2004-05, the unemployment rate of the usual principal status remained about the same in rural or

TABLE 2.27

Unemployment Rates (1983 to 2004-05) All India

Round Year	Male			Female		
	Usual Status	Current Weekly Status	Current Daily Status	Usual Status	Current Weekly Status	Current Daily Status
(1)	(2)	(3)	(4)	(5)	(6)	(7)
Rural						
61st (2004-05)	2.1	3.8	8.0	3.1	4.2	8.7
55th (1999-2000)	2.1	3.9	7.2	1.5	3.7	7.0
50th (1993-94)	2.0	3.1	5.6	1.3	2.9	5.6
43rd (1987-88	2.8	4.2	4.6	3.5	4.4	6.7
38th (1983)	2.1	3.7	7.5	1.4	4.3	9.0
Urban						
61st (2004-05)	4.4	5.2	7.5	9.1	9.0	11.6
55th (1999-2000)	4.8	5.6	7.3	7.1	7.3	9.4
50th (1993-94)	5.4	5.2	6.7	8.3	7.9	10.4
43rd (1987-88	6.1	6.6	8.8	8.5	9.2	12.0
38th (1983)	5.9	6.7	9.2	6.9	7.5	11.0

Source: NSS Report No. 515: *Employment and Unemployment Situation in India* (2004-05).

urban areas for males, but increased by 2 percentage points for females. This implies that there was no improvement in the usual principal status employment.

2. In terms of current daily status, the unemployment rate was 2 percentage points more for females in both the rural and urban areas. This indicates deterioration in female employment. In terms of males, cds rate increased from 7.2 percent in 1999-00 to 8.0 percent in 2004-05 for rural areas. However, there was a slight change in male cds rate in urban areas from 7.3% to 7.5%. The upshot of this analysis is that the major problem of the Indian economy is under-employment and not so much as open unemployment. High usual status of unemployment rate for females in urban areas up from 7.1% in 1999-00 to 9.1% in 2004-05, is however, a cause for concern.

Table 2.28 provides unemployment rates in 2004-05 for rural and urban areas. In both the rural and urban areas, the unemployment rate (CDS basis) was over 8 percent which was quite high. Whereas, in rural areas, the difference in cds rates for males and females indicated minor variations, in urban areas, male CDS rate was 7.5% whereas the female CDS rate was quite high at 11.6%.

TABLE 2.28

Unemployment Rates during 2004-05

Percent (All-India)

	Rural			*Urban*		
	Male	*Female*	*Person*	*Male*	*Female*	*Person*
Usual Status (PS)	2.1	3.1	2.5	4.4	9.1	5.3
Current Weekly Status (CWS)	3.8	4.2	3.9	5.2	9.0	6.0
Current Daily Status (CDS)	8.0	8.7	8.2	7.5	11.6	8.3

Source : NSS Report No. 515 (2004-05).

The usual principal status rate for rural areas was very low at 2.5%, but it was quite significant in urban areas at 5.3%.

State Level Variations in Unemployment Rates (CDS)

Since rural unemployment is of a much larger magnitude than urban unemployment, the data has been arranged in the descending order on the basis of rural CDS rates.

Kerala shows the highest rate of rural unemployment of the order of 25.6 percent in rural areas and 25.2 percent in urban areas. Other states which are higher than the All-India level of 8.2% for rural areas are: Tamil Nadu (15.1%), West Bengal (11.2%), Andhra Pradesh (10.9%), Orissa (10.2%), Punjab (9.7%), Maharashtra (9.3%). Very low CDS rates were observed in Arunachal Pradesh, Uttar Pradesh, Gujarat and Rajasthan. (Refer Table 2.29)

TABLE 2.29

Unemployment Rates According to Current Daily Status in Major States (2004-05)

	Rural	*Urban*
Kerala	25.6	25.2
Tamil Nadu	15.1	8.6
West Bengal	11.2	10.5
Andhra Pradesh	10.9	7.9
Orissa	10.2	15.0
Punjab	9.7	7.5
Maharashtra	9.3	8.8
Chhattisgarh	8.2	7.1
All India	**8.2**	**8.3**
Bihar	6.8	10.0
Karnataka	6.7	6.0
Jharkhand	6.6	8.8
Assam	6.5	9.0
Haryana	6.2	6.9
Himachal Pradesh	5.7	4.9
Jammu & Kashmir	5.6	6.0
Madhya Pradesh	5.6	6.4
Rajasthan	4.4	6.1
Gujarat	4.1	4.7
Uttar Pradesh	3.7	6.3
Arunachal Pradesh	1.4	4.7

Note : Data has been arranged in the descending order on the basis of CDS rates in rural areas.

Source : NSS Report 515, *Employment and Unemployment Situation* in India (2004-05).

In urban areas, cds rates were high in Kerala (25.2%), Orissa (15.0%), West Bengal (10.5%), Bihar (10.0), Assam (9.0%).

Very high rates of unemployment in Kerala, Tamil Nadu, West Bengal, Orissa and Andhra Pradesh need urgent attention.

Unemployment Rate among Youth (Age 15-29 Years)

Table 2.30 provides information regarding youth unemployment for the Age-group 15-29 years. The information pertains to the period 1993-94 to 2004-05. Data reveals that in all the four categories, youth unemployment rates have increased. The situation in urban areas was worse than in rural areas. For urban males the youth unemployment (cds) was 13.7% but for urban females, it was as high as 21.5% in 2004-05. Even in rural areas, youth unemployment rate, though comparatively lower, was still quite high at 12-13% in 2004-05.

It may be noted that unemployment rate among the youth was much higher as compared to that in the over-all population. Secondly, the rate was higher for the urban youth than for the rural youth. Thirdly, compared to the female youth, the unemployment rate for the male youth was lower, and it was substantially lower in urban India.

TABLE 2.30
Unemployment Rates among Youth (15-29 Years)

	1993-94			*1999-2000*			*2004-05*		
	ps	*cws*	*cds*	*ps*	*cws*	*cds*	*ps*	*cws*	*cds*
Rural Male	4.8	5.8	9.0	5.1	7.3	11.1	5.2	6.9	12.0
Rural Female	3.2	4.8	7.6	3.7	6.8	10.6	7.0	7.5	12.7
Urban Male	10.8	11.4	13.7	11.5	12.4	14.7	10.0	11.0	13.7
Urban Female	19.4	18.5	21.2	16.6	16.6	19.1	19.9	18.3	21.5

Source : NSS Report No. 515, *op. cit.*, (2004-05).

Table 2.31 provides information regarding rate of unemployment by level of education for the age group 15-59 years for 2004-05. The data is for usual principal and subsidiary basis. The data reveals that unemployment rate increases with the level of education indicating that the jobseekers become gradually more and more choosers as their level of education increases. It is lowest among the illiterates and higher among the educated.

However, among the educated youth, i.e. those persons who have attained an education level of secondary and above including those who have completed diploma/certificate courses and are in the age group 15-29 years, unemployment rate was very high – 9.1% in rural males and 13.3% in urban males. In contrast, unemployment rates among females were much higher – 20.8% among rural females and 26.7% among urban females.

To sum up, it may be mentioned that over a decade of reform 1993-94 to 2004-05 has failed to reduce unemployment in India and it has moved up to 8.3 percent in 2004-05 as against about 6 percent in 1993-94. The regional picture shows wide variation in cds rates ranging from 25% in Kerala 15%

in Tamil Nadu to 4% in Gujarat and 5% in Himachal Pradesh. Youth unemployment rates were much higher than the overall unemployment rates. The unemployment rates increase with the level of education indicating the poor illiterates are prepared to take up any job that comes their way, but relatively better-off educated persons have become more choosy.

TABLE 2.31

Unemployment Rates Usual Status (Principal + Subsidiary)

	Rural		*Urban*	
Level of Education	*Male*	*Female*	*Male*	*Female*
Not Literate	0.3	0.2	1.0	0.3
Literate and upto primary	1.0	1.1	2.1	2.9
Middle school	1.6	3.4	4.2	8.0
Secondary	3.2	9.5	4.3	13.4
Higher Secondary	4.7	17.1	4.3	15.0
Diploma and Certificate	7.0	20.1	7.7	15.3
Graduate and above	6.2	27.5	5.8	17.2

Source : NSS Report No. 515, *op. cit.*, (2004-05).

Falling Real Wages

C.P. Chandrasekhar and Jayati Ghosh have examined the trend of real wages by categories in 1993-94 prices. (Refer *Business Line,* 28th November 2006). The study reveals the following results:

1. For most categories of regular workers, the recent period (1993-94 and 2004-05) has not been one of rising real wages. While real wages have increased slightly for rural male regular employees, the rate of increase has certainly decelerated compared to the previous period. For all other categories of regular workers, real wages in 2004-05 were actually lower than in 1999-2000. The economy has, therefore, experienced a peculiar tendency of falling real wages along with relatively less regular employment for most workers.
2. Real wages of casual labour appear to have increased slightly in rural areas, although the rate of increase slowed down compared to the previous period. However, for both men and women workers in urban areas, real wages for casual workers on average declined compared to 1999-2000. (Refer Table 2.32)
3. The real expansion in employment has come in the form of self-employment which now accounts for nearly half of the total employment in India. But the shift in employment towards self-

TABLE 2.32

Average Real Daily-wage Earnings of Regular and Casual Workers, All India, 15-59 Years

	1983	1987-88	1993-94	1999-2000	2004-05
(1)	(2)	(3)	(4)	(5)	(6)
I. Regular Salaried Workers					
(a) Rural Male					
Agriculture	17.3	26.1	27.5	44.2	41.1
Non-agriculture	45.5	62.4	66.5	90.8	88.2
All	37.0	53.9	58.5	80.2	83.8
(b) Rural Female					
Agriculture	21.9	19.0	22.8	31.0	31.5
Non-agriculture	26.8	46.4	40.6	91.3	51.6
All	25.0	38.5	34.9	71.8	49.4
(c) Urban Male					
Agriculture	30.6	47.6	51.4	92.9	52.1
Non-agriculture	58.3	72.5	79.2	106.5	101.4
All	57.7	72.3	78.1	102.3	101.0
(d) Urban Female					
Agriculture	23.8	32.9	46.7	38.9	39.6
Non-agriculture	43.0	60.1	62.7	97.3	76.5
All	42.2	60.1	62.3	84.6	76.1
II. Casual Workers					
(e) Rural Male					
Agriculture	16.6	20.1	21.6	25.5	27.8
Non-agriculture	24.1	28.1	30.1	37.5	39.5
All	18.2	22.3	23.2	28.6	31.1
(f) Rural Female					
Agriculture	11.3	13.3	15.1	18.0	19.3
Non-agriculture	11.8	16.3	17.5	23.5	25.8
All	11.3	13.8	15.3	18.5	20.2
(g) Urban Male					
Agriculture	20.8	22.6	25.5	30.3	28.1
Non-agriculture	27.6	30.9	33.8	39.3	38.2
All	26.5	29.4	32.4	38.1	37.3
(h) Urban Female					
Agriculture	12.2	13.2	16.5	19.4	17.2
Non-agriculture	13.1	16.7	19.5	24.7	23.7
All	12.9	15.5	18.5	23.0	21.8

Source : Employment and Unemployment Surveys, National Sample Survey Organization, Various rounds as given by Unni, J. and Raveendran, G., *Economic and Political Weekly,* January 20, 2007.

employment is not a consequence of some pull factor but is rather forced upon the working people due to non-availability of remunerative jobs.

Chandrasekhar and Ghosh, therefore, conclude: "This suggests that a large part of the increase in self-employment— and, therefore, in employment as a whole—is a distress-driven phenomenon, led by the inability to find adequate gainful paid employment."[29] This indicates that shift towards self-employment is part of survival strategies of the working people

Growth Rates of Employment

Data provided in Table 2.33 shows that there is a small recovery in agricultural employment from a practically zero level during 1993-94 to 1999-2000 to 0.83 percent during 1999-2000 to 2004-05. However, there is a stimulus provided to non-agricultural employment from a level of 2.53% during 1993-94 to 1999-2000 to a level of 4.66% during 1999-2000 to 2004-05.

TABLE 2.33
Growth Rates of Employment

(*Percent per annum*)

	1993-94 to 1999-2000	*1999-2000 to 2004-05*
Total agricultural employment	0.03	0.83
Secondary employment	2.91	4.64
Tertiary employment	2.27	4.67
Total non-agricultural employment	2.53	4.66

Source : NSS Report No. 515, *op. cit.*, (2004-05).

Since agriculture still accounts for nearly 60% of total employment in the economy, the relatively high employment growth in secondary and tertiary sectors to a level of 4.66% in 1999-2000 to 2004-05 in unable to significantly change the share of employment towards secondary and tertiary sectors.

10. TREND OF LABOUR PRODUCTIVITY AND SHARE OF WAGES IN VALUE ADDED

Chandrasekhar and Jayati Ghosh have studied the trend of labour productivity. They have calculated net value added per worker (at constant prices) as the measure of labour productivity for the period 1981 to 2003.

The study reveals that labour productivity tripled between 1981-82 and 2003-04 from 0.7 to 2.1 percent. However, the benefits of this sharp increase in labour productivity were largely appropriated in the form of rent, interest and profit incomes by the propertied class, but workers share in value added declined from 0.3 to 0.15 during 1981-82 to 2003-04.

Thus, real wages in organized manufacturing declined by around 11 percent in 2003-04 as against 1995-96. While manufacturing registered a strong growth in production of the order of 5.83% during 1994-95 to 2004-05, falling real wages in the context of rising labour productivity in manufacturing casts a shadow on the reform process whether it can, by any stretch of imagination, be described as "inclusive".

TABLE 2.34
Net Value Added per Worker (In constant prices)

1981	0.71
1986	0.74
1991	1.03
1996	1.75
2001	1.62
2003	2.07

Source : www.macroscan.org

TABLE 2.35
Share of Wages in Value Added

	Wages/NVA
1981-82	0.30
1986-87	0.31
1991-92	0.25
1996-97	0.17
2001-02	0.19
2003-04	0.15

Source : Ghosh, J., www.macroscan.org

11. SUMMING UP

The Survey of economic literature during 1990 to 2004 on the subject of "Poverty, Employment and Growth" reveals two schools of thought—one led by the economists who follow the World Bank-IMF Economic Reforms approach and the other who believe that growth *per se* is not likely to usher

TABLE 2.36
Average Real Wages in Organised Manufacturing

	Rs. In 1993-94 prices
1995-96	11,708
1996-97	10,772
1997-98	10,634
1998-99	9,422
1999-00	9,785
2000-01	10,158
2001-02	9,947
2002-03	9,997
2003-04	10,014

Source : Ghosh, J., www.macroscan.org

in pro-poor growth to take care of the employment and poverty problem. The Planning Commission has also actively participated in the debate and the formulation of the Ninth and Tenth Plans are especially important in this respect.

The profile of poverty not only studied the head-count index but also made use of the Poverty Gap and Squared Poverty Gap to understand the depth of poverty. Datt's study showed that while there is a marked decline in both rural and urban poverty rates between 1973-74 and 1986-87, there is no sign of anything comparable thereafter (i.e. in the post-reform period). Although the urban sector seems to have continued its march of poverty reduction in the process of growth, rural poverty reduction was choked-off by lack of rural growth.

Regarding unemployment, the torch bearers of economic reform held that once the policies of liberalisation, privatisation and globalisation gather momentum, they will accelerate the process of GDP growth and will also increase the growth rate of employment once the teething troubles an over. However, this did not happen and the growth rate of employment in the economy which was of the order of 2.0 per cent per year during 1983 to 1993-94 as per NSS data, sharply declined to less than 1 percent in the period 1993-94 to 1999-00. Critics, therefore, described the process of economic reforms as that of 'Jobless growth'.

Two patterns in employment generation were noticed—one pattern pertained to the period 1983 to 1993-94. In this pattern, nearly 51 per cent of additional employment came from the primary sector, 19 per cent from the secondary sector and 30 percent from tertiary sector. In the other pattern that developed during 1993-94 and 1999-2000, nearly 50 per cent of additional employment was generated in the secondary sector and 73 per cent in the tertiary sector; however, in the agricultural sector, there was a fall in employment by nearly 23 per cent. The post-liberalisation period thus appears to be one which neglected agriculture. The basic question is: Can India afford to adopt the second pattern when agriculture and allied services account for 60 per cent of total employment? Two views were expressed on this issue: one led by Dr. Montek Singh Ahluwalia, Chairman of the Task Force on Employment Opportunities who favoured stepping up GDP growth to 10 per cent as a solution. The other view was led by Dr. S.P. Gupta, Chairman of the Special Group on Targeting Ten Million Employment Opportunities per year, which recommended 60 per cent of the additional job creation by boosting GDP growth to 8 per cent per annum during the Tenth Plan and 40 per cent additional employment opportunities to be created by Special programmes targeted to the poor and unorganised sector of the economy.

Opinion among policy-makers and economists converged towards the Special Group recommendations which were formally accepted by the National Democratic Alliance (NDA) government, but were not seriously implemented. The same policy recommendations have been suggested by the Common Minimum Programme of the UPA Government in 2004, though they have not acknowledged the Special Group as the author of these recommendations.

A close perusal of unemployment rates by household per capita expenditure reveals that the lower consumption groups show much lower UPSS rates of unemployment, but this pattern gets reversed on the basis of CDS criterion. But as expenditure levels improve, there is an increase in unemployment rate on the basis of UPSS criterion and a fall on the basis of CDS criterion. The high degree of CDS unemployment rate is a reflection of the high degree of under-employment among the poor, since the poor cannot afford to remain unemployed as their waiting power is very weak and they take up any job—low paid or high paid, full time or part-time, regular or intermittent.

The structure of employment reveals that the share of organised sector employment which was 7.93 per cent in total employment in 1983 as well as in 1988, declined to 7.1 per cent in 1999-2000. This was due to shedding the load by the public sector to reduce redundancy, but there was a failure on the part of the organised private sector to increase employment to offset the deceleration experienced in the public sector. Besides this, there was a deterioration of self-employment from about 63 per cent in 1977-78 to 56 per cent in 1999-2000, but an increase in casual employment from 30 per cent to over 37 per cent during the same period. The increase in casual employment share is a reflection of the index of deterioration in the quality of employment.

S.P. Gupta, Special Group Report on Employment Policy is unique in the sense that it rejected the reform process as a panacea for all ills of the economy, especially referring to unemployment. To usher an era of zero unemployment and removal of poverty, it rejected the Report of the Task Force headed by M.S. Ahluwalia. Instead, it emphasized that attention be focussed on the unorganised sector which provides employment to 92 per cent of labour force. It was against the policy of 'hire and fire' as the principal instrument for enlarging employment as recommended by the protagonists of economic reform. It underlined the need for improving productivity and job quality of the unorganised sector. It laid emphasis on strengthening agriculture and small and medium industries as the principal contributors to growth and employment. The employment elasticity of the unorganised sector was 3.23 times that of the organised sector. The civil administration in urban areas and panchayats in rural areas have to work hand in hand along with the State to reduce unemployment. All these recommendations find a place in the Common Minimum Programme of the UPA Government.

Bhaumik's study to establish a relationship between NSDP and number of employed shows a negative and statistically significant relation in the pre-reform period. But the same relationship pertaining to post-reform period becomes positive, though statistically insignificant. The increase in the absolute number of unemployed during the post-reform period (from 20.24 million in 1993-94 to 26.43 million in 1999-00) has been visible irrespective of regions and sex of the labour force. However, the all-India picture reveals that segments of labour force representing rural areas suffered relatively more in terms of increasing unemployment in the post-reform period. The study leads us to the conclusion that to effect a reduction in unemployment, growth alone is not sufficient. What matters most is perhaps the quality and composition of growth from the viewpoint of employment expansion.

Datt and Martin studied the relationship between patterns of growth and poverty. Two conclusions emerge from the study: (i) Non-agricultural growth has not been concentrated in the states where it would have had the greatest impact on poverty nationally. Nor has the geographic pattern of agricultural growth been particularly pro-poor. The states with higher growth in agricultural yields were not the key states with higher shares of India's poverty. (ii) Non-agricultural growth was less effective in reducing poverty in states with poor initial conditions in terms of rural development and human resources. The key message of the study is that rapid poverty reduction in India requires more than economic reform. Recent research has brought out that achieving a policy environment conductive to growth interacts multiplicatively with human resource development. It needs to be pointed out that Datt and Ravallion did not include in initial conditions the role of institutional changes introduced by way of land reforms which helped Kerala and West Bengal to usher an era of rapid economic growth both in terms of an increase in agricultural productivity and non-agricultural output per capita during 1993-94 and 1999-00. This, in turn, triggered the process of pro-poor growth resulting in sharp decline in poverty.

The Planning Commission in its *Approach* to *the 11th Five Year Plan* (December, 2006) states: "Using the methodology of the Expert Group on Estimation of Proportion and Number of Poor 1993, the percentage of population below the poverty line is provisionally estimated at 27.8% in 2004-05. Thus the average decline in percentage of population below the poverty line over the period 1993 to 2004 is 0.74 percentage points per year, much less than implied by the official 1999-2000 data. Because of the slower pace of reduction in the percentage of the poor, the estimated number of poor is now estimated be approximately 300 million in 2004-05, larger than the official estimate of 1999-2000."

Data about unemployment rates in 2004-05 reveals that in both rural and urban areas, the unemployment rate (cds basis) was over 8 percent which was quite high.

Data about youth unemployment reveals that during 2004-05, for urban males, the youth employment (cds) was 13.7 percent, but for urban females, it was as high as 21.5 percent. Even in rural areas, youth unemployment rate, though comparatively lower, was still quite high at 12-13 percent.

For most categories of regular workers, the post-reform period (1993-94 to 2004-05) has not been one of rising real wages. While real wages have slightly increased for rural male regular employees, the rate of increase has certainly decelerated compared to the previous period. For all other categories of regular workers, real wages in 2004-05 were actually lower than in 1999-00.

Similarly, for female as well as male casual workers in urban areas, real wages in 2004-05 declined compared to 1999-2000.

The economy has, therefore, experienced a peculiar tendency of falling real wages along with relatively less regular employment for most workers.

The real expansion in employment has come in the form of self-employment which now accounts for nearly half of the total employment, but this is a distress driven phenomenon, led by inability to find regular paid employment.

In short, the economy has succeeded in pushing up GDP growth during the post-reform period, but has failed in effectively reducing poverty and unemployment.

References

1. Singh, Manmohan (2004), Text of Prime Minister Manmohan Singh's address to the nation on June 24, 2004, *Hindu*, June 25, 2004.
2. Planning Commission (1998), *Ninth Five Year Plan (1997-2002)*, Vol. I, p. 30.
3. *Ibid.*, p. 30.
4. *Ibid.*, pp. 30-31.

5. Datt, Gaurav (1999), "Has Poverty Declined since Economic Reforms", *Economic and Political Weekly*, December 11-17.
6. Sen, Abhijit (2000), "Estimates of Consumer Expenditure and its Distribution—Statistical Priorities after NSS 55th Round", *Economic and Political Weekly*, December 16.
7. Visaria, Pravin (2000), "Alternative Estimates of Poverty in India", *Economic Times*, July 29.
8. Planning Commission (2002), *Report of Special Group on Targeting Ten Million Employment Opportunities*, p. 2.
9. Planning Commission (2001), *Task Force on Employment Opportunities*, p. 2.22.
10. Planning Commission (2002), *op. cit.*, p. 2.
11. *Ibid.*, p. 2.
12. *Ibid.*, p. 27.
13. *Ibid.*, pp. 27-28.
14. *Ibid.*, p. 29.
15. *Ibid.*, p. 4.
16. *Ibid.*, p. 7.
17. *Ibid.*, p. 9.
18. *Ibid.*, p. 90.
19. *Ibid.*, p. 10.
20. *Ibid.*, pp. 10-11.
21. Planning Commission (2005), *Mid-Term Appraisal of the 10th Five Year Plan (2002-07)*, p. 263.
22. Bhaumik, S.K. (2003), "Employment in India in the Post-Liberalisation Era", *Indian Journal of Labour Economics*, Vol. 46, No. 1, pp. 86-87
23. *Ibid.*, p. 87.
24. Gaurav Datt and Martin Ravallion (2002), "Is India's Economic Growth Leaving the Poor Behind?", *Journal of Economic Perspectives*, Vol. 16, No. 3, pp. 97-98.
25. *Ibid.*, p. 105.
26. Planning Commission, *Towards Faster and More Inclusive Growth : An Approach to the 11th Five Year Plan*, (December 2006), p. 71.
27. Mahendra, Dev S. and Ravi (2007), Poverty and Inequality: All-India and States, 1983-2005, *Economic and Political Weekly*, February 10, 2007, pp. 519-20.
28. Guruswamy, Mohan and Abraham, Ronald (2006), *Redefining Poverty—A New Poverty Line for a New India*, p. 2.
29. Chandrasekhar, C.P. and Ghosh, Jayati, (2006), Employment Conditions: Working more for less, *Business Line*, November 28, 2006.

Select References

Bhaduri, Amit (1996), "Employment and Labour Market Flexibility and Economic Liberalisation in India", *The Indian Journal of Labour Economics*, Vol. 39, No. 1.

Bhagwati, Jagadish (1993), *Indian in Transition: Freeing the Economy*, Oxford University Press, Oxford.

——— (2001), "Growth, Poverty and Reforms", *Economic and Political Weekly*, Vol. 36, No. 3, July-September.

Bhalla, G.S. and Hazell, Peter (2003), "Rural Employment and Poverty", *Economic and Political Weekly*, Vol. XXXVIII, No. 33.

Bhalla, Sheila (1997), "Trends in Poverty, Wages and Employment in India", *Indian Journal of Labour Economics*, Vol. 40, No. 2.

Bhaumik, S.K. (2003), "Unemployment in India in the Post-Liberalisation Era", *Indian Journal of Labour Economics*, Vol. 46, No. 1.

Chadha, G.K. (2001), "Impact of Economic Reform on Rural Unemployment: No Smooth Sailing Anticipated", *Indian Journal of Agricultural Economics*, Vol. 56, No. 3, July-September.

——— and Sahu, P.P. (2002), "Post-reform Setbacks in Rural Employment: Issues that need further Scrutiny", *Economic and Political Weekly*, Vol. 37, No. 21, May 25.

Chandrasekhar, C.P. and Jayati Ghosh (2006a), "Employment Growth: The latest Trends" *Macroscan: An Alternative Economics*, November 17

——— (2006b) 'Working More for Less', *Macroscan: An Alternative Economics*, November 28.

Datt, Gaurav (1994), "Poverty Alleviation through Rural Public Works: The Experience of Maharashtra Employment Guarantee Scheme", *Indian Journal of Labour Economics*, Vol. 37, No. 4.

——— (1999), "Has Poverty Declined since Economic Reforms", *Economic and Political Weekly*, Vol. XXXIV, No. 50, December 11-17.

——— and Martin Ravillion (2002), "Is India's Economic Growth Leaving the Poor Behind", *Journal of Economic Perspectives*, Vol. 16, No. 3.

Datt, Ruddar (2001), "Economic Liberalisation and its Implications for Employment in India", *Indian Economic Association 84th Conference Volume*, pp. 461-89.

——— (2002), "Employment Policies and the Unorganised Sector", *Indian Journal of Labour Economics*, Vol. 45, No. 2.

——— (2003), *Economic Reforms, Labour and Employment*, Deep & Deep Publications Pvt. Ltd., New Delhi.

——— (2006), Need for Redefining the Poverty Line, *Mainstream*, Vol. XLIV, No. 32, July 29, 2006.

Datta, Meera (1989), "Poverty and Unemployment in Rural India", *Indian Journal of Labour Economics*, Vol. 32, Nos. 3-4.

Etienne, Gilbert (1992), "Employment and Wages in Rural India: the Fight against Poverty in Economic Reforms", *Indian Journal of Labour Economics*, Vol. 35, No. 3.

Ghosh, Jayati (1995), "Employment and Labour under Structural Adjustment", *The Indian Journal of Labour Economics*, Vol. 38, No. 4.

Gupta, S.P. (2000), "Trickle Down Theory Revisited: The Role of Poverty", *Indian Journal of Labour Economics*, Vol. 43, No. 1.

Guruswamy, Mohan and Abraham, Ronald (2006), *Redefining Poverty—A New Poverty Line for a New India.*

Hashim, S.R. (1999), "Employment and Poverty: Some Emerging Issues", *Indian Journal of Labour Economics*, Vol. 42, No. 1.

Krishnan, T.N. (1992), "Population, Poverty and Employment in India", *Economic and Political Weekly*, Vol. 27, No. 46.

Kundu, Amitabh (2000), "Globalising Gujarat—Urbanisation, Employment and Poverty", *Economic and Political Weekly*, Vol. 35, Nos. 35-36

Lalwani, Mahesh, Thomas, Eugene D. (2000), "Incidence of Poverty among Beneficiary Household under JRY: A Case Study of Meghalaya", *Manpower Journal*, Vol. 36, No. 1.

Mahadevia, Darshini (1998), "Informalisation of Employment and Incidence of Poverty in Ahmedabad", *Indian Journal of Labour Economics*, Vol. 41, No. 3.

Mahendra Dev S. (1992), "Employment, Human Development and Rural Poverty", *Indian Journal of Labour Economics*, Vol. 35, No. 1.

——— (1995), "Alleviation of Poverty: Maharashtra Employment Guarantee Scheme", *Economic and Political Weekly*, Vol. 30, No. 41.

——— (1997), "Growth, Employment, Poverty and Human Development: An Evaluation of Change in India since Independence with Emphasis on Rural Areas", *Review of Development and Change*, Vol. 2, No. 2.

——— (2000), "Economic Reforms, Poverty, Income Distribution and Employment", *Economic and Political Weekly*, Vol. 35, No. 10.

——— and Ravi, C. (2007), Poverty and Inequality: All-India and States, 1983-2005, *Economic and Political Weekly*, February 10, 2007.

Mamgain, Rajendra P. (1994), "Alleviating Rural Poverty and Unemployment Problems and Prospects", *Manpower Journal*, Vol. 29, No. 4.

Mehta, Sanat (2000), "No Impact of Economic Reforms on Poverty, Unemployment in India, Where will the Poor go?", *Young Indian*, Vol. 11, No. 11.

Misra, Baidyanathan (1991), "Poverty, Unemployment and Rural Development in Orissa", *IASSI Quarterly*, Vol. 9, No. 3.

Mitra, Arup (1990), "Duality, Employment Structure and Poverty Incidence: The Slum Perspective", *Indian Economic Review*, Vol. 25, No. 1.

——— (1993), "Rural Non-farm Employment, Poverty and Women", *Indian Journal of Labour Economics*, Vol. 36, No. 3.

——— (1994), "India: Employment, Poverty and Economic Policies", *Indian Journal of Labour Economics*, Vol. 37, No. 1.

——— (1994), "Industry, Informal Sector Employment and Poverty", *Indian Journal of Labour Economics*, Vol. 37, No. 3.

Mukhopadhaya, Pundriakaksh (1993), "Population, Poverty and Employment in India", *Economic and Political Weekly*, Vol. 28, No. 16.

Narasaiah, Lakshmi (1996), "Employment and Poverty Alleviation", *IASSI Quarterly*, Vol. 15, No. 2.

Papola, T.S. and Sharma, Alakh N. (1996), "Structural Adjustment, Poverty and Safety Nets: Indian Experience", *Indian Journal of Labour Economics*, Vol. 39, No. 3.

Patnaik, Prabhat (1997), "Some Reflections on Unemployment and Poverty", *Indian Journal of Labour Economics*, Vol. 40, No. 4.

Planning Commission, Government of India (1999), *Ninth Five Year Plan (1997-2002)*.

——— (2001), *Report of the Task Force on Employment Opportunities* (Chairman: M.S. Ahluwalia).

——— (2002), *Report of the Special Group on Targeting Ten Million Employment Opportunities* (Chairman: S.P. Gupta).

——— (2002), *Tenth Five Year Plan (2002-07)*, Vols. I & III.

——— (2005), *Mid-Term Appraisal for the 10th Five Year Plan (2002-07)*.

——— (2006), *An Approach to The 11th Five Year Plan, Towards Faster and More Inclusive Growth*

Radhakrishnan, R. (2002), "Agricultural Growth, Employment and Poverty: A Policy Perspective", *Economic and Political Weekly*, Vol. 37, No. 3.

Rangacharyulu, S.V. (2000), "Analysing Relationship between Employment and Incidence of Poverty", *Manpower Journal*, Vol. 36, No. 1.

Ravallion, Martin and Datt, Gaurav (1996), "India's Checkered History of Fight against Poverty: Are there Lessons for Future?", *Economic and Political Weekly*, Vol. XXXI, Nos. 35, 36 and 37.

Sen, Abhijit (1996), "Economic Reforms, Employment and Poverty: Trends and Options", *Economic and Political Weekly*, Vol. XXXVIII, Nos. 35, 36 and 37.

Sharma, Gurpreet and Singh, A.J. (1999), "Poverty and Unemployment", *Indian Economic Journal*, Vol. 46, No. 4.

Sidhu, H.S. (1991), "Unemployment Poverty Nexus: Another Look", *Indian Journal of Labour Economics*, Vol. 34, No. 2.

Srinivasan, T.N. (2000), *Eight Lectures on India's Economic Reforms*, Oxford University Press, New Delhi.

Sundaram, K. (2001), "Employment and Poverty in 1990s—A Postscript", *Economic and Political Weekly*, Vol. 36, No. 4.

——— (2001), "Employment and Poverty in 1990s—Further Results from NSS 55th Round Employment-Unemployment Survey, 1999-2000", *Economic and Political Weekly*, Vol. 36, No. 32.

Unni, Jeemol (1998), "Non-agricultural Employment and Poverty in Rural India—A Review of Evidence", *Economic and Political Weekly*, Vol. 33, No. 13.

Unni, Jeemol and Raveendran, G. (2007), Growth of Employment (1993-94 to 2004-05), Illusion of Inclusiveness? *Economic and Political Weekly*, January 20.

Waqif, Arif A. (1995), "A Conceptual Approach to National and Regional Harmonisation for Employment Generation and Poverty Alleviation", *South Asian Survey*, Vol. 2, No. 2, World Bank, *World Development Report (2000-01)*, Attacking Poverty.

CHAPTER

3

Living Conditions—Widening Rural-Urban Divide (Wake-up Call for Government)

I. INTRODUCTION

Census data on living conditions indicates that the rural-urban divide is widening. Regarding housing facilities, whereas urban areas have 79 percent permanent houses, this proportion in contrast is only 41 percent in rural areas. Moreover, temporary houses account for only 5 percent in urban areas, but their proportion is as high as 23 percent in rural areas. Drinking water within the premises was available to only 25 percent of rural population, while the figure for urban areas was 65 percent. In urban areas, 88 percent of households are electrified and only 12 percent use kerosene. In rural areas, only 43.5 percent of households have electricity and 55.6 percent depend on kerosene. Bathroom facility was available to 70 percent of urban households, but merely 23 percent rural households had this facility. Only 26 percent of urban households had no latrine, but as against it, 78 percent rural households did not have a latrine. In rural areas, only 4 percent of households had closed drainage, 30 percent open drainage and 64 percent had no drainage. In urban areas, 19 percent of households did not own any of the specified assets, such as radio, television, telephone, bicycle, scooter/motor cycle/moped, car/jeep/van, but in rural areas this percentage was 41 percent. *Census of India (2001) has given a wake-up call to the Government that the development process has strengthened living conditions in urban-India to a much greater extent than in rural-India. The situation in some of the poor and backward states in appalling. We should direct the development process to strengthen rural-India and bridge the rural-urban divide.*

Census 2001 has brought out *Tables on Houses, Household Amenities and Assets.* The publication is useful because it is a complete survey and has demolished several claims made by the Government regarding the quality of housing, the availability of drinking water, electricity in both rural and urban areas. It has also provided state-wise information about houses and household amenities for the different states of India. Useful tables regarding the availability of banking services to households and the availability of specified assets like radio/transistor, television, bicycle, scooter/motor cycle/moped, car/jeep/van have been provided. The tables are useful in understanding the living conditions of households and thus visualizing the magnitude of the task that awaits the Governments, both at the level of the Centre and States to make an effort to improve living conditions.

There are certain tables which are of a subjective nature and need to be analyzed with caution, but quite a large number of tables use objective criteria. For our study, we concentrate only on tables with objective criteria. We propose to give along state-wise break-up of 18 states comprising 95.6 of the total households of the country so that they provide a comprehensive review of the state-level scenario.

2. TOTAL NUMBER OF CENSUS HOUSEHOLDS BY TYPE OF CENSUS HOUSES OCCUPIED

Census 2001 has given a break-up of Census Houses Occupied by type and the corresponding number of households. (Refer Table 3.1). Out of a total of 192 million households, 138.3 million houses are located in rural areas and 53.7 million are located in urban areas. This implies that 72 percent of the total houses are located in rural and 28 percent in urban areas.

But the break-up of houses on the basis of quality of type reveals that out of a total of 99.43 million permanent houses, 56.83 million (57.2%) are located in rural areas and 42.60 million (42.8%) in the urban areas. But in case of semi-permanent houses (57.66 million), 49.40 million (85.7%) are in rural areas and only 8.26 million (14.3%) are in urban areas. The situation regarding temporary houses reveals that out of 34.82 million, nearly 32 million (92%) are in rural areas and only 8 percent (2.8 million) are in urban areas.

TABLE 3.1
Distribution of Households by Type of Census Houses Occupied (2001)

(*In million*)

	Total	*Rural*	*Urban*
1. Permanent	99.43 (100.0)	56.83 (57.2)	42.60 (42.8)
2. Semi-Permanent	57.66 (100.0)	49.40 (85.7)	8.26 (14.3)
3. Temporary (a+b)	34.82 (100.0)	32.01 (91.9)	2.81 (8.1)
(a) Serviceable Temporary	22.10 (100.0)	20.36 (92.1)	1.74 (7.9)
(b) Non-Serviceable Temporary	12.72 (100.0)	11.65 (91.6)	1.07 (8.4)
4. Unclassified	0.05	0.03	0.02
Total	**191.96 (100.0)**	**138.27 (72.0)**	**53.69 (28.0)**

Note : Figures in brackets are percentages of total in a row.
Source : Compiled and computed from *Census of India (2001), Series 1, Tables on Houses, Household Amenities and Assets*, Table H-4 Appendix, p. 173.

Another way of looking at the problem of the quality-composition of housing is to consider the share of each in the houses in rural and urban areas separately.

The data (Table 3.2) reveal that in urban areas, out of 53.7 million total houses occupied, 42.6 million (79.3%) are of a permanent nature, 8.26

TABLE 3.2
Distribution of Households by Type of Census Houses Occupied (2001)

(*In million*)

	Total	*Rural*	*Urban*
1. Permanent	99.43 (51.8)	56.83 (41.1)	42.60 (79.3)
2. Semi-Permanent	57.66 (30.0)	49.40 (35.7)	8.26 (15.4)
3. Temporary (a+b)	34.82 (18.1)	32.01 (23.2)	2.81 (5.2)
(a) Serviceable Temporary	22.10 (11.5)	20.36 (14.7)	1.74 (3.2)
(b) Non-Serviceable Temporary	12.72 (6.6)	11.65 (8.4)	1.07 (2.0)
4. Unclassified	0.05 (0.0)	0.03 (0.0)	0.02 (0.0)
Total	**191.96 (100.0)**	**138.27 (100.0)**	**53.69 (100.0)**

Note : Figures in brackets are percentages of total in the respective column.
Source : Compiled and computed from *Census of India (2001), Tables on House, Household Amenities and Assets*, Table H-4 Appendix, p. 173.

million (15.4%) are of a semi-permanent nature and only 2.81 million (barely 5.2%) are of temporary nature. The total number of unserviceable temporary houses is only 1 million (2%). Obviously, the problem of housing in the urban areas reveals that only 20.6 percent of the total houses need further investment to be converted into permanent houses—the goal of housing policy. Out of them, 15.4 percent need upgradation, i.e. either the walls or the roof has to be converted into a permanent material and 5 percent need to be built afresh. The situation is, therefore, not disturbing and if an urban housing plan with 10-year time-frame is made, it would be possible to meet the goal of 'Housing for All' in the urban areas.

The situation, however, is very different in the rural areas. Out of a total of 138.3 million census houses occupied, 56.8 million (41.1%) are of a permanent nature, 49.4 million (35.7%) are of a semi-permanent nature and quite a significant proportion 23.2 percent (32 million) are of temporary nature. Out of the 32 million temporary houses, 20.4 million are serviceable but 11.6 million are totally non-serviceable. Obviously, the rural housing problem pertains to nearly 81.4 million houses, out of which 49.4 million semi-permanent houses need upgradation and 32 million need to be built afresh. The gigantic nature of the rural housing problem necessitates drawing up a 20-year plan for rural housing, giving priority attention to non-serviceable temporary houses, then to serviceable temporary houses. Along with this, a phased programme of upgrading semi-permanent houses has also to be undertaken.

Table 3.3 provides state-wise picture on housing. Punjab is at the top with 86 percent households having a permanent house and Assam is at the bottom with only 19.7 percent. Since the All-India figure is 51.8 percent permanent houses, states above the all-India average are : Kerala (68.1%), Haryana (65.8%), Gujarat (65.3%), Rajasthan (64.9%), Tamil Nadu (58.5%), Maharashtra (57.8%), Karnataka (54.9%), Andhra Pradesh (54.7%) and UP (53.3%). It would need to be mentioned specially that Rajasthan, though a relatively poor state in terms of per capita NSDP shows a much better performance in having nearly 65% of its houses of a permanent nature. Similarly, Uttaranchal outshines nearly all forward states by having 86.3 percent permanent houses.

On the other hand, West Bengal, a forward state in terms of per capita NSDP and having a CPI (M) Government for nearly 30 years has barely 40.4 percent permanent houses and nearly 60 percent semi-permanent and temporary houses. This indicates gross neglect of "housing policy" in West Bengal.

Among other laggards in permanent housing are Madhya Pradesh (41.6%), Bihar (40.6%), Jharkhand (31.4%), Orissa (27.6%) and Assam (19.7%). A unique feature of Madhya Pradesh (Old) is that as against 37 percent permanent houses, 60 percent are semi-permanent and barely 3 percent are temporary houses. Even in Chhattisgarh which is a very poor region, 72 percent houses are semi-permanent and only 3 percent are temporary. So the major problem in Madhya Pradesh and Chhattisgarh is

TABLE 3.3
Percentage Distribution of Households by Type of Census Houses Occupied

Area Name	Type of census houses					
	Permanent	Semi-permanent	Temporary			Unclassifiable
			Total	Serviceable	Non-serviceable	
(1)	(2)	(3)	(4)	(5)	(6)	(7)
Maharashtra	57.82	34.37	7.74	5.06	2.68	0.07
Punjab	86.10	8.87	5.02	4.11	0.92	0.01
Haryana	65.79	28.25	5.95	4.91	1.04	0.01
Tamil Nadu	58.52	18.15	23.31	19.68	3.63	0.02
Gujarat	65.33	29.54	5.10	3.60	1.50	0.03
Kerala	68.14	21.60	10.21	6.05	4.16	0.06
Karnataka	54.86	35.62	9.49	5.71	3.78	0.02
West Bengal	40.43	37.26	22.27	16.47	5.80	0.04
Andhra Pradesh	54.72	21.30	23.94	17.00	6.94	0.03
Rajasthan	64.94	20.93	14.09	12.35	1.74	0.04
Madhya Pradesh	41.55	55.76	2.69	1.78	0.91	0.00
Chhattisgarh	25.40	72.04	2.55	1.96	0.60	0.00
M.P. (Old)	37.10	60.24	2.65	1.83	0.82	0.00
Uttar Pradesh	53.38	25.62	20.99	16.89	4.09	0.01
Uttaranchal	86.34	6.59	7.06	4.30	2.76	0.01
U.P. (Old)	55.30	24.52	20.18	16.16	4.02	0.01
Assam	19.69	31.27	49.02	2.81	46.21	0.02

Orissa	27.58	25.01	47.40	42.16	5.24	0.01
Bihar	40.73	25.54	33.72	6.31	27.42	0.01
Jharkhand	31.40	57.68	10.92	9.89	1.03	0.00
Bihar (Old)	38.33	33.83	27.84	7.23	20.61	0.01
India	51.80	30.04	18.14	11.51	6.63	0.03

Note : This table excludes institutional households.

Permanent : Houses with wall and roof made of permanent materials. Wall can be G.I., Metal, Asbestos sheets, Burnt bricks, Stone or Concrete, Roof can be made of Tiles, Slates G.I., Metal, Asbestos sheets, Bricks, Stone or Concrete.

Temporary : Houses with wall and roof made of temporary material. Wall can be made of Grass, Thatch, Bamboo, etc. Plastic, Polythene, Mud, Unburnt brick, or Wood. Roof can be made of Grass, Thatch, Bamboo, Wood, Mud, Plastic or Polythene.

Semi-Permanent : Either wall or roof is made of permanent material and other is made of temporary material.

Serviceable temporary : Wall is made of Mud, Unburnt brick or Wood.

Non-serviceable temporary : Wall is made of Grass, Thatch, Bamboo, etc. Plastic or Polythene.

Source : Calculated from Table H-4, Appendix, *Census of India*, 2001, *Series 1, Tables on Houses, Household Amenities and Assets.*

upgradation of semi-permanent houses. It may also be noted that Assam and Orissa have a very high proportion of temporary houses. The situation in Assam is pathetic where 46.2 percent houses are classified as non-serviceable temporary. The other states with very high proportion of temporary houses are Andhra Pradesh (23.9%), West Bengal (22.3%) and Bihar (33.7%).

The upshot of the analysis is that the census data has drawn attention to the utter neglect of housing problem in quite a large number of states. On the Antodaya principle, priority should be given to rectification of temporary housing, especially non-serviceable houses being converted into permanent houses, followed by upgradation of semi-permanent houses. It is one thing to give a slogan "Shelter for all", but it is another thing to develop a good roadmap to reach the goal.

3. PERCENTAGE OF HOUSEHOLDS BY NUMBER OF DWELLING ROOMS

Data provided in Table 3.4 reveals that 3.1 percent of households have no exclusive dwelling room, 38.5 percent have one room, 30 percent have two rooms, 14.3 percent have three rooms, 7.5 percent have four rooms, only 2.9 percent have five rooms and 3.7 percent have six or more rooms.

It we take a minimum of two rooms for a family of five, then even nearly 42 percent of households do not fulfil the criterion of two rooms per household. Obviously, this would require enlargement of housing facilities to meet the housing needs of households with various sizes, keeping in view the availability of a minimum of privacy for the members, especially married couples.

A review of the situation in the rural and urban areas reveals that in rural areas over 43 percent of households do not fulfil the 2-room norm. However, in urban areas, the percentage is slightly lower at 37 percent. Thus, the quality of housing and the availability of a minimum reasonable accommodation does not meet the requirements of over 42 percent of households in India.

Independent Sleeping Room for Married Couples

Table 3.5 provides us an idea whether married couples in India have independent sleeping rooms. Data provided in Table 3.5 reveals that out of 220.3 million married couples living in 192 million households, only 134.0 million, i.e. 60.8 percent have independent sleeping rooms. The situation is slightly better in urban areas and 67 percent of the married couples come in this category, but is rather worse in rural areas where only 58.5 percent of married couples had independent sleeping rooms.

It may also be noted that in rural areas, as the number of married couples in the household increases, the proportion of such couples having independent sleeping rooms declines.

TABLE 3.4

Percentage Distribution of Households by Number of Dwelling Rooms

(All India)

Household Size	*Households having number of dwelling rooms*						
	No exclusive room	*One room*	*Two rooms*	*Three rooms*	*Four rooms*	*Five rooms*	*Six rooms and above*
(1)	*(2)*	*(3)*	*(4)*	*(5)*	*(6)*	*(7)*	*(8)*
			TOTAL				
All	3.11	38.47	29.99	14.35	7.48	2.90	3.70
1	10.58	60.15	19.05	6.08	2.33	0.72	1.08
2	4.31	55.18	26.00	8.56	3.47	1.07	1.41
3	3.58	48.40	29.06	11.38	4.56	1.43	1.59
4	3.19	41.94	31.23	13.55	6.19	1.92	1.99
5	2.89	39.23	32.25	14.28	6.63	2.36	2.38
6-8	2.30	32.67	32.73	16.66	8.70	3.28	3.70
9+	1.70	17.52	24.61	20.03	15.18	7.95	13.03
			RURAL				
All	3.42	39.78	30.17	13.28	7.02	2.76	3.58
1	11.62	60.71	18.73	5.25	2.07	0.63	1.00
2	4.73	57.37	25.82	7.10	2.86	0.87	1.25
3	4.09	51.43	28.75	9.34	3.80	1.18	1.41
4	3.70	45.05	31.21	11.40	5.27	1.61	1.76
5	3.23	41.17	32.53	12.89	5.97	2.07	2.14
6-8	2.48	33.43	33.23	15.92	8.33	3.09	3.52
9+	1.77	17.63	25.02	20.04	14.95	7.88	12.71
			URBAN				
All	2.32	35.11	29.53	17.09	8.67	3.27	4.00
1	8.10	58.83	19.84	8.05	2.96	0.94	1.28
2	3.25	49.58	26.46	12.27	5.03	1.60	1.80
3	2.51	41.98	29.72	15.68	6.18	1.96	1.97
4	2.16	35.62	31.26	17.91	8.06	2.53	2.46
5	2.05	34.43	31.57	17.71	8.26	3.03	2.95
6-8	1.73	29.89	31.17	18.51	10.21	3.87	4.62
9+	1.44	17.14	23.22	19.98	15.94	8.17	14.10

Source : Calculated from Table H-5, *Census of India, 2001, Series 1, Tables on Houses, Household Amenities and Assets.*

TABLE 3.5

Distribution of Households by Number of Married Couples and Number of Married Couples having Independent Sleeping Rooms

(In million)

	Total No. of Households		*Total No. of married couples*		*Total No. of Married Couples having independent sleeping rooms*		*3 as % of 2*
	(1)		*(2)*		*(3)*		*(4)*
	No.	*%*	*No.*	*%*	*No.*	*%*	
India							
Total	192.0	(100.0)	220.3	(100.0)	134.0	(100.0)	60.8
No Married couple	21.3	(11.1)	0	0	0	0	0
1 Married couple	135.0	(70.3)	135.0	(61.3)	81.6	(60.9)	60.4
2 Married couples	26.0	(13.5)	51.9	(23.6)	32.5	(24.3)	62.6
3 Married couples	6.9	(3.6)	20.7	(9.4)	12.6	(9.4)	60.8
4 Married couples	1.9	(1.0)	7.8	(3.5)	4.6	(3.4)	58.9
5 + Married couples	0.9	(0.5)	4.9	(2.2)	2.7	(2.0)	55.1
Rural							
Total	138.3	(100.0)	162.9	(100.0)	95.4	(100.0)	58.5
No Married couple	14.5	(10.5)	0	0	0	0	0
1 Married couple	95.8	(69.3)	95.8	(58.8)	55.6	(58.3)	58.0
2 Married couples	20.2	(14.6)	40.4	(24.8)	24.4	(25.6)	60.3
3 Married couples	5.5	(4.0)	16.4	(10.1)	9.6	(10.0)	58.5
4 Married couples	1.6	(1.1)	6.3	(3.9)	3.6	(3.8)	57.1
5 + Married couples	0.7	(0.5)	4.0	(2.4)	2.2	(2.3)	55.0
Urban							
Total	53.7	(100.0)	57.4	(100.0)	38.5	(100.0)	67.0
No Married couple	6.7	(12.5)	0	0	0	0	0
1 Married couple	39.2	(73.0)	39.2	(68.3)	26.0	(67.5)	66.3
2 Married couples	5.8	(10.8)	11.5	(20.0)	8.1	(21.0)	70.4
3 Married couples	1.4	(2.6)	4.3	(7.5)	2.9	(7.5)	67.4
4 married couples	0.4	(0.7)	1.5	(2.6)	1.0	(2.6)	66.7
5 + Married couples	0.2	(0.4)	0.9	(1.6)	0.5	(1.3)	55.5

Note : Figures in brackets are percentages of total in each category.

Source : Compiled and Computed from Table H-7, *Census of India, 2001, Series I, Tables on Houses, Household Amenities and Assets.*

In urban areas, the situation was relatively more stable and up to 4 married couples in the household, the proportion remained around 67 percent, but with 5 or more married couples, the situation showed a decline in proportion to 55.5 percent.

It may also be noted that as the number of married couples in the household increases, there is a natural desire to set-up a separate household. This explains the declining trend of the proportion of married couples with an increase in the number of married couples in a household. The situation is changing faster in urban areas than in rural areas.

4. DISTRIBUTION OF HOUSEHOLDS BY SOURCE OF DRINKING WATER AND ITS LOCATION

The goal of "Drinking Water for All" suggests that drinking water should be available within the premises for all households but the ground reality as revealed by the Census of 2001 is very different. It is revealed that out of a total of 192 million households, only about 75 million (39 percent) avail of the source of drinking water within the premises; 85 million (44.3 percent) near premises and 32 million (16.7 percent) of households have to obtain water 'away' from the premises, i.e. from over 100 metres in urban areas and 500 metres in rural areas. (Refer Table 3.6)

In rural areas, the situation is much worse. Out of 138 million households, nearly 40 million (28.7 percent) have a source of drinking water within premises, about 72 million (51.8 percent) near premises and 27 million (19.5 percent) away from the premises.

In urban areas, the situation is much better. Out of 54 million families, about 35 million (65.4 percent) have a source of drinking water within premises, 14 million (25.2 percent) near premises and only 5 million (9.4 percent) away from the premises.

Statewise scenario about drinking water access is presented in Table 3.7. The overall picture reveals that Punjab is at the top with 85.5 percent of households having access to drinking water within the premises, followed by Kerala (71.6 percent), Maharashtra (53.4 percent), Gujarat (46 percent) and even a relatively poor state Uttar Pradesh (46 percent). It may be noted that the states have been arranged on the basis of descending order of their per capita NSDP in 1999-00. Two factors seem to play a major role in the access to drinking water—(a) Level of development of the State, and (b) State policies directed towards improving access to drinking water. Although Tamil Nadu, Karnataka, and West Bengal are at a higher level in terms of per capita NSDP, yet their access to drinking water was below the national average of 39 percent within premises. As against them, Uttar Pradesh and Bihar indicated better access to drinking water for their households, though these were states at the lower rung of the ladder in terms of NSDP. Chhattisgarh, Orissa and Jharkhand had barely 19-20 percent households having drinking water within premises. The situation is

TABLE 3.6

Distribution of Households by Source of Drinking Water and its Location

(Million Households)

Location	*Total No. of Households*		*Source of Drinking water*									
			Tap		*Handpumps*		*Tubewells*		*Wells*		*Any other*	
	No.	*%*	*No.*	*%*	*No.*	*%*	*No.*	*%*	*No.*	*%*	*No.*	*%*
(1)	*(2)*	*(3)*	*(4)*	*(5)*	*(6)*	*(7)*	*(8)*	*(9)*	*(10)*	*(11)*	*(12)*	*(13)*
INDIA												
Total	192.0	(100.0)	70.4	(100.0)	68.4	(100.0)	10.7	(100.0)	34.9	(100.0)	7.5	(100.0)
Within premises	74.8	(39.0)	40.0	(56.8)	21.3	(31.1)	3.1	(29.0)	10.0	(28.7)	0.4	(5.4)
Near premises	85.1	(44.3)	25.0	(35.5)	36.6	(53.5)	4.8	(44.8)	15.6	(44.7)	3.1	(40.8)
Away	32.1	(16.7)	5.4	(7.7)	10.5	(15.4)	2.8	(26.2)	9.3	(26.6)	4.0	(33.8)
RURAL												
Total	138.3	(100.0)	33.6	(100.0)	59.7	(100.0)	7.9	(100.0)	30.7	(100.0)	6.3	(100.0)
Within premises	39.7	(28.7)	13.3	(39.6)	16.9	(28.3)	1.6	(20.3)	7.6	(24.8)	0.3	(4.9)
Near premises	71.6	(51.8)	16.9	(50.3)	33.4	(55.9)	4.0	(50.6)	14.6	(47.5)	2.6	(41.2)
Away	27.0	(19.5)	3.4	(10.1)	9.4	(15.8)	2.3	(19.1)	8.5	(27.7)	3.4	(53.9)
URBAN												
Total	53.7	(100.0)	36.9	(100.0)	8.7	(100.0)	2.7	(100.0)	4.1	(100.0)	1.2	(100.0)
Within premises	35.1	(65.4)	26.7	(72.4)	4.4	(50.6)	1.6	(59.3)	2.3	(56.1)	0.1	(7.9)
Near premises	13.6	(25.2)	8.1	(21.9)	3.2	(36.8)	0.7	(25.9)	1.1	(26.8)	0.5	(38.9)
Away	5.0	(9.4)	2.1	(5.7)	1.1	(12.6)	0.4	(14.8)	0.7	(17.1)	0.6	(53.2)

Notes : 1. Any other source includes Tank, Pond, Lake, River, Canal, Spring, etc.

2. Figures in brackets are percentages of the total in the respective group.

3. 'Near premises', i.e. when the location of the available source of water is within a radius of 100 metres in urban areas and 500 metres in the case of rural areas. Away implies availability of source of water beyond the distance prescribed for 'Near premises.'

Source : Compiled and computed from Table H-8, *Census of India 2001, Series 1, Tables on Houses, Household Amenities and Assets.*

TABLE 3.7

Percentage Distribution of Households and their Location for Drinking Water Access

State	Total			Rural			Urban		
	Within Premises	Near Premises	Away	Within Premises	Near Premises	Away	Within Premises	Near Premises	Away
(1)	(2)	(3)	(4)	(5)	(6)	(7)	(8)	(9)	(10)
Maharashtra	53.4	34.3	12.3	38.9	43.9	17.2	73.2	21.2	5.7
Punjab	85.5	11.3	3.2	82.0	13.8	4.2	92.0	6.5	1.5
Haryana	44.5	34.7	20.8	30.7	42.7	26.6	76.0	16.5	7.5
Tamil Nadu	27.1	60.8	12.1	12.0	74.7	13.3	48.3	41.3	10.4
Gujarat	46.5	38.3	15.2	29.3	49.9	20.8	73.5	20.0	6.5
Kerala	71.6	16.4	12.0	69.1	17.4	13.5	78.9	13.7	7.4
Karnataka	31.7	46.4	21.9	18.5	55.4	26.1	56.6	29.6	13.8
West Bengal	32.1	49.9	18.0	23.4	56.1	20.5	53.4	34.7	11.9
Andhra Pradesh	31.3	48.9	19.8	22.8	55.3	21.9	57.2	29.3	13.5
Rajasthan	32.9	43.3	23.8	19.8	51.6	28.6	75.8	16.0	8.2
Madhya Pradesh	24.6	51.2	24.2	14.0	58.7	27.3	55.3	29.4	15.3
Chhattisgarh	19.0	60.3	20.7	11.9	65.8	22.3	49.3	37.0	13.7
M.P. Old	23.0	53.7	23.3	13.4	60.7	25.9	53.9	31.1	15.0
Uttar Pradesh	46.0	44.0	10.0	38.2	50.6	11.2	77.0	17.6	5.4
Uttaranchal	44.8	38.5	16.7	32.7	46.9	20.4	82.0	12.7	5.3
UP (Old)	45.9	43.7	10.4	37.9	50.4	11.7	77.4	17.2	5.4
Assam	37.9	39.7	22.4	33.6	41.9	24.5	63.2	26.3	10.5
Orissa	19.0	50.2	30.8	13.7	53.9	32.4	52.1	27.1	20.8
Bihar	39.6	48.2	12.2	36.3	51.1	12.6	70.5	20.9	8.6
Jharkhand	20.0	55.5	24.5	9.7	63.6	26.7	57.2	26.1	16.7
India	39.0	44.3	16.7	28.7	51.8	19.5	65.4	25.2	9.4

Source : Computed from Table H-8, *Census of India 2001, Series 1, Tables on Houses, Household Amenities and Assets.*

really disappointing in these states, despite over 50 years of planned development.

The situation in rural areas showed wider degree of variation with Punjab at the top with 82 percent of households having access to drinking water and on the other extreme was Jharkhand with a miserably low proportion of 9.7 percent. Chhattisgarh, Karnataka, Rajasthan and Orissa were all below the 20 percent level. It is really amazing that in Tamil Nadu, a relatively much better-off state, barely 12 percent rural households had access to drinking water within the premises. (Refer Table 3.7)

In urban areas, the situation was relatively much better than in the rural areas. The most encouraging feature of the scenario is that Punjab was at the top with 92 percent urban households having access to water within the premises. A number of states which had crossed the 70 percent mark, were Maharashtra, Haryana, Gujarat, Kerala, Rajasthan, Uttar Pradesh and even Bihar. But regrettably, Tamil Nadu was at the bottom with only 48 percent households having drinking water access within premises. Other laggards with less than 60 percent were Karnataka, West Bengal, Andhra Pradesh, Madhya Pradesh, Chhattisgarh, Jharkhand and Orissa.

A close perusal of the data pertaining to rural areas brings out the stark reality that in a number of states more than 25 percent of households have to fetch drinking water after traversing a distance of over 500 metres. These states are: Orissa (32.4%), Rajasthan (28.6%), Madhya Pradesh (27.3%), Jharkhand (26.7%) and Haryana (26.6%). It is really ironical that though Haryana ranks No. 3 in terms of per capita NSDP, it is way behind other states in providing drinking water to its rural population. Only 31 percent of rural households avail of drinking water within premises, nearly 43 percent have access near premises and about 27 percent have access far away. Obviously, the State Government did not pay adequate attention to this problem.

5. THE PROBLEM OF PROVIDING SAFE DRINKING WATER

"As per Census of India, if a household has access to drinking water supplied from a tap, hand-pump/tube well within or outside the premises, it is considered as having access to safe drinking water."[1] Following this definition, the Census 1991 reported that the coverage of households in India having access to safe drinking water was at 62 percent for All-India, over 81 percent for urban households and 56 percent for rural households.

Census of India 2001 has provided data regarding distribution of households by source of drinking water. (Refer Tables 3.8, 3.9 and 3.10). Applying the Census criterion, *Economic Survey* (2003-04) states: "As per Cesus of India 2001 (excluding Jammu & Kashmir), the coverage of households having access to safe drinking water was 77.9 percent comprising 90 percent of urban households and around 73 percent of rural households."[2] It is also stated that National Agenda for Governance of the

NDA Government envisaged provision of safe drinking water to all households by 2004.

The basic question is whether the definition of safe drinking water as given by Census of India is appropriate considering the quality of water provided by handpumps and tubewells? The concept of safe drinking water envisages quality of water whose consumption does not result in water-borne diseases. Judged by this criterion, majority of the handpumps and tubewells are found to be carriers of water-borne diseases and thus cannot be classified in the category of safe drinking water. But such a definition is very handy for the Government because it reduces the burden of the Government to undertake investment to provide safe drinking water.

At the international level, the definition used for safe drinking water includes an improved water source with sustainable access to the population. *Human Development Report* (2004) defines it in the following manner: "The share of population with reasonable access to any of the following types of water supply for drinking : household connections, public standpipes, protected dug wells, protected springs and rain water collection. *Reasonable access* is defined as the availability of at least 20 litres a person per day from a source within 1 kilometre of the user's dwelling."[3]

If we apply the UNDP definition, then majority of the handpumps, unprotected tubewells will not qualify to be included under the category of safe drinking water. Thus, the definition of safe drinking water provided by the Census, as indicated in *Economic Survey (2002-03)* is very weak and exaggerates the coverage of safe drinking water to households. It would be proper, therefore, to consider only tap water and some protected water sources like protected tubewells, and protected handpumps in the category of safe drinking water. This explains, perhaps the reason, why the report on Houses, Household Amenities and Assets of the Census of 2001 has refrained from classifying sources of drinking water as safe or otherwise, but has only classified households on the basis of source of drinking water—Taps, handpumps, tubewells, tanks, ponds, lakes, rivers, canals, springs, etc. (Refer Tables 3.8, 3.9 and 3.10). The Census should have done an exercise to classify various drinking water sources as protected and unprotected to arrive at an estimate of households having access to safe drinking water. The Government estimate of households with safe drinking water at 78 percent is certainly a gross over-estimate.

What should be the goals of drinking water policy?

In our view, the goals of drinking water policy should be the following :

(i) To increase access to tap water to households both within urban and rural areas since it is recognized as the most reliable source of drinking water.

(ii) In case, availability of tap water is not possible, then to instal handpumps—at the individual level within the premises of the

TABLE 3.8

Percentage Distribution of Households by Source of Drinking Water

(Rural)

State	*Source of drinking water*							
	Tap	*Handpump*	*Tubewell*	*Well*	*Tank, Pond, Lake*	*River, Canal*	*Spring*	*Any other*
(1)	*(2)*	*(3)*	*(4)*	*(5)*	*(6)*	*(7)*	*(8)*	*(9)*
Maharashtra	45.54	19.07	3.80	28.46	0.54	1.07	0.82	0.69
Punjab	15.79	77.63	3.49	1.16	0.09	0.19	0.14	1.51
Haryana	37.83	35.73	7.57	16.47	0.70	0.50	0.16	1.04
Tamil Nadu	60.48	20.29	4.52	11.34	1.64	0.41	0.46	0.86
Gujarat	49.09	22.76	5.02	18.27	0.55	0.69	0.29	3.33
Kerala	13.89	1.14	1.84	77.17	0.98	0.70	2.48	1.80
Karnataka	48.48	22.92	9.12	15.56	1.51	1.57	0.43	0.41
West Bengal	7.02	69.24	10.73	11.41	0.22	0.36	0.73	0.29
Andhra Pradesh	40.27	30.85	5.73	19.55	1.20	1.04	0.54	0.81
Rajasthan	21.57	31.26	7.61	30.03	6.40	1.58	0.14	1.39
Madhya Pradesh	10.65	48.02	2.84	35.56	0.31	1.72	0.67	0.24
Chhattisgarh	5.03	59.94	1.19	28.13	0.46	2.19	1.68	1.38
M.P. (Old)	9.01	51.51	2.36	33.38	0.35	1.86	0.97	0.57
Uttar Pradesh	15.96	69.04	0.46	13.96	0.03	0.09	0.14	0.31
Uttaranchal	60.55	21.36	1.14	1.57	1.56	2.37	2.75	8.71
U.P. (Old)	18.41	66.43	0.50	13.28	0.12	0.22	0.28	0.77
Assam	5.44	46.36	4.99	27.03	7.89	5.90	1.39	0.99
Orissa	2.77	31.30	28.81	29.09	2.08	2.95	2.48	0.53
Bihar	1.38	79.95	4.78	13.15	0.02	0.22	0.09	0.41
Jharkhand	2.67	29.94	2.90	58.19	0.35	3.25	1.69	1.01
Bihar (Old)	1.68	68.40	4.35	23.55	0.09	0.92	0.46	0.55
India	**24.29**	**43.20**	**5.74**	**22.23**	**1.28**	**1.33**	**0.93**	**1.01**

Source : Calculated from Table H-8, *Census of India, 2001, Series 1, Tables on Houses, Household, Amenities and Assets.*

TABLE 3.9
Percentage Distribution of Households by Source of Drinking Water

(Urban)

State	*Source of drinking water*							
	Tap	*Handpump*	*Tubewell*	*Well*	*Tank, Pond, Lake*	*River, Canal*	*Spring*	*Any other*
(1)	*(2)*	*(3)*	*(4)*	*(5)*	*(6)*	*(7)*	*(8)*	*(9)*
Maharashtra	89.18	4.49	1.69	3.23	0.24	0.06	0.05	1.06
Punjab	66.81	29.44	2.63	0.22	0.02	0.03	0.09	0.76
Haryana	71.67	22.51	3.13	0.83	0.23	0.08	0.14	1.41
Tamil Nadu	65.40	14.39	6.12	9.61	0.19	0.26	0.42	3.61
Gujarat	83.03	7.09	5.28	1.40	0.02	0.04	0.01	3.13
Kerala	39.87	0.95	2.01	55.95	0.17	0.05	0.12	0.87
Karnataka	78.43	6.19	7.51	6.48	0.28	0.19	0.06	0.87
West Bengal	56.66	22.92	12.71	6.49	0.21	0.05	0.46	0.50
Andhra Pradesh	71.91	11.70	6.55	7.19	0.16	0.13	0.04	2.32
Rajasthan	80.12	10.29	3.11	4.07	0.62	0.07	0.07	1.65
Madhya Pradesh	67.91	13.51	7.14	9.91	0.33	0.23	0.07	0.91
Chhattisgarh	60.01	25.17	3.60	9.74	0.21	0.38	0.27	0.62
M.P. (Old)	66.17	16.08	6.36	9.88	0.30	0.26	0.11	0.84
Uttar Pradesh	54.53	40.99	1.63	1.94	0.10	0.03	0.08	0.69
Uttaranchal	82.28	14.86	0.62	0.24	0.20	0.32	0.21	1.27
U.P. (Old)	56.48	39.16	1.56	1.82	0.11	0.05	0.09	0.73
Assam	31.42	34.24	4.71	24.57	1.68	1.11	1.18	1.10
Orissa	45.91	10.85	15.56	25.21	0.48	0.77	0.50	0.71
Bihar	26.36	57.94	6.93	7.55	0.07	0.12	0.08	0.94
Jharkhand	48.00	16.39	3.81	28.74	0.50	0.87	0.17	1.52
Bihar (Old)	35.99	39.45	5.54	16.98	0.26	0.45	0.12	1.20
India	**68.66**	**16.24**	**5.11**	**7.71**	**0.31**	**0.19**	**0.25**	**1.52**

Source: Calculated from Table H-8, *Census of India, 2001, Series 1, Tables on Houses, Household Amenities and Assets.*

TABLE 3.10
Percentage Distribution of Households by Source of Drinking Water

(Total)

State	*Source of drinking water*							
	Tap	*Handpump*	*Tubewell*	*Well*	*Tank, Pond, Lake*	*River, Canal*	*Spring*	*Any other*
(1)	*(2)*	*(3)*	*(4)*	*(5)*	*(6)*	*(7)*	*(8)*	*(9)*
Maharashtra	64.02	12.90	2.91	17.78	0.41	0.64	0.50	0.85
Punjab	33.61	60.80	3.19	0.83	0.07	0.13	0.12	1.25
Haryana	48.14	31.70	6.22	11.71	0.56	0.37	0.15	1.16
Tamil Nadu	62.53	17.84	5.18	10.62	1.04	0.35	0.44	2.00
Gujarat	62.31	16.65	5.13	11.70	0.35	0.43	0.18	3.25
Kerala	20.40	1.10	1.89	71.85	0.77	0.53	1.89	1.57
Karnataka	58.89	17.11	8.56	12.40	1.08	1.09	0.30	0.57
West Bengal	21.40	55.81	11.31	9.98	0.22	0.27	0.65	0.35
Andhra Pradesh	48.11	26.11	5.93	16.49	0.94	0.81	0.42	1.19
Rajasthan	35.27	26.35	6.56	23.96	5.05	1.23	0.12	1.46
Madhya Pradesh	25.31	39.19	3.94	28.99	0.31	1.34	0.52	0.41
Chhattisgarh	15.49	53.32	1.65	24.63	0.42	1.85	1.41	1.23
M.P. (Old)	22.60	43.08	3.31	27.79	0.34	1.48	0.76	0.63
Uttar Pradesh	23.70	63.41	0.69	11.55	0.05	0.08	0.13	0.39
Uttaranchal	65.89	19.76	1.02	1.24	1.22	1.87	2.13	6.88
U.P. (Old)	26.15	60.88	0.71	10.95	0.11	0.18	0.24	0.77
Assam	9.20	44.61	4.95	26.68	6.99	5.20	1.36	1.01
Orissa	8.73	28.47	26.98	28.55	1.86	2.65	2.20	0.55
Bihar	3.74	77.87	4.99	12.62	0.02	0.21	0.09	0.46
Jharkhand	12.56	26.98	3.10	51.77	0.38	2.73	1.36	1.12
Bihar (Old)	6.01	64.74	4.50	22.72	0.12	0.86	0.42	0.63
India	**36.70**	**35.66**	**5.56**	**18.17**	**1.01**	**1.01**	**0.74**	**1.15**

Source: Calculated from Table H-8, *Census of India, 2001, Series 1, Tables on Houses, Household, Amenities and Assets.*

households and also public handpumps with proper platform and drainage so that the quality of water is not contaminated.

(iii) To convert tubewells and wells into protected drinking water sources so as to ensure a reasonable quality of drinking water and also to arrange for periodic treatment of drinking water drawn from them.

(iv) To protect harvested rainwater in a tank or lake or pond from pollution so that it is reasonably fit for human consumption.

(v) To reduce the distance of the source of drinking water by developing mechanisms by which the share of 'near premises' source is reduced and the share of 'within premises' is increased.

(vi) To provide at least 20 litres of water per day per person in the household.

Data provided by Table 3.8, 3.9 and 3.10 reveal that for the country as a whole, 36.7 percent of households are provided with tap water, 35.7 percent with handpumps, and 5.6 percent with tubewells. Nearly 78 percent of households have access to reasonably protected drinking water sources according to the Census definition.

In urban areas, tap water is available to 69 percent of households, followed by handpumps to 16 percent and tubewells to 5 percent. Obviously, 90 percent of households get access to safe drinking water. However, the situation varies among the states. Maharashtra provides tap water to 89 per cent urban households, followed by Gujarat 83 percent, Rajasthan 80 percent and Karnataka 78 percent. On the other extreme is Bihar which provides tap water only to 26 percent of urban households, Assam 31 percent and Orissa 46 percent. There is a strong need to increase the supply of water through investment in urban water supply schemes. Kerala is a unique case in which 40 per cent of households are provided taps and 56 percent are serviced by wells. There is a need to strengthen tap water supply in Kerala.

Regarding rural areas, the problem of drinking water supply presents a challenge with only 25 percent of population being provided tap water, 43 percent by handpumps and about 6 percent by tubewells for the country as a whole. Tamil Nadu had the unique distinction to provide 60 percent of rural households drinking water through tap, 20 percent through handpumps and 5 percent through tubewells. In other words, about 85 percent of rural households are serviced by reasonably good sources of drinking water. Uttaranchal, Gujarat, Maharashtra and Karnataka also provide nearly 50 percent or more of rural households tap water. But the laggards in developing rural tap water supply are Bihar (1.4%), Orissa (2.8%), Assam and Chhattisgarh (5%), West Bengal (7%) and Madhya Pradesh (9%). It is really heartening that Rajasthan has reached 22 percent of rural households through tap water supply. Ironically, Punjab indicates 78 percent rural households being provided water by handpumps, Bihar (80%),

Uttar Pradesh (69%), West Bengal (69%). There is a strong need to develop water supply through household tap connections in these states to provide good quality safe drinking water.

6. DISTRIBUTION OF HOUSEHOLDS BY SOURCE OF LIGHTING

Census 2001 has compiled data of households by source of lighting. For the country as a whole, for about 56 percent of households, the source of lighting is electricity, for 43 percent, kerosene and for the remaining 1 percent of households, it is solar energy or other oil. Barely 0.3 percent of households had no source of lighting. It would be desirable to examine the picture at the state-level for the urban and rural areas separately.

In urban areas, for India as a whole 88 percent of households use electricity and barely 11.6 percent use kerosene as the source of lighting. Panjab, Maharashtra, Haryana, Gujarat, Karnataka, Andhra Pradesh, Madhya Pradesh, Uttaranchal have crossed 90 percent mark and may be they achieve the goal of cent percent urban electrification in a decade or so. The laggards are Bihar (59%), Orissa (74%), Assam (74%), Jharkhand (76%) and Uttar Pradesh (81%).

The real challenge is in the electrification of rural households. Data provided by Census of 2001 reveals that only 43.5 percent of rural households have electricity as the source of lighting and 55.6 percent depend upon kerosene. Other sources of lighting such as solar energy, other oil, etc. account for barely 0.6 percent and 0.3 percent of households had no lighting. Obviously, the claims of the government regarding rural electrification appear to be very hollow.

But the Government has been basing its campaign of rural electrification on a very weak definition of an electrified village. "A village was considered to be electrified if the electricity is being used within its revenue area for any purpose whatsoever which could include a single connection also."[4] Recently, the Government has decided "to amend the definition of an electrified village to the village where the number of households electrified is at least 10 percent of the total number of households in the village, electricity is provided to public places like schools, panchayat office, health centres, dispensaries, and community centres, and basic infrastructure such as distribution transformer and distribution lines are provided in the inhabited locality as well as the Dalit Basti/hamlet where it exists."[5] As a consequence of the new definition, nearly 1.5 lakh villages are categorized as unelectrified villages. This definition is also extremely weak. Even with 90 percent of households not being electrified, the village could be considered as electrified. The definition should be amended and the condition of at least 50 percent households be electrified in the village should be the criterion. This would reveal how far we are from the target of genuine rural electrification.

TABLE 3.11

Percentage Distribution of Households by Source of Lighting

(Rural)

State	*Source of Lighting*					
	Electricity	*Kerosene*	*Solar Energy*	*Other Oil*	*Any other*	*No Lighting*
Maharashtra	65.17	33.61	0.13	0.24	0.27	0.57
Punjab	89.46	8.95	0.13	0.13	0.25	1.09
Haryana	78.50	20.60	0.22	0.18	0.14	0.36
Tamil Nadu	71.18	28.16	0.20	0.04	0.07	0.35
Gujarat	72.12	26.17	0.21	0.20	0.31	0.99
Kerala	65.53	33.78	0.53	0.06	0.06	0.03
Karnataka	72.16	27.18	0.20	0.06	0.07	0.34
West Bengal	20.27	79.19	0.31	0.04	0.10	0.09
Andhra Pradesh	59.65	39.70	0.18	0.13	0.06	0.28
Rajasthan	44.02	54.67	0.41	0.24	0.12	0.54
Madhya Pradesh	62.32	37.22	0.13	0.08	0.08	0.16
Chhattisgarh	46.11	52.92	0.17	0.09	0.30	0.41
M.P. (Old)	57.58	41.82	0.14	0.08	0.15	0.23
Uttar Pradesh	19.84	79.51	0.39	0.09	0.07	0.09
Uttaranchal	50.35	46.68	2.43	0.07	0.18	0.29
U.P. (Old)	21.51	77.71	0.50	0.09	0.08	0.10
Assam	16.54	83.11	0.18	0.04	0.05	0.08
Orissa	19.35	79.76	0.33	0.06	0.12	0.37
Bihar	5.13	94.48	0.28	0.05	0.04	0.03
Jharkhand	9.99	89.63	0.21	0.08	0.04	0.04
Bihar (Old)	6.25	93.36	0.26	0.05	0.04	0.03
India	**43.52**	**55.61**	**0.29**	**0.11**	**0.16**	**0.31**

Source : Calculated from Table H-9, *Census of India, 2001, Series 1, Tables on Houses, Household Amenities and Assets.*

A close perusal of the data provided in Table 3.11 reveals that states which are above the mark of 50 per cent rural electrified households are: Punjab, Haryana, Maharashtra, Tamil Nadu, Gujarat, Kerala, Karnataka, Andhra Pradesh, Madhya Pradesh and Uttaranchal. The topmost position is enjoyed by Punjab with over 89 percent rural households using electricity as

TABLE 3.12

Percentage Distribution of Households by Source of Lighting

(Urban)

State	*Source of Lighting*					
	Electricity	*Kerosene*	*Solar Energy*	*Other Oil*	*Any other*	*No Lighting*
Maharashtra	94.28	5.06	0.12	0.06	0.13	0.35
Punjab	96.49	2.61	0.14	0.07	0.17	0.52
Haryana	92.94	6.15	0.14	0.14	0.21	0.43
Tamil Nadu	88.00	11.15	0.31	0.03	0.08	0.43
Gujarat	93.39	5.46	0.28	0.07	0.15	0.65
Kerala	84.34	15.08	0.42	0.05	0.07	0.04
Karnataka	90.53	8.78	0.24	0.04	0.07	0.33
West Bengal	79.56	19.52	0.31	0.10	0.20	0.31
Andhra Pradesh	89.99	9.17	0.36	0.07	0.07	0.33
Rajasthan	89.61	9.59	0.11	0.10	0.18	0.40
Madhya Pradesh	92.26	7.14	0.16	0.07	0.11	0.25
Chhattisgarh	82.85	16.54	0.14	0.09	0.10	0.28
M.P. (Old)	90.19	9.21	0.16	0.07	0.11	0.26
Uttar Pradesh	79.92	19.31	0.24	0.09	0.16	0.28
Uttaranchal	90.92	8.38	0.16	0.06	0.15	0.34
U.P. (Old)	80.69	18.55	0.23	0.09	0.16	0.28
Assam	74.29	24.97	0.34	0.04	0.20	0.17
Orissa	74.08	24.29	0.44	0.06	0.15	0.97
Bihar	59.28	39.89	0.41	0.14	0.13	0.15
Jharkhand	75.61	23.77	0.22	0.17	0.10	0.13
Bihar (Old)	66.55	32.72	0.33	0.15	0.11	0.14
India	**87.59**	**11.61**	**0.24**	**0.07**	**0.15**	**0.35**

Source : Calculated from Table H-9, *Census of India, 2001, Series 1, Tables on Houses, Household Amenities And Assets.*

source of lighting. On the other extreme, the laggards are Bihar (5%), Jharkhand (10%), Assam (16.5%), Orissa (19.4%), U.P. (19.8%). Even West Bengal had only 20.3 percent rural households electrified—a very distressing scenario. Rajasthan has reached a level of 44 percent and

TABLE 3.13
Percentage Distribution of Households by Source of Lighting

(Total)

State	Source of Lighting					
	Electricity	*Kerosene*	*Solar Energy*	*Other Oil*	*Any other*	*No Lighting*
Maharashtra	77.49	21.53	0.13	0.17	0.21	0.48
Punjab	91.91	6.73	0.13	0.11	0.22	0.89
Haryana	82.90	16.20	0.19	0.17	0.16	0.38
Tamil Nadu	78.18	21.08	0.24	0.04	0.07	0.38
Gujarat	80.41	18.10	0.24	0.15	0.25	0.86
Kerala	70.24	29.09	0.50	0.06	0.07	0.03
Karnataka	78.55	20.78	0.31	0.05	0.07	0.24
West Bengal	37.45	61.90	0.31	0.08	0.13	0.15
Andhra Pradesh	67.17	32.13	0.22	0.12	0.06	0.29
Rajasthan	54.69	44.12	0.34	0.21	0.14	0.51
Madhya Pradesh	69.98	29.53	0.14	0.08	0.09	0.18
Chhattisgarh	53.10	46.00	0.16	0.09	0.27	0.38
M.P. (Old)	65.34	34.06	0.15	0.08	0.14	0.24
Uttar Pradesh	31.90	67.43	0.36	0.09	0.09	0.13
Uttaranchal	60.33	37.26	1.87	0.07	0.17	0.30
U.P. (Old)	33.54	65.68	0.45	0.09	0.09	0.14
Assam	24.90	74.68	0.20	0.04	0.07	0.10
Orissa	26.91	72.10	0.35	0.06	0.13	0.46
Bihar	10.25	89.31	0.29	0.05	0.05	0.04
Jharkhand	24.30	75.27	0.21	0.10	0.06	0.06
Bihar (Old)	13.88	85.69	0.27	0.07	0.05	0.05
India	**55.85**	**43.30**	**0.27**	**0.10**	**0.16**	**0.32**

Source : Calculated from Table H-9, *Census of India, 2001, Series 1, Tables on Houses, Household Amenities and Assets.*

Chhattisgarh 46 percent. India has, therefore, a long way to go before she can claim genuine rural electrification having been accomplished.

7. DISTRIBUTION OF HOUSEHOLDS ON THE BASIS OF BATHROOM FACILITY, LATRINE WITHIN THE HOUSE AND CONNECTIVITY FOR WASTE WATER OUTLET

Bathroom Facility—Census has provided information regarding availability of bathroom facility within the house. The data provided in Table 3.14, 3.15 and 3.16 reveal that for the country as a whole, 36 percent of households have bathroom facility within the house. This proportion was much higher in urban areas at 70 percent, but was a poor 23 percent in rural areas. So far as rural households were concerned, this proportion was highest in Punjab (62.4%), followed by Kerala (56.5%), Karnataka (48.1%) and Haryana (41.1%). On the other extreme were Chhattisgarh (3.1%), Jharkhand (4.1%), Orissa (4.4%), Bihar (6.1%), Assam (7.9%), West Bengal (9.4%) and Madhya Pradesh (10.9%).

The urban areas showed much better provision of bathroom facility with the national average at 70.4%. States above the national average were Maharashtra, Punjab, Haryana, Gujarat, Kerala, Karnataka, Andhra Pradesh, Rajasthan and Uttaranchal. States with very poor provisioning of bathroom facility in urban areas were Bihar, Orissa, Assam, Jharkhand and West Bengal—all below 60 percent range.

Latrine Facility—For the country as a whole, non-availability of latrine facility was observed for about 64 percent of the total households. In urban areas, this was limited to 26 percent of households, but in rural areas, 78 percent of households did not have latrine facility at all. In Chhattisgarh, this facility was not available to 95 percent households in rural areas, this was followed by Jharkhand (93.4%), Orissa (92.3%), Madhya Pradesh (91%). Kerala was at the top and only about 19 percent of rural households did not have latrine facility. (Refer Tables 3.14, 3.15 and 3.16).

Drainage Systems—The Census of 2001 has classified households on the basis of closed drainage, open drainage and no drainage households. The situation in this regard is far from satisfactory. For the country as a whole, nearly 54 percent households did not have any drainage for waste water outlet. Only 12.5 percent had closed drainage and 33.9 percent had open drainage.

Urban areas have been able to improve drainage system. In urban areas only 22 percent of household had no drainage. Closed drainage was available to 34.5 percent of urban households and open drainage to 43.4 percent. Ironically, the record of Kerala was the poorest in developing drainage system. 69 percent of households did not have any drainage, only 15 percent had closed drainage and 16 percent had open drainage. Uttar Pradesh was at the top in developing drainage system— 26.5 percent of urban households had closed drainage, about 66 percent had open drainage and no drainage households were only 7.6 percent. From the point of view of quality of drainage, Gujarat was at the top with 59.3 percent of urban

TABLE 3.14

Percentage Distribution of Households by Availability of Bathroom and Type of Latrine Within the House and Type of Drainage Connectivity for Waste Water Outlet

(Rural)

State	*Number of households having bathroom facility within the house*	*Type of latrine within the house*				*Type of connectivity for waste water outlet*		
		Pit Latrine	*Water Closet*	*Other Latrine*	*No Latrine*	*Closed Drainage*	*Open Drainage*	*No Drainage*
(1)	*(2)*	*(3)*	*(4)*	*(5)*	*(6)*	*(7)*	*(8)*	*(9)*
Maharashtra	46.09	10.23	5.33	2.66	81.79	5.15	35.99	58.86
Punjab	62.42	26.36	6.39	8.16	59.09	4.24	73.84	21.92
Haryana	41.14	20.46	2.11	6.09	71.34	3.16	68.55	28.28
Tamil Nadu	20.97	4.56	7.36	2.44	85.64	4.28	23.07	72.64
Gujarat	31.36	8.09	11.28	2.29	78.35	6.80	6.86	86.35
Kerala	56.50	12.78	61.99	6.56	18.67	5.77	10.22	84.01
Karnataka	48.07	9.48	4.67	3.25	82.60	4.28	31.11	64.61
West Bengal	9.35	15.35	6.97	4.61	73.07	1.38	14.54	84.09
Andhra Pradesh	27.09	6.39	8.62	3.14	81.85	6.29	35.15	58.57
Rajasthan	20.47	8.10	3.18	3.33	85.39	2.99	20.18	76.83
Madhya Pradesh	10.88	3.88	2.62	2.43	91.06	1.93	17.90	80.16
Chhattisgarh	3.09	1.78	1.83	1.57	94.82	1.42	9.89	88.69
M.P. (Old)	8.60	3.27	2.39	2.18	92.16	1.78	15.56	82.66
Uttar Pradesh	19.92	8.34	1.95	8.94	80.77	5.29	59.70	35.01
Uttaranchal	25.99	16.10	7.17	8.33	68.40	4.50	30.46	65.05
U.P. (Old)	20.25	8.76	2.24	8.91	80.09	5.24	58.09	36.66
Assam	7.87	46.91	8.61	4.04	40.43	0.88	14.11	85.00
Orissa	4.35	3.09	3.29	1.33	92.29	2.55	12.30	85.15
Bihar	6.12	5.97	4.16	3.79	86.09	2.61	32.25	65.14
Jharkhand	4.09	2.12	2.23	2.22	93.43	1.51	16.21	82.29
Bihar (Old)	5.65	5.08	3.71	3.43	87.78	2.35	28.54	69.10
India	**22.83**	**10.30**	**7.11**	**4.51**	**78.08**	**3.91**	**30.27**	**65.82**

Source : Calculated from Table H-10, *Census of India, 2001, Series 1, Tables on Houses, Household Amenities And Assets.*

TABLE 3.15

Percentage Distribution of Households by Availability of Bathroom and Type of Latrine within the House and Type of Drainage Connectivity for Waste Water Outlet

(Urban)

State	Number of households having bathroom facility within the house	Type of latrine within the house				Type of connectivity for waste water outlet		
		Pit Latrine	Water Closet	Other Latrine	No Latrine	Closed Drainage	Open Drainage	No Drainage
(1)	(2)	(3)	(4)	(5)	(6)	(7)	(8)	(9)
Maharashtra	81.60	7.08	44.37	6.63	41.92	45.07	42.51	12.42
Punjab	82.76	20.53	46.52	19.48	13.48	44.97	44.80	10.23
Haryana	75.41	26.48	30.99	23.19	19.34	35.01	53.39	11.59
Tamil Nadu	66.42	11.16	45.47	7.71	35.67	34.56	35.46	29.98
Gujarat	80.62	9.75	62.11	8.69	19.45	59.26	19.03	21.71
Kerala	78.91	11.11	74.76	6.16	7.98	14.85	16.04	69.11
Karnataka	79.15	20.70	44.86	9.67	24.77	41.64	39.33	19.03
West Bengal	58.56	22.89	55.20	6.76	15.15	21.85	45.30	32.86
Andhra Pradesh	78.48	15.10	46.97	16.00	21.93	36.02	46.27	17.71
Rajasthan	71.40	18.21	40.58	17.33	23.89	24.12	56.07	19.81
Madhya Pradesh	63.21	11.89	41.10	14.74	32.26	24.50	51.42	24.07
Chhattisgarh	51.88	5.15	38.82	8.62	47.41	17.12	45.85	37.04
M.P. (Old)	60.72	10.41	40.60	13.40	35.60	22.88	50.20	26.93
Uttar Pradesh	63.76	18.07	31.98	29.96	19.99	26.46	65.91	7.62
Uttaranchal	77.87	26.72	40.82	19.35	13.12	28.36	59.88	11.76
U.P. (Old)	64.75	18.68	32.60	29.22	19.51	26.60	65.49	7.91
Assam	52.98	26.39	58.88	9.33	5.40	9.84	42.78	47.38
Orissa	48.94	9.48	43.05	7.15	40.31	19.61	37.88	42.51
Bihar	43.13	11.37	43.45	14.88	30.31	22.15	46.46	31.39
Jharkhand	54.55	7.41	41.24	18.03	33.32	23.79	48.57	27.64
Bihar (Old)	48.21	9.61	42.46	16.28	31.65	22.88	47.40	29.72
India	**70.40**	**14.60**	**46.12**	**13.00**	**26.28**	**34.50**	**43.37**	**22.13**

Source: Calculated from Table H-10, *Census of India, 2001, Series 1, Tables on Houses, Household Amenities and Assets.*

TABLE 3.16

Percentage Distribution of Households by Availability of Bathroom and Type of Latrine within the House and Type of Drainage Connectivity for Waste Water Outlet

(Total)

State	*Number of households having bathroom facility within the house*	*Type of latrine within the house*				*Type of connectivity for waste water outlet*		
		Pit Latrine	*Water Closet*	*Other Latrine*	*No Latrine*	*Closed Drainage*	*Open Drainage*	*No Drainage*
(1)	*(2)*	*(3)*	*(4)*	*(5)*	*(6)*	*(7)*	*(8)*	*(9)*
Maharashtra	61.12	8.89	21.85	4.34	64.91	22.05	38.75	39.20
Punjab	69.53	24.33	20.40	12.11	43.16	18.46	63.70	17.84
Haryana	51.58	22.29	10.91	11.30	55.50	12.86	63.94	23.20
Tamil Nadu	39.89	7.30	23.22	4.63	64.84	16.89	28.23	54.89
Gujarat	50.56	8.73	31.09	4.78	55.40	27.24	11.60	61.16
Kerala	62.12	12.36	65.19	6.46	15.99	8.04	11.68	80.28
Karnataka	58.87	13.38	18.64	5.48	62.50	17.26	33.97	48.77
West Bengal	23.61	17.53	20.95	5.23	56.29	7.31	23.45	69.24
Andhra Pradesh	39.82	8.55	18.12	6.32	67.01	13.65	37.90	48.44
Rajasthan	32.38	10.47	11.93	6.60	71.00	7.93	28.58	63.49
Madhya Pradesh	24.27	5.93	12.47	5.58	76.01	7.71	26.48	65.81
Chhattisgarh	12.38	2.42	8.87	2.92	85.80	4.41	16.73	78.86
M.P. (Old)	21.00	4.97	11.48	4.85	78.71	6.80	23.80	69.40
Uttar Pradesh	28.72	10.29	7.98	13.16	68.57	9.54	60.95	29.51
Uttaranchal	38.75	18.71	15.45	11.04	54.80	10.37	37.69	51.94
U.P. (Old)	29.30	10.78	8.41	13.04	67.78	9.59	59.60	30.82
Assam	14.41	43.94	15.90	4.81	35.36	2.18	18.27	79.55
Orissa	10.51	3.97	8.79	2.14	85.11	4.91	15.84	79.26
Bihar	9.62	6.48	7.87	4.84	80.81	4.46	33.59	61.95
Jharkhand	15.09	3.27	10.73	5.67	80.33	6.36	23.26	70.37
Bihar (Old)	11.04	5.65	8.61	5.05	80.68	4.95	30.93	64.12
India	**36.14**	**11.50**	**18.02**	**6.88**	**63.59**	**12.46**	**33.93**	**53.60**

Source: Calculated from Table H-10, *Census of India, 2001, Series 1, Tables on Houses, Household Amenities and Assets.*

households having closed drainage, followed by Maharashtra and Punjab (45%) and Karnataka (41.6%).

The drainage situation in rural India, is to say the least, very distressing. Only about 4 percent of households had closed drainage, 30 percent open drainage and 64 percent no drainage. A close perusal of the statewise data about drainage of rural households reveals that virtually closed drainage is conspicuous by its absence ranging from less than 1 percent for Assam to about 7 percent for Gujarat. Regarding the provision of open drainage among rural households, Punjab was at the top (about 74%), followed by Haryana (68.6%). States which have more than 80 percent households with no drainage are: Chhattisgarh (88.7%), Gujarat (86.4%), Assam and Orissa (85%), Kerala and West Bengal (84%) and Jharkhand (82.3%).

8. AVAILABILITY OF SPECIFIED ASSETS

Census of 2001 has presented data about the availability of specified assets. This data is based on six assets, viz., Radio/Transistor, Television, Telephone, Bicycle, Scooter/Motor cycle/Moped, Car/Jeep/Van. It has also provided information about households which possessed none of the specified assets. The information is very useful since it is an indirect measure of the level of poverty or the level of living of a household.

Tables 3.17, 3.18 and 3.19 provide state-wise information on ownership of assets by households classified on rural, urban and total basis.

It would be advisable to consider the proportion of households whom "none of the specified assets" were available. Their proportion for India as a whole was 34.5 percent, for rural areas it was 40.5 percent and for urban areas 19 percent. Obviously, these proportions are higher than the percentage of population below the poverty line reckoned at 27.5 percent for India in 2004-05, 25.7 percent for urban and 28.3 percent for rural areas.

State-wise situation in rural areas presents a very disturbing picture. Even in relatively better-off states like Maharashtra, 50.2 percent of rural households did not have of any of the specified assets, in Gujarat, this ratio was 49.6 percent, in Andhra Pradesh 53.2 percent and in Karnataka 42.9 percent. This only indicates that disparity in income distribution in these states was very high and this explains the high proportion of population with none of the specified assets. Among the poor states, this proportion was expected to be high and this is reflected in the high percentage in this category in Bihar (51.3%), Madhya Pradesh (50.5%), Rajasthan (47.1%) and Orissa (44.4%). It is really heartening, though paradoxical that this proportion was relatively much lower in Uttar Pradesh at 21.4 percent. Punjab again had the distinction that only 13.3 percent of the rural households were in 'None of the specified assets' category but Haryana indicated a much higher proportion at 29.1 percent and Tamil Nadu at 40 percent. There is a need to study the distribution of income and wealth as a result of the growth process, more especially in the post-economic reforms period.

Bicycle is considered as a poor household's means of conveyance. Only about 44 percent of households had a bicycle, the percentage was slightly higher in urban areas (46 percent) and slightly lower in rural areas (42.8 percent). Punjab indicated the highest proportion of rural households having a bicycle (74%), followed by Uttar Pradesh (71.2%), Chhattisgarh (58.2%) and West Bengal (54.3%).

Better-off rural households were shifting to Scooter/Motor cycle/ Moped. In Punjab, 27 percent of the households were in the category, followed by Haryana (13.2%), Gujarat (11.8%), Tamil Nadu (10.7%). All other states fell in the range of 2.5 to 7.5 percent. Car/Jeep/Van were available to only 1.3 percent of the total rural households. The state with highest proportion in this category was again Punjab (3.7%). Quite a number of states, viz., Chhattisgarh, Orissa, Bihar, Jharkhand and Andhra Pradesh indicated a very low figure of 0.5 to 0.6 percent.

Television penetration in rural areas was of the order of about 19 percent. The highest percentage was for Punjab (61.3%), followed by Haryana (44%), Kerala and Uttaranchal (32.3%). The laggards in this regard are Bihar (5.5%), Jharkhand (6.7%), Orissa (9.2%), Chhatisgarh (12.4%), Assam (12.0%) and West Bengal (13.4%).

It may also be noted that the reach of radio/transistor in the rural areas in the poor states is also weak. As against the national average of 31.5 percent, it was only 17.4% in Madhya Pradesh, 21.6% in Chhattisgarh, 21.2 percent in Orissa and 26.5% in Bihar.

The use of telephones in rural areas is limited to 3.8 percent of the households. However, the range of this use varies from 1 percent in Bihar to 15.7 percent in Kerala. Punjab has a second rank with 11.9 percent of households using telephones. The states in which the percentage of households using telephones is very poor, are : Jharkhand (0.85%), Bihar (1.0%), Chhattisgarh (1.0%), Orissa (1.6%), West Bengal (1.8%), Madhya Pradesh (1.95%) and Uttar Pradesh (2.4%).

The situation in urban areas was relatively much better than that of the rural areas. For instance, the proportion of urban households with 'none of the specified assets' was 19 percent, Punjab had the distinction of having the lowest proportion of households in this category (8%) and Bihar had the highest proportion of 32.2%. Even among the poor states, UP indicated a proportion of 15.7 percent, Rajasthan 18.0 percent, Orissa 20.0 percent and Madhya Pradesh 18.0 percent.

The national average for bicycle availability in urban areas was 46 percent. Lowest figure for bicycle was that for Kerala (26.6%), followed by Karnataka (34.5%), Andhra Pradesh (41.5%), Assam (42.5%) and Bihar (45.6%).

The availability of scooter/motor cycle/moped was much higher in urban areas—24.7 percent of households as against only 6.7 percent of rural households. Punjab again was at the top as 40 percent of urban households

TABLE 3.17

Percentage of Households Availing Banking Services and having Each of the Specified Assets

(Rural)

State	*Households Availing Banking Services*	*Availability of Assets*						
		Radio, Transistor	*Television*	*Telephone*	*Bicycle*	*Scooter, Motor Cycle, Moped*	*Car, Jeep, Van*	*None of the Specified Assets*
(1)	*(2)*	*(3)*	*(4)*	*(5)*	*(6)*	*(7)*	*(8)*	*(9)*
Maharashtra	39.42	26.80	24.72	4.38	28.31	7.99	1.61	50.20
Punjab	45.72	38.46	61.26	11.86	74.12	27.01	3.68	13.29
Haryana	42.44	39.22	43.95	6.17	46.22	13.23	2.45	29.09
Tamil Nadu	17.71	38.59	24.33	5.09	39.87	10.74	1.07	40.06
Gujarat	29.86	24.55	21.60	5.53	29.33	11.84	1.82	49.55
Kerala	50.16	58.85	32.26	15.66	15.71	7.39	2.86	29.97
Karnataka	35.21	42.15	21.23	5.69	27.85	7.29	1.36	42.92
West Bengal	27.56	36.67	13.39	1.79	54.28	3.06	1.21	34.04
Andhra Pradesh	30.37	18.43	21.32	3.93	29.96	5.14	0.52	53.16
Rajasthan	23.98	31.67	16.58	3.46	31.67	7.29	1.65	47.08
Madhya Pradesh	21.10	17.38	16.85	1.95	38.25	5.99	0.89	50.46
Chhattisgarh	18.90	21.58	12.54	1.04	58.18	5.85	0.59	35.70
M.P. (Old)	20.46	18.61	15.59	1.68	44.08	5.95	0.80	46.14
Uttar Pradesh	41.90	38.12	16.01	2.41	71.15	6.69	1.48	21.41
Uttaranchal	56.14	51.37	32.27	4.43	25.89	6.16	1.26	30.11
U.P. (Old)	42.68	38.85	16.90	2.52	68.66	6.66	1.46	21.89
Assam	14.98	28.61	12.04	1.88	47.04	3.32	1.15	43.27
Orissa	19.74	21.24	9.23	1.65	49.42	4.52	0.62	44.37
Bihar	18.64	26.49	5.53	1.04	40.12	2.45	0.65	51.34
Jharkhand	21.21	23.54	6.68	0.85	49.26	3.97	0.58	44.30
Bihar (Old)	19.24	25.81	5.79	0.99	42.23	2.80	0.64	49.71
India	**30.11**	**31.49**	**18.91**	**3.77**	**42.78**	**6.67**	**1.29**	**40.49**

Source : Calculated from Table H-13, *Census of India, 2001, Series 1, Tables on Houses, Household Amenities and Assets.*

TABLE 3.18

Percentage of Households Availing Banking Services and having Each of the Specified Assets

(Urban)

State	Households Availing Banking Services	Availability of Assets						
		Radio, Transistor	Television	Telephone	Bicycle	Scooter, Motor Cycle, Moped	Car, Jeep, Van	None of the Specified Assets
(1)	(2)	(3)	(4)	(5)	(6)	(7)	(8)	(9)
Maharashtra	60.01	48.29	70.54	27.32	32.46	20.27	5.76	18.56
Punjab	53.66	41.16	79.67	32.11	67.36	40.22	9.67	8.02
Haryana	51.62	39.81	73.58	27.66	58.81	32.08	8.41	12.56
Tamil Nadu	30.00	50.50	60.72	19.86	46.04	23.60	3.75	21.60
Gujarat	50.32	38.99	65.47	23.34	49.81	35.62	5.95	18.11
Kerala	53.90	60.18	58.47	29.26	26.63	17.80	7.35	18.98
Karnataka	48.96	53.83	66.53	26.06	34.45	27.88	6.27	19.82
West Bengal	59.41	43.47	58.83	18.72	48.43	9.86	3.57	20.39
Andhra Pradesh	33.05	31.33	62.29	22.68	41.53	24.81	3.59	23.99
Rajasthan	44.96	43.02	65.81	22.94	51.16	32.24	5.26	18.00
Madhya Pradesh	47.74	31.11	66.81	18.48	56.03	29.75	4.38	17.99
Chhattisgarh	46.33	30.91	59.63	15.50	66.88	31.93	4.60	17.49
M.P. (Old)	47.43	31.07	65.23	17.82	58.42	30.23	4.43	17.88
Uttar Pradesh	52.96	45.51	60.79	18.33	62.85	25.00	5.32	15.67
Uttaranchal	71.12	44.53	75.59	26.70	46.17	29.66	7.00	12.05
U.P. (Old)	54.23	45.44	61.83	18.92	61.68	25.33	5.44	15.42
Assam	53.30	39.50	55.22	18.85	42.52	16.37	7.33	25.17
Orissa	52.10	38.78	54.54	18.32	67.81	28.71	3.93	20.02
Bihar	47.18	40.01	42.92	13.71	45.62	15.05	3.37	32.18
Jharkhand	62.19	36.49	55.17	12.31	54.11	28.61	4.96	22.57
Bihar (Old)	53.86	38.45	48.37	13.08	49.39	21.09	4.08	27.90
India	**49.52**	**44.47**	**64.26**	**22.97**	**45.98**	**24.70**	**5.63**	**19.02**

Source: Calculated from Table H-13, *Census of India, 2001, Series 1, Tables on Houses, Household Amenities and Assets.*

TABLE 3.19

Percentage of Households Availing Banking Services and having each of the Specified Assets

(Total)

State	*Households Availing Banking Services*	*Availability of Assets*						
		Radio, Transistor	*Television*	*Telephone*	*Bicycle*	*Scooter, Motor Cycle, Moped*	*Car, Jeep, Van*	*None of the Specified Assets*
(1)	*(2)*	*(3)*	*(4)*	*(5)*	*(6)*	*(7)*	*(8)*	*(9)*
Maharashtra	48.13	35.90	44.12	14.09	30.07	13.19	3.37	36.81
Punjab	48.50	39.40	67.69	18.94	71.76	31.63	5.77	11.45
Haryana	45.23	39.40	52.98	12.72	50.05	18.97	4.26	24.06
Tamil Nadu	22.82	43.55	39.48	11.24	42.44	16.09	2.18	32.38
Gujarat	37.83	30.18	38.69	12.47	37.31	21.10	3.43	37.30
Kerala	51.10	59.18	38.83	19.07	18.45	10.00	3.98	27.22
Karnataka	39.99	46.22	36.98	12.77	30.14	14.44	3.07	34.89
West Bengal	36.79	38.64	26.56	6.70	52.59	5.03	1.89	30.08
Andhra Pradesh	31.04	21.63	31.47	8.58	32.83	10.01	1.28	45.93
Rajasthan	28.89	34.33	28.10	8.02	36.23	13.13	2.50	40.28
Madhya Pradesh	27.92	20.89	29.64	6.18	42.80	12.07	1.79	42.15
Chhattisgarh	24.12	23.36	21.50	3.79	59.83	10.82	1.35	32.23
M.P. (Old)	26.87	21.57	27.40	5.52	47.49	11.73	1.67	39.42
Uttar Pradesh	44.12	39.61	25.00	5.61	69.48	10.37	2.25	20.26
Uttaranchal	59.82	49.69	42.92	9.91	30.88	11.94	2.67	25.67
U.P. (Old)	45.03	40.19	26.04	5.86	67.24	10.46	2.27	20.57
Assam	20.53	30.19	18.30	4.34	46.39	5.21	2.05	40.65
Orissa	24.21	23.66	15.49	3.95	51.96	7.86	1.08	41.00
Bihar	21.34	27.77	9.07	2.23	40.64	3.64	0.91	49.53
Jharkhand	30.15	26.37	17.25	3.35	50.32	9.35	1.53	39.56
Bihar (Old)	23.62	27.41	11.18	2.52	43.14	5.11	1.07	46.95
India	**35.54**	**35.12**	**31.59**	**9.14**	**43.67**	**11.71**	**2.50**	**34.48**

Source : Calculated from Table H-13, *Census of India, 2001, Series 1, Tables on Houses, Household Amenities and Assets.*

used the fast moving two-wheeler, followed by Gujarat (35.6%), Haryana (32.1%), Rajasthan (32.2%), Chhattisgarh (31.9%). States with a very low proportion of scooters/motor cycles were : Bihar (15.1%), Assam (16.4%), Kerala (17.8%) and West Bengal (barely 9.9%).

Television penetration was much higher in urban areas since 64.3 percent of households had this asset. In this also, Punjab was at the top with 80 percent of the households having television. States with lower television penetration were: Orissa (54.5%), Assam (55.2%), West Bengal (58.8%) and Chhattisgarh (59.6%).

Telephone availability accounted for 23 percent of urban households at the national level, but states which lagged behind were: Jharkhand (12.3%), Bihar (13.7%), Chhattisgarh (15.5%), Madhya Pradesh (18.5%), Uttar Pradesh (18.3%), Assam (18.9%), West Bengal (18.7%) and Tamil Nadu (19.9%).

It may be mentioned the households may be in possession of a bicycle and motor cycle/scooter/moped and thus, these figures cannot be considered exclusive. Similarly, households having a television may also be having a radio/transistor.

9. BANKING SERVICES

For the country as a whole, 35.5 percent of the households were availing banking services, the proportion was 49.5 percent for urban households and 30.1 percent for rural households. The range of availing banking services in rural areas varied from 71 percent in Uttaranchal to 30 percent in Tamil Nadu. It is really surprising that a relatively developed state like Tamil Nadu should have the lowest proportion of urban households (22.8%) availing of banking services. This is followed by Andhra Pradesh (33.1%), Rajasthan (45%), Chhattisgarh (46.3%), Bihar, (47.2%) and Madhya Pradesh (47.7%)

Nearly similar situation obtains in rural areas. As against the national average of 30.1 percent of households availing of banking services, Assam had the lowest proportion of 15.0 percent, followed by Tamil Nadu (17.7%), Bihar (18.6%), Chhattisgarh (18.9%), Orissa (19.7%) and Jharkhand (21.2%).

10. COMPOSITE INDEX OF WELFARE

An attempt has been made to develop a composite index of welfare on the basis of 8 variables:

(i) Per capital Net State Domestic Product for 1999-00 (at 1993-94 prices).
(ii) Population above poverty line (1999-00)—NSS Data.
(iii) Permanent houses as per 2001 Census.
(iv) Drinking water by Tap (2001 Census).
(v) Lighting of households by Electricity (2001 Census).

(vi) Availability of latrine within the house (2001 Census).
(vii) Availability of bathroom within the house (2001 Census).
(viii) Ownership of at least one of the specified assets—Radio/Transistor, Television, Telephone, Bicycle, Scooter/Motorcycle/Moped, Car/Jeep/Van (as per Census 2001).

Principal Component Analysis was done on the above set of 8 variables called principal components. Factor loadings of different variables of the first two principal components are given in Table 3.20.

TABLE 3.20
Component matrix

	Component	
	1	2
Per Capita NSDP	0.926	-0.112
Population above poverty line (%)	0.924	0.038
Permanent Houses (%)	0.898	0.071
Drinking water by tap (%)	0.708	-0.658
Lighting by Electricity (%)	0.907	-0.292
Latrine (%)	0.714	0.538
Bathroom (%)	0.962	-0.026
At least one of the specified Assets (%)	0.645	0.583

These loadings are used as weights to arrive at the composite indices of welfare. (Refer Table 3.21) Since first principal component itself accounted for more than 70 percent of total variation which is sufficient for conventional norms, it was decided to avoid varimax rotation method, because in our case, the relative values of indices for different states arrived through varimax rotation method are similar.

It may be noted that the ranking of states on the basis of per capita NSDP and the composite index of welfare show variations. This only underlines the fact that while per capita NSDP is an important variable, other variables, some of which are state policy induced and some based on individual preference are important determinants. For instance, states like Maharashtra, Tamil Nadu, Gujarat, Karnataka and Haryana have been keen on providing tap water facility and thus, reducing the time and effort in securing good quality water at the household level. Unfortunately, Kerala and West Bengal did not devote sufficient resources for this vital human necessity. Similarly, providing electricity at the household level has been a high priority policy initiative with some states, but West Bengal lagged far behind, though its ranks in per capita NSDP was higher.

TABLE 3.21

Households Amenities and Assets Along with Per Capita Income and Population above the Poverty Line in India and Composite Index of Welfare

S. No.	Major States	Per Capita NSDP 1999-2000 at 1993-94 prices (Rs.)	Population above Poverty Line (%) 1999-2000	Permanent Houses (2001)	Drinking Water by Tap (2001)	Lighting by Electricity (2001)	Latrine (2001)	Bath Room (2001)	Atleast one of specified assets (2001)	Composite Index Unrotated	Ranks
	(1)	(2)	(3)	(4)	(5)	(6)	(7)	(8)	(9)	(10)	(11)
1.	Maharashtra	23398	74.98	57.8	64.0	77.4	35.1	61.1	63.2	0.70	5.00
2.	Punjab	23040	93.84	86.1	33.6	91.9	56.9	69.5	88.6	1.63	1.00
3.	Haryana	21551	91.26	65.8	48.1	82.9	44.5	51.6	76	1.00	2.00
4.	Tamil Nadu	19141	78.88	58.5	62.5	78.2	35.2	39.9	67.6	0.50	7.00
5.	Gujarat	18685	85.93	65.3	62.3	80.4	44.6	50.6	62.7	0.76	4.00
6.	Kerala	18262	87.28	68.1	20.4	70.2	84.0	62.1	72.8	0.99	3.00
7.	Karnataka	16343	79.96	54.9	58.9	78.5	37.5	58.9	65.1	0.52	6.00
8.	West Bengal	15569	72.98	40.4	21.4	37.5	43.7	23.6	69.9	-0.40	10.00
9.	Andhra Pradesh	14715	84.23	54.7	48.1	67.2	33.0	39.8	54.1	0.08	8.00
10.	Rajasthan	12533	84.72	64.9	35.3	54.7	29.0	32.4	59.7	-0.07	9.00
11.	Madhya Pradesh	10907	62.57	41.5	25.3	70.0	24.0	24.3	57.9	-0.71	12.00
12.	Uttar Pradesh	9765	68.85	53.4	23.7	31.9	31.4	28.7	79.8	-0.47	11.00
13.	Assam	9720	63.91	19.7	9.2	24.9	35.4	14.4	59.4	-1.29	13.00
14.	Orissa	9162	52.85	27.6	8.7	26.9	14.9	10.5	58.7	-1.56	14.00
15.	Bihar	6328	57.4	40.7	3.7	10.3	19.2	9.6	50.5	-1.67	15.00

Notes : States have been arranged in the descending order of per capita NSDP.

1. Planning Commission, *Tenth Five Year Plan (2002-07)*, Vol. III, p. 71.
2. Planning Commission, *Tenth Five Year Plan (2002-07)*, Vol. III, p. 77.

Census of India 2001 Tables on Household Amenities and Assets.

3. Data from Table H-4 Appendix – Permanent households as percentage of census occupied houses.
4. Data from Table H-8.
5. Data from Table H-9.

6&7. Data from Table H-10.

8. Data from Table H-13—Percentage of households owning at least one of the specified assets—Radio/Transistor, Television, Telephone, Bicycle, Scooter/Motor cycle/Moped, Car/Jeep/Van.

Latrine, bathroom and ownership of at least one of the assets, either for recreation or information or as a means of conveyance do add to the quality of living of the household. At private level, households have endeavoured to acquire these amenities.

But whether the houses and housing amenities are policy induced or created out of private preferences, the acquisition of these amenities does improve the quality of living of the households.

On the basis of the combined impact of these 8 variables, Punjab is ranked No. 1 on the basis of composite index. Tamil Nadu which is ranked No. 4 on the basis of per capita NSDP has been pushed down to rank No. 7 on the basis of composite index. Kerala which was ranked No. 6 on the basis of NSDP is pushed up to rank No. 3 on the basis of composite index. It may also be noted that West Bengal which was No. 8 in terms of per capita NSDP has been pushed down to rank No. 10 on the basis of composite index on account of its poor performance in providing housing amenities like permanent houses, drinking water by tap, lighting by electricity, latrine and bathroom.

States with very low per capita NSDP—Madhya Pradesh, Uttar Pradesh, Assam, Orissa and Bihar occupy rank 10 to 15 on NSDP basis as well as on composite index basis. This shows that whereas low NSDP has been a powerful factor in determining housing amenities, state policy induced factors have also been weak in altering or improving their position.

The upshot of this analysis is that per capita NSDP may be considered as an indicator of the level of development but it does not capture in totality the quality of living of the people of a region and thus, there is a need to develop a composite index of welfare so as indicate the quality of living of the people in a state or a region. Such an effort encompasses welfare in a broader sense as compared to NSDP per capita.

11. CONCLUSION

The survey of houses and housing amenities has brought forth a number of issues which need remedial action. It would be appropriate to focus on these issues for future policy direction, more especially in the light of the National Common Minimum Programme accepted by the UPA in 2004.

Firstly, it comes out as a sharp contrast that housing in urban areas has nearly 79 percent permanent houses, but in rural areas this proportion is only 41 percent. Moreover, temporary houses account for only 5 percent in urban areas but they were of the order of 23 percent in rural areas. This suggests that both for upgradation of semi-permanent houses and construction of new houses, the rural areas should get priority over their urban counterpart. Census data has drawn attention to utter neglect of housing problem in a number of states— Madhya Pradesh, Bihar, Jharkhand, Orissa and Assam. There is a high proportion of temporary houses in Andhra Pradesh, West Bengal and Bihar. "Shelter for all" is a good slogan, but it is essential that a road map be developed to achieve this goal in a time-bound manner.

The data also point out that 49 percent of households do not fulfil the norm of two rooms per family, keeping in view the availability of privacy for married couples. Housing policy, more especially for the Economically Weaker Sections of society should keep this in view that the quality of housing should meet minimum reasonable accommodation norms set for a family.

Secondly, drinking water within the premises was available to only 25 percent of rural population, while this figure for urban areas was 65 percent. If we add near premises availability as well, then drinking water was available to 80 percent of households in rural areas and 91 percent of the households in urban areas. The major issue is to make drinking water available within the premises. In rural areas, the degree of variation was very wide—82 percent households in Punjab had access to drinking water within premises as against only 10 percent in Jharkhand. But Chhattisgarh, Karnataka, Rajasthan and Orissa were all below 20 percent. Even for a relatively better off state like Tamil Nadu, this percentage was merely 17 percent.

Besides this, the stark reality is that in a number of states, viz., Orissa, Rajasthan, Madhya Pradesh, Jharkhand and even in Haryana, more than 25 percent of rural households have to fetch drinking water after traversing a distance of over 500 metres.

Thirdly, there are the problems of providing safe drinking water. The Census of India stipulates that if a household has access to drinking water supplied from a tap, handpump/tubewell within or outside the premises, it is considered as having access to safe drinking water. Consequently, *Economic Survey* (2003-04) states that the coverage of households having access to safe drinking water was 77.9 percent comprising 90 percent of urban households and 73 percent of rural households. But this definition of safe drinking water is faulty, judged by the internationally accepted definition in this regard. It would be proper to consider only tap water and some protected tubewells and protected public handpumps in this category. Obviously, the Government estimate of 78 percent households being provided safe drinking water is a gross over-estimate. For this purpose, it is vitally necessary to expand tap water facilities. At present, 25 percent of the rural population is being provided tap water. But Tamil Nadu has the unique distinction of providing 60 percent of rural households tap water. The laggards in developing rural tap water supply to less than 10 percent of households are Bihar, Orissa, Assam, Chhattisgarh, West Bengal and Madhya Pradesh. But as against them, nearly 50 percent or more of rural households in Uttaranchal, Gujarat, Maharashtra and Karnataka provide tap water. There is a strong need to strengthen water supply through household tap connections to provide safe drinking water. India has a long way to go in this regard.

Fourthly, two main sources of lighting are electricity and kerosene. In urban areas, 88 percent households are electrified and only about 12 percent use kerosene. The laggards are Bihar, Orissa, Jharkhand, Assam and to some extent Uttar Pradesh.

In rural areas 43.5 percent of households have electricity and 55.6 percent depend on kerosene. The Government definition of treating a village as electrified if 10 percent of households use electricity is too weak and gives a false sense of satisfaction about rural electrification. This should be amended and the condition of at least 50 percent households being electrified should be used.

States which qualify on the basis of 50 percent criteria of rural electrified households are: Punjab, Haryana, Maharashtra, Tamil Nadu, Gujarat, Kerala, Karnataka, Andhra Pradesh, Madhya Pradesh and Uttaranchal. On the other extreme are laggards like Bihar, Jharkhand, Assam, Orissa and West Bengal. India has a long way to go before she can claim genuine rural electrification having been accomplished.

Fifthly, bathroom facility was available to 70 percent of urban households but merely to 23 percent of rural households. The states lagging behind were Chhattisgarh, Jharkhand, Orissa, West Bengal, Bihar, Assam and Madhya Pradesh.

Sixthly, latrine facility was not available to 26 percent of the urban households, but in rural areas, this proportion was 78 percent. Chhattisgarh, Jharkhand, Orissa and Madhya Pradesh did not provide this facility to over 90 percent of rural households.

Seventhly, regarding drainage, in urban areas only 22 percent of households had no drainage, 43 percent had open drainage and only 35 percent had closed drainage. Ironically, Kerala had the poorest record in developing drainage because 69 percent of households had no drainage, but Uttar Pradesh had the best record with only 8 percent of households with no drainage, 66 percent with open drainage and 26 percent with closed drainage.

In rural areas, only 4 percent of households had closed drainage, 30 percent open drainage and 64 percent no drainage. States with more than 80 percent rural households with no drainage were : Gujarat, Assam, Orissa, Kerala, West Bengal and Jharkhand.

Eighthly, household data has been presented about the availability of specified assets viz., Radio/Transistor, Television, Telephone, Bicycle, Scooter/Motor cycle/Moped, Car/Jeep/Van. Proportion of households whom none of the specified assets were available was 34.5 percent for India, 40.5 percent for rural areas and 19 percent for urban areas. But state-wise situation reveals that in better-off states like Maharashtra, Gujarat, Andhra Pradesh and Karnataka, this proportion ranged between 43 to 53 percent. This only indicates the distortions in income distribution in these states on the path of economic development. Only 44 percent of the households in India did have even a bicycle as a means of conveyance. Telephone availability accounted for 23 percent of urban households at the national level, but the states which lagged behind were Jharkhand, Bihar, Chhattisgarh, Madhya Pradesh, Uttar Pradesh, Assam, West Bengal and Tamil Nadu.

Ninthly, for the country as whole, 35.5 percent of households availed of banking services, the proportion was 49.5 percent for urban households and 30.1 percent for rural households.

Last, but not the last, an attempt has been made to develop a composite index of welfare on the basis of 8 variables. There are significant variations in the ranking of states on the basis of per capita NSDP and the composite index of welfare. Punjab is ranked No. 1 on the basis of composite index. Tamil Nadu which is ranked No. 4 on the basis of per capita NSDP was pushed down to Rank No. 7 on the basis of composite index. Similarly, Kerala was pushed up to Rank No. 3 on the basis of composite index while it ranked No. 6 on the basis of NSDP. West Bengal which ranked No. 8 on the basis of NSDP was pushed down to rank No. 10 on the basis of composite index on account of its poor performance in providing amenities like drinking water, electricity, bathroom and latrine. Composite index captures the quality of living of the people in a much broader sense than NSDP.

To sum up, the message of the Census findings is that the development process has helped urban India to a much greater extent than rural India. We should now direct the development process to strengthen rural India and bridge the rural-urban divide. Gandhi was very forthright in pointing out the exploitation of the rural society by its urban counterpart. Gandhi wrote in *Village Swaraj*: "The British have exploited India through its cities. The latter have exploited the villages. The blood of the villages is the cement with which the edifice of the cities is built. I want the blood that is today inflating the arteries of the cities to run once again in the blood vessels of villages."[6] As a policy statement, Gandhi stated : "The cities are capable of taking care of themselves. It is the villages we have to turn to."[7]

References

1. Government of India, *Economic Survey, 2002-03*, p. 233.
2. Government of India, *Economic Survey, (2003-04)*, p. 224.
3. UNDP, *Human Development Report, (2004)*, pp. 275-76.
4. Government of India, *Economic Survey, (2003-04)*, pp. 174-80.
5. *Ibid.*, p. 179.
6. Gandhi, M.K. (1962), *Village Swaraj*, p. 25.
7. *Ibid.*, p. 26.

CHAPTER

4

Need for Redefining Poverty Line

The debate about redefining poverty has two schools of thought. Among the first school of thought are those economists who are of the view that attempts at upgrading poverty line from time to time have followed a wrong methodology which has resulted in developing a false notion that reduction of poverty is going at a fairly good pace and that by the year 2006-07, as targeted by the Tenth-Plan, India would be able to reduce poverty to a level of 19.34 percent for the country as whole and this implies the total number of poor at end of 2006-07 will be 220 million—about 170 million in the rural areas and 50 million in the urban areas. The Tenth Plan Approach Paper "mandated reduction in the poverty rate by 5 percentage points during the Tenth Plan and another 10 percentage points during the Eleventh Plan." This will still leave more than 11 percent of population, or about 130 million people, below the poverty line in 2012."[1] Professor Utsa Patnaik of JNU has contested the methodology adopted for deriving these estimates. A second school of thought includes a group of economists who argue for redefining the poverty line. Mohan Guruswamy & R.S. Abraham have raised the question of relative poverty in India since India is expected to be a super-economic power by 2020. It would be desirable to understand the poverty scenario during the last 30 years or so.

I. POVERTY SCENARIO IN INDIA

The absolute level of poverty is estimated by standardizing the minimum physical quantities of cereals, pulses, milk, butter, etc. for a subsistence level and then multiplying the physical quantities by price quotations to arrive at a figure of per capita consumer expenditure. It may be noted that as prescribed by the Indian Council of Medical Research (ICMR), these physical quantities should lead to the provision of 2,400 calories per capita for the rural areas and 2,100 calories per capita in urban areas. Obviously, the stipulation of per capita consumer expenditure should result in providing the recommended energy intake in the form of Required Daily Allowance (RDA). This procedure was accepted by the Planning Commission in 1969 and poverty line was fixed at Rs. 20 per capita monthly expenditure at 1960-61 prices. Dandekar and Rath used the criterion of Rs. 15 for rural areas and Rs. 22.5 for urban areas at 1960-61 prices.

Later, the Planning Commission appointed an Expert Group under the Chairmanship of Professor D.T. Lakdawala which submitted its report in 1993. The Expert Group estimated a monthly expenditure of Rs. 49 for rural and Rs. 57 for urban areas at 1973-74 prices. The Expert Group used the Consumer Price Index for Agricultural Labourers (CPIAL) for rural areas and a simple average of Consumer Price Index for Industrial Workers (CPIIW) and the Consumer Price Index for Non-Manual Employees (CPINM) for urban areas. This methodology has been used for updating poverty line and this is given in Table 4.1.

Table 4.1
Poverty Line with base 1973-74

(Monthly expenditure of Rs. per capita)

	Rural	*Urban*
1973-74	49.09	56.96
1977-78	56.84	72.50
1983	89.45	117.64
1987-88	115.43	165.58
1993-94	211.30	274.88
1999-2000	327.56	454.11
2004*	368.00	559.00

* Based on estimated population of 2004 and poverty ratio calculated from using latest National Sample Survey in 2004.

Source : Planning Commission.

It would be of interest to know the total number of poor and poverty percentage in total population. The data reveal that between 1973-74 and 1987-88, though the poverty percentage declined from 54.9 percent in 1973-74 to 44.5 percent in 1983, the total number of poor remained around 320 million. Even in 1993-94, the number of poor was 320 million, since the period 1987-88 to 1993-94 showed a negative decline of poverty percentage of the order of 0.7 percent per annum. The fastest decline in poverty is observed during 1993-94 to 1999-00 at the rate of 3.4 percent per annum and the absolute number of poor declined to 260 million in 1999-00. But during

TABLE 4.2
Percentage of Poor and Total Number of Poor in India Since 1973

Year	*Percentage of Poor (%)*	*Number of Poor (million)*	*Average Annual Rate of Decline (%)*
1973-74	54.9	321	-0.59
1977-78	51.3	329	0.31
1983	44.5	323	0.31
1987-88	38.9	307	1.25
1993-94	36.0	320	-0.7
1999-2000	26.1	260	3.4
2004	23.6	250	0.82

the next five years, though the rate of growth of GDP was of the order of 6.5 percent per annum, number of poor showed a very small decline from 260 million to 250 million, indicating an annual average decline by 0.8 percent during 1999-00 and 2004. Obviously, the rate of poverty reduction slowed down, which raised a question mark about the efficacy of growth-driven strategy that is being followed in the liberalization-globalisation era.

2. METHODOLOGICAL ISSUE

Utsa Patnaik on the basis of National Sample Survey data on per capita monthly expenditure and calorie intake per day has challenged the poverty estimates of the Planning Commission.

Prof. Utsa Patnaik criticizes the Planning Commission for only using expenditure group data to arrive at the number of persons below the poverty line, but just glosses over the calorie intake to ensure that the associated energy intake meets the calorie norm as the basic criterion for determining the level of expenditure at which this can be ensured. Patnaik mentions: "Thus the current data are being used selectively, with only the distribution of persons by expenditure classes being used, and the associated energy intake part being ignored completely. . . . For example, the official price-index adjusted poverty line for 1999-00 for rural areas was Rs. 328 only and this has een applied to the first and last column of Table 4.3 to read the population below this line which came to 27%. No attention was paid to the fact that at this expenditure a person could access only 1,890 calories, over 500 calories per day below the RDA (Required Daily Allowance)."[2] However, if the norm of 2,400 calories is applied, it is revealed that 74.5 percent of population for rural areas was below the poverty line. Thus, the official method of estimation poor leaves out 47.5 percent of total population or around 350 million persons who are actually poor.

TABLE 4.3

Poverty distribution of Persons by per capita Monthly Expenditure and Calorie Intake, 1999-00, All India

Monthly per capita Expenditure (Rs.)	*Calorie intake per day*	*Percentage of total persons*	*Cumulative percentage*
Rural			
Below 225	1,383	5.1	5.1
225-255	1,609	5.0	10.1
255-300	1,733	10.1	20.2
300-340	1,868	10.0	30.2
340-380	1,957	10.3	40.5
380-420	2,054	9.7	50.2
420-470	2,173	10.2	60.4
475-525	2,289	9.3	69.7
525-615	2,403	10.3	80.0
615-775	2,581	9.9	89.9
775-900	2,735	5.0	94.9
900 & more	3,178	5.1	100.0
All	2,149	100.0	
Urban			
Below 300	1,398	5.0	5.0
300-500	1,654	5.1	10.1
350-425	1,729	9.6	19.7
425-500	1,912	10.1	29.8
500-575	1,968	9.9	39.7
575-665	2,091	10.0	49.7
665-675	2,187	10.1	59.8
675-915	2,297	10.0	69.8
915-1120	2,467	10.0	79.8
1120-1500	2,536	10.1	89.9
1500-1925	2,736	5.0	94.9
1925 & more	2,938	5.1	100.0
All	2,156	100.0	

Note : Poverty Line Rs. 327.6 for Rural Areas and Rs. 454.1 for Urban Areas.

Source : National Sample Survey Organisation (1999-00), Report No. 471, Nutritional Intake in India for calorie intake data by expenditure groups and Report No. 454, Household Consumer Expenditure in India—key Results for the distribution of persons.

An Estimate of the Rural Poor has been made on the basis of official estimates and MPCE (Monthly per capita Expenditure) providing 2,400 calories. Since the norm of MPCE for 1973-74 was correctly applied, the estimate of poverty by both the methods works out to be 56.4%. But for year 1993-94 and 1999-00, the official estimates were much lower than that based on MPCE providing 2,400 calories.

TABLE 4.4
Rural Poor and Percent of Rural Population

	1973-74 %	*1993-94 %*	*1999-2000 %*	*MPCE**		
				1973-74	*1993-94*	*1999-2000*
Applying Official Definition (Those with less than MPCE giving 2400 Calories	56.4	74.5	74.5	49	325	570
Official Estimates	56.4	37.3	27.1	49	206	328
Corresponding Calorie Intake	2400	1970	1890			

Source : Calculated from NSS *Reports on Consumer Expenditure, 50th Round 1993-94 and 55th Round 1999-2000.*

* MPCE is Monthly Per Capita Expenditure.

Note that base year 1973-74 is the only year the official definition was correctly applied; in all later years, the nutrition norm is diluted.

Utsa Patnaik concludes her critique with the following observation: "Sometimes to justify the indirect method, it is argued in an illogical manner that the original consumption norm of 2,400 calories was 'too high'. First, it is not 'too high' because the average intake of those below it works out to less than 1,900 calories which is lower than in any other country in the world except the least developed countries. Second, even if it is accepted for the sake of argument that it is 'too high', it does not justify comparing 1999-00 'poverty' figures which are of all those persons below 1,890 calories intake, to those below 1,970 calories in 1993-94 and below 2,400 calories intake in 1973-74."[3]

3. REDEFINING POVERTY LINE— BASIC NEEDS APPROACH

Mohan Guruswamy and Ronald Joseph Abraham of the Centre for Policy Alternatives, New Delhi have highlighted the distinction between poverty and hunger. Guruswamy *et. al.* state: "Poverty is an economic condition. Hunger is a physical condition that arises out of severe economic condition. While the definition of hunger in terms of calories can remain constant, the definition of poverty is relative to the present levels of general prosperity. . . . The present official poverty line is based only on calories and hence accounts for little else but the satiation of one's hunger. It would have been more accurate to define this as a *starvation line,* as that is exactly what it is."[4] (Emphasis Added)

The official poverty line should be renamed as 'starvation line' since apart from providing 650 grams of foodgrains per day, it makes very little provision for the other essentials of life, such as nutrition and balanced diet, provision for health, electricity and cooking fuels, clothing and miscellaneous expenditure pertaining to education, shelter and other minimum levels of expenditure to sustain life, such as travelling, washing and stitching of clothes, durable consumer goods, some expenditure on furniture, etc. A realistic and proper definition of poverty line should, therefore, include all the basic needs of human life so as to ensure a minimum level of quality.

Thus, the claim made by the Government that poverty ratio has declined from 54.9 percent in 1973-74 to about 25 percent in 2004 is spurious and gives a false sense of satisfaction to Indian polity. A dynamic concept of poverty line should, therefore, incorporate basic human needs approach and should not limit itself to minimum calorie intake needed for subsistence.

Guruswamy and Abraham have made the following components of basic human needs to arrive at a new poverty line for India which is claimed to be one of the fastest developing economies of the world.

1. Nutritional Norms and Cost Involved

On the basis of the recommendations of National Institute of Nutrition (NIN) under the aegis of Indian Council of Medical Research, it is highly important that a balanced diet be provided so as to prevent underweight among children under age 5. It may be noted that as per the *Human Development Report (2005)*, 47 percent children under age 5 are underweight. Similarly, 21 percent of total population is undernourished in 2000-02. It may also be observed that in China, only 10 percent children are underweight and 11 percent of total population is undernourished during 2000-02. Obviously, India is lagging behind China in nutritional status. Mohan Guruswamy has made an effort to determine the cost of a balanced nutritious diet for an average Indian to be Rs. 573 person.

2. Expenditure on Health

India spends only 1.3 percent of GDP on the provision of public health, but the private expenditure on health is 4.8 percent of GDP in 2002. Since according to the Health Ministry, barely 20 percent of Indian population is covered by public healthcare, the poor are forced to take recourse to the private sector. The 'Universal Insurance Scheme' which is targeted to meet the needs of the poor to pay annually Rs. 365 per person and an individual can get insured for all inpatient medical-care upto a sum of Rs. 30,000. This implies that Rs. 365 per annum or Rs. 30 per capita is the cost of health expenditure for the poor in India. Guruswamy includes a sum of Rs. 30 per person per month as the legitimate expenditure for obtaining healthcare.

3. Expenditure on Clothing

In fact, clothing requirements of children, men and women necessitate different norms for clothing. Similarly, weather conditions necessitate different norms for summer and winter. In the estimate prepared by Guruswamy, seasonal requirements have been disregarded for the sake of simplicity. The clothing requirements have been calculated at Rs. 207 per person per annum or Rs. 17 per month.

4. Energy Consumption

A housing unit with two bedrooms, a kitchen is the basis of Guruswamy to calculate energy consumption. It is assumed that each house has an electric connection. On the basis of minimum needs approach, each home needs a few basic electric fittings—four bulbs and two fans. It is further assumed the ceiling fans work for 12 hours a day—8 hours during night and 4 hours during day. On the basis of these minimum requirements, per capita monthly expenditure on electricity has been calculated as Rs. 175 per month per family. Assuming a norm of 5 members of the family, this works out to be Rs. 35 per month per person.

The other component of energy consumption is cooking fuel. National Family Planning Survey (1998-99) shows that at the all-India level nearly 74 percent of the population uses wood, crop residues, dung cakes and coal as cooking fuels. This proportion is 91 percent for rural areas and 30 percent for urban areas. But all these fuels cause indoor pollution and cause such diseases as tuberculosis, asthma, heart diseases and respiratory disorders. But the poor cannot afford LPG which is considered as a clean cooking fuel, as this fuel is the prerogative of the middle class and affluent sections.

Moreover, state support towards LPG has been rising over time but kerosene has been witnessing a reduction in state support. Kerosene is a more affordable substitute for the poor. The monthly per capita expenditure on Kerosene has been calculated at Rs. 20 per capita per month. This is based on the assumption that a family gets 10 to 12 litres of kerosene per month on ration cards. For a family of 5 persons, a typical family consumes 2.2 litres per head and it is being sold at a subsidized price of Rs. 9 per litre. Assuming that all families are able to obtain their quota of kerosene on ration cards, the monthly expenditure on kerosene comes to Rs. 20 per person.

Thus, the total per capita monthly energy requirements entail an expenditure of Rs. 55—for electricity consumption Rs. 35 and for cooking fuel Rs. 20.

5. Miscellaneous Expenditure

Miscellaneous Expenditure includes cost on travel, purchase of books and stationery for school going children, expenditure on certain social ceremonies like birth, death or festivals, etc., purchase of consumer goods, furniture, fixtures for family needs, etc., it is expected that miscellaneous expenditure works out at Rs. 820 per family per month or Rs. 164 per capita.

These calculations are based on the basic needs approach at minimum levels. The purpose is not to provide only for subsistence, but to move towards a more humane level of life.

Summing up, the minimum costs on the assumption of basic needs approach work out to be Rs. 840 per month or Rs. 4,200 per month per family [(i) Balanced nutritious diet Rs. 574; (ii) Health Insurance Expenditure Rs. 30; (iii) Clothing Rs. 17; (iv) Energy consumption Rs. 55 and (v) Miscellaneous Expenditure Rs. 164.]

On the basis of the holistic approach regarding the poverty line inclusive of basic needs, Mohan Guruswamy has calculated that "69% of India's population is below the poverty line i.e. over 71 crore persons. This has to be seen against the official figure of 26 percent persons below the poverty line, i.e. nearly 2.65 times. The situation in rural India is appalling with 84% of the rural population below the more holistic poverty line; it is certainly better in urban India at a round 42 percent.

World Bank on the basis of the international poverty lines at the rate of $1 per day has calculated in its *World Development Report (2005)* that in India for the year 1999-00, people below this poverty line were of the order of 34.7% and if we use the norm of $2 per day, then 80% of the Indian population was below the poverty line.

CONCLUSION

The following conclusions emerge from the analysis of poverty line. *Firstly,* the procedure of upgrading poverty line on the basis of price index needs a review and this should be accompanied by the norm of calorie intake. *Secondly,* the basis of poverty line was decided four decades ago in 1969. For a developing economy with an aspiration of becoming a super-economic power by 2020, it is all the more necessary to develop a basic needs approach poverty line, instead of a uni-dimensional poverty line based on calorie intake of food primarily which is only a starvation line. This will entail greater effort on the part of the state to take steps that the benefits of rapid economic growth reach 'aam adami' (common man) to use a phrase of the Congress manifesto. Then, it will shake us out of our complacency about poverty in India. We have miles to go before we sleep.

REFERENCES

1. Planning Commission, *Tenth Five Year Plan (2002-07)*, Vol. 1, p. 7.
2. Patnaik, Utsa, Food Security Situation in India, *Young Indian*, May 21-27, 2005.
3. *Ibid.*, p. 8.
4. Guruswamy, Mohan and Abraham, Ronald Joseph (2006), Redefining Poverty—A New Poverty Line for a New India, *Young Indian*, April 1-7, 2006, p. 10.

CHAPTER

5

Unorganised Sector and Informalisation of the Indian Economy

The National Commission for Enterprises in the Unorganized Sector (2007) states: "There is no doubt that this "shining India" has expanded in the past and is still expanding at a very high rate. But this picture is spoiled by virtually stagnant consumption expenditure and miserable working and living conditions of the 77 percent of our population who are poor and vulnerable . . . . This is the other world which can be characterized as the India of the common people . . . whom the growth process, by and large, by-passed." The Planning Commission Special Group (2002) provided the answer to alleviate the situation: "The only answer to the situation is to increase productivity and job quality of the unorganized sector. It means that all attempts should be made to implement those policies, which will release the basic growth constraints and by ensuring a level playing field for this sector."

I. UNORGANISED SECTOR AND INDIA'S INFORMAL ECONOMY

At the outset, it would be advisable to understand the concept of the unorganised sector. It may also be clarified that the terms organized and unorganised sector in India are used interchangeably with formal and informal sector at the international level as recommended by the ILO.

There has been lack of clarity and uniformity in the use of the term. The Central Statistical Organisation defines unorganised or informal sector consisting of enterprises who producing for the market do not have more than 20 employees (without power) or 10 employees (with power). The workers of these enterprises are not registered under any legal stipulation like the Industrial Disputes Act of 1948, etc. and can, therefore, be included in the household sector (and hence within the informal sector) as per the System of National Accounts (SNA) 1993.

Thus, employment within the unorganised sector has hitherto been derived as a residual of the total workers minus the workers in the organized sector as reported by the Director-General of Employment and Training (DGET). It may, however, be mentioned that DGET figures do not include informal/unorganised employment in the organized sector—a phenomenon which is becoming increasingly significant in the Indian economy. To that extent, there is an element of under-estimation in the determination of unorganised sector employment in the economy.

The National Commission for Enterprises in the Unorganised Sector (NCEUS) set-up by the Government of India considered various aspects of the matter and defined the unorganised sector in the following manner:

"The unorganised sector consists of all unincorporated private enterprises owned by individuals or households engaged in the sale and production of goods and services operated on a proprietary or partnership basis and with less than ten total workers."[1]

Following this definition, in agriculture, only the plantations and other types of organized agriculture (i.e. corporate or co-operative farming) are excluded. Thus, a very large part of the workers engaged in agriculture are included.

Secondly, the NCEUS defined unorganised or informal employment as follows:

"Unorganised workers consist of those working in the unorganised enterprises or households, excluding regular workers with social security benefits, and the workers in the formal sector without any employment/social security benefits provided by the employers."[2]

This definition excludes casual or contract workers and thus captures unorganized sector employment in a more realistic manner.

2. SIZE OF THE UNORGANISED SECTOR

NCEUS prepared estimates of employment in the unorganised sector. As on January 2005, the total employment (principal and subsidiary) in the Indian economy was 458 million, of which the unorganised sector accounted for 395 million, i.e. 86 percent of the total workers in 2004-05.

However, a distinction has been made by the NCEUS in organized sector/unorganised sector employment and organized and unorganised worker. The unorganised sector refers to enterprises which employ less than 10 workers. But the unorganised workers refer to workers who are employed whether in the organized or unorganised sector but are not covered for social security benefits.

From the data given in Table 5.1, it is evident that out of 62.6 million employed in the organized sector, 29.1 million are unorganised workers applying the criterion of social security benefits. Similarly, out of 395 million workers employed in the unorganised sector, 1.4 million workers avail of social security benefits and are, therefore, classified as organized workers. After applying the two criteria, out of a total employment of 457.5 million workers, only 34.9 million are entitled for social security benefits, i.e. 7.6 percent of the total workers in 2004-05 and the remaining 422.6 million (92.4 percent) are treated as unorganised workers. Comparing this, with 1999-00, it is revealed that though during 1999-00 and 2004-05, total employment in the economy increased from 397 million to 458 million, i.e. an increase by 61 million during the 5-year period, the number of organized workers remained stagnant at 35 million and the entire increase of employment was in the category of unorganised workers. NCEUS, therefore, sums up the situation as under:

TABLE 5.1

Total Employment Sector-wise (million)

	Informal/ Unorganized workers	*Formal/ Organized workers*	*Total*
		1999-2000	
Informal/Unorganised Sector	341.3 (99.6)	1.4 (0.4)	342.7 (100.0)
Formal/Organized Sector	20.5 (37.5)	33.6 (62.2)	54.1 (100.0)
Total	361.8 (91.2)	35.0 (8.8)	396.8 (100.0)
		2004-2005	
Informal/Unorganised Sector	393.5 (99.6)	1.4 (0.4)	394.9 (100.0)
Formal/Organized Sector	29.1 (46.6)	33.5 (53.4)	62.6 (100.0)
Total	422.6 (92.4)	34.9 (7.6)	457.5 (100.0)

Note : Figures in brackets are percentages.

Source : NSS 61st Round (2004-05), and NSS 55th Round (1999-00), Employment-Unemployment Survey: Computed by NCEUS.

"What this means in simple terms is that the entire increase in the employment in the organized sector over this period has been informal in nature, i.e. without any job or social security. This constitutes what can be termed as informalisation of the formal sector, where any employment increase consists of regular workers without social security benefits and casual or contract workers again without the benefits that should accrue to formal workers."[3]

Categories of Workers among the Unorganised Workers

(a) Wage Workers

Wage workers are persons employed for remuneration among the unorganised workers, directly by employers or through agencies or contractors. Wage workers include casual and temporary workers or those employed by households including domestic workers. Wage workers also include regular workers in the unorganised sector.

(b) Self-employed in the Unorganised Sector

There are workers who operate farm or non-farm enterprises or engage in a profession or trade, either on own account, individually or with partners, or as home-based workers. Own account workers include unpaid family workers also.

Both the categories of workers face different kinds of vulnerabilities or risks and thus are referred to as weaker sections of society. They suffer from two types of vulnerabilities – job insecurity or social insecurity or both. Regular workers in the unorganised sector are those working for others and getting in return salary or wages on a regular basis. These workers suffer from social insecurity due to sickness or injury or old-age and are not entitled to any social security against these vulnerabilities. They enjoy, however, job security. As against them, temporary, casual or contract workers suffer from job insecurity as well as social insecurity.

Home Workers as a Distinct Category

The International Labour Organisation (ILO) in 1996 defined a home worker who carried out work for remuneration in the premises of his/her choice, other than the work place of the employer, resulting in a product or service as specified by the employer, irrespective of who provided equipment, materials or inputs used. These workers, therefore, work under the 'putting out system'. Mostly, homeworkers have to purchase, repair and maintain their own tools or machines, and bear the costs of some inputs (e.g. garment workers often have to buy their own thread), transportation to and from the contractor to obtain work and then handover the finished product, and also provide space within their homes to carry out the tasks of production.

According to NSS (1999-00), homeworkers constituted 8.2 million workers out of a total of 69 million self-employed workers, among them, 4.8 million (58.5 percent) are women. Available studies show that in the manufacturing sector in India, product outsourcing from large firms to small firms is on the increase. Homeworkers constituted about 12 percent of all self-employed workers in 1999-00, but they have grown in numbers as a consequence of greater resort to outsourcing. But no later estimate is yet available.

TABLE 5.2
Number and Proportion of Workers in the Unorganised Non-agricultural Sector (1999-2000)

	No. millions			*Percentage*		
	Male	*Female*	*Total*	*Male*	*Female*	*Total*
Self-Employed						
(a) Independent workers	49.5	11.2	60.7	93.6	70.0	88.0
(b) Home workers	3.4	4.8	8.2	6.4	30.0	12.0
All self-employed (a+b)	52.9	16.0	68.9	100.0	100.0	100.0
All unorganised non-agricultural workers	87.9	22.5	110.4			

Source : NCEUS Report (2007), *op. cit.*, p. 241, Appendix A1.4.

Out of a total of 110 million unorganised non-agricultural workers, about 69 million, i.e. 62 percent are self-employed. Among the self-employed, 88 percent are independent workers and 12 percent are home-based workers.

Data given in Table 5.3 reveals that out of 458 million workers, the proportion of self-employed workers is 56.5 percent (258 million) and casual workers are 28.3 percent (130 million). Taken together, these two categories which are the most vulnerable among workers constituted about 85 percent. The remaining 69 million workers were regular workers (15 percent).

However, the proportion of self-employed in the unorganised sector was 64% (253 million) out of a total of 395 million workers and that of casual workers was 29 percent (116 million). Taken together, these two most vulnerable groups accounted for 93 percent among the unorganised sector. Regular workers accounted for only 7 percent. This provides a vivid overview of the pathetic state of unorganised workers in which 93 percent of workers suffered from job as well social insecurity. Among the organized workers, the situation was relatively better where 69 percent were regular workers and barely 31 percent were self-employed and casual workers.

The situation in the agricultural sector was appalling where 99 percent of the workers were either self-employed and casual workers and only 1 percent were regular workers. However, in the non-agricultural sector, 6 percent were self-employed and casual workers and 34 percent were regular workers.

The unorganised sector in agriculture accounted for 99.4 percent of self-employed and casual workers devoid of security whatsoever. However, in the non-agricultural sector, this proportion was as high as 83 percent.

TABLE 5.3

Size and Distribution of the Organized and Unorganised Sector Workers by Industry and Status 2004-05

	Agriculture			*Non-agriculture*			*All*		
	Organised	*Unorganised*	*Total*	*Organised*	*Unorganised*	*Total*	*Organised*	*Unorganised*	*Total*
(1)	*(2)*	*(3)*	*(4)*	*(5)*	*(6)*	*(7)*	*(8)*	*(9)*	*(10)*
Number of Workers (Million)									
SE	2.3	163.9	166.2	2.9	89.2	92.1	5.2	253.1	258.2
RW	1.3	1.5	2.8	41.9	24.8	66.7	43.2	26.4	69.5
CW	2.5	87.4	89.9	11.7	28.1	39.8	14.2	115.5	129.7
Total	6.1	252.8	258.9	56.5	142.1	198.5	62.6	394.9	457.5
Percentage Distribution of Workers									
SE	38.1	64.8	64.2	5.1	62.8	46.4	8.3	64.1	56.5
RW	20.1	0.6	1.1	74.3	17.4	33.6	69.0	6.7	15.2
CW	41.8	34.6	34.7	20.7	19.8	20.0	22.7	29.2	28.3
Total	100.0	100.0	100.0	100.0	100.0	100.0	100.0	100.0	100.0
Percentage of total	**2.4**	**97.6**	**100.0**	**28.4**	**71.6**	**100.0**	**13.7**	**86.3**	**100.0**

Note : SE = Self-employed; RW = Regular Worker; CW = Casual Worker.

Source : NSS 61st Round 2004-05, *Employment-Unemployment Survey. Computed.*

The overall scenario that emerges is: In the economy, the unorganised sector workers constituting 86 percent of the total workforce suffer from very insecure working conditions. It is this group that deserves maximum support for improving their living conditions.

3. POVERTY, VULNERABILITY AND NON-ORGANISED SECTOR EMPLOYMENT—THE HIGH DEGREE OF CORRELATION

NCEUS has made an attempt to categorise the population of the country into six groups based on consumption expenditure.

"Extremely poor" are those with a per capita per day consumer expenditure of three-fourth of the official poverty line (i.e. an average of Rs. 8.9 per capita per day (pcpd). In 2004-05, the second group "poor" are those between the Extremely poor and up to the official poverty line (average expenditure of Rs. 11.6 pcpd); the third is called the "Marginally Poor" with per capita consumer expenditure of only 1.25 times the poverty line (i.e. Rs. 14.6 pcpd); and the fourth called "Vulnerable" have per capita consumer expenditure of only two times the poverty line (i.e. Rs. 20.3 pcpd). In 2004-05, the Extremely Poor constituted 6.4 percent, the Poor 15.4 percent, the Marginally poor 19.0 percent. These three constituted 41 percent of the total population. If the "vulnerable" are added to this group, the total accounts for 77 percent of total population. NCEUS Categorised this 77 percent, totaling 836 million people, with an income of roughly below $2 PPP, as the poor and vulnerable sections of the population. (Refer Table 5.4)

It may be noted that whereas there is slow decline in the population of the poor and vulnerable from 82 percent in 1993-94 to 77 percent in 2004-05, there is in contrast an increase in total population of the poor and vulnerable from 732 million to 836 million during the same period. This implies that there is no gain in the total burden of the poor and vulnerable.

As against this, there is an increase in the middle and high income groups which stood at 254 million in 2004-05 compared to 162 million in 1993-94.

Making a strong indictment of the growth process, the NCEUS mentions:

> **"There is no doubt that this "Shining India" has expanded in the past and is still expanding at a very high rate. But this picture is spoiled by a virtually stagnant consumption expenditure and miserable working and living conditions of the 77 percent of our population who are poor and vulnerable. . . . This is the other world which can be characterized as the India of the Common People, constituting more than three-fourths of the population and consisting of all those whom the growth process has, by and large, bypassed."[4] (Emphasis added)**

TABLE 5.4
Population in Different Expenditure Classes

(*In million*)

S. No.	*Expenditure Class*	*1993-94*	*1999-00*	*2004-05*
(1)	(2)	(3)	(4)	(5)
1.	Extremely Poor (up to 0.75 PL)	103	87	70
2.	Poor (0.75 PL to PL)	172	174	167
3.	Marginally Poor (PL to 1.25 PL)	168	200	207
4.	Vulnerable (1.25 PL to 2 PL)	290	349	392
5.	Middle Income (2 PL to 4 PL)	139	167	210
6.	High Income (>4 PL)	24	26	44
7.	Extremely Poor and Poor (1+2)	274	262	237
8.	Marginal and Vulnerable (3+4)	458	549	599
9.	Poor and Vulnerable (7+8)	732	811	836
10.	Middle and High Income (5+6)	162	193	253
	Total	894	1,004	1,090
	Expenditure Class		*Percentage Share and average consumer expenditure per capita per day in Rs. (pcpd)*	
1.	Extremely Poor (up to 0.75 PL)	11.5	8.7	6.4 (9)
2.	Poor (0.75 PL to PL)	19.2	17.3	15.4 (12)
3.	Marginally Poor (PL to 1.25 PL)	18.8	19.9	19.0 (15)
4.	Vulnerable (1.25 PL to 2 PL)	32.4	34.8	36.0 (20)
5.	Middle Income (2 PL to 4 PL)	15.5	16.7	19.3 (37)
6.	High Income (>4 PL)	2.7	2.6	4.0 (93)
7.	Extremely Poor and Poor (1+2)	30.7	26.1	21.8 (11)
8.	Marginal and Vulnerable (3+4)	51.2	54.7	55.0 (18)
9.	Poor and Vulnerable (7+8)	81.8	80.7	76.7 (16)
10.	Middle and High Income (5+6)	18.2	19.3	23.3 (46)
	Total	100.0	100.0	100.0 (23)

Notes : 1. Figures in bracket denote average consumer expenditure per capita per day in Rs.
2. PL refers to Poverty Line.

Source : Computed from unit level data of NSS 61st Round 2004-05, NSS 55th Round 1999-2000 and NSS 50th Round 1993-94, Employment-Unemployment Survey.

By and large, workers in the unorganised sector coming for informal work are of the order of 836 million or 77 percent of the population. They constitute 92 percent of workforce employed in the informal or unorganised sector of our economy. Thus, there is a close correlation between the poor and vulnerable groups with the unorganised sector or informal economy.

4. ESTIMATE OF ORGANISED AND UNORGANISED WORKERS

Out of a total of 458 million workers, agricultural workers constituted 259 million (56.6% of total) and non-agricultural workers were about 199 million (43.4% of total). Out of 458 million workers, males constituted 310 million (67.7% of total) and females accounted for 148 million (32.3% of total).

Data provided in Table 5.5 reveals that unorganised workers constituted 92.4% of the total workforce, accounting for about 423 million workers. As against them, the organized sector workers constituted 7.6% of the total workforce and were only of the order of 35 million. This indicates that the development process pursued in India during the last six decades has not been able to reduce the share of unorganised workers in the economy.

TABLE 5.5

Distribution of Organised and Unorganised Workers (2004-05)

	Total (million)	*% of total*
Total Workers	**457.5**	**100.0**
(a) Agriculture	258.9	56.6
(b) Non-agriculture	198.5	43.4
Organised Workers	**34.9**	**7.6**
(a) Agriculture	2.9	0.6
(b) Non-agriculture	32.0	7.0
Unorganised Workers	**422.6**	**92.4**
(a) Agriculture	256.0	56.0
(b) Non-agriculture	166.5	36.4

Source : NCEUS (2007), *op. cit.*, p. 200.

Among the 423 million workers in the unorganised sector, agricultural workers constituted 256 million (56.0 percent) and non-agricultural workers were of the order of 167 million (36.4%). Among 35 million organised workers, merely 3 million were agricultural workers and 32 million were non-agricultural workers.

Poverty Ratios among Organised and Unorganised Workers

According to NSS 61st round on the basis of 30-day uniform recall period, the poverty ratio for the country as whole in 2004-05 was 27.5%. However, it was 28.3% in rural areas and 25.7% in urban areas.

TABLE 5.6
Poverty Ratios among Unorganised and Organised Workers (2004-05)

		Unorganised workers	*Organised workers*	*All workers*
Agricultural	**Total**	**20.5**	**13.8**	**20.4**
Non-agricultural	Rural	17.2	3.5	15.7
	Urban	23.7	4.3	19.6
	Total	**20.4**	**4.1**	**17.8**
All	Rural	19.2	5.4	18.7
	Urban	25.1	4.5	21.0
	Total	**20.4**	**4.9**	**19.3**

Source : NCEUS (2007), *op. cit.*, p. 24.

Overall poverty ratio among all workers was of the order of 19.3%, but there was sharp difference in the poverty ratio among unorganised standing at 20.4% as against the organised at a low level of 4.9%.

However, in agriculture, the poverty ratio among all workers was 20.4%, and among unorganised workers, it was 20.5% and among organised workers was 13.8%. This shows that poverty ratio among unorganised workers in agriculture was relatively much higher than poverty even among organised workers.

In the non-agriculture sector, poverty ratio was 20.4% among unorganised workers in comparison to merely 4.1% among organised workers. This indicates among the non-agricultural workers, unorganised sector poverty ratio was five times more that that of the organised workers.

Poverty Ratios by Nature of Employment

Sharp differences in poverty ratios among casual workers, self-employed and regular workers exist in the non-agricultural sector.

Among the three types of workers, poverty ratios among casual workers were the highest, followed by self-employed workers and they were the lowest among regular workers. However, it may be noted that poverty ratio among unorganised workers were much higher than among their counterparts in the organised sector. But difference in the poverty ratios among regular workers in the urban organised sector at a low of 6.8% as against 20.2% the unorganised workers was the sharpest—3 times in

TABLE 5.7

Poverty Ratios among Non-agricultural Workers by Nature of Employment (2004-05)

	Rural		*Urban*	
	Organised	*Unorganised*	*Organised*	*Unorganised*
Casual Workers	21.9	23.1	35.0	41.5
All workers	**11.2**	**17.2**	**10.4**	**24.1**
Self-employed	11.2	15.9	11.4	21.4
Regular workers	5.2	11.5	6.8	20.2

Source : NCEUS (2007), *op. cit.*, p. 25.

comparison. The casual workers were the worst sufferers in the urban areas, as their poverty ratio was 35% among organised workers and 41.5% among unorganised workers.

5. SELF-EMPLOYED WORKERS IN NON-AGRICULTURAL SECTOR

Indian economy is dominated by 'self-employed' workers. On the basis of latest data for 2004-05, self-employed workers account for 56.5 percent of the labour force—the single highest group in the categorization of workers followed by casual workers (28.3%) and regular workers (15.2%). They fall in two categories those employed in agriculture constituting of farmers marginal, small and big who work in agriculture on their own and obtain a major part of their income from own cultivation and not wage labour. They are included in the unorganised sector and their number has been estimated at 166 million for 2004-05.

On the other hand, there are quite a large number of self-employed in the non-agricultural sector and they were around 92 million in 2004-05. Self-employed workers are grouped into three categories:

(a) *Own Account Workers*: They work on their own using their labour power. To eke out a better living, they stretch their work for longer hours. This phenomenon is referred to as *'self-exploitation'* by Chayanov, a Russian economist.

(b) *Unpaid family workers*: These persons do contribute their labour but do not get any separate remuneration. Their contribution becomes a part of the family income.

(c) *Employers,* i.e. those who hire at least one wage worker, but the total number of hired workers is less than 10, to use the definition provided by the National Commission for Enterprises in the Unorganised Sector.

Table 5.8 reveals that as a proportion of all workers, self-employed

TABLE 5.8

Percentage of the Self-employed Workers in Unorganised Non-Agricultural Sector (2004-05)

	Rural			Urban			Total		
Employment Status	*Male*	*Female*	*Total*	*Male*	*Female*	*Total*	*Male*	*Female*	*Total*
(1)	*(2)*	*(3)*	*(4)*	*(5)*	*(6)*	*(7)*	*(8)*	*(9)*	*(10)*
1. Own Account Worker	50.2	38.6	47.6	47.0	35.4	44.7	48.6	37.1	46.2
2. Unpaid family labour	9.1	37.7	15.4	11.1	26.1	14.0	10.1	32.3	14.7
3. Employer	1.0	0.3	0.8	3.5	0.6	3.0	2.3	0.4	1.9
Total self-employed (1+2+3)	**60.3**	**76.6**	**63.9**	**61.6**	**62.1**	**61.7**	**61.0**	**69.8**	**62.8**
All workers	**100.0**	**100.0**	**100.0**	**100.0**	**100.0**	**100.0**	**100.0**	**100.0**	**100.0**

Source : Computed from NSS 61st Round, 2004-05, Employment-Unemployment Survey.

workers account for about 63 percent. The contribution of females being about 70 percent and of males around 61 percent. Share of the self-employed is much higher among women in rural areas, while in urban areas, it is more or less equal for men and women.

On the basis of income, the NCEUS has classified self-employed in two broad categories:

Low income self-employed who are closer to or marginally above casual workers	*High income self-employed who are closer to or higher than regular workers*
1. Handloom weavers (mostly women)	1. Independent professionals (such as doctors, lawyers, artists and accountants)
2. Chikan workers (mostly women)	2. Shop owners in urban areas
3. Street vendors	3. Rice mill owners
4. Food processors	4. Workshop owners
5. Rickshaw pullers	5. Commission agents
6. Rag pickers	6. Brokers of real estate, housing, etc.
7. Beedi rollers (mostly home workers)	7. Owners of small hotels and restaurants.
8. Agarbati-makers (mostly women)	
9. Potters	
10. Bamboo product makers	

Two Types of Enterprises

Majority of the Enterprises (87 percent), are own-account workers (OAEs), in rural areas they account for nearly 94 percent.

TABLE 5.9
Percentage of Enterprises and Total Workers by Enterprises Size, 1999-2000

Establishment Type	*Enterprises*			*Workers*		
	Rural	*Urban*	*Total*	*Rural*	*Urban*	*Total*
1. OAE: Owner Operator	61.8	51.9	57.5	40.1	27.2	33.8
2. All OAEs	94.2	78.4	87.4	87.5	58.7	73.4
3. Establishments 2-5 workers	5.2	18.4	10.9	9.5	29.8	19.4
4. Establishments 6-9 workers	0.7	3.1	1.7	3.0	11.6	7.2
Total (2+3+4)	**100.0**	**100.0**	**100.0**	**100.0**	**100.0**	**100.0**

Note : OAEs are enterprises with no hired worker. Establishments are enterprises with hired workers.

Source : Computed from NSS 55th Round 1999-00, Informal Sector Enterprises.

Besides them, establishments with hired workers, about 11 percent had 2-5 workers and less than 2 percent had 6-9 workers.

There is concentration of workers in OAEs, 73% in all areas, and 87% in rural areas. They include both owner operated and family labour. In fact single owner operator enterprises account for 34 percent of workers, other OAEs use family labour also. 19 percent workers are in establishments which have at least one hired worker and 2-5 total workers. About 7 percent are in such establishments with at least one hired worker and 6-9 workers.

It may be noted that concentration of workers in own account enterprises (OAEs) is a much lower in urban areas— 58% as against rural areas accounting for 87%.

On the whole it may be mentioned that OAEs constitute 87 of the informal enterprises with 73 percent of all workers engaged in them.

Value of Assets and Gross Value Addition in OAEs

OAEs have very low average value of assets, about Rs. 39,000 per enterprise. The OAEs mainly use their own fixed assets with 85% and 60% of them reporting not using any hired assets in rural and urban areas respectively.

Gross value addition per worker in OAEs is just Rs. 19,000 per year or merely Rs. 1,583 per month. In urban areas, the gross value addition is Rs. 26,100 per year or Rs. 2,175 per month, while it is about Rs. 14,000 per year or Rs. 1,167 per month in rural areas.

At the prevailing price level in the year 2000, a rural family required Rs. 328 per capita per month to cross the official poverty line. Considering the average size of a family at 5, a rural family requires Rs. 1,640 per month to cross the poverty line. As against it, in urban areas, Rs. 454 per capita are required to cross the poverty line. An average family requires Rs. 2,270 per month to cross the poverty line. In both cases, gross value addition per worker is less than the required average family expenditure to keep its head above the poverty line. NCEUS, therefore, rightly concluded: *"Over-all, a large percentage of enterprises were mainly engaged in some form of survival operations rather than carrying on with a business activity in the proper sense of the term."*[5] (Emphasis added)

The major problems faced by OAEs were shortage of credit, lack of marketing and infrastructural facilities and competition from larger units. However, nearly 30% of OAE operators felt they did not have any serious problem.

Self-employed Establishments with Hired Workers

Average value in fixed assets in the establishments with hired workers is nearly Rs. 3 lakhs as against Rs. 39,000 in OAEs. Obviously, their scale of operation is much better than that of OAEs. In fact, average value of fixed assets in larger establishments with 6-9 workers is even higher than Rs. 6

lakhs. The return to assets in these larger units is also higher since they are enabled to use a higher value of fixed assets well.

TABLE 5.10

Gross Fixed Assets Per Enterprise and Gross Value Addition Per Worker in Establishments—1999-2000

(in Rupees)

Employment Size	*Fixed assets per enterprise*			*Gross value added per worker*		
	Rural	*Urban*	*Total*	*Rural*	*Urban*	*Total*
2-5 workers	1,18,272	2,86,658	2,41,663	27,414	38,707	35,906
6-9 workers	2,16,603	7,45,336	6,32,165	22,803	54,253	47,854
All establishments	**12,934**	**3,53,209**	**2,95,013**	**26,303**	**43,061**	**39,068**

Source : NSS 55th Round, 1999-2000, Informal Sector Enterprises.

Similarly, gross value addition in establishments using hired labour is Rs. 39,000 which is nearly double that of the OAEs. Moreover, establishments in urban area have even much higher value addition which only shows that the nature of products manufactured in urban establishment does make a difference.

To sum up, self-employed is a very broad category and thus it conceals a good proportion of workers who are only *'disguised wage workers'*. In the absence of alternative avenues of employment, tiny enterprises operate with the help of family labour or just one or two hired workers. They are, therefore, survival enterprises for a very large number of workers whose share is even larger than the wage workers in the Indian economy. What is of crucial importance is to understand the self-exploiting nature of these family enterprises by lengthening their working hours and working on practically all days in a year.

There is a need to provide access to credit, marketing and infrastructure. In some areas, especially handlooms, there is a need to improve technology.

Although enterprises using 6-9 workers are relatively better since their fixed capital is estimated at Rs. 3 lakhs in 2000, still they are much below the limit of Micro-enterprises who have been defined as having a threshold limit of Rs. 25 lakhs under the Micro, Small and Medium Enterprises Act of 2005.

Consequently, promotional measures should be designed and implemented so that more credit is made available to them to improve their technology and competitive strength. There is a need to strengthen human capital as well by spending more on health and education of these workers so that the poor people working in them can improve their level of living by higher earnings.

6. AGRICULTURAL LABOURERS

Agricultural labourers were estimated at 87 million in 2004-05 constituting about 34 percent of 259 million agricultural workers, i.e. farmers and agricultural labourers. The agricultural labourers are characterized by poor physical and human capital and also high poverty levels.

Wage level of agricultural labourers was as low as Rs. 43 per manday in 2004-05. The non-agricultural wage rates were about 1.5 times that of agricultural wage. Gender disparity is also high and the ratio of female wages to male agricultural wages has remained unchanged at about 0.70 since 1993-94 up to 2004-05, indicating that male wages are 1.4 times the female wages. There has been a decline in the growth rate of wages of casual agricultural workers during the nineties as compared to eighties.

TABLE 5.11
Wages and Growth Rates of Wages of Casual Agricultural Workers

Wage Rate (Rs./manday)		*Growth Rates (percent/year)*	
1993-94	33.7		
1999-2000	40.0	1993-94	2.9
2004-05	42.6	2000-05	1.3

Source : NSS 50th, 55th and 61st Rounds for 1993-94, 1999-2000 and 2004-05.

TABLE 5.12
Disparities in Agricultural Wages

	Ratio of female wage rate to male wage rate	*Ratio of agricultural to non-agricultural wage*
1993-94	0.70	0.66
1999-2000	0.71	0.62
2004-05	0.69	0.65

Source : NSS 50th, 55th and 61st Rounds for 1993-94, 1999-00 and 2004-05.

Minimum wages and agricultural wages—As per the Minimum Wage Act, 1948, the first National Minimum wage was fixed at Rs. 66 irrespective of the rural-urban location. The second is the minimum wage of Rs. 49 for rural areas as proposed by the National Commission for Rural Labour (NCRL). However, the prevailing wage rates were often observed to be much lower than either of these minimum wage norms. *In 2004-05, about 91 percent of agricultural labourers received wage rates below the National Minimum wage and about 64 percent below the NCRL norm of minimum wages fixed for rural areas. This is a very distressing scenario in view of high GDP growth rates observed in recent years in the Indian economy.*

Pattern of employment shows that growth rate of employment stagnated at 0.2 percent per annum during 1994-00. NCEUS analyzing the factors for this stagnation of employment mentions: "Prime among these was a lower investment in irrigation, drought proofing and agricultural research because of which there was no intensification of farming in rain-fed and dry-land areas."[6] As consequence, between 1993-94 and 2004-05, there was a decline in the number of days of wage employment available per year to agricultural labourers from 224 to 209. This further reduced the annual earning of agricultural labourers.

TABLE 5.13

Wage Employment Days for Rural Agricultural Labourers in a year

	1993-94	*1999-2000*	*2004-05*
Male	244	235	227
Female	196	199	184
Total	224	220	209

Source : NSS 50th, 55th and 61st Rounds for 1993-94, 1999-2000 and 2004-05.

7. BONDED LABOUR

Bonded labour or forced labour implies compelling a person to accept employment at wages or remuneration which is much less than the legally prescribed minimum wage or at times, even without any payment, in lieu of debt. Even after the enactment of Bonded Labour System (Abolition) Act, 1976, bonded labour has continued according to National Commission on Rural Labour (NCRL) 1991. Nearly 89 percent of the bonded labourers were in agriculture who mainly belonged to Scheduled Castes and Scheduled Tribes who were kept in bondage by rich agricultural landholders. Being poor, they have to borrow at high rates of interest. Since the wages received by them are very low, they are unable to pay the debt. As a result, a vicious circle is created between poverty and bonded labour. NCRL (1991) stated very clearly: "The kernel of bondedness lies in unrepayble debt and loss of freedom to seek alternate employment through the market process."

There are no precise estimates regarding the size of bounded labourers. The researchers and social workers believe a high incidence of bonded labour. But the Annual Report of the Ministry of Labour and Employment (2006-07) reported that incidence of bonded labour in 2005-06 is only 397 cases. According to NCEUS, "While bonded labour was considered a thing of the past, prevalent in a colonial era, it has been found that *new forms of attachment have been rising in developed agriculture, the phenomenon of a 'U' shaped relationship between labour attachment and agricultural development, i.e. after an initial decline as agriculture develops, it starts to increase at later stages."*[7] (Emphasis added)

Despite the law abolishing bonded labour, the work of relief and rehabilitation has been a slow process, mainly because of the inherent difficulties in the identification of bonded labour.

To sum up, agricultural labourers are the most vulnerable section of the agrarian population. In view of the low wages received by agricultural labour and only for about 200 days in a year, his income remains very low to have basic needs for his family. The Minimum wages Act is more often observed in breach, rather than in compliance. Consequently, it has failed to provide the much-needed relief. There is no social security mechanism to help. Agricultural labourers have not succeeded in forming unions except in a few states. In the absence of social security for the informal sector and particularly for agricultural labourers, their condition remains grim.

8. WORKING CONDITIONS OF FARMERS

Out of 166 million farmers, about 143 million, i.e. 86 percent belong to the category of marginal and small farmers (owning les than 2 hectares). Their produce is so low that they are able to maintain only a subsistence level of living. Consequently, many are forced to seek wage employment to supplement their income. These framers have very little access to credit and mostly depend on medium and large farmers or money lenders, trading agents, etc. for credit which is available at very high rates of interest. Not being able to actualize price gains of agricultural produce, they continue to remain poor. During the nineties, the Government support, particularly of investment in irrigation, research and extension facilities has been declining. After the Green Revolution, there has not been any breakthrough in agricultural technology and thus productivity deceleration has been identified as the most important underlying factor responsible for the decline in agricultural output.

Credit, Indebtedness and Suicides

Small and marginal farmers households need credit to meet the consumption needs so as to maintain subsistence as well as for production purposes to meet the rising costs of cultivation. But unfortunately, they are able to get a relatively small proportion of credit from institutional sources like Government, co-operative societies and banks, and have to depend on non-institutional sources like moneylenders, traders, relatives and friends. Need it be mentioned that institutional credit is available at relatively lower rates of interest and non-institutional credit is available at higher rates of interest.

TABLE 5.14
Percentage Distribution of Loans by Farm Size and Sources, 2003

Source of Loan	*Sub-marginal less than 0.4 ha.*	*Marginal 0.41 to 1.00 ha.*	*Small 1.01 to 2.00 ha.*	*Medium-large Above 2 ha.*
1. Government	3.9	3.8	1.7	1.4
2. Co-operative Society	14.1	17.0	20.5	22.8
3. Bank	24.4	32.0	35.4	42.6
Total Institutional (1+2+3)	**42.2**	**52.8**	**57.6**	**66.8**
4. Agricultural/professional money lender	32.4	30.8	25.9	20.0
5. Trader	4.9	4.6	4.2	6.0
6. Relatives and friends	15.2	9.1	8.8	5.2
7. Doctors, lawyers and other professionals	1.4	0.7	0.8	0.8
8. Others	3.6	2.0	2.6	1.2
Total : Non-institutional (4 to 8)	**57.6**	**47.2**	**42.4**	**33.2**

Source : NSS 59th Round, Situation Assessment Survey of Farmers. ha. : hectare(s)

Data given in Table 5.14 shows that with an increase of farm size, the proportionate availability of institutional credit increases. It was 42.4% for sub-marginal farmers and was about 67 percent for medium and large farmers. Conversely, the proportion of dependence on non-institutional credit was 57.6% for sub-marginal farmers but it declined as the size of the farm increases and was only 33% for medium-large farmers.

TABLE 5.15
Percentage of Outstanding Loans by Purpose, 2003

Farm Size	*Consumption Expenditure*	*Productive Purpose Expenditure*	*Total*
Sub-marginal	61	39	100
Marginal	43	57	100
Small	29	71	100
Medium-Large	20	80	100

Note : Productive purpose included both current production expenditure and capital expenditure.

Source : NSS 59th Round, Situation Assessment Survey of Farmers.

Purpose of Loans

Table 5.15 reveals that loans for productive capital expenditure as a percentage of total loans outstanding increase with farm size. The share of loans for consumption on unproductive purposes such as marriages and other consumption expenditure was much higher for sub-marginal farmers at 61% and for marginal farmers was 43%. As against it, the 80% of the loans taken by medium and large farmers were for productive purpose.

Since the loans for sub-marginal and marginal farmers were at very high rates of interest from non-institutional lenders, they increased the burden of debt. These poor farmers with very low capacity found it impossible to repay them and thus, borrowed more for the payment of interest as well. Consequently, the vicious circle of indebtedness and poor repaying capacity pushed quite a large number to commit suicides. A very large number of suicides were committed by farmers in Punjab, Andhra Pradesh, Karnataka, Maharashtra and Kerala. In most cases, the suicide victims were small and marginal farmers.

Mr. Bhanuji Rao in his article 'the noose of debt' (*Business Line*, 8th August 2006) has presented data on the rise of suicides during the period 1995 to 2002. "By any standard, it is a sad state of affairs to see several thousand farmers committing suicides, with the number rising too fast—from 10,000 to 25,000—in just seven years, to be taken lightly."

TABLE 5.16

Share of Farmers Suicides in Total Suicides in India

	Total number of suicides	*Estimated Number of suicides by farmers*	*Percent by farmers*
(1)	*(2)*	*(3)*	*(4)*
1995	89,178	10,719	12.0
1996	88,241	13,730	15.6
1997	95,829	13,617	14.2
1998	1,04,713	16,010	15.3
1999	1,10,587	16,079	14.5
2002	1,54,000	25,071	16.3

Note : Column 2 is from Google Search on suicides and column 2 is from an article by Mr. Sharad Joshi (*Business Line*), May 31, 2006.

Tata Institute of Social Sciences (TISS) in its study of 644 suicides in Vidharbha (Maharashtra) reported: 83 percent of suicides were committed by small and medium landholders. The causes of suicides were common: Repeated crop failure, inability to meet the rising cost of cultivation and indebtedness. The TISS report stated: "The other important points were the mismatch between the cost of production and the low minimum support price or the market price leading to huge losses; debt, from a low Rs. 10,000 to Rs. 3 lakhs and the inevitability of half the amount borrowed from private lenders who *charge an usurious 5 percent per month*."[9] (Emphasis added)

Irrigation and Input use

According to the report of Planning Commission Steering Group (2007), declining public investment in irrigation has been one of the major reasons for the declining agricultural productivity during the nineties. However, larger farmers capitalized on cheaper sources, e.g. higher percentage of irrigation from canals which is cheaper irrigation option while small farmers have to rent water. Besides this, the small farmers have to rent out mechanical equipment/implements which adds to the cost of cultivation.

The Tenancy Issue

To augment their holdings, a large number of farmers lease in land. In this respect, it may be stated that tenancy reform had the perverse impact of driving tenancy underground, and making it more difficult for tenants to lease land on secure and reasonable conditions. It is really strange that upper stratum of tenants usually pay cash rents, while the tenants-at-will usually remain sharecroppers, paying 50% of the produce as rent. It was really distressing to find that share of recorded tenancy was neglible, 0.74 percent in 2003. This clearly shows that tenant cultivators are highly vulnerable. NCEUS suggests that new law should be framed to protect the rights of both landowners and tenants. Moreover, banks should not insist on copies of land records for credit purposes.

To salvage the working conditions of farmers, especially marginal and small farmers, NCEUS recommends the following initiatives:

(a) To expand the network of institutional credit facilities in the rural areas and the credit needs of small and marginal farmers are met through earmaking credit for the group.

(b) Introduction of a universal social security system as a support for farmers, more especially the landless and marginal and small farmers. Such a system provides for health expenses, life and unemployment insurance and old-age pensions.

(c) Land reforms particularly related to tenancy laws, land leasing, distribution of ceiling surplus land is urgently needed.

9. ACTION PROGRAMME FOR THE UNORGANISED SECTOR

The National Commission for Enterprises in the Unorganised Sector (NCEUS) was the first initiative taken by the Central Government to study in-depth the problems of the unorganised sector and recommend measures to improve the state of affairs in this sector which provides employment to 93 percent of workforce. The main task before NCEUS was to suggest:

(a) Measures necessary for bringing about improvements in the productivity of enterprises and generation of large scale employment opportunities;
(b) Labour laws in the informal sector consistent with labour rights; and
(c) Expansion in the security system available for labour in the informal sector.

The Commission has recommended the following action programme for the unorganised sector:

A. Protective Measures for Unorganised Workers

Two sets of measures are recommended in this regard:

(1) Ensuring Minimum Condition of work which include the following:

Salient Features of Minimum Conditions of Work Proposals

- Eight-hour working day with half-hour break
- One paid day of rest per week
- National minimum wage for all workers in the unorganised sector, not covered by the Minimum Wages Act
- Piece rate wage to equal time rate wage
- Women work to be paid at par with men
- Deduction in wage rate to attract fines
- Right of unorganised workers to organise
- Safety equipment and compensation for accident
- Protection from sexual harassment
- Provision of child-care and basic amenities at the workplace

(2) *Minimum level of social security*—NCEUS recommends two comprehensive bills separately for agricultural and non-agricultural workers providing the following benefits:

(a) *Life Insurance*: Rs. 30,000 for natural death or Rs. 75,000 in the event of accidental death or total disability;
(b) *Health insurance*: Hospitalization for each worker and his family members, costing Rs. 15,000 a year with Rs. 10,000 per ailment in designated hospitals; and

(c) *Old age security*: All BPL (Below the poverty line) workers will get a monthly pension of Rs. 200 at the age of 60 plus; all workers other than BPL will be entitled to provident fund.

The proposed scheme is expected to cost Rs. 1,095 per worker per year for 30 crore workers in the unorganised sector. The total cost of the scheme for both agricultural and non-agricultural workers will be Rs. 33,950 crores at 2006-07 prices after full coverage—(Rs. 19,400 crores for agricultural workers and Rs. 13,950 crores for non-agricultural workers). Workers below the poverty line (BPL) will be exempt from contribution and their share will be borne by the Central Government; and other workers will contribute Re. 1 per day and the Central and State governments each will pay Re. 1 per day. On the assumption that GDP will grow at the rate of 8 percent in the next five years, the cost of the scheme would be 0.20 percent of GDP in the year of its inception. This will rise to 0.48 percent of GDP in 2010-11 when all the unorganised workers are expected to be covered.

B. Package of Measures for the Marginal and Small Farmers

The Commission recommends that during the Eleventh Plan period, the Government focuses a targeted programme to help small and marginal farmers. The Government could take as its priority tasks the development of area specific irrigation schemes; crop procurement, measures for reducing risks, formation of self-help groups (SHGs) for farmers with respect to irrigation resources, inputs and marketing arrangements; tenancy reform and group farming. The Government can also undertake technological platforms which could be accessed by such farmers.

1. Emphasis on Accelerated Land and Water Management

The Commission is of the view that in rainfed areas, the watershed development programmes are of crucial importance and have a high benefit cost ratio. About 45 million hectares have been covered under watershed development programme so far, while about 75 million hectares remain to be covered. The Commission recommends accelerated expansion of watershed development programmes and Rainfed Area Programmes to revive agriculture in rainfed agricultural land on which a large number of the rural poor are dependent, as an immediate priority.

2. Credit for Marginal-Small Farmers

The Commission recommends that priority sector lending guidelines of the RBI should be amended and a 10 percent quota, out of the 18 percent presently assigned for agriculture, be fixed for farmers with landholding below 2 hectares.

Besides this, 20-40 percent of marginal and small farmers are excluded from formal financial sector due to lack of *patta* and title decades. The Commission recommends that the such farmers be extended credit on the basis of certificates issued by panchayats. To reduce the risk of default, the Commission is of the view that the Government may set-up a Credit Guarantee Fund (CGF) in NABARD, on the lines of the CGF set-up by the Ministry of Micro, Small and Medium enterprises which provides Guarantee cover on loans to small units.

3. *Farmer's Debt Relief Commission*

To alleviate the distress faced by farmers with respect to 31 districts, in four states of Andhra Pradesh, Maharashtra, Karnataka and Kerala, the Government has launched a special package of debt relief. To help other states as well, the Commission recommends the setting up of Farmers Debt Relief Commissions. The Central Government, as a part of the relief package, could extend assistance to State Commissions on a 75:25 basis.

C. Measures to Improve Growth of Non-Agricultural Sector

1. *Improve Credit Flow to the Non-agricultural Sector*

The Commission recommends in a detailed manner measures to improve access of bank credit for micro and small enterprises. At present, the priority sector targets are as follows:

Agriculture 18 percent, weaker sections 10 percent, and others including micro and small enterprises 12 percent. There is no specific target for small and micro-enterprises. The Commission recommends that an explicit target of 10 percent be set for lending to micro and small enterprises. Within this, a 4 percent target be set-up for micro-enterprises with capital investment up to Rs. 5 lakhs. Since the priority sector quota for agriculture is 18 percent (of which 10 percent should be reserved for small and marginal farmers), and another 10 percent as recommended for small and micro-enterprises, this would leave a quota of 12 percent from the total priority sector allocation of 40 percent, which in the Commission's view, should be allocated for socio-economically weaker sections, for purposes of housing, education, professions etc. with a loan ceiling of Rs 5 lakhs.

2. *Creation of a National Fund for Unorganised Sector (NAFUS)*

The Commission recommends an agency be created for the development of unorganised sector which shall be called *National Fund for the Unorganised Sector (NAFUS)* with an initial corpus of Rs. 5,000 crores, contributed by Central Government, public sector banks, financial sector institutions and other government agencies. The target group of the fund would be micro-enterprises, with focus on those below an investment of Rs. 5 lakhs. These constitute 94 percent of small enterprises in the country but they receive only 2 percent of Net Bank Credit despite providing employment to 70 million people and contributing 30 percent of industrial production.

3. *Upscaling of Cluster Development through Growth Poles*

The Commission recommends the development of 'growth poles' for the unorganised sector, based on concept of a cluster of clusters with public-private partnership. This recommendation involves an upscaling of cluster development efforts through the provision of common infrastructure, service centers, etc. designed to take the existing cluster development approach to the next level. The Commission believes that clusters once developed would lead to multiplier effect on production and employment in rural areas.

The Commission also recommends that 'growth poles' should be given the same incentives currently being offered to Special Economic Zones.

D. Measures to Expand Employment and Improve Employability Programmes

1. *Expand Employment through Self-employment Programmes*

The Commission recommends that target of employment under self-employment schemes should be raised to 5 million per year as against 2 million per year proposed by the Eleventh Plan.

2. *Universalise and Strengthen NREGA*

The Commission recommends the extension and universalisation of National Rural Employment Guarantee Programme to all districts in the country. At present, NREGA programme covers 330 districts. The Commission, in this respect, recommends that on the employment front, the cap on employment for 100 days a year to be provided per household should be removed and the programmes should be purely demand based, on the lines of Maharashtra Employment Guarantee Scheme.

3. *Improving the Employability through Skill Development*

The Commission noted the 'skill development initiatives' (SDI) being provided at present at a total cost of Rs. 550 crores. The objective of the scheme is to provide training to school leavers, existing workers, ITI graduates to improve their employability. On an average, an expenditure of Rs. 5,000 per person is expected to be incurred on training imparted and certification of trainees under SDI Scheme.

The Commission recommends that though DGET scheme is a step in the right direction, it should be expanded through a supplementary on-the-job training-*cum*-employment assurance programme for an additional sum of Rs. 5,000 per person to be provided as one-time payment as an incentive to any employer who is willing to provide on-the job-training for skill enhancement to at least one year to the trained worker.

10. ASSESSMENT OF NCEUS RECOMMENDATIONS

The National Commission on Enterprises by the Unorganised sector (NCEUS) is the first major attempt by the Central Government to address the issues related to unorganised sector. The NCEUS Report studies in-depth the wide ranging issues pertaining to the enterprises in the unorganised sector and also studies in-depth the wide range of issues pertaining to the enterprises in the unorganised sector and also studies issues related with wages, employment, social security and growth of this sector which employs 93 percent of workers. The Report is a strong indictment of the policies pursued after the introduction of LPG model of development in the Indian economy since 1991. It emphasizes the fact that the development process has failed to reduce the size of the unorganised workers standing at 423 millions in 2004-05, i.e. 92.4% of the total labour force. It has merely benefited 35 million, i.e. 7.6 percent workers in the organised sector. Moreover, 91% of workers are denied the benefit of National Minimum Wage fixed at Rs 66 under the Act and 64% below the NCRL norm of Rs. 49 fixed for the rural areas. It has brought out the stark reality of 836 million people, i.e. 77% of the population whose income is below $ 2 PPP, as the poor and vulnerable sections of the population.

The Report is a landmark in making recommendations pertaining to the lot of 423 million workers in the unorganised sector. Since it has also framed two bills—one for agricultural workers and the other for non-agricultural workers, it has done commendable spade work and thus, left very little leeway for the Central Government to delay the measures pertaining to the action programme for the unorganised sector. The Commission needs the appreciation of the neglected sections to take up their cause and make a concerted effort to improve the lot the workers in the unorganised sector who have been bypassed by the reform process.

However, the Commission is guilty of not acknowledging the *Report of the Special Group on Targeting Ten Million Employment Opportunities per year* appointed by the Planning Commission which submitted its Report in May 2002, under the stewardships of Dr. S.P. Gupta, the then member of the Planning Commission. The Special Group stated in a forthright manner : *"The only answer to the situation is to increase productivity and job quality of the unorganised sector. It means that all attempts should be made to implement those policies, which will release the basic growth constraints and by ensuring a level playing field for this sector. . . . In the attempt to increase labour productivity, more emphasis should be laid on the growth of this sector, rather than for substitution of labour with capital. Further, to improve the job quality and its security, major changes in legislation will be needed regarding social security measures, working conditions, minimum wages and protection of labour interests."*[10]

It is really strange that the Commission neglected the earlier attempt to boost the unorganised sector. Whether this is deliberate or unintentional, is only known to Dr. Arjun Sen Gupta and other illustrious members of the Commission. Since the Report was prepared under the NDA government, but could not be implemented, is no reason for ignoring its findings and recommendations.

A close perusal of the NCEUS recommendations reveals that some of the recommendations are distant goals which cannot be realized in the near future. The entire set of minimum conditions of work—eight-hour working day with a weekly holiday, national minimum wage of all workers in the unorganised workers, equal wages for men and women, child-care and basic amenities at workplace—is an attempt to implement the concept of decent work. These conditions do not exist even in the organised sector. Moreover, after the introduction of economic reforms, these conditions are being violated with impunity. The Report itself accepts that casual workers now account for about 23 percent of all workers in the organised sector even, then the first priority should be convert casual workers into regular workers and later take up the question of decent work. 'Regular work for all' should be the primary goal and then gradually the country should move towards 'decent work for all'.

Regarding 'bonded labour', the findings of the Commission are very weak. The Commission should have involved organizations like Gandhi Peace Foundation and Bandhua Mukti Morcha headed by Swami Agnivesh to prepare a plan for the effective abolition of bonded labour which it has failed to do. It only depended on Labour Ministry Annual Reports which are totally unreliable in this area. The Action Programme of the Commission blacks out any recommendation in this regard.

Despites weaknesses here and there, it may be stated that the Report of National Commission on Enterprises in the Unorganised sector is a unique document which intends to give Reforms a human face and as such, it should be welcomed. The Government should take steps to implement the Report and provide necessary financial support for the purpose. It would be desirable to give this task to a separate Ministry so that unorganised enterprises and workers in these are able to attain the goals set by the Commission in its two Bills.

References

1. National Commission for Enterprises in the Unorganised Sector (2007), *Report on Conditions of Work and Promotion of Livelihoods in the Unorganised Sector,* p. 3.
2. *Ibid.,* p. 3.
3. *Ibid.,* p. 4.
4. *Ibid.,* p. 8.
5. *Ibid.,* p. 53.
6. *Ibid.,* p. 125.
7. *Ibid.,* p. 129.
8. Bhanoji Rao, The Noose of Debt, *Business Line,* August 8, 2006.
9. *Ibid.,* p. 2.
10. Planning Commission (2002), *Report of the Special Group on Targeting Ten Million Employment Opportunities,* pp. 10-11.

CHAPTER

6

India as an Economic Superpower (Myth and Reality)

During the last decade, a perception is growing in the world that China and India are becoming two major economic superpowers in the world. Consequently, business firms, more especially multi-national corporations, are moving towards India and China so as to take advantage of the prevalent and fast growing market in these two countries. Accompanied with this phenomenon is rise of business tycoons in India. According to *Forbes List 2007*, India added to its list 14 new billionaires taking its total to 36. The combined net worth of these 36 billionaires was of the order of $191 billion—equal to one-fourth of India's GDP. Simultaneously, there is the growth of the Indian middle class which is, according to a study by the National Council of Applied Economic Research (NCAER), around 28.4 million households by 2009-10. The income range of the middle class has been defined as Rs. 2 lakhs to Rs. 10 lakhs per annum. This implies that by 2009-10, about 153 million persons will be covered in the middle class. Along with this, 3.8 million households comprising a population of 20 million are estimated to be rich, i.e. an income level of over Rs. 10 lakhs per annum.

All these developments have created an impression in the world that India is growing as an economic superpower and so the mad such towards India by big business all over the world.

I. INDIA EMERGING AS AN ECONOMIC SUPERPOWER

To understand the situation, it would be worthwhile to examine the Gross National Income on Purchasing Power Parity basis (PPP) of the world's economies with a total GNI (PPP) above $1,000 billion. Table 6.1 provides information for 13 economies which fall in this range. GNI (PPP) has been used since it provides us an idea about the size of the market in the country.

TABLE 6.1

GNI and Per Capita of GNI of Select Countries in 2005

Country	*Population (Million)*	*GNI*		*GNI PPP*	
		$ Billion	*$ Per Capita*	*$ Billion*	*$ Per Capita*
1. USA	296	12,970	43,740	12,438	41,950
2. China	1,305	2,264	1,740	8,610	6,600
3. Japan	128	4,988	38,980	4,019	31,410
4. India	**1,095**	**793**	**720**	**3,787**	**3,460**
5. Germany	82	2,852	34,580	2,409	29,210
6. UK	[illegible]	[illegible]	[illegible]	1,000	[illegible]
7. France	[illegible]	2,170	[illegible]	1,855	30,540
8. Italy	57	1,725	30,010	1,657	28,840
9. Russian Fed.	143	639	4,460	1,523	10,640
10. Spain	43	1,100	25,360	1,120	25,820
11. Korean Republic	48	765	15,830	1,055	21,850
12. Canada	32	1,052	32,600	1,040	32,220
13. Mexico	103	753	7,310	1,034	10,030

Note : Countries have been arranged in the descending order on the basis of GNI (PPP).
Source : World Bank, *World Development Report (2007).*

Although GNI (PPP) per capita of India in 2005 was only $ 3,460, but on account of the large size of its population of the order of 1,095 million, GNI (PPP) was of the order of $3,787 billion and thus, India was ranked at No. 4 in the world. USA was ranked at No. 1, followed by China and Japan. But even though India was fourth in the world in total GNI, in terms of per capita GNI, USA was 12 times that of India, Japan 9 times that of India and China 1.9 times that of India.

Table 6.2 reveals that the Indian economy experienced an average annual growth of GDP the order of 6 percent during 1990-2000 and it further improved to 6.9 percent during 2000-05. Along with this, the population growth rate during 2000-05 came down to 1.5 percent per annum.

Obviously, India can be ranked at No. 2 in GDP growth during 1990-2005, only next to China which experienced a growth rate of a little over 10 percent in GDP during 1990-2005. GDP growth in India has been further rising and has been reckoned at 9.2 percent during 2006-07. Consequently, India can take pride along with China for being reckoned among the fastest

TABLE 6.2
Growth Rates of GDP in Selected Economies

Country	Average Annual GDP Growth		Average Annual Population Rate (%)	
	1990-2000*	2000-05†	1990-04*	2000-05†
1. USA	3.5	2.8	1.2	1.0
2. China	10.6	9.6	0.9	0.6
3. Japan	1.3	1.3	0.2	0.2
4. India	**6.0**	**6.9**	**1.7**	**1.5**
5. Germany	1.8	0.7	0.3	0.1
6. UK	2.7	2.3	0.3	0.2
7. France	2.0	1.5	0.4	0.6
8. Italy	1.6	0.7	0.1	-0.1
9. Russian Fed.	-4.7	6.2	-0.2	-0.4
10. Spain	2.6	3.1	0.7	1.4
11. Korean Republic	5.8	4.6	0.8	0.5
12. Canada	3.1	2.6	1.0	1.0
13. Mexico	3.1	1.9	1.6	1.0

Source : * World Bank, World Development Indicators (2006), and
† World Development Report (2007).

growing economies of the world. With population growth rate declining to 1.5% during 2000-05, the per capita GDP growth will also get accelerated and if this trend continues for over the next two decades, the gap between the per capita GDP of India as compared with the high income economies of the world will further narrow down. India has, therefore, to keep up its momentum of GDP growth to rise to the level of 10 percent so as to level up with the growth rate in China. Thus, the whole question boils down to sustaining this high GDP growth rate during the next two decades.

2. RISE OF BIG BUSINESS TYCOONS IN INDIA

In the sixties and the Seventies, there was a big debate in India regarding the growth of monopolies and all this led to the passage of the Monopolies and Restrictive Trade Practices Act (1970). All proposals of new investment or expansion of investment were referred to the MRTP Commission for clearance. But the Industrial Policy of 1991 dismantled all these restrictions and freed big business to undertake heavy investments.

This led to the emergence of a large number of billionaires in India. Forbes (2007) has included 36 billionaires from India with a total networth of $ 191 billion (Rs. 8,60,000 crores). In the world, according to *Forbes 2007*, there are 946 billionaires, out of which India has a share of 36 (3.8 percent of total). It may be noted that India has surpassed Japan with only 24 billionaires with a networth of $64 billion. Even China had 24 billionaires in 2007.

Table 6.3 provides a list of Indian billionaires in Forbes list (2007). Among the Indian billionaires, Lakshmi Mittal is at the top with a networth

TABLE 6.3
Ranking of Indian Billionaires in Forbes Billionaire List (2007)

World Rank	*Name*	*Age*	*Net worth $ Billion*
(1)	*(2)*	*(3)*	*(4)*
5	Lakshmi Mittal	56	32.0
14	Mukesh Ambani	49	20.1
18	Anil Ambani	47	18.2
21	Azim Premji	61	17.1
62	Kushal Pal Singh	76	10.0
[illegible]	Sunil Mittal	49	9.5
88	Kumar M. Birla	39	8.0
88	Shashi and Ravi Ruia	NA	8.0
114	Ramesh Chandra	67	6.4
137	Pallonji Mistry	77	5.6
210	Adi Godraj	64	4.1
214	Shiv Nadar	61	4.0
279	Dilip Shanghvi	51	3.1
287	Cyrus Poonawalla	65	3.0
287	Indu Jain	70	3.0
349	Kalanithi Maran	41	2.6
349	Grandhi Rao	57	2.6
390	Savitri Jindal	57	2.4
390	Tulsi Tanti	49	2.4
407	Subhash Chandra	56	2.3
432	Uday Kotak	48	2.2
458	Baba Kalyani	58	2.1
488	Malvinder & Shivinder Singh	NA	2.0
557	Narayana Murthy	60	1.8
618	Anurag Dikshit	35	1.6
618	Venugopal Dhoot	55	1.6
664	Vijay Mallya	51	1.5
664	Jaiprakash Gaur	76	1.5
717	Vikas Oberoi	36	1.4
754	Nandan Nilekani	51	1.3
799	S. Gopalakrishnan	51	1.2
840	Pradeep Jain	41	1.1
840	Keshub Mahindra	83	1.1
840	Rahul Bajaj	68	1.1

Source : Forbes List of Billionaire (2007).

of $32 billion, followed by Mukesh Ambani ($20.1 billion) and Mr. Anil Ambani ($18.2 billion). Although Mukesh Ambani ranks at No. 14 in the world and his brother Anil ambani at No. 18, but if the combined wealth of the two Ambani brothers is taken together, they surpass Lakshmi Mittal and would be at No. 4 position in the world.

The new billionaires have amassed wealth from media to computer software, from real estate to liquor. Among them, the prominent names in computer software are Azim Premji of WIPRO, N. Narayana Murthy of INFOSYS, Nandan Nilekani, G. Gopalakrishnan and Shiv Nadar of HCL.

A good number of developers or builders have also found a place in the billionaires list. The notable among them are Kushal Pal Singh of DLF, Ramesh Chandra of Unitech, Grandhi Rao of GMK, Jaiprakash Gaur for JP Associates, Vikas Oberoi for Oberoi Construction and Pradeep Jain of Parsvanath developers.

The new crop of billionaires which has come up after 1990 has surpassed several big names in he list of big business houses like Birlas, Singhania, Bajaj, Mafatlal, Mahindra & Mahindra, to quote only a few, who were considered industrial giants during 1970s and 1980s. From among the big names in 1970s, the only ones which could find a place in the Forbes list are Kumar Mangalam Birla, Indu Jain of Bennet Coleman & Co. and Pallonji Mistry of Construction, Adi Godrej, Vijay Mallya, Rahul Bajaj and Keshub Mahindra.

1980s witnessed the rise of Dhirubhai Ambani, Shashi and Ravi Ruia and Baba Kalyani of engineering.

Quite a large number of billionaires in the Forbes List blossomed after the introduction of economic reforms in 1991. Besides the Software giants, they were: Subash Chandra of Zee, Sunil Mittal of Bharti Group, Tulsi Tanti of Suzlon, Uday Kotak of Kotak Mahindra, Kalanithi Maran of Sun media group and Savitri Jindal of steel. There was a meteoric rise in the case of many families.

The Billionaire Club spearheads the corporate sector in India. Out of them, the top 8 account for a total networth of $ 123 billion. This accounts for 64.3 percent of total networth of all the 36 Indian billionaires. This indicates the growth of monopoly capital in India in which top 8 billionaires are in possession of nearly two-third wealth of all the billionaires.

3. MYTH AND REALITY OF INDIA AS AN ECONOMIC SUPERPOWER

An economic superpower may have a hundred billionaires, but the basic question that stares in the face of the country's polity and economy is: Do the billionaires impact on the state of unemployment, poverty, deprivation, hunger in the country? If the level of the masses does not improve, but only a very small section of the country's population appropriates economic resources in their favour, then the country cannot claim to be a real economic superpower, though it may parade its handful of billionaires as symbols of this great power. It would be worthwhile to examine the reality of the status of economic superpower in India.

First of all, consider the employment situation in the country. Total employment in the organized sector declined from 273.7 lakhs in 1994 to 264.4 lakhs in 2004, indicating a annual average negative growth rate of 0.38 percent. But classifying it further into public sector and private sector reveals that the rate of growth of employment in the private sector moved tardily from 0.44% during 1983-94 to 0.61% during 1994-2004. Obviously, large business houses are not able to generate employment which is higher than the increase in labour force. The contribution of the billionaires in this regard is, therefore, disappointing.

TABLE 6.4

Employment in Organized Sector in India

(Lakh Persons as on 31st March)

	1994	*2004*
Public Sector	194.45	181.97
Private Sector	79.30	82.46
Total	273.75	264.43
Growth Rate of Employment		
	1993-94	*1994-04*
Public Sector	1.53	-0.80
Private Sector	0.44	0.61
Total	1.20	-0.38

Source : Government of India, *Economic Survey (2006-07).*

According to National Sample Survey data, both the usual status and current daily status unemployment have increased during 1999-00 and 2004-05, the increase is sharper in the case of females than of males. CDs unemployment in 2004-05 has increased to nearly 9 percent in 2004-05.

Secondly, if we consider the poverty ratio, then on the basis of uniform recall period, poverty ratio declined from 36% in 1993-94 to 27.5% in 2004-05. In absolute terms, there were 300 million persons who live below the poverty in 2004-05. Among them, the very poor (those are below 75% of the poverty line) were 115 million, the obvious conclusion is: the extent of decline in poverty ratio in the post-reform was only 0.70 percent annum (1994-2004) as against 0.85 percent in the pre-reform period (1983-94). The slow down in poverty decline is due to a significant increase of inequality in the post-reform period. Thus, there was an enclave type development in post-reform period, which pushed growth rate further, but failed to percolate its effects among the poor.

Thirdly, National Family Health Survey (2005-06) reveals certain startling facts:

1. *Anaemia among children and adults:* 79.2% children in the age 6-35 months were found to be anaemic and this percentage was higher for rural areas at 81.2 percent. Besides this, 56% of married women in the age group 15-49 years were found to be anaemic. Among married men in the age group 15-49 years, 24.3% were found to be anaemic.

TABLE 6.5

Percentage of Households with Basic Amenities (2005-06)

	Total	*Rural*	*Urban*
Have Electricity	67.9	93.1	55.7
Use piped drinking water	42.0	71.0	27.9
Have access to toilet facility	44.5	83.1	25.9
Live in a pucca house	41.4	74.1	25.5

Source : National Family Health Survey (2005-06).

2. Percentage of children who are stunted (too short for age) was 38%, and those who were wasted (too thin for height) was 19%. Similarly, under-weight children under age 3 were as high as 46 percent. This does not reflect well about the health of the nation.
3. A look at the availability of basic facilities reveals that only 68 percent households had electricity—93% in urban areas and merely 56 percent in rural areas. Piped drinking water was available to only 42% of total population only 42% of total population—71% in urban and only 28% in rural areas. Toilet facility was available only to 45% of the total population—83% in urban and 26% in rural areas.

   A pucca house was available to only 41% of the population—74% in urban and 26% in rural areas. The upshot of the analysis is that Bharat (Rural India) suffers grievously in the lack of civic facilities and only 25% rural population has access to piped drinking water, toilet facility and a pucca house. The situation is better in India (urban areas) where nearly 3/4th of the population has access to basic civic amenities.
4. In 2004, about 20% of the population was undernourished.
5. Low birth rate babies (weight less than 2.5 kg. at the time of birth) were of the order of 30%.
6. India ranks at No. 126 on the basis of human development index (HDI) in 2004. Its HDI was 0.611—among the medium HDI countries in the range 0.5-0.8.

Thus, we have a 'shining India' with 36 billionaires, a booming rich and middle class of the order of nearly 150 million which sucks away the major benefits of high growth rate. On the other hand, there is a 'suffering India' living more especially in rural areas and slums in urban areas which has a population of over 900 million. The myth of being a economic superpower explodes when we look at the living conditions of 900 million. Unless the condition of the vast majority of Indian population improves, it would be downright improper to consider India as a real economic superpower.

Khuswant Singh, eminent journalist made a very scathing comment in *Hindustan Times*, dated 17th November 2007 : "It was as ironical a coincidence as could be, what in American slang is known as a double whammy—two slaps on the face. India, which is counted *among the poorest of the poor nations of the world, should also produce the richest of the rich."*

CHAPTER

7

Opening Retail Trade for FDI (A Retrogressive Measure)

Recently, a controversy has arisen about opening the Retail Trade for foreign direct investment FDI. UPA Government led by the Congress Party is in favour of permitting FDI in retail trade. The idea was mooted by the Finance Minister but due to strong opposition by left parties, the Government made a tactical withdrawal. Recently, the Prime Minister has again said that the Government would soon initiate the process of opening FDI in retail trade.

To understand the implications of the FDI in retail trade, it would be desirable to understand the size and structure of retail trade and the groups of persons involved in it. The opposition to this idea is mainly due to its labour displacing effects which would result in loss of jobs and to sacrifice the interests of employment in favour of MNCs engaged in retail trade to enhance their profits.

I. SIZE AND STRUCTURE OF INDIA'S RETAIL SECTOR

Since trade is a part of the service sector, we present data about the share of the various components of GDP in the service sector. Table 7.1 presents the share of service sector and its different sub-sectors in GDP for 2003-04. It may be noted that service sector which accounted for 48 percent of GDP in 1993-94 improved its position to 56.5 percent in 2003-04 and became the leading sector of the Indian economy. Within the various sub-sectors, trade (wholesale and retail) improved its position from a share of 11 percent in GDP in 1993-94 to 14.5 percent in 2003-04.

TABLE 7.1
Components of Service Sector in India

	GDP at 1993-94 prices (Rs. crore)		*Share in GDP (%)*		*Growth Rate during 1993-94 to 2003-04*
	1993-94	*2003-04*	*1993-94*	*2003-04*	
Construction	40,593	74,819	5.2	5.2	6.3
Trade	**93,206**	**208,121**	**11.9**	**14.5**	**8.4**
Hotels and Restaurants	6,613	15,992	0.8	1.1	10.0
Railways	9,648	15,836	1.2	1.1	5.1
Other Transport	32,063	64,240	4.1	4.4	7.2
Communications	9,420	61,370	1.2	4.3	20.6
Banking and Insurance	41,665	97,871	5.3	6.8	8.9
Real Estate, ownership of dwellings and business services	[illegible]	[illegible]	[illegible]	[illegible]	5.9
Public Administration	43,639	85,847	5.6	5.6	7.0
Other Services	49,996	106,937	6.4	9.2	7.9
Total GDP in Service Sector	374,809	810,515	48.0	56.5	7.8
GDP of the Economy	781,345	1,430,548	100.0	100.0	6.2

* Including storage.

Source : Compiled and computed from CSO, *National Accounts Statistics (2005).*

According to the Government of India, *Economic Census (1998),* the number of workers employed in retail trade was 18.54 million, out of which 10.65 million (57.4%) was in the urban sector and 7.89 million (42.6%) was in the rural sector. (Refer Table 7.2)

Out of the total employment of 18.54 million, nearly 60 percent were in Own Account Enterprises and nearly 11 percent were in Non-Directory Enterprises employing between 1 to 5 workers and nearly 29 percent were in Directory Enterprises (DEs) employing 6 or more workers. Obviously, retail sector indicates a preference for own account enterprise, i.e. family businesses.

According to another estimate, unorganized retail trade employs nearly 3.95 crore persons. Adding to this, 5 lakh workers in organized retail trade, the number of workers engaged in total retail trade is of the order of 4 crores (40 million). Given the size of labour force at 378 million as on 31st March 2002, retail trade provided employment to 10.6 percent of the labour force. Thus, this sector is very important from the point of view of providing employment.

TABLE 7.2
Number of Workers Engaged in Retail Trade by Type of Enterprises in India

Type of Enterprise	*No. of Workers Employed (Million)*			
	Rural	*Urban*	*Total*	*Percentage*
OAE	6.04	5.14	11.18	60.3
NDE	0.44	1.58	2.02	10.9
DE	1.41	3.93	5.34	28.8
All	**7.89 (42.6)**	**10.65 (57.4)**	**18.54 (100.0)**	**100.0**

OAE : Own Account Enterprises.
NDE : Non-Directory Enterprises consisting of establishments employing at least one but not more than 5 employees.
DE : Directory Enterprises, those employing at least six persons.
Source : Government of India, *Economic Census (1998).*

Employment in Organized Retail Trade

The total employment in organized trade (wholesale and retail) rose from 4.48 lakhs to 4.91 lakh between 1992-93 and 2001-02, giving an annual

TABLE 7.3
Total Employment in Organized Wholesale and Retail Trade

(Lakh Persons)

Year	*Wholesale and Retail Trade*		*Total*	*Percentage Share*	
	Public Sector	*Private Sector*		*Public Sector*	*Private Sector*
1992-93	1.48	3.00	4.48	33.0	67.0
1993-94	1.61	3.01	4.62	34.8	65.2
1994-95	1.62	3.08	4.70	34.5	65.5
1995-96	1.62	3.17	4.79	33.8	66.2
1996-97	1.64	3.17	4.81	34.1	65.9
1997-98	1.64	3.21	4.85	33.8	66.2
1998-99	1.63	3.23	4.86	33.5	66.5
1999-2000	1.63	3.30	4.93	33.1	66.9
2000-01	1.63	3.39	5.02	32.5	67.5
2001-02	1.56	3.35	4.91	31.8	68.2
Growth rate of Employment	0.6	1.8	0.9		

Source : Compiled and computed from *Monthly Abstract of Statistics*, No. 7, Vol. 5.7, July 2004, Central Statistical Organization.

average growth rate of 0.9 percent. In the public sector, employment remained practically stagnant after 1993-94, around 1.6 lakh persons. However, the growth rate of employment in organized trade in the public sector was a meagre 0.6 percent per annum during 1992-93 and 2001-02. In the private sector, the situation was slightly better and annual employment growth rate was 1.9 percent during the 9-year period.

Table 7.3 also provides data about organized retail trade in the public sector and the private sector. Two-thirds of employment in organized retail trade was provided by the private sector and nearly one-third was the share of the public sector. There is a slight improvement in the share of private sector from 65.2 percent in 1993-94 to 68.2 percent in 2001-02. Consequently, the share of the public sector has declined from 34.8 percent in 1993-94 to 31.8 percent in 2001-02.

Undeveloped Nature of Employment in the Organized Retail Trade

In India, retail trade predominantly exists in the unorganized sector which accounts for 98 percent of the retail trade. While the organized sector accounts for only 2 percent. As compared with this, organized sector accounts for 90 percent of retail trade in USA, 80 percent in U.K., 70 percent in Western Europe. Even in some of the under-developed countries, organized retail trade accounts 40 percent in Brazil, 35 percent in South Korea, 20 percent in China, but only 2 percent in India.

TABLE 7.4
Share of Organized Sector in Retail Trade

	Percentage of Total Trade
U.S.A.	90
UK	80
Western Europe	70
Thailand	40
Brazil	40
China	20
India	2

Most unorganized retail consists of traditional forms of retailing in India, such as kirana Shops, paan/beedi shops, hardware stores, daily convenience stores and bazars. But so far big business has not entered retail trade. Even in wholesale markets, businessmen of medium range predominate. In contrast, in highly developed countries, organized retail trade is monopolized by global giants like Wal-Mart, Tesco, Kingfisher, Carrefour and Ahold which intend to expand their hold in India.

Size of Trade Sector in India

Total size of the trade sector in GDP at current prices was Rs. 91,324 crores in 1993-94 (13.1% of GDP) and it improved to 3,45,000 crores in 2003-04 (15.2% of GDP). This gives an average annual growth rate of 14.2 percent. The share of the unorganized retail sector works out to the Rs. 3,38,100 crores (at the rate of 98 percent of total trade). This huge size of the unorganized retail sector is sought to be captured by multinational giants like Wall-Mart by making entry into the retail sector.

TABLE 7.5
Size of Retail Trade

(Rs. crores at current prices)

	Retail Trade	*% of GDP*
1993-94	91,324	13.1
2000-01	2,75,302	14.5
2003-04	3,44,998	15.2

Source : Same as for Table 7.3.

Density of Retail Sector

Federation of Indian Chamber of Commerce and Industry (FICCI) has prepared an estimate of the outlets in the retail sector. Between 1996 and 2001, retail outlets increased from 8.54 million to 11.16 million—an increase of 30.6 percent. With 11.16 million retail sector outlets, India has the highest retail density of 11 per 1,000 persons. In fact, this is due to the fact that capital-labour ratio is very low. Quite a number of unemployed persons or even otherwise, seeking avenues of employment consider it a very convenient route to create self-employment. Mr. Mohan Guruswamy *et. al.* believe that this is a sector of forced employment. They are of the view: "One of the principal reasons behind the explosion of retail outlets and its fragmented nature in the.country is the fact that retailing is probably the primary form of disguised unemployment/underemployment in the country. Given the already overcrowded agriculture sector, and the stagnating manufacturing sector, and the hard nature of and relatively low wages of jobs in both, many million Indians are virtually forced into the services sector. Here, given the lack of opportunities, it becomes almost a natural decision for an individual to set-up a small shop or store, depending upon his/her means and capital. And thus, a retailer is born, seemingly out of circumstances rather than choice." (*Economic and Political Weekly,* February 12-18, 2005, p. 620). This statement does not wholly account for the expansion of the retail sector, because as the economy expands its output in various sectors like foodgrains, other crops and manufacturing, they

TABLE 7.6
Growth of Outlets in Retail Trade

(*Million*)

	Food Retailers	*Non-food Retailers*	*Total*
1996	2.77	5.77	8.54
1997	2.94	6.04	8.98
1998	3.12	6.33	9.45
1999	3.30	6.67	9.97
2000	3.48	7.05	10.53
2001	3.68	7.48	11.16

Source : FICCI.

necessitate a growth of the retail sector as well to reach the ultimate consumers. However, some employment may be the consequence of unemployment and quite a large number of under employed persons, depending upon their capacity to invest, set-up a small retail shop or store initially and if successful, may expand it further as they are able to generate or mobilize more resources.

2. THE CONTROVERSY REGARDING OPENING OF RETAIL SECTOR FOR FDI

Opening of retail trade for FDI is supported by the Government represented by Mr. P. Chidambaram, Finance Minister and the Prime Minister as well. The Government is supported by Industry Associations like FICCI and CII. However, the left parties and the Swadeshi Jagran Manch are vehemently opposing this move since it is alleged that such a step will deprive and displace millions of persons engaged in this trade. It would be appropriate to understand the arguments of both sides so as to have a correct assessment of the situation.

In a report jointly prepared by McKinsey & Company and the Confederation of Indian Industry (CII), it has been estimated that in case, retail trade is opened to FDI, India holds the potential of becoming a $300 billion market by 2010. According to FICCI study, the total turnover of India's trade, both organized and unorganized sector taken together, as on 2003 was Rs. 11,00,000 crores or $245 billion. Taking it to a level of $300 billion implies a growth rate of 2.9 percent per annum. This is a very modest increase considering the average growth rate of the economy to be of the order of 7 percent per annum during 2003-2010. This can be achieved even by Indian retailers, both organized and unorganized working together. Secondly, the McKinsey–CII report only talks about the growth in trade volume if global retail giants like Tesco, Kingfisher, Wal-Mart, Carrefour and

Ahold are allowed to operate in this sector. It only implies an outflow of funds to multinational giants, but the effects of this policy in terms of displacement of employment opportunities have not been studied by FICCI. Already the period of economic reforms has been considered as a period of jobless growth, but in the case of retail trade, it is likely to turn out as one of negative employment growth. The question of examining the need for enlarging trade via multinationals *vis-a-vis* its labour displacing effects has to be seriously examined.

In this context, it has to be realized that size of retail giants like Wal-Mart has to be kept in view. For instance, as per the Annual Report of Wal-Mart, its turnover in 2004 was $256 billion. This implies that this was bigger than the total turnover of trade of $245 billion in India. However, the net profit of Wal-Mart in 2004 was $9 billion and it employed only 1.4 million persons. As against it, the total employment in the retail market in India was 39.5 million in 2003, according to the FICCI study. Wal-Mart had 4,806 stores, of these 1,355 stores were outside USA. The average size of a Wal-Mart store was 85,000 sq.ft. and the average turnover was around $51 million. Compare it with India, where out of 11 million stores, only 4 percent had an average size of more than 500 sq. ft. As against the average turnover of $51 million of Wal-Mart store, the average turnover of India's store was Rs. 11.0 lakhs or merely $24,450. Our stores are lilliputs compared with the large size of Wal-Mart stores. This average is the result of the combination of organized and unorganized sectors. In 98 percent of the retail sector trades like small paan and beedi shops, the small trader selling groceries or cloth or other articles of daily consumption, this average is much smaller.

The upshot of the study of comparative size of multinational stores with Indian stores only reveals that even organized sector retail outlets will not be able to face the onslaught of foreign competition when it comes, not to speak of the small traders in the unorganized sector.

Consumer's Interest Argument

Another argument put forward in favour of multinational traders is that they will, reaping the economies of scale, be able to sell goods at cheaper prices, thus benefiting millions of consumers. This argument needs to be examined in the light of experience in several countries. The strategy of retail sector giants is that in the initial stages, they keep lower prices so as to drive out competitors. This may continue even for 2-3 years, since these giant retailers have deep pockets. Once the domestic retailers are forced to close their shops, the giant multinationals start increasing their prices. In UK, retail companies operated by multinational companies charged 40 percent higher prices, but in the absence of alternative, the consumers have to pay higher prices. Once a monopoly or oligopoly situation is created, the giant multinationals buy cheap and sell dear.

In the agricultural sector, these companies are encouraging contract farming and as a consequence, they will be able to force farmers to sell cheap to multinationals, which will in turn sell them at higher prices to consumers. As Nick Robbins wrote in the context of East India Company: "By controlling both ends of the chain, the company could buy cheap and sell dear." Thus, domestic producers and consumers would not be benefited, once the multinational retail giants are able to create a monopoly position. This is generally referred to 'predatory pricing' in economic literature. In short, opening of retail trade to FDI will not benefit the consumer, though it may in the initial stages, give a deceptive feeling of some benefit.

Impact on Employment in Retail Trade

Even if Wal-Mart were to open a Wal-Mart store in each of the 35 cities with a population of over 1 million in India, Wal-Mart will be able to create a turnover of Rs. 8,030 crores with an employment of only 10,000 employees (assuming per employee turnover of $1,75,000 per employee in a Wal-Mart store outside USA and each store with a turnover of $51 million). It has been estimated that even if giant multinational retailers were to cover 20 percent of our retail trade, which is not an over-estimate, they will employ only 1.8 lakh persons, driving nearly 8 million persons out of unorganized retail sector. The employment displacing effects on retail trade are very considerable and there is a need to study this question deeply, rather than gamble in opening the retail trade to retail giants to repent later.

3. INTERNATIONAL EXPERIENCE

It has to be remembered that countries like China, Thailand and Malaysia which opened their retail sector to FDI were forced to reverse this policy and enact new laws to control the entry of giant retail players in the retail sector. According to All China Federation of Trade Unions, as a result of the entry of multinational companies, the domestic retail trade is shrinking. The Chinese Newspapers have been stressing this point that indigenous retail market is facing extinction. Moreover, a good number of Chinese producers had to stop their production because competition from Wal-Mart reduced their margins to such a low level that the domestic producers found it impossible to sustain themselves.

Even in advanced countries, opposition to the entry of US Retail Giants has started. In France, as against a level of 30 years ago, the number of retail shops has declined to 17 percent. In Denmark, during a period of 10 years (1982 to 1992), about 30 percent of small retail shops were closed as a result of competition of US retail giants. It is estimated that in the subsequent 10 years, only 3,000 retail shops will be left in Denmark.

Even within US, Wal-Mart has to face strong criticism. The municipal corporations of California and Chicago have imposed a ban on opening of Wal-Mart stores. Even in the big cities of France and Germany, Wal-Mart is required to obtain permission from local authorities to open a new store. Even in Japan, South Korea and France, the foreign retail traders are banned to enter the trade in petroleum products, rice, tobacco, salt, fresh vegetables, meat and intoxicants.

4. GOVERNMENT STRATEGY TO BREAKTHROUGH THE IMPASSE

The Government has initiated a new strategy to force a breakthrough to the resistance of the left parties to open FDI in the retail sector. The strategy is simple: Opening up of retail to FDI will be restricted to food items with the farmers being projected as the direct beneficiaries. According to the strategy, the farmers would be allowed to sell their produce directly to multinationals instead of bringing it to the *Mandi*. This will eliminate middlemen operating in the *Mandis* and will benefit the farmers in the form of better prices for their produce. Since farmers outnumber small traders, this may result in giving a big push to opening food items for FDI retail. In the wake of continuing opposition by the left, the new strategy is likely to have a two-fold impact: Firstly, it would blunt the argument of the left since small traders would not lose their livelihood by the new policy because all non-food items, accounting for 60 percent of retail trade, will still be out-of-bounds for FDI. Secondly, the Government has argued that FDI will help in setting up cold chains to eliminate wastage of vegetables and fruits which is of the order of 40 percent, this will be a substantial argument for a breakthrough.

In case, the strategy of the Government succeeds, it will imply the entry of multinationals in retail trade. However, its success will depend on two conditions: Foreign retail giants, if they enter into contract with farmers to pick up agricultural produce, at prices higher than those given by wholesale buyers in mandis, they will be able to control retail trade in food items, by assuring the farmers better prices than their competitors. It has been observed in recent years that farmers are able to realize better prices from food processing industries owned by multinationals like Nestle. But if the multinationals after sometime also start exploiting the farmers due to their monopoly power, the farmers may reject selling their produce to them. It is all a question of sharing the benefits. Indian wholesale buyers can also in competition start paying better prices to farmers, and thus retain their hold.

It is difficult to predict the outcome. It will depend on attitude of foreign retail giants and the Indian wholesale buyers in mandis. It is argued that competition between them may benefit Indian farmers. If this benefit is short-lived, the strategy may end in fiasco.

5. CONCLUSION

The Government should not hastily plunge into the opening of FDI in retail sector since it is definitely going to affect employment adversely. Its employment displacing effects should be carefully studied. The spurious argument advanced for helping the consumer will only be a short term phenomenon. In the long-run, even the consumers will be forced to pay through their nose as a result of the creation of monopoly. Paul Etgart, former director of the giant UK retailer TESCO warned: "Indian retail business should not be fooled by partnership offers by global retail giants because they want 100 percent control and eventual ownership." He further advised Indians "to urge your government to retain your strict FDI regulations, for global retail giants are very smart and clever to tackle local, cultural and political obstacles. India must beware" (Developing Retail Sector, India Told', *The Hindu*, January 21, 2005).

Recently, there have been violent protests by small traders against big retail giants. As a result of these violent protests, the UP Government headed by Ms. Mayawati decided to close down all Reliance Fresh retail stores. This was done to protect the jobs of small retailers and their employees. This is bound to have an effect in other states. Congress Party is also having rethinking on this issue, since Commerce Minister Kamal Nath recently said that the Government cannot ignore the employment displacing effects of opening retail to big business—Indian as well as foreign. There is need for a thorough re-examination of the policy towards retail trade.

India should evolve its own model of retail trade keeping in view the issue of employment as the Central focus and should heed the warning given by the policies of retail trade in which devastating effects on employment were observed even in developed countries like US, France and Japan.

CHAPTER

8

Single-brand Retail FDI (Rhetoric and Reality)

The controversy regarding the opening of the retail sector to FDI has again been revived with the announcement of the Government to allow 51 percent FDI in Single-brand retail. Although the Government had earlier announced that it would not open the retail sector to FDI without consultation with left parties, but on hindsight it appears that it was only a tactical retreat. The major purpose was to develop a sugar-coated pill to sell the policy of allowing FDI in retail. The Government, thus, as a matter of strategy announced that it only intends to open FDI to single-brand companies. Consequently, the controversy has been revived.

I. FDI POLICY AND RETAIL SECTOR

Outlining the policy at the Davos meet on January 27, 2006, Commerce and Industry Minister Mr. Kamal Nath said, "FDI policy was domestic driven and that foreign investment should not replace or displace employment as the country is committed to FDI being directed towards job creation." Mr Kamal Nath got support form US Ambassador to India, Mr. David Mulford when he said in an interview to PTI: "Why does Left oppose opening of retail to FDI? Are they opposed to farmers and business guys and other getting credit developing their livelihoods and their businesses?" On the Left's argument that opening up the retail sector would result in small traders losing their livelihood, Mr. Mulford said, " *I recognize there are complicated problems because of the innate structure of your current small shop sector*. But surely, you know, we have found in other countries that large retailers and small shopkeepers can co-exist perfectly well." (*Economic Times*, 30 January 2006) Emphasis added.

Both the Commerce Minister and US Ambassador are singing the same tune that opening 51 percent FDI retail would not displace employment and that it would be beneficial to the Indian economy to acquire resources from big multi-nationals in retail. Mr. Kamal Nath is either oblivious of the ground reality about the prevailing employment situation in the country or is just closing his eyes to the ground level situation. Even after a decade and half of the progress of economic reforms in India, as per latest data provided by the 61st round of the National Sample Survey, current daily status (CDS) rate of unemployment was 8.3 percent for India in 2004-05—8.2 percent for rural areas and 8.3 percent in urban areas. This obviously indicates that there was a deterioration in unemployment during 1999-2000 and 2004-05, although GDP growth picked up further to touch a level of 7.4 percent in 2004-05. How long can the people of India (Aam Adami) be fed on the false plea that economic reforms may lead to higher level of unemployment in the short-run, but in the medium term, they will reduce unemployment. Fifteen years is certainly not a short period, it has to the thought of as a medium term. Obviously, as against the rhetoric of economic reforms, the hard reality is that the reforms process has failed to bring about any reduction in the rate of unemployment. Rather it has resulted in an increase in the rate of unemployment to a high level of over 8.3 percent.

According to a Cris Infac study, "The organised retail industry is on a high growth trajectory, and is expected to grow at 25-30 percent per annum in the next five years. The market size is forecast to grow to Rs. 1,09,500 crores by 2009-10 from Rs. 35,000 crores in 2004-05. The basic question is : If the Indian economy grows by 7 to 7.5 percent per annum, the growth of organised retail industry by 25-30 percent will only mean poaching by the organised sector into the unorganized sector, viz., Kirana shops and convenience stores. Data about growth of employment only shows that the organised sector showed a zero or sometimes negative growth of employment and the entire growth of employment has recently been witnessed in the unorganized sector. This being the hard reality, would it be proper to open FDI retail further to foreign players. To pursue policies of labour displacement, while paying lip sympathy to the employment objective has been the hall mark of the economic policies in the reform period.

Regarding the US Ambassador's support to the Government policies, it may be stated that His Excellency, Mr David Mulford should have remained within the limits of diplomatic propriety and refrained form making comments on the attitude of the Left parties in opposing the opening of the retail sector. He has himself accepted that "There are complicated problems there because of the innate structure of your current small shop sector." Let me explain the innate structure. Firstly, it is one thing to talk of unemployment in a developed economy like USA with a highly developed social security system which includes unemployment doles, and another thing to understand the implications of unemployment in a developing country like India in which over 93 percent of the labour force engaged in unorganized sector does not have any system of social security. It is a question of survival for the small traders. Secondly, there is the question of co-existence of large corporate sector *vis-a-vis* unorganized sector. There is a shrinkage of the share of the unorganized sector in net domestic product from 70 percent to 57 percent during the last two decades, but there has been an increase in employment share of unorganized sector form about 89 percent to 93 percent. Obviously, the organized sector has failed to absorb workers from the unorganized sector, rather the process of casualisation of the workers both in the organised and unorganized sector has witnessed a sharp increase. Co-existence of the large corporate sector with the unorganized retail should not tilt the scales against the unorganized retailer. The common man, therefore, asks a legitimate question: For whom are economic reforms intended? For the weak or for the privileged few. The answer is not hard to find: Economic reforms by unleashing the process of liberalization have helped only the privileged. They have failed to bring about the much-needed balance between growth, employment and equity.

2. FDI IN RETAIL NOT CRUCIAL FOR THE GROWTH OF INDIAN ECONOMY

The big question before the country is: should it allow big business—Indian or foreign—to continue to pressurize the Government under various pretexts to open areas which were earlier the preserve of the small retail sector. The basic issue is : Is FDI in retail such a crucial area which deserves entry of big multi-nationals? For the country FDI should be welcome in infrastructure, in heavy industry, in the energy sector etc. which will increase our productive capacity to have GDP growth rate of 8-10 percent on a sustainable basis. The country has adequate capacity to run its retail business in an efficient manner. Opening FDI retail will only legitimize the profits of big multi-nationals, without helping the small trader in the country.

This fact has become obvious when it is argued that single-brand retail FDI will help in establishment of more luxury malls. It will imply more good-looking shops. Ultimately, FDI will not help us in enlarging our productive capacity in either manufacturing or infrastructure sectors. It is simply aimed at serving the interests of big business and cater to the needs of upper middle class and affluent sections of our society.

Meaning of Single-brand Retail

Another relevant issue is : What is single-brand retail? Does it mean a single product or a whole range of products sold under a brand name? It may be noted that food and grocery stores share 76 percent of the spending by the consumers and 99 of this market is in the unorganized sector. Wall-mart is a brand name in its own right and thus can sell all grocery and food products and several other non-food items under a single-brand name. Similarly, other big foreign retail companies like Tesco, Kingfisher, Correfour and Ahold can also sell all their products and use a single brand. The giant retailers, once they are permitted to open shop in India, will establish full-fledged outlets even in small towns. It would not be possible to prevent this process of penetration in the Indian retail market. It was the duty of the Government to specify what 'single-brand' is. But it appears that the intention of the Government is not to make it explicit. This would leave elbow room for the Government to further broad-base the concept of 'single-brand' to accommodate a whole range of extensions. Single-brand is a device used by the Government to facilitate the entry of foreign retail giants in the Indian retail market. Once this is done, permitting them to enlarge their area of operation will be relatively more easy.

CPM polit bureau, therefore, criticized the single-brand retail FDI proposal that it is a clandestine way to open doors to foreign retail giants. "The stipulation that it will be for single-brand shops does not mean it will imply to single product only but can cover a variety of products." CPM leader Mr. Sitaram Yechury said: "We are opposed to FDI in retail sector. . . . The Government says it will allow FDI in branded goods. But it is a loose term as anything can be branded. We want the Government to specify the items where FDI is allowed."

Similarly BJP leader Sh. V.K. Malhotra, deputy leader of the opposition in Lok Sabha said: The cabinet decision is a "cruel joke" on small business. "This move is going to hit small traders and business hard. It is a cruel joke on them. We will oppose it hard in Parliament" when it comes before it for consideration.

International Experience

Moreover, international experience in opening retail to big multi-nationals reveals that in the initial phase, the Giant retailers charge lower prices to capture the market. They have deep pockets and can bear losses in the short period. But once the market share is captured, they raise prices and recover the losses. It has to be kept in mind that countries like China, Thailand and Malaysia which opened their retail sector to FDI, were forced to reverse this policy and enact new laws to control the entry of retail giants. The retail companies operated by MNCs charged 40 percent higher prices. Thus, they even appropriate more profits at the cost of the consumer.

Indian Big Business in Retail

But there is a related issue. Reliance Industries announced that the board has approved the initial phase of setting up various retail outlets like hyper-markets, supermarkets, convenience stores and specialty stores in select cities covering all the geographic regions in the country at an estimated cost of $750 million. By mid-2006, the Company is likely to start 50 big stores in 22 cities across five states, including Maharashtra, Gujarat, Andhra Pradesh, Punjab and West Bengal. It will mean an investment of Rs. 20,000 to Rs. 30,000 crores. The question which has not been seriously considered by either the Government or the opposition or even by the left parties providing support to the Government is: if FDI in retail sector would hit the small trader and kirana shops, then it could be argued that even the entry of Indian big business in retail would produce the same kind of results as contemplated in opening FDI in retail. Already, quite a number of big players like Big Bazars and Pantaloon outlets, Lifestyle, Trent and Globus have started appropriating the retail market share. In India, there are estimated to be 11.1 million retail outlets, but the organised retail accounts for less than 3 percent. Indian big business, which traditionally left retail trade to unorganized retail consisting of kirana shops, paan/beedi stores, hardware stores, daily convenience stores and bazars is now directing its attention to capture a much larger share in this sector. The modern organised retail accounts for a very small segment, that is around Rs. 30,000 crores and growing at over 30 percent in urban and semi-urban markets. If this process is allowed in an unhindered manner, the Indian retail Giants will in the next decade swallow a big proportion of retail trade, nearly 50 percent by 2016.

Need for a National Policy on Retail Trade

The moot question is: If entry of the FDI in retail is likely to hit unorganized retail, the entry of Indian big business is also likely to produce the same effect. The retail trade provides employment to nearly 40 million or nearly 11 percent of labour force. Obviously, serious thought should be given to the employment displacing effects of permitting big business—Indian or foreign in the retail sector. This is not to suggest that the unorganized retail sector be not modernized, but to suggest that the modernized retail sector be promoted to grow and join the organised sector. The government should evolve a suitable policy for allocating space at subsidized rates to small retailers, provide credit and help the small trader to introduce modern technology in retail. Such a policy, if designed, would reconcile the growth, employment and equity objectives of national policy in a harmonious manner.

During recent years, small traders attacked Reliance Fresh outlets in the various states of India. It was alleged that big business houses are damaging employment in retail, more especially hitting the interests of small traders. Mayawati Government in Uttar Pradesh ordered big business houses to close their retail outlets because they pose a threat to the maintenance of law and order. Following this ban, Governments in other states are also compelled to do some rethinking on this issue because the country is forced both from the point of view of political and economic necessity to find a solution of the difficult and important problem of unemployment. This is the big question.

CHAPTER

9

Special Economic Zones (SEZs)

Special Economic Zones (SEZs) denote geographical areas which enjoy special privileges as compared with non-SEZ areas in the country. The main motivating force for setting up SEZs came from the Ministry of Commerce with a view to boost exports by attracting both Indian and foreign corporates to undertake investment in these areas. Earlier Export Processing Zones are now also being converted into Special Economic Zones. Accordingly, the Government has converted Export Processing Zones (EPZ) located at Kandla and Surat (Gujarat), Santa Cruz, Mumbai (Maharashtra), Falta (West Bengal), Chennai (Tamil Nadu), Vishakhapatnam (Andhra Pradesh) and NOIDA (Uttar Pradesh) into SEZs.

1. OBJECTIVES OF SETTING UP SEZs

The main argument to establish SEZs is to promote exports by concentrating resources in some pockets (designated as SEZs). The policy was introduced in April 2000 to provide internationally competitive and hassle-free environment for exports. The units may be set up to manufacture goods or render services. The unit in the SEZ area has to be a net foreign exchange earner, but no conditionality has been imposed to export a specified proportion of the output.

SEZ can be set-up in the public sector, private sector or joint sector or even by state governments in collaboration with any corporate.

2. SPECIAL PRIVILEGES FOR SEZs

SEZs are duty-free enclaves of development and are deemed as foreign territories for purpose of trade, duties and tariffs. The policy offers several fiscal and regulatory incentives to developers of the SEZ as well as to the units within these zones.

Corporations in SEZs will not have to pay any income tax on their profits for the first 5 years and only 50% of the tax for two years thereafter. The concession of paying only 50% of the tax can be extended for another three years if half of the profit is reinvested in the corporation. Besides, income tax benefit, units in SEZ shall be exempted from a host of other taxes and duties like customs duty, excise duty, service tax, Value Added Tax (VAT), dividend tax, etc.

For SEZ developers, all raw materials from cement to steel to electrical parts shall be exempt from any tax/duty. All imports for developing SEZs shall be exempt from any custom duties.

For SEZs, the Government will acquire vast tracts of land and provide it to the corporations or developers. A basic condition is that 25% of the area of SEZ must be used for export related activities and the remaining 75% of the area can be used for economic and social infrastructure. All the benefits and concessions of SEZ can be availed of for the whole area.

The list of authorized operations include roads, housing apartments, convention centres, cafeterias and restaurants, airconditioning, telecom and other communication facilities and recreational facilities.

Sector-specific SEZs will be allowed to have additional operations including hotels, schools and educational & technical institutes. Multi-product SEZs will also be allowed to have ports, airports and golf-courses.

Sector-specific developers of SEZs will be allowed to have 7,500 houses, hotels with a total of 100 rooms, a 25-bed hospital and schools and other educational institutions and a multiplex up to 50,000 sq. meters. Multi-product SEZs will be allowed to build 25,000 houses, a 250 room hotel and a hospital with 100 beds and a multiplex of 2,00,000 sq. metres.

For sector specific SEZs, the applicant's net worth has to be a minimum of Rs. 50 crores while the minimum investment criterion is Rs. 250 crores. To qualify for developing a multi-product SEZ, the net worth has to be at least Rs. 250 crores and the minimum investment in the project Rs. 1,000 crores. For applying for IT SEZs, net worth of applicant has to be Rs. 100 crores.

SEZs would be exempt from the application of labour laws so that they can attract entrepreneurs to set-up industrial units. Thus, Labour Commissioners will have no jurisdiction to inspect SEZs, even to implement safety and environmental norms in these units. All industrial units and other establishments in SEZs shall be declared, "Public Utility Service" in which any strike shall be illegal. This implies that SEZs will not comply with the provisions of the Industrial Disputes Act, 1947. They will, however, have the freedom to employ contract labour to any extent. The Contract Labour (Regulation & Abolition) Act is also proposed to be amended to include certain peripheral activities.

3. SEZ POLICY MOTIVATED BY THE CHINESE EXPERIENCE

China established in 1980 special economic zones (SEZs) in 14 coastal cities. The main purpose was to provide a dual role for SEZs to act as "Windows" in developing the foreign-oriented economy, thus, generating foreign exchange by boosting exports and importing advanced technologies. Consequently, SEZs became "radiators" in accelerating economic development. In these zones, to attract foreign investment, custom duties and income tax were eliminated. This helped China to improve the coastal regions and thus accelerate the development of these regions. The policy helped to attract foreign-funded enterprises to invest over $30 billion in China and over 5,000 domestic enterprises from all over the country to invest about 20 billion Yuan in SEZ regions. As a result, six pillar industries took firm roots in China. They are: automobiles and spare parts and components, micro-electronics and computers, household electrical appliances, bio-medicines and optical, mechanical and electrical products. All the SEZ units were developed by the State and not by private corporates or individuals.

However, the rapid growth of coastal regions of China did not get transmitted to the provinces of hinterland. As a consequence, a divide emerged between the rich and affluent coastal regions and the poor regions of the hinterland in China. In other words, instead of developing growth with equity, China promoted growth with inequity and disparities between the rich and the backward region widened. Neither did the benefits of urban development percolate to the rural areas. The Government of China has realized its mistake of promoting exclusive growth of coastal areas and thus, the Eleventh Five Year Plan of China beginning from 2006 set as its major goal: balancing urban and rural development and development among regions. On March 5, 2006, Wen Jiabao, Premier of the State Council set forth the following major tasks of the 11th Plan: to implement a policy of getting industry to support agriculture and cities to the country-side so as to bring about a rapid and significant change in the overall appearance of the country-side. Secondly, while carrying forward the development of western region, China will implement the strategy of rejuvenating north- east China and the Central region. In nutshell, developed regions should assist and stimulate the development of under-developed regions. This is an admission of the weaknesses of following the policies of exclusive development with special economic zones.

4. PRESENT STATE OF SEZ AND FUTURE PROGRAMMES

The status report of the SEZs as per availability of information till end July 2007 is as under:

1. Formal approval has been granted to 362 SEZs so far, out of which 133 have been notified.
2. Total investment made so far has been of the order of Rs. 43,125 crores, according to Mr. G.K. Pillai, Union Commerce Secretary in a seminar organised by *Industrial Economist* at Chennai on 23rd July 2007.
3. Total employment generated was merely of the order of 35,053. This implies that investment-employment ratio was Rs. 1.23 crores per unit of employment.

Status Report on SEZs

Granted formal approaval	362
Notified	133
Yet to be notified	229
Operational SEZs	75
Investments in these SEZs	Rs. 43,125 Cr.
Employment generation	35,053
Estimated investments by March 2008	Rs. 100,000 Cr.
Estimated direct employment by March 2008	100,000

It has been also projected that by March 2008, SEZ units investments would cross Rs. 1 lakh crores leading to the creation of 1 lakh jobs. This implies that SEZ units investment employment ratio will come down slightly to Rs. 1 crore per unit of employment. From this projection, it is obvious that SEZ units are highly capital intensive.

During 2004-05, the total exports from the Special Economic Zones were of the order of Rs 18,655 crores. This works out to be 4.97% of the country's total exports (Rs. 3,75,340 crores). During 2005-06, it was

TABLE 9.1

Export Performance of EOUs and SEZ Units

Year	*SEZ Units*		*EOUS*		*Total Exports*	
	Rs. crores	*US$ Million*	*Rs. crores*	*US$ Million*	*Rs. crores*	*US$ Million*
2004-05	18,655 (4.9)	4,140 (4.8)	37,488 (9.9)	86,343 (9.8)	3,75,340 (100.0)	85,536 (100.0)
2005-06	22,309 (4.9)	4,984 (4.8)	37,658 (8.2)	8,506 (8.3)	4,56,418 (100.0)	1,03,091 (100.0)

Note : Figures in brackets are percentages of total exports in terms of Rupees and US $ respectively.

Source : Compiled and Computed from data provided by Export Promotion Council and RBI Bulletin July 2007.

Rs. 23,309 crores. In 2005-06, it would be of order of 4.88% of total exports (Rs. 456,418 crores).

Thus, total exports from SEZs (Special Economic Zones) and EOUs (Export Oriented Units) functioning earlier was 14.8% of total exports in 2004-05, out of which the share of SEZs was 4.9% and that of EOUs was 9.9%. In 2005-06, the share of SEZs remained stagnant at 4.9% and that of EOUs declined to 8.2%, in the total exports of SEZs and EOUs taken together at 13.1%. Since there are no export obligations on SEZs, the EOUs may not also fulfil their export obligation. Given the scenario, SEZ units exports growth may continue to be low despite very rosy expectations.

Lured by the heavy incentives, a large number of industrial houses and developers—Indian as well as foreign—are pushing their applications to the state governments to approve new proposals, but the sharp apprehensions and the critique of SEZ policy has forced government to do some rethinking on the issue, though Mr. Kamal Nath, Minister of Commerce is very keen to promote development via SEZ route.

5. CRITIQUE OF SEZ POLICY

The critique of SEZ policy has emerged from within the UPA government as well as from the left parties and even independent sources. It would be relevant to review the debate going on.

Firstly, the Finance Minister Mr. P. Chidambaram disagreed with the Commerce Minister on issues of key concessions, land use and the future of existing export-oriented units. A study made by the National Institute of Public Finance and Policy (NIPFP) found that the Government will lose Rs. 97,000 crores in tax revenues during 2005-10 as a consequence of the tax concessions to SEZ units. This works out to be an annual average loss of Rs. 19,400 crores to the state exchequer. The IMF Chief economist estimates that the loss of revenue to the public exchequer will be of the order of Rs. 1,75,000 crores. These figures are being quoted by the Left that the SEZ policy needs a review because it is bound to add to fiscal deficit whereas the Finance Minister was making efforts to reduce the budget deficit every year. The Reserve Bank of India has also expressed its reservations about it. The basic questions is: shall these tax concessions bring about any dramatic change in giving an impetus to the export growth? The fact that the SEZ projects in 2004-05 were able to provide exports barely to the tune of Rs. 18,655 crores (4.9 percent of the total exports) indicates the capacity of these units to accelerate exports. In contrast, the small scale sector provided exports of the order of Rs. 1,24,416 crores during 2004-05 or 34.4 percent of the total exports. The question which the nation must decide is: should it promote the SME sector which has much greater potential or the SEZ units which contribute relatively much less in terms of foreign exchange earnings? Although Mr. Chidambaram is being dubbed as a conservative *vis-a-vis* the reformists but there is much more sense in his point of view. Mr. Narendar Pani observes in this connection: "The FM knows that he will be in trouble if the economy as a whole does not do well, while the Commerce Minister concerns are only with export-oriented industries that are expected to benefit from SEZs." (Narender Pani, SEZs as a Chinese Puzzle, *Economic Times*, September 22, 2006). The basic issue is that the assumption of closer links between sectors benefiting from globalisation and the rest of the economy, has not been validated by international experience.

The second issue pertains to acquiring huge tracts of prime agricultural land for SEZ units. For instance, the UP Government had given a corporate house 2,500 acres of land in Dadri to set-up a power plant which required only 50 acres. Similarly, West Bengal Chief Minister has handed over prime agricultural land for the Tata Small Car Manufacturing unit at Singur. This land was capable of producing three crops a year. Moreover, acquisition of land is done at prices determined by the Government and not market prices which is the legitimate right of the farmers. Obviously, this was being done to feed rich industrial houses and developers at the cost of poor farmers. Congress President Mrs. Sonia Gandhi felt seriously disturbed about the way things were going on. She laid down the following guidelines for congress-ruled states on the 23rd September 2006.

"Prime agricultural land should not normally be diverted to non-agricultural uses. Industry requires land. But this must be done without jeopardizing agricultural prospects."

She added "farmers must be compensated well for their land, rehabilitation policies must be strengthened to reassure displaced people, and farmers could perhaps be given a stake in projects set-up on land acquired from them."

Following the indictment of SEZ policy by the Congress President, whereas the Left felt that its stand was vindicated, ministers within the UPA were keen to do a U-turn and declare that they were already following these guidelines. On September 25, 2006, Commerce Minister Mr. Kamal Nath announced that "the Board of Approval for SEZ has made it mandatory that no proposal for setting up SEZs on prime agricultural land be cleared." The Agricultural Minister Mr. Sharad Pawar said: "The government's idea of acquiring land at government rates was not good. The concept of economic development by putting the farmers out on the streets is not welcome." Pawar expressed his unhappiness about the policy of state governments deciding the price at which farmers sell land to private companies. "Actually it should be between the industrialists and the farmers. If at all the government is involved, then it should ensure that the farmers get the rightful compensations and also some share (at least 12.5 percent) of the developed land."

Mrs. Sonia Gandhi's guidelines produced an electrifying effect and the UPA ministers started singing a different tune on the policy of protecting the interests of farmers.

Thirdly, a related question is about the land use. To stipulate only 25 percent land for export-related industrial purpose and the rest for infrastructure, housing, parks, golf-courses appears to be totally unjustified.

Moreover, to suggest the construction of 25,000 housing units in a multi-product SEZ implies that instead of boosting manufacturing and rendering services for exports, the developers will be given total freedom to make enormous profits from housing. It would, therefore, be proper to lay down norms of land use and insist that at least 50% land in a SEZ will be used for industrial production, 25% for related infrastructure and only 25% is made available for other facilities like schools, a hospital, a housing complex for workers employed in SEZ and recreational facilities.

Fourthly, the question of exemption from labour laws is another vital issue. In order to attract industrialists—Indian as well as foreign, state governments are over-bending to promise SEZs from exemption of labour laws. What does this imply?

This implies that state Labour Commissioners have no jurisdiction over factories in SEZs. The power of the Labour Commissioner will be transferred to the Development Commissioner and the Labour Commissioner will be required to take permission from the Development Commissioner to enter SEZ, even for inspection of 'safety and environmental norms within the factory.'

Mr. Mahesh C. Agarwal, Chairman—Managing Director of Brijbasi Hi-tech Group in his article states in a very forthright manner: "So workers are completely at the mercy of the factory owners in the SEZs, and they either have to accept the inhuman and fascist conditions prevailing therein or lose their livelihood. The working conditions in the units set-up in the SEZs are appalling, as expected and there is often no restriction even on the length of the working day." (*Sar Economist*, September 2006, p. 40)

But the irony is that the Left parties which earlier had an uncompromising stand on the application of labour laws *vis-a-vis* the Government, are also having second thoughts on this question. Indications to this effect were noted in an article titled "Marxism and Left Front government's efforts of Industrialization" published recently in the party organ *Desh Hitaishai* by Benoy Kumar, a member of the CPM Central Committee where he argues: Bengal alone cannot afford to refuse the abolition of labour laws. If it does so, industries will come up in other states, thereby adversely affecting the interests of the working class. "If states like Maharashtra, Gujarat, Karnataka and Tamil Nadu announce that they will abolish labour laws as desired by the Centre and if the working class there fails to resist such a move, what will our state government do? If we insist on maintaining labour laws in our SEZs, there will be no industries here." (*Hindustan Times*, September 19, 2006).

The attitude of both the Centre and the State Governments on the application of labour laws is very questionable. The blame game is of no use, the states putting the responsibility on the Centre and vice versa. The real issue is: When SEZs are provided land by the Government at below the market rate, they are provided exemption from a host of taxes, custom duty, excise duty, service tax, VAT, etc. are these not sufficient incentives for them as against non-SEZ industrial units, then what is the justification of providing exemption from labour laws. Giving the industrialists power to exploit the workers and force them to work in inhuman conditions shall be violative of Article 38(1) of our Constitution which states: "The State shall strive to promote the welfare of the people by securing and protecting as effectively as it may a social order in which justice, social, economic and political, shall inform all the institutions of the national life." Should the state forget its duties to provide citizens the 'right to work' and ensuring a 'decent standard of life' and full enjoyment of leisure?

Lastly, the country will be divided into two separate groups—SEZ and non-SEZ areas. Experience of locational preference with huge relative reduction in taxes and duties as also cost reduction on account of exemption of labour laws shall prompt industrial units to shift from non-SEZ to SEZ areas. This implies that net additions to total investment will be less than the projected level by the advocates of SEZ.

To conclude: There is a need to have a reconsideration of SEZ approach to industrialization and export promotion. The Finance Minister and the Reserve Bank of India do not see any justification in having a system of differential taxation in SEZ and non SEZ areas causing an erosion of tax revenues ranging from Rs. 1,00,000 crores to Rs. 1,75,000 crores according to different estimates. Moreover, the earlier policy of exempting tax revenues if new industrial units in the hinterland are set up to mitigate the additional costs required was justified. But most of the SEZ units are planned around the metropolitan towns. For instance, Reliance wants to set-up Maha Mumbai SEZ, the second largest SEZ in the world—after Shenzhen in China— spread over an area of 35,000 acre. Nearly 100 villages covering 1.5 lakh families face eviction in view of the notices served by the Maharashtra Government. A government official admitted: "The entire region is the states' rice bowl. Almost every family in these villages cultivates paddy though majority of them are small and marginal farmers making land acquiring process more complicated." (Report in *Economic Times*, 2nd October 2006). Reliance has also proposed another multi-product SEZ in Haryana spread over 25,000 acres. Similar proposals of setting up SEZs in the vicinity of major metropolitan towns are also under consideration of state governments. Why should the government subsidise the big business houses—both Indian and foreign—at the cost of the farmers, is the moot question.

Earlier the poor villagers have been suffering due to big power dams and Narbada Bachao Andolan (NBA) took up the cause of their rehabilitation. Social reformers have now taken up the cause of displacement of poor farmers by providing very low rates of compensation for acquiring their land. For instance, Jagatsinghpur steel project by POSCO has already been allotted 1,100 acres of agricultural land for Rs. 25,000 per acre falling within the fertile delta of Mahanadi by the Government of Orissa. This is a very low rate of compensation for the ousted farmers.

Moreover, the experience of China suggests that the Chinese hinterland is still lagging, now even more so against the glamorous coastal regions. The

Chinese have, therefore, decided to have a course correction in Eleventh Five Year Plan.

While in the Approach Paper of the 11th Five Year Plan, India set-up as its primary goal "Towards Faster and More Inclusive Growth," in practice through the policy on SEZ we are setting up "iniquitous enclaves" of development which will result in "exclusive growth." Bringing out the flaws in SEZ Policy, *Business Line* in its editorial states: "The history of discrete or locational tax exemptions suggests a shift in investments not an addition; firms tend to move productive capacities to low-tax regions instead of adding fresh investments. . . . But even if that were not the case, the SEZ concept is still faulty because it creates opportunities for the few. . . . Historically, the export processing zones have been poor exporters and even poorer foreign exchange earners compared to domestic tariff area; now, the SEZs are required to perform even less in terms of forex earning while being given more, precisely at a time when the overall economy with all its constraints and bottlenecks is performing excellently." (*Business Line* editorial, September 26, 2006 titled Iniquitous Enclaves). On the one hand, India intends to emerge as a first-rate super-economic power by 2020, but on the other hand, it will have third-rate labour with deteriorating economic conditions with no income security or employment security or social security in SEZs which are destined to become industrial enclaves with super-profits. Does this all match with our concept of so-called inclusive growth? Whereas the ILO has set 'decent work' as their goal, we are generating forces which lead to 'indecent work' as their goal. It may be noted the Second National Commission on Labour in its Report (2002) clearly stated that it was not in favour of granting any exemption from labour laws in respect of establishments in export promotion zones or special economic zones.

Mr. Rahul Bajaj, Chairman, Bajaj Auto Ltd. criticizing the SEZ policy mentions: "I believe that on the balance the SEZ Act and rules currently in force may not ensure that the nation would gain significantly. As they stand, they are possibly providing incentives to units in SEZs disproportionate to the incremental benefits that may accrue to the nation." (Some straight talk on SEZs, *Economic Times*, October 4, 2006). There is a need to impose stiffer obligations on SEZas so as to justify the incentives. "With a stiffer export obligation of 60-75% of production, 60-75% reservation of land for production units and logical and fairer land acquisition process, SEZs may serve the ends that they should serve."

India should also give special attention to the fact that while giving preference to the objective of export promotion, it does not weaken the objective of 'food security'. Mr. Mangal Rai, Director-General, Indian Council of Agricultural Research has drawn attention to the question of food security and warned: "Since land area is limited and agricultural land is the most precious, one must be very careful. One will have to take into cognizance the long-term effects of the food security of this country. Food security is an integral part of national security."

CHAPTER

10

Development, Displacement and Rehabilitation

I. SEZ EXPERIMENT OF WEST BENGAL

After the introduction of the concept of Special Economic Zones as the vehicles of rapid industrialization, a mania has gripped several state governments to follow this route of rapid industrial progress. Big business houses—Indian as well as foreign multinationals—have formed a beeline to get big proposals approved by the State. CPI(M) led West Bengal Government is the single state in which SEZ have become a major controversy. On the one extreme is Chief Minister Budhadeb Bhattacharjee who showed unflinching determination to push the idea forward. On the other, there was Trinmool Congress led by Mamta Banerjee who was sternly opposed to the manner in which the State Government pushed its single track agenda, more especially in Singur for Tata Small Car Project and later in Nandigram for Salim Chemicals Project. The chief instrument employed to acquire land for big business houses was Land Acquisition Act of 1894 which authorised the state government to acquire land for "public purpose."

It would of interest to understand the size of acreage which was proposed to be brought under SEZ in West Bengal. According to a rough estimate prepared by D. Bandyopadhya, former secretary, Rural Development, West Bengal who played a seminal role in implementing 'Operation Barga', it involves an acquisition of 1,40,000 acres in 9 districts which include Midnapur (37,297 acres), West Midnapur (26,134 acres),

Howrah (26,500 acres), Darjeeling (25,200 acres), South 24-Parganas (13,318 acres), North 24-Parganas (5,743 acres), Hoogly (6,247 acres), Nadia (365 acres), and Jalpaiguri (161 acres). The state government took upon itself the responsibility to acquire land and hand it over to the big business houses. CPI(M) government underplayed the resistance of the peasants to part with their land since it was the only source of livelihood. The ruthless manner in which the West Bengal Government and the CPI(M) cadres went out to suppress this resistance created a strong resistance culminating in the establishment of Save Land from Acquisition Movement.

The reign of terror let loose by CPI(M) government and cadres led to a very strong resistance and even the CPI(ML) joined hands with the peasantry. The claim made by the Chief Minister that 96 percent of the cultivators had willingly given up their land for public purpose was found patently incorrect even by the Leftist intellectuals and the Citizens Council which visited Singur and Nandigram.

Prof. Sumit Sarkar, an eminent leftist historian who visited Singur made a categorical denunciation of the CPI(M) government in the following words:

> "As a lifelong Leftist, I am deeply shocked by the recent events in countryside of West Bengal. . . . Three things became very clear, because of which the West Bengal government's version cannot be accepted. One, land far from being infertile or monocropped, as has been stated repeatedly, is extremely fertile and multi-cropped. . . . Two, there is no doubt that the vast bulk of the villagers we met are opposed to the take-over of land and most are refusing compensation. . . . Three, we found much evidence of force being employed, particularly on the night of September 25 and December 2, 2006."
>
> "Clearly, the whole thing had been done without consultation with very little transparency, and in a very undemocratic manner."

Left intellectuals and journalists who formed the Citizens Committee on Singur and Nandigram included Colin Gonsalves, senior Supreme Court Advocate, Professor Sumit Sarkar, an eminent historian, Mr. Sumit Chakravarty, Editor, *Mainstream*; Krishna Mazumdar, Delhi University and Tanikar Sarkar, Jawaharlal Nehru University. The Citizen's Committee made startling findings:

> "Our impression was that the people of Nandigram are prepared for a very hard struggle. It is being waged with remarkable communal amity and with participation from all political groups, many of whom had been CPM just the other day."
>
> "We found a determined peasant movement in Singur, peaceful so far, except for some recent attacks on the fence surrounding the land.

Villagers are determined to fight on, regardless of the costs to themselves." (*Mainstream*, February 9-15, 2007)

The Citizen's Committee concluded:

"Large segments of erstwhile CPM members and supporters are deeply alienated, against the Party and the Government. Muslims are terribly offended about misinformed aspersions cast at the Jamiat as communal and they are not satisfied by the invitation offered to their leaders by the Party leadership to come and discuss the matter. We concluded that the apprehensions of the peasants are fully justified as industries these days do not produce large number of jobs. There are alternative sites that can be acquired for industrialization without damaging agriculture and village communities."

The Citizen's Committee warned the CPM Government:

"We urge the ruling front to reconsider their land acquisition policy, to talk to all segments of the people and to listen seriously to their arguments. They need to think seriously about alternative sites for industrialization that would not lead to the displacement of peasants. *They need to think, in consultation with the people, about the alternative forms of development. Otherwise, a civil war may ensue.*" (Emphasis added, as reported in *Mainstream*, February 9-15, 2007).

Tissue of Lies by the CPM Government of West Bengal

Mr. Budhadeb Bhattacharjee, the Chief Minister made two assertions:

1. 96 percent of peasants voluntarily surrendered their land for industrialization.
2. Only one percent of the land in West Bengal is not cultivable.

The first statement that "96 percent of peasants voluntarily surrendered their land" did not go down the throat of even its allies like CPI, RSP and Forward Bloc, not to speak of the opposition party like Trinmool Congress, social activists like Medha Patkar and even left intellectuals who openly opposed the policies of the CPM.

Secondly, according to the Bureau of Applied Economics and Statistics of West Bengal, the uncultivable land is a little over 18 percent. In absolute terms, it is over 1.5 million hectares which means 3.7 million acres. D. Bandyopadhay therefore asserts: "How could the Chief Minister so brazenly make an incorrect statement that no uncultivable land was available for the purpose of industrialization in West Bengal?" The loss of multi-cropped fertile land would mean loss in terms of foodgrains production. Experts are of the view that the average production of foodgrains in West Bengal is a little over 1 tonne per acre. This would imply that West Bengal's loss of foodgrains from SEZ would be of the order of 1.5 lakh tonnes. This can create a serious shortage of foodgrains in the coming years.

Issues Related to Land Acquisition *versus* Livelihood

The Government of West Bengal used the Land Acquisition Act, 1894 to acquire land for industries. The plea given by the Government is the concept of 'public purpose'. The concept of public purpose in the view of the economists is related to the provision of 'public goods' and this includes highways, bridges, rural roads, hydro-electric dams, schools, colleges, universities, hospitals, etc. In other words, it includes land acquired for the creation of economic and social infrastructure. Professor Manoj Pant of Jawaharlal Nehru University, therefore, questions the public purpose concept of West Bengal Government. He asserts: "One can classify in this (public purpose) category national highways, bridges, rural roads, etc. But obviously the state acquiring land for a "Tata Car" or "Salim Chemicals" can hardly be justified under "public interest." (*Economic Times*, January 10, 2007)

Second issue pertains to loss of livelihood and the compensation. There is no doubt that the principal source of livelihood of farmers is land, and if land is acquired, they lose the source of their livelihood. Not only that, in West Bengal, the land is actually cultivated by Sharecroppers (bargadars) who are not the owners of land. They also lose their livelihood. The question is: Should the farmers and sharecroppers together be rehabilitated or should the state take care of only the land owners? Medha Patekar who spearheaded the Narmada Bachao Andolan says: "Displacement has been invariably without rehabilitation. The land Acquisition Act, 1894, a law made during the British rule, is still being used in a shameless manner for acquiring not only properties, but also the livelihood of people in exchange for meager amount of cash." (Acres for heartache, *Hindustan Times*, 29th January, 2007)

Thus, the issue pertains to the quantum and manner of compensation. Should the amount of compensation be decided by the State or should it be related to the prevailing market value of land? Should sharecroppers whose livelihood is also affected be compensated? If so, the manner and quantum of compensation should be decided on this basis.

Market Value *versus* State-Regulated Value

The experience of acquisition of land for SEZ suggests that Reliance Industries is buying land at a rate of about Rs. 20 lakhs per acre for its Haryana SEZ project while the open market price is Rs. 28 lakhs per acre. But the situation in Dadri and Greater NOIDA areas of UP is much worse where the farmers have to sell land at about Rs. 10-12 lakhs per acre whereas the average market price is Rs. 25 lakhs. It means that the farmers get between 40-50 percent of the market price as compensation. This is downright unjust, but the strange fact is that the so-called "Samajwadi Party" was on the side of industrialists and in the name of industrialization, it permitted the industrialists to exploit the farmers. Thus, it ruthlessly suppressed the agitation by farmers in Dadri and did not permit former Prime Minister V.P. Singh to enter Dadri.

In West Bengal, the CPI(M) government started acquisition of land on behalf of the industrialists at a regulated price which was much lower than the market price. It employed the arm of the state to force peasants to surrender land for SEZ projects at Singur and Nandigram which led to massive protests and forced the CPI(M) government to retreat. The movement against the SEZ project gathered massive momentum throughout West Bengal and even the Left Front Chairman Biman Bose recently observed that if the agitation continues further and if the ideological moorings are allowed to be loosened even more, the CPI(M) could be doomed for ever.

The lesson learnt by the CPI(M) appears to be that over-enthusiasm shown by the State Government in favour of industrialization could result in a political backlash which the party cannot afford since it threatens its own existence. Since bargadars (Sharecroppers) were the main force behind the uprising in Singur and Nandigram, the CPI(M) Government is considering a New Formula which puts bargadars (Sharecroppers) at par with landholders.

At present, while landowners get 75 percent of the value of land according to market price as compensation, bargadars get only 25 percent. This is creating a lot of resentment as it is the bargardars who till land and take 75 percent of the crop while giving 25 percent to the owners. The Government is considering a formula to increase compensation for bargadars to 75 percent to bring them at par with landowners. In other words compensation will be 150 percent of value of land. While 25 percent of the additional burden would be borne by the Government, the remaining burden will be borne by the industrial house.

Although a final shape has not been given to the New Formula, the CPI(M) hopes that if the industrial houses agree to bear the additional burden of compensation, the Government would be able to take the wind out of the sails of the opposition.

The massive agitation in Singur and Nandigram in West Bengal had its repercussions in other states like Orissa, Maharashtra, Haryana, etc. The farmers are becoming increasing conscious about their exploitation by industrial houses and developers. Therefore, the attempt to deny land and protest against forced acquisition. The Orissa Government has informed POSCO that it will not use force to persuade farmers to vacate their lands for POSCO's steel project. The onus of acquiring land will henceforth be on POSCO and the POSCO officials have to inform people about rehabilitation and resettlement packages and persuade farmers to give up their lands voluntarily.

Maha Mumbai SEZ is to be built on 11,696 hectares or nearly 29,000 acres of land and this project will displace one lakh persons from 45 villages. Obviously, awakened by protests elsewhere, the people likely to be ousted from the villages expressed their resentment before the Parliamentary Panel on Special Economic Zones that visited the State.

2. POINTS OF CONSENSUS ON REHABILITATION REGARDING SEZ

The controversy over land acquisition for SEZ and the churning going on at various levels has resulted in a broad consensus on the following points:

1. States should give preference to barren and wastelands for SEZ purposes. Although the industrial houses prefer plots near metropoles where infrastructure is available, it would be a much better policy to utilize wastelands and reduce costs of acquisition and develop infrastructure in barren and wastelands. After all Jamshedji Tata established TELCO & TISCO in a barren and uninhabited area.
2. Even if the acquisition of land becomes necessary for the purpose of minimum area requirement for the SEZ, then single crop land should be acquired and double-crop or multi-crop land should not exceed 10 percent of the total area required for SEZ.
3. The area required for each SEZ should be re-examined and a minimum of 50% should be for industrial purpose and the rest for other purposes, instead of having only 25% area for industrial purpose. In case, this is not done, then SEZ becomes a 'land grab scheme' through the backdoor". As Mr. Arvind Kumar, IT Secretary, Maharashtra Government said: "SEZ are nothing but tools for the elite to grab more property and should cease to exist. Such land grab practices do not augur well for this country and should be stopped immediately."
4. Landowners of both monocrop and double-crop or multi-crop land should, besides compensation, be allotted small plots in the vicinity of SEZ so that when the area develops as an industrial centre, they can set- up auxiliary workshops for repair and maintenance, or create other ancillary units or services nearby the SEZ area. This will at a later stage help the flow of income to persons who sacrificed their land.
5. In case, it is not possible to allot plots of land to the persons displaced by industry, it should be incumbent on the industrial houses to train at least one member of the family and provide a job in the industry so that the loss of livelihood is compensated in a significant manner. Alternatively, the displaced farmers and share croppers should be given shares in the industrial firm with a lock-

in period of 20-30 years since the purpose is to provide for long-term benefits to ousters.

6. it would not be wise to provide tax concessions for all businesses in SEZs. This would mean a loss of revenue of the order of Rs. 1,60,000 crores. Moreover, it will create a division between SEZ and non-SEZ companies and there would be a shift of investment from non-SEZ to SEZ. This will imply less real increase of investment for the country, though the advocates of SEZ would claim much higher increase. In this connection, Gujarat Chief Minister Narendra Modi has suggested that only 'core activities' in SEZ should be eligible for tax concessions. All other services like accommodation and hotels, restaurants for employees or recreational facilities should not be eligible for tax exemptions. There should be no encouragement to a real estate play, but support to solid, substantial business which enhances the manufacturing capacity of the economy.
7. Those industrial houses which agree to develop barren and wasteland for industrial purposes should be provided additional concessions and support by the Government in the form of speedy development of infrastructure.

Following nation-wide protests over land-acquisition by states for SEZs, the Central Government imposed a freeze on fresh approvals of SEZ, despite the fact that a number of developers had bought machinery and employed workers. The Central Government's promise of finalizing a new rehabilitation policy to provide better compensation to the displaced has been put on hold in view of elections to various state assemblies. There appears to be threat of a democratic backlash. This temporary and intentional delay is understandable. But the real issue is: what should be the guiding principle of the new rehabilitation policy? In words of President John F. Kemedy, whether you are administering a government or managing a business, ask not what farmers can do for you; ask what you can do for them. Following this principle alone can usher in 'inclusive growth', the main objective outlined in the Eleventh Five Year Plan.

3. IS THE SEZ POLICY FLAWED?

The over-enthusiasm to push the SEZ policy as the instrument of rapid industrialization has come against the roadblocks, more especially in West Bengal, where Chief Minister Buddhadeb Bhattacharya tried to ride rough shod over the livelihood of thousands of landowners, bargadars and landless Labourers. It was a threat to their livelihoods since fertile multi-cropped land was the principal source of their sustenance. Instead of listening to their grievances and concerns and finding solution of the problem in a democratic manner, the CPI (M) government tried to crush their resistance by sheer brute force. Over two thousand police men along with CPI (M) cadres on the 14th March, 2007 launched an unprecedented offensive, villagers were beaten, their houses were torched and a wave of ruthless suppression was unleashed to teach a lesson to those who were determinedly opposing land acquisition by the Government in Nandigram. As reported in the Press, the police firing led to the killing of 14 persons and hundreds were injured. Mr. Gopalkrishna Gandhi, Governor of West Bengal expressing his 'sense of cold horror' decided to do some plain speaking. "I was saddened at what I saw here. People are in shock. They are not getting proper treatment. Some of them need to be shifted to Kolkata." Normally, the Governors do not to choose to do plain speaking, but the tragedy at Nandigam was so gruesome, that the Governor, the chosen man of the Left front government, decided to question: "What is the public purpose served by the use of force that we have witnessed today?" The Calcutta High Court took *suo motto* cognizance of tragic incidents at Nandigram and ordered CBI to probe the incident.

The alliance partners of the Left Front the CPI, the Revolutionary Socialist Party (RSP) and Forward Block (FB) accused the Chief Minister: "The CM is running a one-party rule in the State instead of a coalition government." They described the police action in Nandigram as disgrace for the Left government. The Chief Minister kept all the alliance partners in dark about vital policy decisions. The CPI, RSP and FB threatened to pull out of the Government if such a state of affairs continued in the coalition. The CPI (M) patriarch Mr. Jyoti Basu in a very curt manner told Buddhadeb Bhattacharya: "What they (CPI, RSP and Forward Bloc) are saying is right. I also feel that the CPI (M) is running a one-party rule in the state. It does not look like a coalition government at all." Chiding the Chief Minister, Mr. Basu said: "Who ordered the firing? Who decided to send the police? You must own up responsibility of what has happened. . . . You are running this government in an arrogant manner." The pressure of the alliance partners of the Left-front Government was so strong that the CPI(M) government had to buckle in and announce that all SEZ proposals are put on hold. It will wait for the Centre to announce a "socially balanced" SEZ Policy.

In a very strong article, Mr. A.B. Bardhan, General Secretary, CPI said: CPI was of the view that SEZs were neither necessary not inevitable for the growth of industries. "It is only a method by which monopolists, MNCs and big businesses can grab large tracts of land and indulge in real estate speculation and at the same time enjoy a package of concessions."

The impact of events at Singur and Nandigram has begun to be felt in other states as well. In Orissa, the Government has washed its hands off land acquisition and told POSCO to enter into deals with farmers directly for land acquisition. In Maha Mumbai SEZ, the farmers are not willing to accept Reliance Package of land acquisition. A visit to 45 villages by a team of the *Economic Times* revealed that the ground reality is very different. The villagers had the same grievances. Firstly, the company was eyeing for their prime land. Second, the price Reliance is paying is a pittance. As against

Reliance offer of Rs. 10 lakh per acre, Cidco was offering Rs. 5 crores for the same piece of land. Third, they are promising job to only one member in the family. As of now, the whole family including all sons, their wives and kids are making a living out of the land. We earn enough for all.

The basic question: Is the SEZ policy flawed? There is ample evidence to show that there is a need to have a fresh look in view of feedback from affected farmers, share croppers etc. There are various points while need consideration:

1. According to the Statistical Abstract (2002) of the Central Statistical Organisation, India has 18 million hectares (44.5 million acres) of culturable waste lands and 25 million hectares (61.7 million acres) of fallow lands. Taken together, they account for 43 million hectares (106.2 million acres) of culturable waste and fallow lands. Obviously, there is enough waste and fallow land available for industrialization. Instead of setting up SEZ on multi-cropped land, it would be advisable to use waste and fallow lands for the purpose. This shall reduce the cost of land acquisition which can be used to develop infrastructure. The industrialists, however, have to move away from the Metropoles, but this is what it should be because such a policy will assure minimum birth pangs and also reduce concentration of industries. The state can help and even subsidise the development of infrastructure in the form of roads, electric energy, water supply, etc.
2. The policy of granting massive tax concessions in the form of exemptions from excise, custom duties, service tax and corporation tax should be abandoned. This, according to a Finance Ministry estimate, is expected to result in a revenue loss of Rs. 1,60,000 crores. This amount should be used to build infrastructure so as to facilitate the process of industrialization.
3. SEZ should not be declared foreign territory and exempt from the application of all labour laws. After all, what is the purpose of industrialization? It is to provide employment in industry and wean away persons dependent on agriculture. Exemption from labour laws is likely to create inhuman conditions of employment. This cannot be the policy of a welfare state which is not tired of talking about improving the life of the *Aam Admi* (common man).

States have now sent the ball in the court of the Central Government to frame a "socially balanced" policy on SEZ. It is no use blindly following China which has only 5 such special economic zones, but in India, there is a plan to have 362 special economic zones. Unlike China, in a democratic country like India, it is not possible to ruthlessly muzzle the voice of the displaced people, in favour of generating profits for the industrial and business classes and developers.

The Central government is drawing its own lessons from the setbacks suffered in elections in Maharashtra, Punjab and Uttarakhand. The Group of Ministers on SEZ is likely to opt for a following policy frame:

(a) The government should not be seen as a middleman in the land acquisition process.
(b) A "strong stress" should be laid on fallow and wastelands instead of farmlands to build industrial projects.
(c) Instead of compensating only landowners, the Government should take care of the interests of displaced land owners, bargadars (share croppers) and agricultural labourers as well.
(d) Instead of treating the farmers as the enemies of industrialization, a more harmonious relationship need to be developed between farmers, industrial and business houses and developers by including them in a more significant manner in the process of development.
(e) Even if it become inevitable to acquire certain lands, the displacement and rehabilitation package along with the process of implementation shall be publicly announced to take care of the concerns of the affected parties.

There is a need to have a course correction of the flawed SEZ policy to save the country from conflict and pave the way for a smooth process of industrialization. A U-turn from a policy of land to the tiller to a policy of land to the miller can boomerang on the State if it decides to disregard the interests of farmers, share croppers and landless labourers and also impact food security in the country.

4. SOME RECENT DEVELOPMENTS IN THE EVOLUTION OF SEZ POLICY

Following clashes in Nandigram and Singur in West Bengal, the issue of developing a new SEZ Policy was referred to the Central Government. On the recommendations of a Group of Ministers, the Government has, as a first initiative laid down two conditions:

Firstly, the Government has prescribed a ceiling of 5,000 hectare for any SEZ proposal. State Governments may, however, prescribe lower ceiling.

Secondly, a minimum of 50 percent of the land has been set as minimum processing area. (Although originally only 25 percent of land was prescribed as processing area, later it was enhanced to 35 percent)

But other issues have not yet been resolved. In the meanwhile, opposition to acquire land spread to Orissa, where a giant project like the POSCO mines and steel is under implementation. Even resistance by farmers developed in the Mukesh Ambani's Navi Mumbai Zone SEZ. Not only that, in Haryana, the farmers are demanding higher compensation for acquiring land and also a strong and meaningful Resettlement and Rehabilitation Policy for those whose livelihood would be affected.

In India, so far 362 SEZ proposals have been formally approved by the Department. Of these, 133 have been notified and 229 proposals were cleared for notification. Decision on Mukesh Ambani's Navi Mumbai Zone has also been approved while imposing certain conditions..

The major charges levelled by the resistance movement to SEZ are:

First, driven by private investment decision, it has no limits other than profit perception. It is, therefore, necessary to reconsider the meaning of public purpose so as to expand the notion of "public purpose" to include infrastructure and public utility facilities.

The State must evolve new norms of compensation for an expanded list of affected persons, which should include owners of land and also tenant cultivators who are the principal producers in agriculture.

The basic issue is to further the interests of the society by promoting the process of industrialization, and also ensure fairplay to the seller (the farmers) and other stakeholders like tenants whose livelihood would be threatened. Mr. Ashok Upadhyay poses the problem in the right perspective when he asserts: In India, the economic miracle has engendered a dramatic reversal of factor supply, "capital is available on tap, land, is not, in any case not for the requirements of the next wave of economic growth. Unless it can reconcile conflicting interests over land acquisition consensually and transparently, New Delhi must expect more clashes such as those at Nandigram and Kalinganagar and Pune.: (*Business Line,* Has development landed India in a crisis?, May 18, 2007)

The Government is working on a proposal under which people giving up their land could get 20 percent of rehabilitation grant in the form of shares of companies for which land has been acquired. Besides this, preference in handing out the contracts from the units, in shops and wage employment will be given to affected persons.

Secondly, the applicability of Resettlement and Rehabilitation (R&R) Policy is to be enlarged to include all cases of involuntary displacement—not merely those hit by project displacement but also those losing houses, livelihood and adversely affected otherwise.

Thirdly, the proposed Land Acquisition Amendment Bill should redefine public purpose to include strategic purposes relating to navy, military and airforce and any other work vital to the State. This would cover public infrastructure such as electricity, communication, mining, water supply and public facilities.

Fourthly, it also proposed to have public purpose include cases of "persons" (meaning any company or association or body of individuals, whether incorporated or not) where land is required for purposes "useful for the general public."

There can be controversy over the last category "useful for the general public," because the Government has lot of discretion and it can declare any undertaking to qualify for SEZ under it. However, there is no final word on it as yet as the debate is going on and the Government has to make up its mind about the various criteria for determining public purpose.

There are some basic differences between China and India on the development of SEZ. Firstly, China set-up its first SEZ in 1980 and thereafter developed a total of only 5 SEZs and all were promoted by the Government. In India, out of 362 SEZ, none of those who have been formally approved is to be developed by the Government. This has given a strong feeling that Government is pandering to the interests of big private sector companies and developers by announcing a very large number of tax concessions and also declaring SEZs as foreign territory for non-applicability of labour laws, it is not advisable to give foreign territory status to SEZ units.

Secondly, the SEZs were established at strategic locations in China where they were close to ports or major industrial locations, so that they could fulfil the objective of promoting exports. But in India, SEZs have been sanctioned in a very large number of locations and without a focused purpose. Consequently, people have doubts over the real intent behind SEZ.

Thirdly, over-enthusiasm shown by the Government to permit SEZ in a variety of products and forcing large acquisition of land to be transferred to big business, Indian as well as foreign, resulted in the creation of mistrust about the intentions of the Government. People were not convinced that there would be large scale employment generation in SEZs. Rather the perception that got strengthened was that the creation of SEZ units will imply greater loss of jobs and livelihood for the poor and relatively much smaller increase of jobs. In other words, the net employment effect of SEZ was perceived as negative.

To sum up: India has been carrying forward the process of industrialization since the Second Five Year Plan started in 1956. Big industrial units were established in steel, fertilizers, shipbuilding, aircraft manufacture and several other basic and heavy industries related to infrastructure, and large tracts of land were acquired. But Government had established a relation of trust and thus, the process moved on smoothly, because it was motivated by 'public purpose'. Moreover, for industrial units to be established in backward areas, Government provided incentives and tax concessions. Consequently, there was enthusiasm about industrialization of the country. Private sector also got strengthened to set-up units, once basic infrastructure was made available.

The Government has failed to create a sense of enthusiasm and motivation among the people about SEZs as the major vehicles of industrialization. Rather they are seen as promoting 'crony capitalism' in the country, as symbols of generating inequalities and totally inclined towards MNCs and big Business Houses to earn huge profits. There is, therefore, a need for course correction. SEZ alone cannot be the answer for rapid growth. They can only be supplements in the process of growth. If this view is acceptable, there is a need to bring about a balance between SEZ and non-SEZ units and thus, rationalization of incentives and tax concessions has to be undertaken, rather than tilting the balance only in favour of SEZ units.

The basis difference between China and India is that whereas China operates under a single party rule, India has a vibrant multi-party democracy. In this political structure, the Government cannot ignore the perceptions of the people towards 'welfare' and 'public purpose'. Consequently, it would be prudent to develop a unique SEZ model within the socio-political framework of the country, rather than blindly imitating China.

> "Do not sell your fertile land for any SEZ or for any economic activity. I do not want to see any farmer landless. I know what it means as I too come from a farming family." He said at a function recently. While acknowledging the importance of SEZs for growth, he said instead of acquiring fertile lands at government rates, official agencies and industry should make farmers their partners : 'Let them give them equity shareholding according to their land ownership at existing market value.'"
>
> —A.P.J. Abdul Kalam
> Former President of India
> as reported in *Hindustan Times*,
> 22nd December 2007

CHAPTER

11

Parliamentary Standing Committee Report on Special Economic Zones

Parliamentary Standing Committee on Special Economic Zones (SEZs) consisting of 31 members submitted its Report in June 2007. The Committee had representatives from the Congress, RJD, CPI-M, CPI, Trinmool Congress, Samajwadi Party and BJP. Besides the political parties, representatives from various major ministries, trade unions, corporate houses like WIPRO, INFOSYS, Reliance and some NGOs deposed before the Committee, chaired by senior BJP leader Murli Manohar Joshi. The unique feature of the Report is that it was able to reconcile the views of divergent groups and thus develop a unanimous report which is considered as exhaustive, democratic and fair to all stakeholders taking into view their concerns and those of the country.

I. FINDINGS AND RECOMMENDATIONS OF THE STANDING COMMITTEE

It would be of interest to study the findings and recommendations of the Report.

The concept of Special Economic Zones (SEZs) is not new since they were considered as growth catalysts with the philosophy of export-led growth in several countries like China Indonesia, Philippines, Iran, Jordan, Poland, Pakistan, South Korea, Thailand, Russia, Kazakhstan, Ukraine, etc. Even USA had around 285 Free Trade zones. The total number of SEZs in the world is around 3,000, though China had only 6 of them along the coastal region, being operated by the Government.

In India, while passing the SEZ Act in May 2005, the following objectives of SEZs were laid down:

- Generation of additional economic activity;
- Promotion of exports of goods and services;
- Promotion of investment from domestic and foreign sources;
- Creation of employment opportunities; and
- Development of infrastructure facilities.

After the promulgation of the SEZ Act, the government cleared 401 proposals, (237 "formal approvals" and 164 "in-principle" approvals).

But, as the Committee notes, "the reception to SEZs among various Indian stakeholders has not been on the expected lines. There have been voices of dissent, and at same places violent protests. A section of the farmer community, whose lands are being acquired for setting up SEZs, is particularly agitated and aggrieved with the policy. *There is an imperative need to understand the cause of the farmers' agitation and grievance.*" (p. 117)

Undue Haste in Approving SEZ Proposals

The Government, more especially the Commerce Ministry has been guilty of approving SEZ proposals in haste, without examining the proposals in detail and taking care of the comments of State governments. The Committee, therefore feels that *no further SEZs should be notified till the SEZs Act and the Rules made thereunder have been amended in such a manner that would make it people-friendly, besides the objective of export-led industrial growth.* (p. 118)

Concerns of the Ministry of Agriculture

The Ministry of Agriculture stated that total cultivated land in the country decreased from 185 million hectares in 1980, to 183 million hectares in 2003. The per capita availability of land declined from 0.27 hectare to 0.18 hectare, and non-agricultural use of land increased from 19.66 million hectares to 24.48 million hectares during the same period.

During 1980-81 and 1990-91, the average annual increase in non-agricultural use of land was 1.68 lakh hectares, whereas during the 5-year period 1999-2000 to 2003-04, the average annual increase in non-agricultural use became 2.25 lakh hectares.

During the last few years, the average overall productivity of land especially, cereals, coarse cereals and pulses, etc. has been stagnant. But 127 million cultivators and 107 million agricultural labourers are dependent on land for their livelihood. Diversion of agricultural land to non-agricultural purposes would be detrimental to the food security of the country. Moreover, it is estimated that diversion of 1,000 hectares of cultivated land to non-agricultural use can deprive 900 cultivators and 760 agricultural labourers of their livelihood.

The National Commission on Farmers headed by Dr. M.S. Swaminathan, the world renowned agricultural scientist also emphasized the importance of conserving agriculture land in the following terms:

> "Prime farm-land must be conserved and should not be diverted for non-agricultural purposes like the Special Economic Zones. Such special programmes should be assigned on waste and/or land affected by salinity and other abiotic stresses. . . . It is in our national interest that agriculture and industry both prosper in a mutually reinforcing manner." (p. 35)

Recommendations of the Standing Committee

In view of the over-whelming weight of the evidence, the Standing Committee recommended:

(i) There should preferably be a ban on the use of irrigated double crop or multi-crop land for setting up SEZs.
(ii) Normally, only waste and barren lands should be used for setting up SEZs.
(iii) If it becomes unavoidable to make use of cultivated land, only single-crop, rain-fed land should be used. The percentage of such land should not exceed 20% of the total area of a multi-product SEZ. In respect of SEZs other than multi-product ones, the ceiling could be 40%.
(iv) It should be mandatory for the Developer to obtain permission of the State Government for purchasing single crop cultivable land for SEZ use.

"With regard to availability of uncultivable land, as per land use classification of the country, barren and uncultivable land is available to the extent of 18 million hectares. In many of the coastal states, land near the coast is saline, which is not good for cultivation. This is the area where SEZs or any other industrial enterprise can be set-up. This will not affect our food security. China has developed SEZs in the coastal areas." (p. 39)

The Standing Committee was surprised to note that the Ministry of Agriculture is not represented on the Board of Approval for SEZ. Being an important stakeholder, the Ministry of Agriculture must be represented on the Board.

(i) Release of Land Locked in Closed Industrial Units

The Committee noted the fact that recommendations for liquidation of 1,254 private sector units, 31 Central PSUs and 41 State PSUs were pending in various High Courts. The Government may consider unlocking and recycling of land and assets of closed industrial units under liquidation. This available unlocked land of the closed units can be used for setting up SEZs by a suitable mechanism. Similarly, land acquired for Growth Centres and other schemes, which have not been found sustainable, may be diverted for SEZs.

(ii) Minimum and Maximum Area for Various Types of SEZ

The SEZ Act prescribes a minimum area for various types of SEZs but does not prescribe any maximum area for them. The Standing Committee has laid down a maximum area limits as well. (Refer Table 11.1 on p. 223)

The Standing Committee held the view that under the present system, the Developers may be tempted to acquire more area than is necessary, particularly for developing profitable support activities in the non-processing area. It is, therefore, necessary to prescribe a maximum area also for various types of SEZs, with the condition that at least 50% of the area will be used as "processing area." This condition should not be relaxable.

(iii) Checking the Mad Rush for IT SEZs

The Committee noted that 148 out of 237 SEZs so far were IT SEZs. This mad rush of IT SEZs was due to the attempt by the IT units to avail of the benefit of tax holidays for 10 years under the SEZ Act, which otherwise cannot be availed by the IT companies beyond 2009. The Committee is of the view that if the existing tax benefits to the IT sector are extended for ten years, this mad rush for SEZs in the IT Sector would automatically stop. *The Committee recommended that the Government should take a decision an extending the tax holiday to IT sector for a further period of 10 years to control this situation.*

(iv) Putting a Cap on SEZs Region-wise

The state-wise distribution of 237 approved SEZ proposals reveals that only four states taken together, namely Maharashtra, Andhra Pradesh, Karnataka and Tamil Nadu, account for 146 SEZs, i.e. over 60% of total SEZ approvals. On the other hand, the states like Bihar or North Eastern States have not received any such proposals.

The Committee noted the tendency of concentration of SEZs in already developed states and regions. This is not in consonance with our accepted goal of balanced regional development. The Committee, therefore, recommended that *there is a need for putting over-all and region-wise caps on the SEZs. These caps can be revised after a few years, considering the experience of the functioning of SEZ.*

TABLE 11.1
Minimum Area for Various Types of SEZs

	Type	*Minimum Area*	*Minimum Area for Special States/UTs*
	(1)	*(2)*	*(3)*
1.	Multi-product	1,000 hectares	200 hectares
2.	Multi-services	100 hectares	100 hectares
3.	Sector Specific	100 hectares	50 hectares
4.	IT	10 hectares and minimum built up area of 1 lakh sq. meters.	10 hectares and minimum built up area of 1 lakh sq. meters.
5.	Gems and Jewellery	10 hectares and minimum built up area of 50,000 sq. meters.	10 hectares and minimum built up area of 50,000 sq. meters.
6.	Bio-tech and Non-conventional energy*	10 hectares and minimum built up area of 40,000 sq. meters.	10 hectares and minimum built up area of 40,000 sq. meters.
7.	Free Trade and Warehousing Zone (FTWZ)	40 hectares and minimum built up area of 1 lakh sq. meters.	40 hectares and minimum built up area of 1 lakh sq. meters..

* Includes solar energy equipment/cell, but excluding SEZs for non-conventional energy production and manufacturing.

Source : Parliamentary Standing Committee on Commerce, 83rd Report on the *Functioning of Special Economic Zones (2007)*, p. 126.

TABLE 11.2

Proposed Maximum Area Limits for Various Types of Special Economic Zones

Type	*Maximum Area*		*Maximum Area for Special States/UTs*
	with an element of cultivable land	*Only waste land*	
1. Multi-product	2,000 ha.	5,000 ha.	500 ha.
2. Multi-services	200 ha.	500 ha.	200 ha.
3. Sector Specific	200 ha.	500 ha.	200 ha.
4. IT	20 ha.	50 ha.	20 ha.
5. Gems and Jewellery	20 ha.	50 ha.	20 ha.
6. Bio-tech and Non-conventional energy*	20 ha.	50 ha.	20 ha.
7. Free Trade and Warehousing Zone (FTWZ)	100 ha.	200 ha.	100 ha.

Note : ha stand for hectares

Source : *Op. cit.*, (2007), pp. 126-27.

(v) Need for Replacement of Land Acquisition Act, 1894 by a Modern Legislation

The Committee was of the view that *'public purpose'* as defined under the Land Acquisition Act of 1894 did not address the problems of displacement of farmers who are paid notoriously low rate of compensation for their land. Not only the land-owners, but the sharecroppers and agricultural labourers who are actually engaged in cultivation also lose their livelihoods. It is, therefore, necessary that Land Acquisition Act of 1894 be replaced by a modern legislation which should be more transparent and people-friendly and take care of the problems of the affected persons due to land acquisition.

Moreover, 'public purpose' needs to be redefined. Unless the public purpose for which the land is being acquired involves an over-riding interest like defence/national security, the acquisition should take place with the consent of affected parties. Further, a National Relief and Rehabilitation Act should be enacted to provide a comprehensive package to those deprived of their lands.

The Committee, therefore, recommended that the new policy and legislation should be finalized expeditiously. The Committee outlined the dimensions which may be kept in view while deciding new reliefs and compensation.

1. Monetary compensation should be only a part of the compensation package and should be calculated on the prevailing market rates. To ensure, this, the State Governments should prescribe minimum prices for land in various areas, which should reflect the market rate, and review/revise these periodically. Thereupon, whether the land is acquired by the Government or the SEZ developers, the acquisition/purchase price should be higher than the minimum price fixed by the Government.
2. It should be ascertained from the land-owner and his co-workers including sharecroppers and agricultural labourers, as to how they propose to resettle/rehabilitate themselves. The Government should provide assistance to the affected persons accordingly, by way of an adequate resettlement allowance, employment, training, bank loan, etc.
3. Where the impact of acquisition is felt beyond the pale of land-owners and their co-workers, provision should be made to rehabilitate the affected community as a whole.

(vi) Multi-product SEZ and the Need for Involving the Displaced Persons in the Development Process of SEZ

Multi-product SEZ, to be viable, would be in the nature of industrial townships and thus may result in massive displacement of people. It would be, therefore, more desirable if these people, instead of being compensated, become a part of the development process of SEZ. The Standing Committee recommended that this may be done in the following manner:

1. Land should be taken from the land-owners on lease so that they get a one-time lump sum premium, followed by periodic rentals for sustenance. If the land is on lease, it reverts to the lesser in case SEZ fails or is dissolved for any reason.
2. At least one family member of the land-owner should be offered employment in the SEZ venture. It should be the responsibility of the developer to arrange necessary training of that person in skill acquisition.
3. Similarly, the whole range of agricultural workers, rural artisans, etc. depending on farming activities and connected with the acquired land should be given suitable employment in the "processing" or "non-processing" areas in keeping with their skills. They should also be imparted training as necessary.
4. The feasibility of allotting equity shares to the land-owners in the Developer's Company should also be considered.

(vii) Master Plan for SEZs

The Committee has suggested that the SEZs should have a Master Plan for civic amenities, which would determine the areas for residential space, the commercial areas, the green area, roads and pathways, etc. for an integrated development of an SEZ. In this regard, Indian planners must take note of the fact that one of the earliest Chinese SEZs at Shenzhen used to be a small village and it grew to a city of 10 million within a short span of 20 years. The Government should, therefore, enunciate a clear policy with regard to governance issues pertaining to areas surrounding SEZs.

(viii) Housing for SEZ Workers

Apprehensions have been expressed that large SEZs are being planned by various developers for real estate exploitation, particularly when the location of SEZs is in the vicinity of cities like Delhi and Mumbai. The Committee recommended that provisions may be made in the SEZ Act/ Rules that assets, including housing, created in the non-processing area would meet and subserve the requirements of those working in the processing area only and not for anyone else.

The Committee further elaborated that in the giant SEZs, the residential complexes should be built, not only for the management and office staff, but also for workers. If the workers are forced to stay outside the SEZ area, it would lead to proliferation of shanty towns in the neighbouring areas.

(ix) Tax Exemptions Need Rationalization

The SEZ Act provides for exemptions, drawbacks and concessions for the entrepreneurs as well as developers of the SEZs. Private developers would be able to derive tax exemptions from direct taxes for a period of 10 years for their operations in non-processing area. Since the developer's activities do not result in enhancement of exports, such tax concessions are not justified. The Committee, therefore, recommended that fiscal incentive, unrelated to exports, should not be granted. Tax benefits should be granted only for exports activities and infrastructure development.

The Finance Ministry estimated, based upon first 70 SEZ proposals, a total loss of tax revenue worth Rs. 1,02,621 crores from 2006-07 to 2009-10. Out of this, loss of direct tax revenue was estimated to be Rs. 53,740 crores and loss of indirect taxes Rs. 48,881 crores. For 237 formally approved SEZs, the revenue loss would be of much greater magnitude. The *Committee recommended a review of tax concessions for this purpose and SEZ entrepreneurs and developers should be separated for tax concessions. By withdrawing tax concessions to developers would reduce the loss to a significant extent as also meet the purpose of export promotion for which SEZ have been designed.*

(x) Level Playing Field for Domestic Industry vis-a-vis SEZ

Fears have been expressed that that providing large number of tax concessions to SEZs results in reducing costs to SEZ entrepreneurs by 40%

to 50% and this would have negative impact on domestic industry. The SEZs could act as a disincentive and dampener for Domestic Tariff Area (DTA) business. *The Committee held the view that a level playing field should be provided to the domestic industry vis-a-vis SEZs.*

(xi) No Dilution in the Implementation of Labour Laws in SEZs

Section 49 sub-section (1) of the SEZ Act empowers the Central Government to decide if any of the provisions of the SEZ Act (other than Sub-section 54 and 56), on any other Central Act or any rules or regulations made therefore or any notification or order issued or direction given thereunder shall or shall not apply to SEZs. However, this proviso restricts the power of the Central Government to laws, rules, regulations, notifications, orders and directions relating to matters other than those relating to trade unions, industrial and labour disputes, welfare of labour, including conditions of work, provident funds, employers liability, workmen's compensation, invalidity and old-age pensions, and maternity benefits applicable in any Special Economic Zone. However, SEZ Act permits the State Governments to delegate powers under the Industrial Disputes Act to Development Commissioner and to declare SEZs as Public Utility Services. Moreover, the Model SEZ Act for the State Governments, framed by the Centre, contains a list of exemptions clauses in labour laws, including the Minimum Wages Act and the Contract Labour (Regulation and Abolition) Act.

The Standing Committee recommended that *deviation from the SEZ Act and SEZ Rules, as well as the Model Act for State Governments should be corrected, to ensure that no dilution of labour laws occurs."* (p. 139)

Moreover, it was pointed out that the functions of Grievance Redressal Officer (GRO) in a SEZ should not be performed by the Development Commissioner or any officer under him. It was suggested that the GRO should be an independent person or body, having the confidence of all the parties. The Committee opined that " *no body should be allowed to be a judge in his own cause, and, therefore, the functions of the GRO should be taken away from the Development Commissionerate by making suitable changes in the SEZ Act."* (p. 140)

"The Labour Conciliation Machinery should be separate, the Development Commissioner should not take on the role of the Labour Commissioner. He may be assisted by an officer of the State Government, who has the experience in dealing with labour issues. *The idea should be to make applicable the labour laws of the land in each SEZ."* (p. 140)

(xii) Widening the Composition of the Special Economic Zone Authority

SEZ Act provides for the constitution of a Special Economic Zone Authority (SEZA) which has the following functions: (a) the development of infrastructure in the SEZ, (b) promoting exports from the SEZ, (c) reviewing the functioning and performance of the SEZ, (d) levy user or service charges or fees or rent for the use of properties belonging to the authority, and (e) performing such other functions as may be prescribed.

Presently, SEZA comprises of six members with the Development Commissioner, as its Chairperson. Other five members include three officers of the Central Government and two entrepreneurs or their nominees, all to be nominated by the Central Government. The Standing Committee observed: "The composition of the Special Economic Zone Authority seems to be narrow, in as much as it does not appropriately represent different constituents involved in the functions of SEZs. Moreover, the provision of 1/3rd members, i.e. two including the Chairman, also seems to be inadequate.

The Standing Committee recommends that "the composition of the authority should be expanded to represent some more stakeholders. At least one nominee of the Developer, two nominees of the concerned State Government, one nominee of resident workers, one financial expert and one security expert may be included in the composition of the Authority. One half of the total members may form the quorum for its meetings." (p. 141.)

2. APPRAISAL OF THE REPORT ON SEZ FUNCTIONING

Parliamentary Standing Committee Report on the *Functioning of Special Economic Zones* is a very comprehensive and sensitive document. It is comprehensive because it takes into account consideration of food security, defence, loss of massive tax revenue due to a plethora of exemptions indiscriminately granted both to entrepreneurs and developers, composition of Board of Approvals for SEZ projects, need for replacement of Land Acquisition Act (1894) by a more modern legislation for SEZ, and providing level playing field for industry in Domestic Tariff Area (DTA) and SEZs. It is a sensitive document because it voices the concerns of the farmers, sharecroppers and other co-workers who are the stakeholders in the implementation of SEZ policy. It endeavours to build democratic structure of the Special Economic Zones Authority (SEZs) by widening its composition to include various stakeholders, in place of the bureaucratic structure of six nominees of the Central Government, without even including any representative of the State Government, developers and workers. The Report is likely to come up for discussion in the Parliament. There are certain issues which require further consideration by the Government and the people of the country, more especially the issues pertaining to labour rights, welfare and representation on the authorities of Special Economic Zone.

First issue pertains to the attitude of the State Governments towards the Standing Committee itself. It was highly distressing to note following observations of the Committee:

> *"The role of the State Government or the local administration should have been to facilitate the Sub-committee to meet the affected people, especially the farmers, who had come to express their grievances before the Sub-committee. However, they were prevented from meeting the Sub-committee by the administration staff itself.* It created the impression that the local administration at those places did not want the Sub-committee to meet the farmers and to go into the question of land use, land sale and rehabilitation. The Committee expects the State Governments to ensure that in such cases co-operation from their local administration is forthcoming." (p. 124, emphasis added)

It is really distressing to read such a straight indictment of the local administration and the State Governments. It appears that the Committee showed decorum in this regard and did not precipitate the issue then and there. In case of their search for truth, the Committee should have devised its own procedure and used some extra-ordinary measures to meet the affected farmers, by planning a visit to the villages from which the farmers had come to meet the Sub-committee.

Secondly, there are two issues which require immediate action. It has been argued that Land Acquisition Act (1894) has become outdated because it was designed by the imperialist power to facilitate acquisition of land to suit their objectives. The situation has dramatically changed after independence. Most politicians believe, and rightly so that this act needs replacements by a modern legislation. The Government also concedes the need for doing so, but has not initiated any concrete steps to prepare a draft for the consideration of the Parliament. In this context, the Standing Committee should have done a great service, had it applied its energies in preparing draft legislation. Similar is the case of framing the National Relief and Rehabilitation Act. It is now accepted by all political parties that besides the landowners, there are other stakeholders like sharecroppers, landless labourers and co-workers whose livelihood is seriously affected by displacement. It would have been in the fitness of things that the representatives of all political parties should have applied their mind to prepare the draft of Relief and Rehabilitation Act and with this, *fait accompli,* forced the government to address this issue in the interests of providing sustenance to affected persons during the interim period of their rehabilitation. Such a step would have gone a long way to resolve this important issue which has become a hindrance to progress on industrial front.

Thirdly, the question of declaring SEZ as a 'public utility service' and thus abrogating the application of Labour Laws also needed serious consideration. It is very easy for the Commerce Minister to say that export activity and thus SEZs should be declared as 'public utility' but to defend it with convincing arguments has been its shortcoming. In post-independent

India, public utilities have acquired a connotation, and expanding its frontiers to declare any activity as public utility cannot be justified, though Mr. Kamal Nath may use this term to overcome a hurdle in a very irresponsible manner. To take garb under this clause, and prevent the application of Minimum Wages Act and Contract Labour (Regulation & Abolition) Act would not stand the test of public scrutiny.

Fourthly, we present below a table prepared on the basis of data provided by the State Governments regarding the relative proportions of permanent, temporary, casual/contract labourers employed in SEZs in various states.

TABLE 11.3
Nature of Employment in SEZ

State	*Permanent*	*Temporary*	*Casual/Contract*	*Total*
Gujarat	3,206	11,143	4,752	19,101
	(16.8)	(58.1)	(24.9)	(100.0)
Madhya Pradesh	998	562	257	1,817
	(54.9)	(30.9)	(14.2)	(100.0)
Tamil Nadu	12,906	3,650	3,389	19,945
	(64.7)	(18.3)	(17.0)	(100.0)
Kerala	5,445	1,552	825	7,822
	(69.6)	(19.8)	(10.6)	(100.0)

Note : Figures in brackets are percentages of total.

Source : Compiled from 83rd Report of the Parliamentary Standing Committee (2007) on the *Functioning of Special Economic Zones.*

A close perusal of the data given in Table 11.3 reveals that Kerala had the lowest proportion of Temporary and Casual/Contract labour of the order of 30.6%, Tamil Nadu 35.3%, Madhya Pradesh 45.1% and Gujarat as high as 84.3% in this category. The basic question is: what should be the maximum permissible limit of temporary and casual/contract labourers? If labour is needed, why should security of employment be denied to it, so as to enhance the profits of entrepreneurs and developers? Does labour have a right to a reasonable share in value-added? Or should we permit the entrepreneurs and developers to amass huge wealth, while denying labour its legitimate right? The Supreme Court has already laid down guidelines that if a temporary/casual employee has worked for 240 days in a year, he/she shall have to be made permanent because it proves the continuous need of the person concerned. India, as a democratic welfare state, has to pay due attention to the problems of the oppressed and exploited, failing which democracy will cease to have any meaning for *aam admi* (common man).

Fifthly, the Standing Committee mentions in one of its recommendations: "Development Commissioner should not take on the role of Labour Commissioner." (p. 14.) But the question is: Who gave the Development Commissioner the role of the Labour Commissioner? Obviously, it is the SEZ Act. Instead, it would have been far better to recommend that SEZ Act should be amended to separate the powers of the Development Commissioner and empower the Labour Commissioner to ensure the application of Labour Laws in SEZ. This would have been more in consonance with the noble spirit with which the Report has been written.

Proposed Composition of the Special Economic Zones Authority

Development Commissioner (Chairman)	
Central Government nominees	3
Nominees of Entrepreneurs	2
Nominee of Developer	1
Nominees of State Government	2
Nominee of Resident Workers	1
Financial Experts	1
Security Expert	1

Lastly, the composition of Special Economic Zones Authority is very undemocratic. The Committee have taken note of it and recommended its expansion from six members to twelve members. However, in the proposed composition given below, entrepreneurs and developers have been provided 3 nominees, but resident workers only 1 nominee. This token representation will not ensure better labour participation. The accepted principle in Labour Economics is equality of membership between employers and labour. Following this, there should be three representatives of labour. Moreover, the history of trade unionism reveals that nominated internal members never exhibited the zeal to pursue the cause of labour in an effective manner. It is the external members who have shown better bargaining power. It is, therefore, necessary that the share of workers in SEZA be reconsidered, and it should be raised to three, one from among the workers and two representatives of trade unions. Once the principle is accepted, the modalities of representation can be worked out.

To conclude, it may be stated that the Standing Committee Report on SEZ is a path breaking document which indicates the direction in which the country must move if it wants to pursue industrialization with a human face. It is an attempt to take care of problems that are likely to arise if industrialization is pushed ruthlessly without taking care of concerns of the displaced families. In that sense, the Report does commendable service to the nation. To advance the path outlined in the Report, there are some areas in which gaps have to be filled up. In our appraisal, we have drawn attention of the policy-makers to urgently take up the question of designing a modern legislation on Land Acquisition and also framing a Relief and Resettlement Policy which helps those who are displaced, leading to a smooth transition to new sources of livelihoods.

There is the also a great need to usher in policies in the functioning of SEZ so that workers are assured a fair deal in the value added in SEZ. They cannot be treated as foreign enclaves in which entrepreneurs and developers shall have unlimited freedom to exploit labour and maximize profits.

APPENDIX

REHABILITATION AND RESETTLEMENT POLICY, 2007

People displaced from their homes for developmental projects can look forward to getting various benefits including up to 20 per cent of their compensation package in the form of shares of the project with the Government according to national policy on Rehabilitation and Resettlement (R&R) finalized by the UPA government on October 11, 2007.

With prior approval of the Government, the proportion of share can be as high as 50 percent of the rehabilitation grant and compensation amount. This package could ease resolution of disputes over land acquisition as witnessed in Tata's projects in West Bengal and Orissa; Posco's project in Orissa and other proposed special economic zones in various parts of the country.

The new policy, which replaces the National Policy on Resettlement and Rehabilitation for Project Affected Families, 2003, is aimed at striking a balance between need for land for developmental activities and protecting the interests of the land owners and others whose livelihood depends on the land involved. In other words, benefits under the new policy shall be available to all affected persons and families whose land, property or livelihood is adversely affected by land acquisition. These could be tenants, the landless, the agricultural and non-agricultural labourers, artisans, and others dependent on the land.

The benefits under the new policy include: land-for-land; preference for employment in the project to at least one person from each family; training and capacity building for suitable jobs and self-employment; scholarships for education of eligible persons from the affected families; preference to groups or co-operatives of the affected persons in the allotment of contracts and other economic opportunities in or around the project site.

The policy also entails wage employment to the willing affected persons in the construction work in the project; housing benefits including houses to the landless affected families.

It provides for financial support to the affected families for construction of shops, working sheds, transportation costs, temporary and transitional accommodation, and comprehensive infrastructural facilities and amenities including education, health care, drinking water, roads, electricity, sanitation, religious activities, cattle grazing, and other community resources.

The benefits have been linked to the Consumer Price Index.

Life-time monthly pension to the vulnerable such as the disabled, destitute, orphans, widows, unmarried girls, abandoned women, or persons above 50 years of age is also built in the package. Special provision for the STs and SCs include preference in land-for-land for STs followed by the SCs;

a tribal development plan, which will also include a programme for development for alternate fuel and non-timber forest produce resources.

R&R Committees would be formed at the district and project level with representatives from the affected families including women, voluntary organisations, panchayats and local elected representatives. There would be post-implementation social audits of the R&R schemes and plans.

For effective monitoring of the progress of implementation of R&R plans, provisions have been made for a national monitoring committee, a national monitoring cell, mandatory information sharing by the States and UTs with the national monitoring cell, and oversight committees in the Ministries/Departments concerned for each major project.

A National Rehabilitation Commission shall be set-up by the Union Government, which will be duly empowered to exercise independent oversight over the rehabilitation and resettlement of the affected families.

Highlights of the New Policy on Rehabilitation and Resettlement (2007)

- National Rehabilitation Commission, ombudsman for grievance redressal and Rehabilitation and Resettlement Committee for each project.
- Consultation with *gram sabhas* compulsory.
- Social impact Assessment of displacement of 400/200 families in plains/hill areas.
- Tribal Development Plan for displacement of 200-plus tribal families.
- If possible, land for land compensation and housing benefits for those who lose house.
- Option for affected families to take 20%-50% compensation with government approval.
- Preference in project jobs and one job per nuclear family, support for skill development.
- Rs. 500 monthly pension for destitute, widows, unmarried girls.

Land Acquisition Amendment Bill, 2007

- Land can be acquired for public purpose. It also includes strategic purposes vital to the state and public infrastructure such as electricity, water supply. However, if land remains unutilized for five years, it will revert to government.
- Rate of compensation not to be less than floor price fixed by the state or average of higher prices paid in 50% of land sale cases.
- Persons with tenancy rights recognized entity for proportionate share in compensation.

According to the policy, land acquired for a public purpose cannot be transferred to any other purpose but a public purpose, and that too, only with prior approval of the Government. If land acquired for a public purpose remains unutilized for the purpose for five years from the date of taking over the possession, it shall revert to the Government concerned. It states: when land acquired is transferred for a consideration, 80 percent of any net unearned income accruing to the transferor, shall be proportionally shared with the persons from whom the lands were acquired, or their heirs.

One of the objectives of the policy is to minimise displacement of people and to promote non-displacing or least-displacing alternatives. It also recommends that only the minimum necessary area of land commensurate with the purpose of the project should be taken, and the use of agricultural land for non-agricultural purposes should be kept to the minimum; multi-crop land should be avoided and irrigated land use should be kept to the minimum for such purposes. Projects may preferably be set-up on wastelands or unirrigated lands.

Critics have raised certain problems in the process of implementation. For instance, land-for-land promise is subject to the limitation of the availability of Government land. Secondly, the promise of providing employment for one-job per member family in the new project depends on the suitability of the candidate, and availability of jobs matching with the ability of the person seeking jobs. Thirdly, the Government's proposal that 80 percent of any future gains on land transfer should be shared with original landowners or their heirs, is much more difficult to implement, moreso, if there is a dispute among the heirs about the inheritance of the property of the original owner. Lastly, the idea of giving landowners the option of taking 20 percent of compensation in the form of shares is also beset with operational difficulties. Some unscrupulous promoters may allot such shares which may turn out to be worthless pieces of paper.

A democratic government, however, cannot afford to remain totally silent about the genuine grievances of the affected persons. From that point of view, the Government's initiative indicates its sensitivity to the problems raised in the implementation of SEZ. In stead of decrying the Government proposal, it would be much more prudent to suggest ways and means for finding a solution to this difficult problem.

CHAPTER

12

Emerging Structure of Indian Economy : A Statewise Analysis

Introduction

Indian economy has observed a growth pattern in which share of GDP in service sector has moved far ahead of the share in the secondary sector (industry). This is at variance with the historical pattern of development observed in developed countries. It is also at variance with the pattern observed even in developing countries which are similarly placed. On the structure of distribution of labour force, whereas in developed countries, there was a significant transfer of labour force to industry during the period of industrialization and later to sharp increase in the employment of labour force in the post-industrialization period to the service sector, the Indian economy has only marginally transferred its labour to industry and services, and continues to have nearly 60 percent of the labour force employed in agriculture. Obviously, India's pattern of development presumably indicates a pre-mature emergence of the service sector as the major contributor to GDP. Since most of the states in the Indian Union can be compared to many of the countries of Europe in size and population, it was thought desirable to study the changing structure of different states in the process of development.

I. HISTORICAL EXPERIENCE OF STRUCTURAL CHANGE IN DEVELOPED ECONOMIES

Structural changes take place in economies as the process of economic development proceeds further and gathers momentum. These structural changes result in changes in the proportion of national product and of the labour force. The most common pattern of structural change follows a sequence of a shift from agriculture to industry and then to services. These structural changes are observed both in the relative shares of national product and in labour force.

According to economists like Colin Clark and AGB Fisher, the basic argument in support of structural changes in national product is that as income levels increase, the proportion of income spent on food shows a decline and that on non-food items (or manufactures) shows a relatively higher increase. At still higher level of income, there is a high proportion of income spent on services. In other words, low income elasticity of demand for agricultural products, tends to shift the pattern of production in favour of manufactures which have high income elasticity of demand. According to Fisher, there is a saturation level for the demand for manufactures. Clark argued that demand for manufactured goods saturates, setting at around 20 to 25 percent, and, with a continuing fall in the demand for agricultural products, there is an increase in the demand of services.

Shift in demand pattern is thus the result of differences in elasticity of demand. Shift in the pattern of demand does impact on transfer of labour force from agriculture to industry and subsequently to services. But Baumol (1967, 2001), however, argued that employment or shift in labour force is not the consequence of a change in final demand, but is the result of differential productivity growth. Increasing share of labour force employed in services has, however, been attributed by most economists to low productivity in services as compared to manufacturing.

TABLE 12.1

Output and Employment Shares in Selected Developed Economies (2002)

Country	*Shares in Output (%)*			*Shares in Employment (%)*		
	Agri-culture	*Industry*	*Services*	*Agri-culture*	*Industry*	*Services*
United Kingdom	1	26	73	1	25	74
United States	2	23	75	2	24	74
France	2	22	76	3	25	72
Japan	1	31	68	5	31	64
Germany	1	30	69	3	33	64
Italy	3	29	69	5	32	63
Australia	4	26	69	5	21	74

Source : World Bank (2004), *World Development Indicators.*

Table 12.1 reveals great similarity in the pattern of output and employment shares among the seven selected countries. Firstly, share of agriculture in their GDP was less than 5 percent indicating that agriculture accounts for a very small portion of total output. Similarly, the share of labour force in agriculture was below 5 percent. Secondly, the share of industry in GDP was in the range of 22 to 30 percent. Likewise, the share in employment by industry ranged between 21 to 33 percent. Thirdly, the share of services in GDP ranged from 69 to 76 percent. Also it may be observed that the share of employment was in the range of 63 to 74 percent. From this, the broad picture that emerges is as follows: With a shift of GDP from agriculture to industry, there was a nearly proportionate shift in employment. Similarly, a rise in the share of services in GDP was accompanied by a proportionate increase in employment.

2. GDP AND EMPLOYMENT SHARES IN SELECTED DEVELOPING COUNTRIES

Table 12.2 provides information regarding shares of GDP and Employment among agriculture, industry and services in selected developing countries. To indicate the relative levels of development, GDP per capita figures on purchasing power parity (PPP) basis have also been given so as to understand the pattern of demand propelling output shares. The data reveal wide variations in the output and employment pattern. The Republic of Korea shows GDP shares which are very close to those of a developed economy. The share of agriculture is just 3 percent and that of services is 62 percent. the share of industry was also quite high at 33 percent. Indonesia, Thailand, Philippines and Malaysia indicated a nearly similar pattern of output in which the share of agriculture ranged between 10 to 17 percent, that of industry between 32 to 49 percent and that of services between 40 to 46 percent. India and Pakistan share a very similar pattern of output with GDP shares in agriculture in the range of 22-23 percent, in industry 23 to 27 percent and in services 51 to 53 percent. But employment share of agriculture is 61 percent in India, that of industry was 17 percent and of services only 22 percent. In Pakistan, share of employment in agriculture was 48 percent, that of industry 18 percent and of services 34 percent.

A very striking feature of the output pattern is that with an increase in GDP per capita (PPP), the share of agriculture showed a very strong inverse correlation, but this was not observed in the GDP share of industry and services. This implies that with an improvement in GDP (PPP), the share of industry and services depended on other factors and policies pursued by a country. For instance, China has increased its share of industry to a level of 46 percent and is described as the 'Manufacturing Hub of the world', while India seems to have specialized in IT Sector and thus has become a BPO Centre of the world, resulting in a sharp increase in the share of the service sector.

TABLE 12.2

GDP and Employment Shares in Selected Developing Countries

Country	GDP per capita (PPP) 2003	Shares in Output (%)[1]			Shares in Employment (%)[2]		
		Agriculture	Industry	Services	Agriculture	Industry	Services
(1)	(2)	(3)	(4)	(5)	(6)	(7)	(8)
1. Korea, Republic	18,000	3	35	62	10	28	62
2. Malaysia	8,970	10	49	42	18	32	50
3. Thailand	7,450	10	44	46	46	21	33
4. China	4,980	13	46	41[4]	47	22	31
5. Philippines	4,640	14	32	53	37	16	47
6. Indonesia	3,210	17	44	40	44	17	39
7. India	2,880	22	27	51	61[3]	17[3]	22[3]
8. Pakistan	2,040	23	23	53	48	18	34

1. Per capita GDP and GDP shares are for 2003. Per capita GDP figures are on PPP basis.
2. Employment shares are for 2000.
3. For India, employment shares are taken from IAMR, Manpower Profile (2004) and are based on National Sample Survey, Report No. 481, Employment and Unemployment in India, July 2001-June 2002, 57th Round.
4. Data for China pertains to 2004 as revised by the Eleventh Five Year Plan (2006-10).

Source : World Bank, *World Development Indicators (2004) and (2005).*

However, the employment pattern provides a very different picture. A substantial reduction in the share of agriculture in total employment could be observed in the case of Korean Republic and Malaysia to a level of 10 percent and 18 percent respectively. These countries had a high share of employment in services in the range of 50% and 62% respectively. Obviously, there is a greater shift of employment in services than that of in industry. Philippines indicates that whereas its share in employment in agriculture declined from 52 percent to 37 percent between 1980 and 2001, its share in industry remained stagnant as about 16 percent and the entire decline in the share of agricultural employment by 15 percent was absorbed by an increase in services from 33 percent to 47 percent during this period.

India and Pakistan shared a high proportion of employment in agriculture, i.e. 61 percent and 48 percent respectively. In both countries, the share of employment in industry was at lower level of 17-18 percent, but the service sector indicated 34 percent share in Pakistan and merely 22 percent in India. Even though the GDP share in services of India shot up to 51 percent, yet the share in employment was merely 22 percent. Obviously, output employment ratio in India remained very high, indicating a capital-intensive pattern of growth in the service sector.

3. CHANGING PROFILE OF GDP AND EMPLOYMENT OF WORKFORCE IN INDIA

Changing profile of GDP in India during 1950-51 to 2001-02—over a period of 51 years is given in Table 12.3. The data reveal that GDP from the primary sector (viz., agriculture and allied entities like forestry and fishing) declined form 59 percent in 1950-51 to 46 percent in 1970-71 and thereafter, sharply declined 24 percent in 2001-02. This was partially neutralized by an increase in the share of the secondary sector from 13 percent in 1950-51 to about 22 percent in 1970-71 and further increase to about 27 percent in 2001-02. But the biggest hike in GDP share occurred in case of services from about 27 percent in 1950-51 to 32 percent in 1970-71 to 49 percent in 2001-02. The emerging structural change in GDP shares witnessed a big decline in the share of agriculture, coupled with a modest increase in the share of industry and a much sharper increase in the share of services which now account for nearly half of the total GDP.

But the question arises: Did this structural shift in GDP share have an impact on the employment pattern or distribution of workforce in India? Data provided in Table 12.4 based on the various rounds of the National Sample Survey reveals that the share of workforce deployed in agriculture declined from 74 percent in 1972-73 to about 61 percent in 2001-02. Along with this declines, the share of employment in industry increased from 11.2 percent in 1972-73 to 14.9 percent in 1993-94 and further to 17.1 percent in 2001-02. Also the share of services in total employment increased form 14.6 percent in 1972-73 to 22.1 percent in 2001-02.

TABLE 12.3
GDP at Factor Cost by Industry of Origin (at 1993-94 Prices)—All India

(*Rs. crores*)

Year	*Primary*	*Secondary*	*Tertiary*	*Total*
1950-51*	83,154 (59.2)	18,670 (13.3)	38,642 (27.5)	1,40,466 (100.0)
1960-61*	1,12,848 (54.8)	34,239 (16.6)	59,016 (28.6)	2,06,103 (100.0)
1970-71	1,37,320 (46.3)	64,258 (21.6)	95,331 (32.1)	2,96,909 (100.0)
1980-81	1,59,293 (39.2)	95,055 (23.7)	1,46,753 (36.6)	4,01,128 (100.0)
1990-91	2,23,114 (32.2)	1,88,601 (27.2)	2,81,115 (40.6)	6,92,871 (100.0)
2001-02	3,04,666 (24.0)	3,38,165 (26.7)	6,25,114 (49.3)	12,67,945 (100.0)

* For 1950-51 and 1960-61, Primary Sector includes agriculture, forestry, fishing and mining & quarrying, but figures for 1970-71, 1980-81, 1990-91 and 2001-02 include mining & quarrying in the secondary sector, instead of the primary sector.

Source : Government of India, *Economic Survey (2004-05)* and Central Statistical Organization as reported in RBI, *Handbook of Statistics of the Indian Economy (2004-05).*

The upshot of this analysis is that whereas GDP share of agriculture declined sharply, the corresponding decline in employment share did not take place in India. Meanwhile, GDP share of industry registered a very small increase of 5 percent during the last three decades (1970-71 to 2001-02). But the corresponding increase in employment share was only 6 percent during the same period. This only indicates that the process of industrialization failed to absorb excess labour in agriculture in the expansion of industry. Thirdly, share of services in GDP increased sharply to about 50 percent, but they also failed to register a sharp increase in employment which was barely 5 percent as against an 18 percent increase in GDP during 1970-71 and 2001-02. From this it follows that Indian did not experience sequence in the growth of GDP and employment in industry during the process of industrialization, but skipped to the post-industrialization phase of increasing its share of GDP as well as employment in services, though a relatively much smaller increase in employment in the service sector took place.

TABLE 12.4
Distribution of Working Force by Industry Division

(*All India*)

Industry Division	*Total*			
	1972-73	*1983*	*1993-94*	*2001-02*
Agriculture				
Agriculture Forestry, Fishing and Hunting	74.0	68.1	63.9	60.8
Industry				
Mining and Quarrying	0.4	0.6	0.7	0.5
Manufacturing	8.8	10.7	10.6	11.9
Electricity, Gas and Water	0.2	0.3	0.4	0.2
Construction	1.8	2.3	3.2	4.5
Sub-total	**11.2**	**13.9**	**14.9**	**17.1**
Services				
Wholesale and Retail trade and Restaurants and Hotels	5.0	6.9	7.6	10.5
Transport, Storage and Communication	1.8	2.5	2.9	3.5
Other Services	7.8	8.8	10.7	8.1
Sub-total	**14.6**	**18.2**	**21.2**	**22.1**
Activities not Classified	0.2	0.4	—	—
Total	100.0	100.0	100.0	100.0
Total Employment (Million)	**236.3**	**302.8**	**372.1**	**428.2**

Figures relate to usual status of individuals.

Workforce covers those involved in gainful activity regularly + those involved in gainful activity occasionally.

Source : National Sample Survey Organization, 27th, 32nd, 38th, 43rd, 46th, 48th and 50th Rounds with reclassification of Shares of agriculture, industry and services as given in IAMR, ManpowerProfile in India (2004).

4. GDP, EMPLOYMENT AND PRODUCTIVITY PER WORKER IN INDIA

In Table 12.5, we present data about GDP and employment growth in India for the period 1972-73 to 2001-02. From this, we have worked out productivity per worker at 1993-94 prices. Data reveals that there is an increase in the growth rate of productivity per worker by 1.7 % in Primary, 2.0 % in Secondary and 2.9 % in the Tertiary Sector during the 29-year period (1972-73 to 2001-02).

TABLE 12.5
Gross Domestic Product, Employment and Productivity Per Worker in India

Gross Domestic Product

(*Rs. crores at 1993-94 prices*)

Year	*Primary*	*Secondary*	*Tertiary*	*Total*
1972-73	1,33,699	62,699	1,01,918	2,98,316
	(44.8)	(21.0)	(34.2)	(100.0)
1993-94	2,62,059	1,85,070	3,34,216	7,81,345
	(33.5)	(23.7)	(42.8)	(100.0)
2001-02	3,33,274	3,09,557	6,25,114	12,67,945
	(26.3)	(24.4)	(49.3)	(100.0)

Distribution of Employment

(*In million*)

Year	*Primary*	*Secondary*	*Tertiary*	*Total*
1972-73	174.8	26.4	35.1	236.2
	(74.0)	(11.2)	(14.8)	(100.0)
1993-94	240.4	52.8	78.9	372.1
	(64.6)	(14.2)	(21.2)	(100.0)
2001-02	260.4	73.2	94.6	428.2
	(60.8)	(17.1)	(22.1)	(100.0)

Productivity per Worker

(*Rupees at 1993-94 prices*)

Year	*Primary*	*Secondary*	*Tertiary*	*Total*
1972-73	7,649	23,749	29,036	12,630
1993-94	10,901	35,051	42,359	20,998
2001-02	12,798	42,289	66,080	29,611
CAGR between 1972-73 and 2001-02	1.7	2.0	2.9	3.0

Disparity Ratios in Productivity per Worker

Year	*Primary*	*Secondary*	*Tertiary*
1972-73	1.0	3.1	3.8
1993-94	1.0	3.2	3.9
2001-02	1.0	3.3	5.2

Sources : 1. Data for sectoral distribution of GDP was taken from CSO as given in *Economic Survey (2004-05)*.

2. Data for distribution of labour force was taken from IAMR, *Manpower Profile India (2004)*.

3. Productivity per worker is calculated by dividing GDP with the total number of workers in the respective sector.

It may also be noted that disparity ratio in productivity per worker which was 1:3.1 between primary and secondary sector in 1972-73 increased slightly to 3.3 in 2001-02. But the disparity ratio between primary and tertiary sector increased from 3.8 in 1972-73 to 5.2 in 2001-02. These differentials in productivity explain why the absorption of workers in secondary and tertiary sectors has been lower in India. It also repudiates the commonly held belief by the economists that increasing share of labour force in services is due to low productivity in services as compared to manufacturing.

The question arises: How does one explain the growth of India becoming a post-industrial 'service economy', without passing though the major phase of industrialization, spearheaded by manufacturing? A very plausible explanation is: Technological changes during the last few decades have induced an increase in demand for services even at relatively lower levels of per capita income. Moreover, development of communication technologies and reduction of the barriers to commodity flows and movement of people, specially skilled persons due to impact of globalization, have produced demonstration effects resulting in shifting the pattern of demand in developing countries in favour of those prevailing in developed countries much earlier than the historical experience would justify. As consequences, both the production and consumption of services have shown a quantum jump. Unfortunately, the pattern of production of services which is capital-intensive has failed to bring about a significant proportion of the workforce to services even. In an overall view, pattern of GDP growth did not bring about a shift in employment pattern to either industry (manufacturing) or services.

5. DIFFERENCES IN DISTRIBUTION OF NSDP IN DIFFERENT STATES

While considering the differences in distribution of NSDP and Employment into Agriculture, Industry and Services, it is necessary to define the various broad divisions. The Economic and Political Weekly Research Foundation includes the following:

1. Agriculture covers agriculture, forestry, logging and fishing.
2. Industry covers mining & quarrying, manufacturing, electricity, gas and water supply and construction.
3. Service sector includes all other sectors in the Net Domestic Production by economic activity, viz., Transport, storage and communications, trade, hotels and restaurants, banking & insurance, real estate ownership of dwellings and business services, public administration and other services.

There is a controversy about mining and quarrying. In our analysis, mining and quarrying has been included in industry and not in agriculture, though some believe that mining and quarrying should appropriately be a part of the primary sector. Similarly, following EPW Research Foundation, we have included construction alongwith manufacturing as a part of industry and not in services as the CSO has done in its classification.

Table 12.6 provides an overall view of distribution of NSDP as well as employment into agriculture, industry and services. The figures of per capita NSDP for 2000-01 have also been juxtaposed.

There is a general agreement among economists that a higher level of per capita NSDP suggests the attainment of a higher level of development. The states have been arranged in descending order in terms of per capita NSDP.

A study of the Table 12.6 reveals the following:

A comparison of Punjab and Maharashtra reveals that these two states vary widely different pattern of distribution of NSDP. Punjab contributes 40.5 percent of NSDP from agriculture in 2000-01, while Maharashtra contributes only 13.7 percent from agriculture. Obviously, prosperous agriculture in Punjab following the Green Revolution has shown a higher share of agriculture, whereas relatively Maharashtra which remained relatively unaffected by the Green Revolution has shown a small share from agriculture. This is evident from the fact that whereas per hectare yield of foodgrains in Punjab was 4,040 kgs, in Maharashtra, it was a meagre 874 kgs. If foodgrains yields can be used as a proxy for the development of agriculture, then it was natural that the share of agriculture in Punjab NSDP was bound to be higher than that of Maharashtra.

Haryana has shown that in 2000-01, with 33 percent of share of NSDP in agriculture, its share in industry was about 26 percent and that in services was nearly 41 percent. This change in distribution of shares can be explained by a higher yield of foodgrains per hectare to sustain a still high share in agriculture in 2001-02, though it has declined significantly from about 63 percent in 1960-61. The improvement in NSDP share in industry has been modest from about 16 percent in 1960-61 to 19 percent in 1980-81, merely three percent in a span of 20 year and this improved further to 26 percent in 2000-01. It only implies that some acceleration in industrialization did take place during the last two decades or so. But there was a sharp escalation in the share of the service sector form about 21 percent in 1960-61 to about 41 percent in 2001-02, but out of this increase of nearly 20 percent, nearly 15 percent increase was witnessed during 1980-81 to 2000-01. To sum up, Haryana continued to be a primarily agricultural state till 1980-81, by improved very tardily in industry, but saw a big jump in the service sector.

Tamil Nadu and Gujarat both indicate a sharp decline in the share of agriculture. While Tamil Nadu improved its share in industry to 32 percent in 2000-01, Gujarat accounted for still higher share of NSDP in industry to 38 percent. But in both cases, the share of the service sector improved sharply—47 percent in the case of Gujarat and about 50 percent in the case of Tamil Nadu.

TABLE 12.6

Relative Shares of Net Domestic Product in Agriculture, Industry and Services of India (1960-61 to 2000-01) Major States

Sl. No.	State	Per capita NSDP at factor cost (Rs.) 2000-01	Year	Percentage share of Agriculture, Industry and Services in NSDP			
				Agriculture	Industry	Services	Yield of food grains kgs/hectare (2001-02)
(1)	(2)	(3)	(4)	(5)	(6)	(7)	(8)
1.	Punjab	15,048	2000-01	40.5	22.5	37.0	4,040
			1980-81	49.5	18.5	32.0	
			1960-61	54.0	15.6	30.4	
2.	Maharashtra	14,211	2000-01	13.7	32.8	53.5	874
			1980-81	27.7	35.5	36.8	
			1960-61	41.6	26.7	31.7	
3.	Haryana	13,822	2000-01	33.0	26.3	40.7	3,128
			1980-81	54.2	19.4	26.4	
			1960-61	62.7	16.4	20.9	
4.	Tamil Nadu	13,017	2000-01	18.6	31.8	49.6	2,209
			1980-81	25.4	34.0	40.6	
			1960-61	51.9	17.7	30.4	
5.	Gujarat	12,489	2000-01	15.0	38.1	46.9	1,414
			1980-81	39.9	28.1	32.0	
			1960-61	41.6	26.0	32.4	

(Contd.)

TABLE 12.6 (*Contd.*)

(1)	(2)	(3)	(4)	(5)	(6)	(7)	(8)
6.	Karnataka	11,900	2000-01	30.0	23.5	46.2	1,212
			1980-81	45.4	21.4	33.2	
			1960-61	60.4	16.0	23.6	
7.	Himachal Pradesh	11,029	2000-01	24.4	33.1	42.5	NA
			1980-81	49.9	19.1	31.0	
			1960-61	NA	NA	NA	
8.	Kerala	10,510	2000-01	25.1	19.7	55.2	NA
			1980-81	39.1	24.5	36.4	
			1960-61	55.6	15.6	28.8	
9.	Andhra Pradesh	10,195	2000-01	30.0	23.0	47.0	2,102
			1980-81	45.6	17.6	36.8	
			1960-61	NA	NA	NA	
10.	West Bengal	9,796	2000-01	26.5	21.2	52.5	2,424
			1980-81	31.6	30.3	38.1	
			1960-61	40.5	26.3	33.2	
11.	Rajasthan	8,104	2000-01	27.5	28.6	43.9	1,099
			1980-81	50.3	20.0	29.7	
			1960-61	56.2	16.6	27.2	
12.	Madhya Pradesh	7,195	2000-01	27.6	29.6	42.8	1,148
			1980-81	52.1	21.9	26.0	

(*Contd.*)

13. Jammu & Kashmir	7,385	2000-01	36.6	12.2	51.2	NA
		1980-81	47.0	1.3	39.7	
		1960-61	67.6	8.8	23.6	
14. Assam	5,943	2000-01	38.7	21.0	40.3	1,460
		1980-81	48.4	11.2	40.4	
		1960-61	56.4	19.7	23.9	
15. Orissa	5,562	2000-01	34.4	18.4	47.2	1,399
		1980-81	53.2	17.6	29.2	
		1960-61	NA	NA	NA	
16. Uttar Pradesh	5,570	2000-01	35.7	21.4	42.9	2,164
		1980-81	52.0	15.6	32.4	
		1960-61	NA	NA	NA	
17. Bihar	3,879	2000-01	32.0	24.7	43.3	1,664
		1980-81	51.1	21.5	27.4	
		1960-61	53.6	15.0	31.4	

Notes : 1. Agriculture covers Agriculture, Forestry, Logging and Fishing.
Industry covers Mining and Quarrying, Manufacturing, Electricity, gas and water supply and construction.
Services cover all the other sectors in the Net Domestic Product Distribution by economic activity.

2. Per capita NSDP at factor cost figures for 2000-01 have been taken from Reserve Bank of India, *Hand book of Statistics on the Indian Economy (2004-05)*.

3. Percentage shares of agriculture, industry and services have been taken from Economic and Political Weekly Research Foundation (2003), *Domestic State Product of States of India (1960-61 to 2000-01)*.

4. Relative Shares for 1960-61 are at 1960-61 prices and those for 1980-81 are at 1980-81 prices series, but for 2000-01, they were at 1993-94 prices.

5. States have been arranged in the descending order of per capita NSDP for 2000-01.

6. For yield of foodgrains per hectare, data has been taken from Ministry of Agriculture, *Agricultural Statistics at a Glance (2004)*.

7. For Bihar, NSDP distribution is for 1999-2000.

Karnataka has developed a pattern in which the share of the service sector shot up to 46 percent in 2001-02 as against only 24 percent in 1960-61, but its share in industry remained low at about 24 percent in 2000-01 as against 16 percent in 1960-61. There is a continuous decline in the share of agriculture from 60 percent in 1960-61 to 45 percent in 1980-81 and 30 percent in 2001-02. This implies that the share of agriculture was halved during the last four decades. But Karnataka has broadly followed the Indian model that it moved on to a post-industrial 'service economy' without passing through the phase of industrialization.

Kerala, Andhra Pradesh, West Bengal have also more of less followed the Karnataka Model or broadly Indian Model, and with a decline in the share of agriculture in NSDP, the share of the service sector improved much faster than that of industry.

Rajasthan and Madhya Pradesh both indicate a significant decline in the share of agriculture, but there has been an increase in the share of industry to 29-30 percent, but the service sector ranged between 43-44 percent in 2000-01. This indicates that though the service sector was the dominant sector, yet its level remained relatively less with respect to other states like Kerala, West Bengal, Tamil Nadu and Maharashtra.

Jammu & Kashmir, by its very nature is a special category state. There was a sharp decline in the share of agriculture from about 68 percent to about 37 percent, but its share in industry remained at the lowest level of 12 percent, but there was a big jump in the share of services from 24 percent in 1960-61 to about 51 percent by 2000-01. The disturbed political climate, restrictions on Indian businessmen to invest in Kashmir and the growing terrorism were the factors restricting the industrial development of the state. Tourism and other services allied with tourism did lead to a big jump in the share of the service sector.

Coming to very poor states like Assam, Orissa, Uttar Pradesh and Bihar, the share of agriculture in NSDP declined but ranged between 32 to 39 percent in 2000-01. However, the share of industry did not pick up significantly and ranged between 18 percent and 25 percent. Share of the service sector in these three states viz., Assam, Uttar Pradesh and Bihar ranged between 40-43 percent in 2000-01. It was only in the case of Orissa that its share in service sector rose to 47 percent, but this was the consequence of a very small shares in industry to 2000-01 at a level of merely 18 percent.

From a review of the change in the structure of NSDP in various states, the broad conclusions that emerge are:

But for Punjab where there was a relatively much slower decline in the share of NSDP in agriculture, most of the states in our survey indicated a sharp decline. Punjab and Haryana, the main beneficiaries of green revolution witnessed higher share in NSDP for agriculture in the range of 30 to 41 percent. In contrast, industrialized states like Maharashtra, Gujarat and Tamil Nadu experienced steep fall in the share of agriculture to a level of 14-19 percent, much lower than the All India figure of 24 percent

The share of industry indicate a significant increase in Maharashtra, Tamil Nadu and Gujarat to a level of 32 to 38 percent, thus enabling them to switch over to service sector.

However, whereas the process of industrialization did start in other states, but rate of industrialization was not sufficiently high-ranging between 20 to 30 percent. Jammu & Kashmir indicate very little growth in industry share. Orissa, a very poor state, remained a laggard in its march towards industrialization.

Service sector became the driver and the magnet for several states like Maharashtra, Tamil Nadu, Gujarat, Karnataka, Kerala and West Bengal and its share ranged over 50 percent. In relatively poor states like Rajasthan, Madhya Pradesh, Assam, Orissa, Uttar Pradesh and Bihar, the service sector did become a leading sector, but not to the same level as in forward and richer states.

Productivity in agriculture was a dominant factor in the determination of the share of agriculture in NSDP. If a big push is given to agriculture in backward states with lower per capita NSDP, it can further stimulate the growth of the service sector, and also improve the share of industry.

However, there is a word of caution in interpreting the data in Table 12.6. The figures for 2000-01 are based on 1993-94 prices, for 1980-81 at 1980-81 prices and for 1960-61 at 1960-61 prices. We have, therefore, used only the percentage shares of NSDP for agriculture, industry and services, on the assumption that even if a continuous state level series was available at constant prices for the 40 year period, it would not be significantly different from that presented here.

6. DISTRIBUTION OF NSDP IN VARIOUS STATES IN THE POST-REFORM PERIOD (1993-94 TO 2003-04)

Data of distribution of NSDP in the post-reform period in Primary, Secondary and Tertiary sector at 1993-94 prices is presented in Table 12.7. From the absolute figures provided for various states in the survey, percentage distribution has been calculated. An indication of the percentage change in each sector has also been indicated.

A close perusal of the data reveals the following:

But for Jammu and Kashmir where the share of the primary sector increased by a nominal 0.3 percent, in all other states, the share of the primary sector has shown a decline. This decline was much sharper in the case of Kerala (15.1%), Haryana (13.0%), Himachal Pradesh (12.7%), Bihar (12.3%), Karnataka (12.3%) Orissa (12.1%) and Tamil Nadu (11.9%). However, this decline was modest in the case of Andhra Pradesh (9.5%), West Bengal (9.2%), Punjab (7.7%), Maharashtra (6.5%), Uttar Pradesh (6.2%), Rajasthan (5.5%) and Gujarat barely (1.8%).

The question that needs to examined is: how is this decline distributed in favour of the secondry sector or the tertiary sector. A close perusal of the data reveals that in the case of Maharashtra, there was a decline in the share

TABLE 12.7

Components of Net State Domestic Product at Factor Cost (At 1993-94 prices)

(Rs. crores)

Sl. No.	State	Year	Primary	Secondary	Tertiary	Total
(1)	(2)	(3)	(4)	(5)	(6)	(7)
1.	Punjab	1993-94	13,052	5,368	8,647	27,067
		2003-04	16,075	8,703	14,843	39,621
		1993-94	(48.2)	(19.8)	(32.0)	(100.0)
		2003-04	(40.5)	(22.0)	(37.5)	(100.0)
		% Change	**-7.7**	**2.2**	**5.5**	
2.	Haryana	1993-94	8,276	4,971	6,174	19,421
		2003-04	10,285	8,874	15,640	34,,799
		1993-94	(42.6)	(25.6)	(31.8)	(100.0)
		2003-04	(29.6)	(25.5)	(44.9)	(100.0)
		% Change	**-13.0**	**-0.1**	**13.1**	
3.	Maharashtra	1993-94	21,069	33,236	48,462	1,02,767
		2003-04	22,680	41,392	97,500	1,61,572
		1993-94	(20.5)	(32.3)	(47.2)	(100.0)
		2003-04	(14.0)	(25.6)	(60.4)	(100.0)
		% Change	**-6.5**	**-6.7**	**13.2**	
4.	Gujarat	1993-94	10,322	15,287	16,952	42,561
		2003-04	19,910	30,593	38,160	88,663
		1993-94	(24.3)	(35.9)	(39.8)	(100.0)
		2003-04	(22.5)	(34.5)	(43.0)	(100.0)
		% Change	**-1.8**	**-1.4**	**3.2**	
5.	Tamil Nadu	1993-94	13,243	16,916	21,484	51,643
		2003-04	11,733	25,833	48,006	85,572
		1993-94	(25.6)	(32.8)	(41.6)	(100.0)
		2003-04	(13.7)	(30.2)	(56.1)	(100.0)
		% Change	**-11.9**	**-2.6**	**14.5**	
6.	Karnataka	1993-94	13,863	9,102	14,017	36,982
		2003-04	16,114	14,533	33,321	63,968
		1993-94	(37.5)	(24.6)	(37.9)	(100.0)
		2003-04	(25.2)	(22.7)	(52.1)	(100.0)
		% Change	**-12.3**	**-1.9**	**14.2**	
7.	Himachal Pradesh	1993-94	1,502	1,103	1,645	4,250
		2003-04	1,686	2,566	3,192	7,444
		1993-94	(35.3)	(26.0)	(38.7)	(100.0)
		2003-04	(22.6)	(34.5)	(42.9)	(100.0)
		% Change	**-12.7**	**8.5**	**4.2**	
8.	Kerala	1993-94	7,638	4,896	11,318	23,852
		2003-04	6,704	7,762	25,271	39,737
		1993-94	(32.0)	(20.5)	(47.5)	(100.0)
		2003-04	(16.9)	(19.5)	(63.6)	(100.0)
		% Change	**-15.1**	**-1.0**	**16.1**	

(Contd.)

TABLE 12.7 (Contd.)

(1)	(2)	(3)	(4)	(5)	(6)	(7)
9.	Andhra Pradesh	1993-94	18,570	10,765	22,320	51,655
		2003-04	23,428	20,081	45,023	88,532
		1993-94	(36.0)	(20.8)	(43.2)	(100.0)
		2003-04	(26.5)	(22.7)	(50.8)	(100.0)
		% Change	**-9.5**	**1.9**	**7.6**	
10.	West Bengal	1993-94	16,792	10,894	20,712	48,398
		2003-04	22,875	18,772	48,145	89,792
		1993-94	(34.7)	(22.5)	(42.8)	(100.0)
		2003-04	(25.5)	(20.9)	(53.6)	(100.0)
		% Change	**-9.2**	**-1.6**	**10.8**	
11.	Rajasthan	1993-94	10,196	7,327	11,454	28,977
		2003-04	15,374	12,776	23,618	51,768
		1993-94	(35.2)	(25.3)	(39.5)	(100.0)
		2003-04	(29.7)	(24.7)	(45.6)	(100.0)
		% Change	**-5.5**	**-0.6**	**6.1**	
12.	Madhya Pradesh	1993-94	14,568	7,253	12,115	33,936
		2003-04	17,332	14,034	21,399	52,765
		1993-94	(42.9)	(21.4)	(35.7)	(100.0)
		2003-04	(32.8)	(26.6)	(40.6)	(100.0)
		% Change	**-10.1**	**5.2**	**4.9**	
13.	Jammu & Kashmir	1993-94	2,042	990	2,469	5,501
		2003-04	2,899	871	3,985	7,755
		1993-94	(37.1)	(18.0)	(44.9)	(100.0)
		2003-04	(37.4)	(11.2)	(51.4)	(100.0)
		% Change	**0.3**	**-6.8**	**6.5**	
14.	Assam	1993-94	5,670	2,606	5,210	13,486
		2003-04	5,982	3,293	9,437	18,712
		1993-94	(42.1)	(19.3)	(38.6)	(100.0)
		2003-04	(32.0)	(17.6)	(50.4)	(100.0)
		% Change	**-10.1**	**-1.7**	**11.8**	
15.	Orissa	1993-94	7,163	3,324	5,716	16,203
		2003-04	7,834	5,298	11,253	24,385
		1993-94	(44.2)	(20.5)	(35.3)	(100.0)
		2003-04	(32.1)	(21.7)	(46.2)	(100.0)
		% Change	**-12.1**	**1.2**	**10.9**	
16.	Uttar Pradesh	1993-94	29,160	14,060	27,715	70,935
		2003-04	33,534	20,606	41,870	96,010
		1993-94	(41.1)	(19.8)	(39.1)	(100.0)
		2003-04	(34.9)	(21.5)	(43.6)	(100.0)
		% Change	**-6.2**	**1.7**	**4.5**	
17.	Bihar	1993-94	10,677	1,809	8,294	20,780
		2003-04	12,647	3,183	16,518	32,348
		1993-94	(51.4)	(8.7)	(39.9)	(100.0)
		2003-04	(39.1)	(9.8)	(51.1)	(100.0)
		% Change	**-12.3**	**1.1**	**11.2**	

Notes : 1. Owing to differences in methodology of compilation, data for different States/ Union Territories are not strictly comparable.

2. Figures in brackets are percentages of total NSDP in the row.

Source : Compiled and computed from CSO data provided by RBI, *Handbook of Statistics on the Indian Economy (2004-05).*

of secondary sector by 6.7 percent and the entire decrease in the share of the primary and secondary sector was compensated by a sharp increase in the share of tertiary sector.

In the case of Haryana, share of the secondary sector was stagnant during the reform period and the tertiary sector was expanded by 13 percent in response to decline in the share of the primary sector.

The case of Tamil Nadu also reveals that the share of secondary sector during the 10-year period of reforms period (1993-94 to 2003-04) declined by 2.6 percent and that of the tertiary sector showed a big increase by 14.5 percent.

The case of Karnataka was similar to that of Tamil Nadu, which indicated a decline in the share of the secondary sector by about 2 percent and a big increase in tertiary sector by 14 percent.

In case of Kerala, there was a decline in the share of primary sector by 15 percent and a marginal decline in the share of secondary sector by 1 percent, but the tertiary sector recorded the highest increase by 16 percent.

In case of West Bengal, there was a decline in the share of primary sector by 9.2 percent and a small decline in the share of the secondary sector by 1.6 percent and this was accompanied by a significant increase in the share of tertiary sector by 10.8 percent.

Jammu & Kashmir indicated a big decline in the share of the secondary sector by 6.8 percent, but the increase in the share of tertiary sector was very modest at 6.5 percent. This was probably due to absence of a conducive climate for boosting investment in industry in view of the threat to security and peace.

In Assam, the tertiary sector indicated an increase by 11.8 percent while the secondary sector suffered a marginal decline in the share by 1.7 percent.

Orissa and Bihar also witnessed a closely similar situation with a marginal decline in the share of the secondary sector by about 1 percent and a rise in he share of the tertiary sector by about 11 percent.

Madhya Pradesh appears to be the single state in which a decline in the share of the primary sector by 10 percent was shared equally by an increase in the secondary and tertiary sector by 5 percent each.

Himachal Pradesh presents another unique example where the decline in the share of primary sector by about 13 percent was compensated to the extent of 9 percent by industry (secondary sector) and only 4 percent by the tertiary sector.

Punjab, Andhra Pradesh and Uttar Pradesh represent another category where a fall in the share of the primary sector by 6-9 percent, was barely compensated to the extent of 2 percent by secondary sector and the remaining part of 4-7 percent was provided by the tertiary sector.

The upshot of the analysis is that the state level scenario about the sectoral changes broadly supports the All-India picture that during the post-reform period (1993-94 to 2003-04), India witnessed a slow transition to industrialization by improving the share of the secondary sector and in many cases, it is a case of de-industrialization, but the states bypassing industry shifted to the post-industrial 'service economy'. In the case of states like Himachal Pradesh and Punjab, the secondary sector did improve its condition marginally, and did play a significant role in this transition. Tertiary sector has also improved its position substantially and played a leading role, though this sector has lagged behind the overall achievement of the country to 50 percent level.

7. RELATIVE SHIFT IN THE SHARES OF NSDP AND EMPLOYMENT IN AGRICULTURE, INDUSTRY AND SERVICES

Table 12.8 provides data about the percentage shares of NSDP for 2000-01 and employment for 1999-00 for agriculture, industry and services. From these figures, output employment ratios (O/L) have been derived. These ratios indicate productivity per unit of labour. The per capita NSDP for 2000-01 at 1993-94 prices as an indicator has been juxtaposed and the states have been arranged in a descending order on the basis of per capita NSDP

It is expected that states with a higher per capita NSDP should be able to reduce their share of NSDP in agriculture and consequently raise their share in industry if they were passing through the phase of industrialization. This should also help to transfer labour from agriculture to industry. However, if the state has switched over to the post-industrial service economy before completing the process of industrialization, then a larger share of GDP should be derived form the service sector and a larger proportion of labour should also be absorbed in the service sector.

A close perusal of the data reveals that there does not exist a uniform pattern in India that abides by the experience of developed countries.

Take for instance, Punjab and Haryana—the two states which spearheaded the Green Revolution. As against the share of 40 percent in NSDP for agriculture in 2000-01, the corresponding share in employment in Punjab was 53.4 percent; and similarly with 33 percent share in NSDP for agriculture of Haryana, agriculture supported about 54 percent of labour force. Both these states had high output employment ratio of 0.76 and 0.61 respectively in agriculture. In Punjab, the NSDP share in industry was 22.5 percent and employment share was 20 percent. In Haryana, a nearly similar situation prevailed and the state indicated its percentage share in NSDP at 26 percent for industry with an employment share of 20 percent. Consequently the share of the service sector in NSDP remained between 37-40 percent, but the employment share was about 26-27 percent.

But in contrast, Maharashtra which enjoyed a second place in terms of per capita NSDP in 2000-01, had a small proportion of NSDP being generated from agriculture viz., 14 percent, but it carried a heavy burden of labour employed at around 57 percent in agriculture. But with 33 percent share of industry in NSDP, its share in employment was barely 18 percent. In case of services, their proportion in NSDP was 53 with a labour absorption of around 26 percent. This implies that output labour ratio in Maharashtra for agriculture was only 0.24 for agriculture, 1.85 for industry and 2.1 for services. O/L ratio indicates a low level of development in agriculture, a high O/L ratio for industry shows a capital intensive pattern of industrialization and much higher capital intensive pattern in post-industrial service sector. Maharashtra is an example of agricultural backwardness, accompanied by industrialization, and entry into post-industrial service economy. In other words, it has an asymmetry in the relative shares of agriculture, industry and services.

The pattern of development in Gujarat follows a more or less similar pattern to that of Maharashtra. Tamil Nadu, however, has been able to reduce its labour force employed in agriculture to 47 percent, though NSDP share stood at 19 percent. Its NSDP share in industry was 32 percent with employment share of 27 percent, but its share of NSDP for services was quite high (50%) with an employment share of 26 percent. it is also a case of a state with a relatively less backward agricultural economy jumping on to become a post-industrial service economy.

Kerala showed a singularly different pattern with NSDP share derived from agriculture declining to 25 percent accompanied by low employment share of 40 percent. This was accompanied with 27 percent share in employment in industry and 33 percent in services. There is no doubt that Kerala with NSDP share of 55 percent in services, has also entered the post-industrial service economy, but there is less disparity in labour force distribution as also in the output labour ratio in the three sectors.

West Bengal has also followed a more of less similar pattern like Kerala with the share of NSDP agriculture going down to 27 percent with an employment share being brought down to 47 percent. Service sector continues to be the driver of NSDP in West Bengal with a share of 53 percent with about 28 percent share of labour absorbed in industry. Industry has languished in West Bengal with 21 percent share of NSDP with 25 percent share of labour indicating a comparatively lower level of labour productivity. The flight of capital due to aggressive trade unionism accounted for the low NSDP share of services. There is no doubt that labour productivity in agriculture has improved in West Bengal, but this is very low in comparison with green revolution states in India. The State Government is now making amends for its past mistakes.

Then there a group of backward states, viz., Andhra Pradesh, Rajasthan, Madhya Pradesh, Jammu & Kashmir, Assam, Orissa, Uttar Pradesh and Bihar which have a very high proportion of labour force dependent on agriculture with Assam accounting for 60 percent and Bihar and Madhya Pradesh account for nearly 75 percent. The share of the service sector in NSDP ranges from 40 percent in Assam to 51 percent in Jammu & Kashmir. As against it, the share of industry in NSDP ranges from as low as 12 percent in Jammu & Kashmir and 18 percent in Orissa to 29 percent in

Table 12.8

Relative Shares of NSDP and Employment in Agriculture, Industry and Services

State	Per capita NSDP Rs. 2000-01	Percentage share of NSDP at 1993-94 prices as (2000-01)			Percentage share of Employment (1999-2000)			Output Employment ratios (O/L)		
		Agriculture	Industry	Services	Agriculture	Industry	Services	Agriculture	Industry	Services
	(1)	(2)	(3)	(4)	(5)	(6)	(7)	8=2/5	9=3/6	10=4/7
1. Punjab	15,048	40.5	22.5	37.0	53.4	20.1	26.6	0.76	1.12	1.39
2. Maharashtra	14,211	13.7	32.8	53.5	56.6	17.7	25.7	0.24	1.85	2.08
3. Haryana	13,822	33.0	26.3	40.7	53.8	19.9	26.4	0.61	1.32	1.54
4. Tamil Nadu	13,017	18.6	31.8	49.6	47.2	26.8	26.0	0.39	1.19	1.91
5. Gujarat	12,489	15.0	38.1	46.9	60.1	17.4	22.5	0.25	2.19	2.08
6. Karnataka	11,900	30.3	23.5	46.2	63.1	15.7	21.2	0.48	1.50	2.18
7. Himachal Pradesh	11,029	24.4	33.1	42.5	69.6	15.2	15.2	0.35	2.18	2.80
8. Kerala	10,501	25.1	19.7	55.2	40.0	26.7	33.2	0.62	0.73	1.66
9. Andhra Pradesh	10,195	30.0	23.0	47.0	66.3	13.4	20.2	0.45	1.72	2.33
10. West Bengal	9,796	26.5	21.2	52.5	46.6	25.3	28.1	0.57	0.84	1.88
11. Rajasthan	8,041	27.5	28.6	43.9	67.6	17.1	15.3	0.41	1.67	2.87
12. Madhya Pradesh	7,195	27.6	29.6	42.8	74.5	10.5	15.0	0.37	2.82	2.85
13. Jammu and Kashmir	7,385	36.6	12.2	51.2	62.9	15.2	21.9	0.58	0.80	2.33
14. Assam	5,943	38.7	21.0	40.3	60.5	8.6	30.9	0.64	2.44	1.30
15. Orissa	5,562	34.4	18.4	47.2	71.6	14.1	14.3	0.48	1.30	3.30
16. Uttar Pradesh	5,570	35.7	21.4	42.9	63.7	16.5	19.8	0.56	1.30	2.17
17. Bihar	3,879	32.0	24.7	43.3	74.0	10.7	15.3	0.43	2.31	2.83
All India	10,308	25.5[1]	24.0[1]	50.5[1]	60.8[2]	17.1[2]	22.1[2]	0.42	1.40	2.29

Notes : 1. All India distribution of NSDP is taken from CSO (2005), *National Accounts Statistics.*

2. Represents the mean of 23 states as given in Planning Commission, *Tenth Five Year Plan, 2002-07*, Vol. III, p. 75.

3. Percentage distribution of NSDP for various states has been taken from Economic and Political Weekly Research Foundation, *Domestic State Product of States in India (1960-61 to 2000-01).*

4. Percentage share in Employment has been taken from Employment and Unemployment data on CD-ROM for year 1983, 1993-94 and 1999-00 by NSSO, New Delhi.

Rajasthan. In view of high share in employment in agriculture, the shares of employment in industry and services together fluctuate between 25 percent to 40 percent. Obviously, the situation in these states is a low level of equilibrium in both NSDP and employment. The low level of productivity in agriculture, failure to move towards industrial or post-industrial service economy has been experienced in these states. Some of these states are making efforts to boost productivity in foodgrains—Andhra Pradesh 2,102 kgs and Uttar Pradesh 2,164 kgs per hectare, all other states have been operating at much lower levels of productivity. Moreover, in these states, there is a pressing need to intensify the rate of growth in industry and services, but unless a second Green Revolution in agriculture is not achieved, progress towards industrialization and post-industrial economy will also be restrained.

8. CONCLUSION

The survey of NSDP and employment shares in various states reveals a wide disparity. In Punjab and Haryana, the high share of NSDP from agriculture was the result of high productivity in agriculture with a small reduction of employment share in agriculture. However, the relatively high shares of NSDP in agriculture in poor states like Andhra Pradesh, Rajasthan, Madhya Pradesh, Jammu & Kashmir, Uttar Pradesh and Bihar were due to backwardness of agriculture, low levels of development in industry and services but these states have a very high proportion of workforce dependent on agriculture, with very small proportion drawing their livelihood from industry and services. Kerala and West Bengal, though medium level states in per capita NSDP indicate relatively lower share of NSDP originating from agriculture (25%) and over 50 percent from services and about 20 to 21 percent in industry.

There is a need to study the production and employment pattern of every state and evolve suitable policies to strengthen agriculture in the first instance which provides livelihood or employment to nearly two-third to three-fourth of the labour. A break-through in agriculture will provide a push to industry and services as a consequence of the increase in labour and land productivity in agriculture. The industry sector (or more popularly manufacturing) has lagged behind the growth in services. This transition witnessed in most of the states to a post-industrial 'service economy' without passing through a process of industrialization has been noted as a major weakness of the outcome of the development process undertaken in the country during the last 50 years. State level analysis indicates the policy directions that should be pursued in future so that sectoral disparities in NSDP and employment pattern are reduced.

The terms agriculture, industry and services in this paper correspond to the meaning of primary, secondary and tertiary sector, unless indicated otherwise.

References

Ajit Singh (2005), 'Manufacturing Services, Jobless Growth and Informal Economy : Will services be the new Engine of Growth in India?', Presentation in a Seminar at ILO, New Delhi, 16th February.

Baumol, W.J. (1967), Macroeconomics of Unbalanced Growth : The Anatomy of Urban Crisis, *Americal Enonomic Review*, Vol. 57.

———, (2001), "Paradox of the Services: Exploding Costs, Persistent Demand in Ten Raa and R. Schetkatt (eds.), The Growth of Service Industries: *The Paradoxof Exploding Costs and Persistent Demand,* Cheltenham, Edward Elgar.

Fisher, A.G.B. (1939), 'Production: Primary, Secondary and Tertiary', *The Economic Journal,* Vol. XV, Government of India (2005), *Economic Survey* (2004-05).

IAMR, *Manpower Profile India* (2004).

Papola, T.S. (2005), Emerging Structure of the Indian Economy—Implications of Growing Inter-Sectoral Imbalances, Presidential address, 88th Annual Conference of the Indian Economic Association, December 27-29.

Rangrajan, C. (2006), Employment and Growth, V.V. Giri Memorial Lecture, New Delhi

Reserve Bank of India (2005), *Handbook of Statistics of The Indian Economy,* (2004-05).

World Bank (2004), and (2005), *World Development Indicators.*

CHAPTER

13

Prime Minister's Critique of Reforms

I. ECONOMIC REFORMS—GROWTH *VERSUS* EQUITY

Mani Shankar Aiyer, not caring for the fact that he was a Minister in the UPA Government made a strong critique of reforms when he asserted: In the name of reforms, the country was propelling growth that only benefits big industrialists, leaving the vast majority of Indians and the small scale industry in a state of neglect and deprivation. The benefits of growth reach only the rich and the poor continue to be poor. Mr. Aiyer's comments were accepted by quite a number of persons in the Congress who felt that the growth process divided the country into a 'Shining India' and a 'Suffering India', to put it in the language of left critics. Mr. Aiyer quoted a journalist: Masses determine who will rule India, but the classes determine the policies of the government.

On May 1, 2007, Prime Minister Manmohan Singh joined the debate while inaugurating the Campus of the Institute for Studies in Industrial Development when he said; "*I was struck by a comment in the media* that most of the billionaires among India's top business leaders operate in obligopolistic markets, and in sectors where the government has conferred special privileges on a few. This sounds like crony capitalism. Are we encouraging crony capitalism? Is this necessary phase in the development of modern capitalism in our country? Are we doing enough to protect consumers and small businesses from the consequences of modern capitalism in our country." (Emphasis added)

Referring to problems faced by small and medium enterprises, the Prime Minister said: "Do we have a genuine level playing field for all businesses? What should be done to project a greater degree of competitiveness in industrial sector?

Underlying the need for a level playing field, Mr. Singh said there was a need to focus on the role of small and medium enterprises in industrial development. "We cannot depend on a few large industrial houses and capitalists for driving our industrial process. The employment intensive nature and the greater regional spread of small and medium enterprises makes them an attractive option for our industrial growth processes."

Subsequently, Prime Minister Manmohan Singh in his inaugural address at the Annual Session of the Confederation of Indian Industry on May 24, 2007, told India Inc to break cartels and abstain from ostentatious consumption and greed in their quest for profit maximization and warned business that growing income inequalities could lead to social unrest. To quote the Prime Minister:

> "The operation of cartels by groups of companies to keep prices high must end. It is unacceptable to obstruct the forces of competition from having free play. It is even more distressing in a country where the poor are severely affected by rising commodity prices. *Cartels are a crime and go against the grain of an open economy.*" (Emphasis added)

The Prime Minister added: "Maximization of profits should be within the bounds of decency and greed."

Commenting on the vulgar display of wealth by the rich in lavish weddings and other social ceremonies, he said, "they were a blatant expression of wasteful expenditure. Such vulgarity insults the poverty of the less privileged; it is socially wasteful and it plants seeds of resentment in the minds of have-nots."

The Prime Minister cautioned India Inc. on the high level of remuneration for its promoters and senior executives.

The Prime Minister exhorted industry to fight corruption at all levels. "Corruption need not be the grease that oils wheels of progress. There are many successful companies today that have refused to yield to this temptation. Others must follow."

Reminding industry of their corporate social responsibility, Dr. Manmohan Singh suggested a 10-point charter of social responsibility.

Presenting the government's Report to the people for 2004-07, the Prime Minister emphasized: "High national income growth alone could not address the challenges of employment generation or poverty reduction." All policies of the UPA Government were guided by the strategy of "inclusive growth." He listed his government's achievements—high economic growth rate, increase in outlays of education and health, remunerative prices for farmers and massive investments for rural development and agriculture.

PM's 10-point Charter for Corporate Social Responsibility

1. Respect workers and invest in their welfare.
2. Undertake corporate social responsibility.
3. Implement affirmative action and offer jobs to SCs, STs and OBCs.
4. Resist excessive remuneration of promoters and senior executives. Avoid conspicuous consumption.
5. Invest in people and their skills.
6. End cartels that keep high prices.
7. Invest in eco-friendly technologies.
8. Promote enterprise and innovation.
9. Fight corruption at all levels.
10. Promote socially responsible media.

2. REACTIONS TO THE PM'S SUGGESTION TO INDUSTRY

Reacting to the Prime Minister's suggestions to the corporates to resist excessive remuneration to promoters and senior executives, CII and Assocham responded that the decision on remuneration should be left to the companies themselves. Mr. Sunil Bharti Mittal said: CEO's salaries could not be legislated. There is shortage of skills in key areas, especially in the service industry that is seen in high salaries, but the cases of high salaries are few. In short, industry circles dismissed the PM's suggestion of restraining CEO's salaries and promoters remuneration and suggested that it should be left to market forces.

Both the CPM and BJP criticized the PM's speech by stating: Most of the government's policies were aimed at benefiting the industrialists. His appeal to industry was only for "public consumption". Within the Congress circles, the opinion was divided. Official spokesperson welcomed the PM's rhetoric, but quite a section of the Congress leaders felt that there is a need for course correction and move in the direction of growth and social justice. In case, this is not done and the price rise in essential commodities continues, it would be very difficult for the government to win the confidence of *aam admi* (common man).

It would be of interest to outline the major steps needed on two issues: (a) Ending cartels so as to check high prices; and (b) to restrain the sharp like in the remuneration of promoters and high salaries of CEO's.

Both the issues are related to Corporate Social Responsibility—a modern version of Gandhi's idea of trusteeship. This idea has remained a pious sentiment and the reaction of the Chambers of industry is: Salaries cannot be legislated. They should be left to the companies, meaning thereby market forces.

3. GROUND REALITY AND NEED FOR STRONG ACTION

What are the ground realities in this regard: A look at the Annual Remuneration of the top executives in 2004-05 reveals that the corporate heads are appropriating heavy amounts in the form of salaries and commissions. Top 20 CEOs, several of whom are promoters of the companies, received a heavy amount of Rs. 187 crores in 2004-05 as salaries including commissions. The Ambani Brothers—Mukesh and Anil of Reliance Industries Ltd. together siphoned of Rs. 43.44 crores in 2004-05. Similarly, four top CEOs of Hero Honda Motors Ltd. got over Rs. 52.54 crores. The range of the salary of the top CEOs in 20 top companies is between Rs. 4 crores and Rs. 20 crores. If the salary of the lowest paid employee is Rs. 5,000 per month, then the CEO's annual remuneration works out to be in range of 1:667 and 1:3,333 times.

When the CEOs draw such hefty amounts, they are also obliged to pay heavy amounts to other managers and professionals employed in their companies at various levels

So the common argument is: Let us raise the rate of growth of the economy to 8-10 percent. Ultimately, all will benefit. So don't worry about the poor. But the hard reality is that salaries of executives are growing at the rate of 15% per annum in the private sector in India, but as against it, "according to the Annual Survey of Industries, real wages stagnated or declined even for workers in the organized industry, although managerial and technical staff did secure large increase."

"The wage share in our organized industrial sector has halved after 1980's and is now among the *lowest in the world.* One reason for this is increasing capital intensity of the organized sector, another is outsourcing." (*Approach to the 11th Five Year Plan,* p. 73).

The Prime Minister emphasized the goal of "inclusive growth." However, ILO Report on *Labour and Social Trends in Asia and the Pacific (2006)* brings out the stark reality that between 1990 and 2002, there was a decline in real wages in manufacturing in India by 22 percent, despite an increase in manufacturing labour productivity of over 84 percent over the same period. Obviously, this implies that the fruits of economic reforms are pocketed by the upper echelons in the private sector, while labour is denied its due. Ironically, the salaries of managerial and technical staff have been increasing at the rate of 15% per annum. The question which the critics pose is: Are we promoting 'inclusive growth' or 'exclusive grwoth'? The poor, therefore, look upon themselves as the victims of development. Their perception is: Under the garb of promoting competition, real wages of labour have declined. Their livelihood is being snatched in rural areas by the policy of Special Economic Zones (SEZs), as promoters of rapid industrialization. The tribals are victims of a policy which gives contracts to big forests contractors, and thus deprives the tribals of their ancestral right on forests as a means of livelihood. It is, therefore, imperative that the state must turn its attention to the poor so as to transform the poor from being victims of development to partners of development. This is the challenge for the government. Prime Minister should, therefore, shed the idea of 'trusteeship' or 'Corporate Social Responsibility' and devote his attention to undertake concrete steps to improve the lot of the poor—urban as well as rural. This can be done by a programme of empowering the rural poor and tribals in development projects, and not excluding them. Besides this, profit maximization has to be tempered to reasonable levels by linking wages to productivity. For this, there is a need to take legislative action. It would be a folly to leave everything to market forces. State intervention is a necessity.

Strong Action to End Cartels

Dr. Manmohan Singh urged Corporate India to "desist from non-competitive behaviour. The operation of cartels by groups of companies to keep prices high must end. It is unacceptable to obstruct the forces of competition from having free play." None of the chambers of industry responded even by a verbal commitment that they will themselves initiate action in this regard. Experience the world over suggests that unless the state took effective and direct action against cartels, concrete results could not be obtained. The US Government used the 'leniency principle' to break cartels. The principle is simple, it grants lenient treatment to a member of the cartel to blow the whistle on the conspiracy, provide vital evidence against it and co-operate with the competition authority in the investigation. The principle is not new, it is simply the application of 'approver principle' in the Indian Criminal Law to the economic domain. Of the 50 cartels cases pending in USA in 2005, over half resulted from disclosure by 'whistle blowers' or 'leniency applicants'. It has also been reported that since 1997, the US authorities obtained over $2 billion and in 2002 alone, the total jail sentences amounted to 10,000 days, the average jail sentence rising to 18 months!

Some of the most notorious cartels were busted with the help of leniency applications. The Global Vitamins Cartel led to penalties of $500 million on Hoffman-La Roche and $225 million of BASF, plus prison term for senior executives. Rhone Pouplence, the leniency applicant, escaped punishment. Seeing the spectacular success of the leniency programme, the European Commission, the UK, Canada, Germany, France, Brazil, Japan, Mexico, Korea and Australia took similar action.

The basic question is: Did the Prime Minister direct the Competition Commission of India (CCI) to initiate strict action against them. Mr. Vinod Dhall, acting chairman and member of the CCI laments: "In India too, the Competition Act, 2002 contains stringent provisions against cartels. Unfortunately, the Act's enforcement sections are yet to come into force, awaiting as they are, pending amendments to the Act. Till then the Competition Commission of India (CCI) cannot inquire into alleged cartels, or other violations of the Act." (Vinod Dhall, Blowing the Whistle on Cartels, *Economic Times*, May 29, 2007)

The sincerity of the Government stands exposed that even after five years of the passage of the Competition Act (2002), its provisions are yet awaiting enforcement. A fine example of hypocrisy!!

To sum up: the Government must act decisively on both issues. Mr. N.R. Narayanamurthy, CEO, Infosy propagating without any perceptible effect, that the salary of the topmost CEO should be fixed between 15 to 20 times the lowest pay in the organization. This can help the government in several ways: Firstly, it will stop or at least slow down the exodus of competent executives, both technical and managerial from the public sector to the private sector. Secondly, it will facilitate the Government to review the entire structure of salaries after intervals of 10 years by the appointment of Pay Commission. The jurisdiction of the Commission should be extended to both the public sector an the private sector so that talent gets evenly distributed. Let it be clearly understood that even in the United States, *New York Times*, editorial "A say on Executive pay" (May 26, 2007) has pointed out that the chasm between excessively paid corporate executives and the average worker in US and the deleterious effects it has produced is being put under a scanner. Shareholders of increasing number of companies are demanding their prior concurrence for pay packages, and US Congress is said be thinking of a law to keep emoluments within the limits of decency. It is only effective state policies that can deliver the goods. Time has come to demonstrate that the government will not exhaust itself with mere barking, but will also bite if its suggestions are ignored. Similarly, the Cartels have to be busted as early as possible to save the common man from the adverse effects of high prices. Let direct action replace pious statements.

There is a need to reconsider economic reform agenda so that growth and social justice are effectively reconciled and state policies do not encourage, to use PM's words, crony capitalism. Let us provide level playing field to small and medium industries, provide incentives to enterprises creating more employment. The whole gamut of policies need a review.

CHAPTER

14

Eleventh Five Year Plan and Inclusive Growth

I. OBJECTIVES AND TARGETS AND POLICIES OUTLINED

The Planning Commission presented a draft of the Approach to the 11th Five Year Plan (2007-08) in January 2006. This draft was considered by the National Development Council and in the light of observations of the NDC, a final version of the Approach to the 11th Plan titled *"Towards faster and More Inclusive Growth"* has been presented in December 2006. The document accepts that though the Tenth Plan (2002-07) has accelerated annual average GDP growth rate to 7.2 percent, it has not been able to address the problems of the common man. To quote the Approach to the 11th Five Year Plan." This performance reflects the strength of our economy and the dynamism of the private sector in many areas. Yet, it is also true that economic growth has failed to be sufficiently inclusive, particularly after the mid-1990s. Agriculture lost its growth momentum from that point on and subsequently entered a near crisis situation. Jobs in the organized sector have not increased despite faster growth. The percentage of our population below the poverty line is declining but only at a modest pace. Malnutrition levels also appear to be declining, but the magnitude of the problem continues to be very high. For too many people still lack access to basic services such as health, education, clean drinking water and sanitation facilities without which they cannot claim their share in the benefits of growth."[1]

The document hastens to add: "Rapid growth is an essential part of our strategy for two reasons: Firstly, it is only in a rapidly growing economy that we can expect to sufficiently raise the incomes of the mass of our population to bring about a general improvement in living conditions. Secondly, rapid growth is necessary to generate the resources needed to provide basic services to all."[2]

The Planning Commission has suggested that "growth can accelerate to around 9 percent over the 11th Plan period, provided appropriate policies are put in place. With population growing at 1.5% per year, 9% growth in GDP would double the real per capita income in 10 years. This must be combined with policies that will ensure that this per capita income growth is broad based, benefiting all sections of the population, especially those who have thus far remained deprived."

The main economic indicators of the 11th Plan are summarized in Table 14.1.

TABLE 14.1

Macro-economic Indicators for the 11th Five Year Plan

	10th Plan (Actual)	*11th Plan (Average)*
1 Growth Rate of GDP (%)	**7.2**	**9.0**
(a) Agriculture	1.7	4.0
(b) Industry	8.3	10.5
(c) Services	9.0	9.9
2. Investment rate (% of GDP) of which	**27.8**	**35.0**
(a) Public	6.7	10.2
(b) Private	21.1	24.9
3. Domestic Saving Rate (% of GDP) of which	**28.2**	**32.3**
(a) Household	22.8	22.0
(b) Corporate	4.5	6.1
(c) Public Sector Enterprises	4.2	3.0
(d) Government	–3.2	1.2
4. Current Account Balance (% of GDP)	**0.2**	**-2.8**
5. Government Fiscal Balance (% of GDP)	**-8.0**	**-6.0**

Source : Planning Commission (2006), *An Approach to the 11th Five Year Plan*, p. 18.

With overall GDP growth target of 9%, the target for agricultural growth has been fixed at 4%, for industry 10.5% and services at 9.9%. Compared with the 10th Plan, target for agriculture has been more than doubled, but for industry, there is a small increase from 8.3% to 10.5% and for services from 9% to 9.9%.

The Plan projects that the growth rate of 9% of GDP could be achieved with an investment rate of 35.1 percent. Thus, the capital-output ratio has been assumed to be 3.9.

To step up the rate of investment to 35.1%, the country needs to improve the domestic saving rate to 32.3%, thus, by implication, admitting 2.8 percent of foreign savings.

The Plan document states: "A feasible objective is to accelerate from 8% growth at the end of 10th Plan to 10% by the end of the 11th Plan, yielding an average GDP growth rate of about 9% in the 11th Plan. . . . The structure of growth should also be such as to promote a wide spread of benefits. Doubling agricultural GDP growth to around 4%, is particularly important in this context. This must be combined to promote rapid growth in non-agricultural employment so as to create 70 million job opportunities in the 11th Plan. If these objectives are achieved, the percentage of people in poverty can be reduced by 10 percentage points by the end of the Plan period."[3]

On the external front, the Approach document estimates that current account deficit will become negative to the extent of 2.8 percent of GDP.

Education, Health and Other Essential Services

For promoting inclusive growth, the 11th Plan must extend access to public services such as health, education, clean drinking water, sanitation etc. which are currently denied to large parts of our population, especially in rural areas.

The provision of good quality education is the most important equalizer for the economy. The Eleventh Plan, therefore states: "Education is the most critical input for empowering people with skills and knowledge and for giving them access to productive employment in the future. The 11th Plan should ensure that we move towards raising public spending in education to 6% of GDP, which is an NCMP commitment. It must fulfill the constitutional obligation of providing free and compulsory elementary education of good quality to all children upto age 14."[4]

Sarva Shiksha Abhiyan (SSA)—Almost 100% enrolment of 6-14 year old, the major objective of SSA (education for all) is likely to be achieved by 2007. Enrolment however, is the first step. Children must also complete eight years of schooling and this continues to be a major challenge. The drop-out rate in primary schools for the country as a whole was around 31% in 2003-04 and it was much higher in many states. Drop-out rates for both boys and girls of all social groups must be reduced sharply, if not eliminated altogether.

Noting the poor quality of human and physical infrastructure, the 11th Plan states: "We should also note that just 28% of our schools had electricity in 2005 and only about half had more than two teachers or two classrooms. Only 40% of primary school teachers were graduates and 30% had not even completed Higher Secondary."[5] Quoting a study by *Pratham*, an NGO, the Plan document mentions: "38 percent of the children who have completed four years of schooling cannot read a small paragraph with short sentences meant to be read by a student of class II. About 55% of such children cannot divide a three digit number by a one digit number."

Secondary Education: Universalization of elementary education alone will not suffice in the knowledge economy. A person with merely 8 years of schooling will be as disadvantaged in a knowledge economy dominated by ICT as an illiterate person in modern industry and services. The 11th Plan must therefore aim to progressively raise the minimum level of education to high school or class X level.

The Plan notes that at present, private aided and unaided schools account for 58% of the total number of secondary schools and 25% of the student population. But public school education being costly, government schools account for 75% of enrolment of secondary schools. To meet the needs of children from poor families who complete primary education, it is necessary that the quality of government schools be improved.

Technical or vocational Training: India has 5,000 Industrial Training Institutes (ITIs) under the Ministry of Labour and 7,000 vocational schools under the Ministry of Human Resource Development. According to the 11th Plan, the total capacity of these vocational Training Institutes is a mere 2 to 3 million and there is a need to enlarge their capacity to 15 million. ITIs in India cater to around 40 skills compared with 4,000 in China. There is a need to strengthen Public Private Partnership models and involve industry to design such courses keeping in view the State-of Art Technology.

Higher and Technical Education: Although India has a well developed and comprehensive higher education system, yet it caters to only 10% of the relevant age group going to the universities and colleges, although in many developing countries, the comparable ratio is between 20 and 25 percent.

There should be three objectives in this regard—*expansion, inclusion and excellence.* It is a matter of deep concern that 6 to 8 states account for 60 percent of the engineering colleges or bio-tech R & D labs. The Eleventh Plan while undertaking expansion of higher education should take care of the regional divide and bridge it. Secondly, there is a need to make higher and technical education more inclusive by using various measures. The Central Government is taking measures to extend the coverage of deprived classes by expanding reservations besides SCs and STs to Other Backward Classes (OBCs). However, while doing so, the creamy layer among all deprived classes be excluded, so that really deprived can take benefit from it. Besides this, the availability of educational loans and scholarships can also enable the poor among the upper classes to benefit from higher education and thus, rise in the social ladder. Thirdly, there is a need to develop the quality of education in both privately-managed and publicly-managed higher education institutions. To achieve all the three objectives, it would be necessary to pump more resources in higher education. The beneficiaries of the higher educational outputs, viz., the State and the Corporate sector should strengthen the quantum of resources needed for the purpose.

On the external front, the Plan projects an average increase of imports by 12.1 percent. Hopefully, it projects an increase of exports by 16.1 percent.

Even then, on current account, the Plan projects a negative balance of the order of 2.6 percent of GDP.

Health, Education and Other Essential Services

In the matter of health, there are large gaps in the availability of health services such as maternal and child care, clean drinking water and access to basic sanitation facilities for the mass of our population, especially the poor, who do not have minimum access.

Bharat Nirman

Bharat Nirman is a time-bound action plan in rural infrastructure development for a 4-year period (2005-09). The main goals set out in the programme are as under:

Irrigation	: To create 10 million hectares of additional irrigation capacity.
Rural Roads	: To connect all habitations (66,802) with population above 1,000 (500 in hilly areas) with all-weather roads.
Rural Housing	: To construct 60 lakh houses for rural poor.
Rural Water Supply	: To provide potable water to all uncovered habitations (55,067) and also cover slipped back and water quality affected habitations.
Rural Electrification	: To provide electricity to all un-electrified villages (1,25,000) and to connect 23 million households below the poverty line.
Rural Telephony	: To connect all remaining villages (66,822) with a public telephone.

Some of the services e.g. education and healthcare are available in the private sector, but their supply being very costly, they are beyond the reach of the common man. Obviously, bulk of burden of providing these services has to be borne by the public sector funding.

The Tenth Plan also mentions: "The delivery of these services is poor and those responsible for delivering the services cannot be held accountable." For the purpose of improving accountability in rural areas, the Plan proposes more active supervisation by the Panchayati Raj Institutions (PRIs). The help of NGOs need to be taken in urban areas. For secondary and higher education and also for tertiary healthcare, other methods of monitoring have to be devised to improve accountability.

To enlarge and improve the quality of education, health and related essential services will require an enhancement in public spending. Both the

MONITORABLE SOCIO-ECONOMIC TARGETS OF THE 11TH PLAN

Income and Poverty

- Accelerate growth rate of GDP from 8% to 10% and then maintain at 10% in the 12th Plan in order to double per capita income by 2016-17
- Increase agricultural GDP growth rate to 4% per year to ensure a broader spread of benefits
- Create 70 million new work opportunities
- Reduce educated unemployment to below 5%
- Raise real wage rate of unskilled workers by 20 percent
- Reduce the headcount ratio of consumption poverty by 10 percentage points

Education

- Reduce dropout rates for children from elementary school from 52.2% in 2003-04 to 20% by 2011-12.
- Increase literacy rate for persons of age 7 years or more to 85%
- Lower gender gap in literacy to 10 percentage points
- Increase the percentage youth of the relevant age-group going to higher education from the present 10% to 15% by the end of the 11th Plan.

Health

- Reduce infant mortality rate (IMR) to 28 and maternal mortality rate (MMR) to 1 per 1000 live births.
- Reduce Total Fertility Rate to 2.1
- Provide clean drinking water for all by 2009
- Reduce malnutrition among children of age group 0-3 to half its present level.
- Reduce anemia among women and girls by 50% by the end of the 11th Plan

Infrastructure

- Ensure electricity connection to all villages and BPL households by 2009 and round-the-clock power by the end of the Plan.
- Ensure all-weather road connection to all habitation with population 1000 and above (500 in hilly and tribal areas) by 2009, and ensure coverage of all significant habitation by 2015.
- Connect every village by telephone by November 2007 and provide broadband connectivity to all villages by 2012.

Provide homestead sites to all by 2012 and step up the pace of house construction for rural poor to cover all the poor by 2016-17.

Central and State Governments should endeavour to increase budgetary allocations for these services.

Accelerating Agricultural Growth to 4% of GDP

Accelerating GDP growth in agriculture to around 4 percent as envisaged in the Eleventh Plan, is not an easy task. Actual growth of agricultural GDP, including forestry and fishing was only 1.7% per annum during the Tenth Plan. The challenge posed is to more than double agricultural growth rate achieved in the 10th Plan. This will require efforts on many fronts:

Firstly, prices of agricultural products have failed to keep pace with the costs and as a consequence, profitability in agriculture has declined. This would necessitate state intervention to improve the prices of agricultural produce. For this purpose, the Eleventh Plan recommends amendments in the Agricultural Produce Marketing Committee Acts and also facilitate contract farming.

Secondly, it is necessary to shift from a focus on productivity of individual crops to a focus on enhancement of farm incomes, recognizing the farm as a multi-product system. This would require diversification of crops so that value-added crops are encouraged.

Thirdly, the National Commission on Farmers has recommended that the rate of public investment in agriculture is to be stepped up, more especially in irrigation, watershed development, rural road connectivity and rural electrification.

11th Plan Approach targets to bring an additional 11 million hectares under irrigation – 5.5 million from major & medium irrigation, 3.5 million hectares through minor irrigation and about 2 million hectares through ground water development.

The Plan has estimated that the revitalization of agriculture so as to achieve the target of 4% growth would require the provision of Rs. 80,000 crores. The Approach Paper has suggested that besides additional allocation, the resources should be supplemented by Employment Guarantee Programme.

Fourthly, another and major recommendation of the 11th Plan approach is to recognize the need for land reform. In this connection, 11th Plan mentions: "Lack of recognized tenancy rights makes it difficult for *de facto* tenants to get credit from formal sources. Tenants without legal rights do not have proper incentive to develop land and this explains part of yield gap."[6]

Fifthly, there is a need to identify the knowledge deficit in agriculture. This will require revitalization of agricultural extension system linking with improvement of Krishi Vikas Kendras (KVKs) in every district. For this purpose, soil testing to inform farmers of micro-nutrient deficiencies should be greatly expanded.

Sixthly, there is a need to review the policy of supplying free electric power to farmers which only encourages excessive use of water. Similarly, the present system of fertilizer subsidy is not well-balanced and this results in excessive use of nitrogenous fertilizer which reduces productivity in the longer term. "These are politically sensitive issues but ignoring them only make the problem worse," says the Approach Paper.

Seventhly, inadequate access to credit is a major problem affecting most farmers often pushing them into the hands of moneylenders who charge exorbitant rates. To alleviate the situation, co-operative credit system needs to be revitalized. According to the Approach Paper, "The Central Government has indicated its willingness to provide resources to recapitalize the system provided state governments agree to a framework in which the credit co-operatives are effectively depoliticized."

Lastly, over the longer term, agricultural research must be revitalized to ensure full exploitation of scientific advances which make it possible to improve productivity in various agro-climatic zones. The Central Government should in this regard implement the recommendations of the Swaminathan and Mashelkar Committees.

Industrial Sector Growth Target Fixed at 10%

"Accelerating GDP growth to 9% in the 11th Plan will require industry to grow at 10.5% and manufacturing at 12%. This calls for a substantial increase in investment in the industrial sector, combined with technological upgradation and modernization to achieve efficiency levels needed to survive in an increasingly competitive world.

The 11th Plan Approach Paper states: "Indian manufacturing is highly dualistic, with the organized sector producing 67% of manufacturing value added but employing only 12% of all workers in manufacturing. . . . A clear priority for the 11th Plan is to encourage the organized sector to employ more labour and, simultaneously, to improve productivity in the unorganized sector."[7]

"Labour intensive mass manufacturing based on relatively low skill levels provides an opportunity to expand employment in the industrial sector. China has done exceptionally well in this area and has opened up the world market in which we could compete effectively."[8]

It would be, therefore, appropriate to shift focus towards medium and small enterprises (MSEs). Agro-processing, sericulture and a host of other industries can be developed through encouraging MSEs. A cluster approach can help increase viability by providing these units with infrastructure, information, credit, and support services of better quality at lower costs.

11th Plan draws attention to the problems generated by Special Economic Zones (SEZs) when it states: "there is lack of a level playing field between manufacturing units within SEZs and in the Domestic Tariff Area, and that there can be large loss of revenue on account of tax concessions for export of goods and services that are already being exported without such concessions. These concerns need to be addressed and where necessary adequate safeguards put in place."[9]

The Approach Paper recommends further reform measures to achieve these objectives: The inflexibility of our labour laws may be denying us the opportunity to expand employment in organized manufacturing sector. This is a sensitive issue but the Central Government should initiate a dialogue with labour leaders to evolve a consensus.

The policy of progressive dereservation of industries for small scale production has reduced the list of reserved industries form about 800 to 326. The policy should be accelerated in the 11th Plan.

Although industrial licensing has been virtually eliminated, residual entry barriers remain in sugar, petroleum refining and drug industry. These should be progressively eliminated.

Infrastructure Development

Lack of infrastructure is a major constraint on economic development and must be tackled on a priority basis by both the Centre and the States. Action on rural infrastructure is as important as action on strengthening urban infrastructure.

"Preliminary exercises suggest that investment in infrastructure defined as road, rail, air and water transport, power generation, transmission and distribution of telecommunication, water supply, irrigation and storage will need to increase from 4.6% to around 8% of GDP in the 11th Plan period."[10] This will place heavy burden on the public sector because the private sector investment is not likely to be available in these areas.

Bharat Nirman

Lack of rural infrastructure is high priority for inclusive growth and Bharat Nirman programme was conceived by the UPA government as the major instrument for its promotion. It needs to be reinforced in the 11th Plan so that critical targets for irrigation, rural road connectivity, rural drinking water, rural housing and rural telecom connectivity can be met.

Urban Infrastructure

Rapid economic growth will inevitably lead to greater urbanization. Unfortunately, the state of urban infrastructure in the country has deteriorated to an extent that we are not able to fully benefit from these economies. Poor urban infrastructure inflicts severe hardship on people. Congested roads, poor public transport, inadequate availability of water, improper treatment of sewage, uncollected solid waste and above all grossly inadequate housing that forces more than 50% of our urban population to live in slums, all these decrease the quality of life and lower the well-being of urban population. They also affect foreign investment because India cannot expect to make a favourable impression on foreign investors.

To improve urban infrastructure, the UPA government has launched on December 3, 2005 the Jawaharlal Nehru National Urban Renewal Mission (JNNURM) for a 7-year period beginning from 2005-06. It aims at integrated development of infrastructure services in 63 cities to improve civic amenities on universal access basis to urban poor. The scheme involves a total allocation of Rs. 50,000 crore to be provided by the Central Government as Additional Central Assistance in the form of 100% grant as a percentage of project cost from 35% (for Mega cities) to 90% (for North Eastern states).

Power Sector development is critical for industrial growth and the real problem is with the distribution system. This is entirely in the hands of state governments and they should give top priority to improving performance of distribution companies.

Public Private Partnerships (PPPs) are very desirable as a supplement to the effort of private sector. PPPs can sometimes run into controversies if the private partner is seen to have received unduly favourable treatment. It is, therefore, essential to evolve a framework for public private partnerships based on principles which ensure that PPPs are seen in public interest. This can be done by ensuring that the terms of concession agreements are transparent and protective of public interest, and also that there is robust competitive bidding so that least cost options are chosen. This approach has been adopted by the Centre in roads, ports, airways and railways. State governments should adopt a similarly transparent approach to ensure that PPP projects succeed.

Bridging the Divides in the Society

The strategy of inclusive growth can command broad-based support, only if it seen to bridge the prevailing divides. The Eleventh Plan has identified four major divides:

(i) Divide between the rich and the poor.
(ii) Divide with regard to access to essential services.
(iii) Rural-Urban divide.
(iv) Regional Divide.

Growing divide between the rich and the poor

Estimation of Proportion and Number of poor (on the basis of methodology of the Expert Group, 1993), the percentage of population below the poverty line in 2004-05 is provisionally estimated at 27.8% in 2004-05."[11] Since 36% of the population was below the poverty line in 1993 the average decline in percentage of population below the poverty line over the period 1993 to 2004 is 0.74 percentage points per year, much less than implied by the official 1999-2000 data. Because of the slower reduction in the percentage of poor, the absolute number of poor is now estimated to be approximately 300 million in 2004-05, larger than the official 1999-2000 estimate of 260 million.

Underlining the slow reduction of poverty, 11th Plan states: "Although growth of non-agricultural GDP has been much higher, its benefits do not compensate for a deceleration in agricultural growth. In fact, much of the poverty reduction during 1999-2005 is because food prices hardly increased. The outcomes would therefore have been much better, had agricultural growth been more rapid."[12]

Employment

"The average daily status unemployment rate which had increased form 6.1% in 1993-94 to 7.3% in 1999-00, increased further to 8.3% in 2004-05."[13] A matter of serious concern is that this has been associated with a sharp increase in unemployment (from 9.3% in 1993-94 to 15.3% in 2004-05) among agricultural labour households which represent the poorest groups."

"Non-agricultural employment expanded robustly at an annual rate of 4.7% during 1999-2005 but this growth was entirely in the unorganized sector and mainly in low productivity self-employment. Employment in the organized sectors actually declined despite fairly healthy GDP growth."

. . . "According to the Annual Survey of Industries, real wages stagnated or declined even for workers in the organized industry although managerial and technical staff did secure large increase."

"The wage share in our organized industrial sector has halved after the 1980's and is now among the lowest in the world. One reason for this is increasing capital intensity of the organized sector, another is outsourcing."[14]

The 11th Plan estimates an increase of 65 million in labour force. Adding to this, the backlog of 35 million, the total number of unemployed will be of the order of 100 million. The Plan intends to create 65 million job opportunities. Thus, the backlog of unemployed at the end of the 11th Plan will be of the same order as 35 million at the start of the Plan. To achieve this, non-agricultural employment would need to accelerate to 5.8% per annum from 4.7% in 1999-2005. Obviously, the entire burden of creating employment in the non-agricultural sector will be borne by the unorganized sector, because with the most optimistic assumptions, the employment in organized sector will increase by barely 2 million, if past trends on the capital intensity ratio continue.

A basic and long standing concern relates to whether the growth strategy will bypass the poor, excluding them from the benefits of growth. This is obvious from the fact that the much higher growth of non-agricultural GDP is not trickling down to the poor, because agriculture is now accounting for 22 percent of GDP, but is supporting 60 percent of the labour force. In view of this scenario, the rate of decline of poverty despite a sharp increase of GDP growth to over 7 percent has slowed down or is at best, very modest.

Rural-urban divide and Growing Gap with Respect to Access to Essential Services

"Another divide that needs to be bridged is between the rural and the urban population. Data from NSS survey show that the ratio of urban to rural per capita consumption increased form 1.62 in 1993-94 to 1.76 in 1999-00 and further to 1.91 in 2004-05, which suggests that the rural urban divide is widening especially since the NSS probably does not fully capture consumption by the rich, particularly in urban areas. If the comparison is extended to gaps in availability of the essential services, the chasm is much deeper."[15]

Among other essential services are included (a) disparity in health and nutritional status, (b) education and skills and (c) availability of clean drinking water. The 11th Plan proposes to act decisively on both fronts. In case of rural areas, the effort is being made through Bharat Nirman; in the urban areas, Jawaharlal Nehru National Urban Renewal Mission (JNNURM) launched in 2005-06 is directed to improve urban services to the poor.

Even in urban areas, massive problems have emerged as a result of rapid growth of urban population. Even clean drinking water is not available to all. There is increasing growth of slums, there are regular breakdowns of power supply and there is increasing shortage of residential housing, more especially for the poor and the migrant population from rural areas.

Regional Divide

There is a growing gap between the richer and poor states in terms of overall GDP and per capita GDP growth rates. This has caused regional divide. The growth performance across states has varied and the performance of the poor states which have poor infrastructure has been disappointing. As a consequence, poor states failed to attract investment – both Indian and foreign.

However, there is convergence in educational and health indicators across states. The gap between the better performers and poorer states has narrowed. These improvements in infrastructure must be complemented by improvements in infrastructure and other elements which make for a pro-investment environment.

"Equally important is the emergence of large differences within states with many districts in states that are otherwise performing well suffering from severe backwardness. The causes of backwardness of districts are familiar. These are typically districts with rainfed agriculture or extensive land degradation, generally poor infrastructure and connectivity and low human development indicators. Many of these districts also have large tribal populations, where problems of tribal rights in forest areas have remained unresolved and contribute to persistent dissatisfaction."[16] In many of these districts, there is rise of Naxalism which poses a threat to the stability of the country.

To take care of the regional imbalance both among the states and within the states, the Government has launched a new programme to be funded by Backward Regions Grant Fund which will be applicable to identified districts.

2. CRITIQUE OF THE 11TH PLAN APPROACH

The 11th Plan Approach visualizes "Faster and more inclusive growth" as its objective. This, by itself is a welcome development that after a period of a decade and half of reforms initiated in 1991, it is being realized that the reform process has widened disparities between the rich and the poor, it has slowed down reduction of poverty to a modest figure of 0.74 percent for the period 1993-94 and 2004-05, it has resulted in a rise of unemployment from about 6 percent in 1993-94 to 7.32 percent in 1999-00 and further to 8.3 percent in 2004-05. Besides, it has sharpened the rural-urban divide as well as the regional divide between the fast growing forward states and slow growing backward states. The iniquitous growth that the reform process had generated was shaking the political foundation of the Indian society and there was a need for a course correction. Failure to do this would pose a serious threat to the UPA Government which rode to power on the plank of helping *Aam admi* (common man).

The question arises: Does the Approach Paper really address the concerns which it has chosen to redress?

The Approach document has fixed a target of pushing up overall GDP growth during the 11th Plan to an average rate of 9.0 percent, this will be achieved by boosting growth of agriculture to about 4 percent after a disappointing growth of 1.7 percent during the 10th Plan, and by pushing up growth of industry to 10.5 percent and services to 9.9 percent. It would be good to recall that industry indicated a growth rate of 8.3 percent and services to 9.0 percent during the 10th Plan. Obviously, in industry and services, the 11th Plan intends to improve growth rates only marginally, it is only by doubling growth rate in agriculture that its target of 9 percent growth is likely to be fulfilled. This implies that the success of the 11th Plan will be determined by the success in achieving growth targets in agriculture, moreso, when agriculture still continues to provide livelihood to 58 percent of our population. To that extent, the strategy indicates that the concept of 'inclusive growth' is a part of Eleventh Plan framework.

Reduction of Poverty—The basic Issue

But inclusive growth would become a reality only if there is a rapid decline in poverty coupled with rapid reduction of unemployment in the 11th Plan. A close reading of the Approach Paper reveals that there appears to be a very weak political will exhibited by the planners.

On the question of setting a target of poverty reduction, the Approach Paper mentions: "We can do this by aiming at doubling the real income of the average Indian in less than ten years time and also committing ourselves to reduce poverty to less than 10 percent in the same period." The Plan document has admitted that the percentage of poverty in 2004-05 is about 28 percent and thus, the 11th Plan intends to reduce it by 10 percent by 2017. This would imply a rate of reduction of poverty by about 1 percent during 2004-05 and 2016-17. This is even less than the decline in poverty observed during 1973-74 and 1986-87 when the average growth rate of GDP ranged around 5 percent.

There is another problem raised by Mohan Guruswamy et. al. about the definition of poverty line. "While the definition of hunger in terms of calories can remain constant, the definition of poverty is relative to the present levels of general prosperity...the present official poverty line is based only on calories and hence accounts for little else but the satiation of one's hunger. It would have been more accurate to define this as a *starvation line*, as that is exactly what it is."[17] (Emphasis added). The Planning Commission, thus, intends to reduce starvation line up to 10 percent by 2017. For providing a basic minimum, poverty line needs to be redefined in terms of basic needs approach. While India is aiming to become a super economic power by 2020, it will only reduce starvation by that date. In the light of this, India should adopt the International Poverty Line of $2 per day as the basis of determining the percentage of people in poverty. As per the *Human Development Report* (2005), on the basis of $1 per day, for the year 1999-00, people below the poverty line in India were of the order of 34.7% and if we use the norm of $2 per day, then 80 percent of the Indian population was below the poverty line. The present poverty line on the basis of calories does not even meet the rock bottom standard of poverty set at $1 per day, not to speak of reaching the standard of $2 per day basis on basic needs approach. The Planning Commission should, therefore, upgrade the poverty line to reach international standards as it intends to do in other sectors of manufacturing, services and yield of output in agriculture. It should not seek a false sense of satisfaction that it has been able to effectively reduce poverty.

Unemployment Problem

The 11th Plan estimates the new additions to the workforce would be the order of 65 million during the Plan period. If we add the 35 million backlog of unemployment, total employment requirement works out to 100 million. The Plan intends to create 65 million jobs. Consequently, the backlog of unemployed at the end of the 11th Plan will continue to be of the same order as at beginning of the Plan. The reduction of unemployment depends on two factors—achievement of pushing agricultural growth to 4 percent and increasing the absorptive capacity of the small and medium enterprises. The planners do not have any hope from the organized sector to generate more jobs. Whereas the growth objective is too ambitious in agriculture since it calls for more than doubling the growth achieved in the 10th Plan, there is likely to be shortfall in generation of employment in agriculture. While in industry, the 11th Plan identifies the problem, it has not suggested a concrete strategy to strengthen the small and medium enterprises. The rhetoric is not backed by policy support.

The 11th Plan Approach Paper is a rehash of the Report of the *Task Force on Employment Opportunities* (2001) headed by Dr. Monek Singh Ahluwalia, the then member, Planning Commission who is at present the Deputy Chairman of the Planning Commission. The Task Force suggested measures like the boosting of private sector investment in agriculture, development of integrated agricultural complexes and food parks by the corporate sector, giving contracts, to agro-companies for developing degraded wastelands, encouraging large industrial units, including MNCs to participate in the development of food processing industries, and involving large firms in various activities like construction, retail trade and road transport among others. In other words, the total task for employment generation should be given to the corporate sector. For facilitating this process, the Report suggested the total de-reservation of small industries in the next four years and the reform of the labour laws by deleting chapter VB of the Industrial Disputes Act so as to give the employers the right to hire and fire. The Report was considered to be anti-labour and most of its recommendations were thought to be employment restricting, rather than employment generating. The policy makers did not formally reject this Report, yet it was sidelined by appointing S P Gupta Special Group on Targeting 10 Million Employment Opportunities per year in September 2001.

The Special Group headed by Dr. S.P. Gupta highlighted the fact that since 93 percent of the labour force is employed in the unorganised sector, all attempts should be made to improve productivity and job quality of the unorganised sector. More emphasis should be laid on the growth of the unorganised sector, rather than substituting labour by capital. The Special Group pointed out that out of 7 percent of total employment in the organized sector, the share of the private sector was only 2.5 percent. The public sector is already shedding its excess labour. If the private sector is given the right to hire and fire by amending labour legislation, the immediate effect, according to the Special Group, would be more of firing rather than hiring. On the basis of international experience and imperative need of our country, the Special Group brought out the fact that small and medium industries (SMEs) should not only co-exist with large industries but should become the principal contributors of growth and employment.

The 11th plan, however, continues to recommend the complete de-reservation of small scale industries and thus withdraw reservation from 326 items which are still reserved. It continues to harp on labour law reform, even after acknowledging that there is no hope from the organized sector to generate additional employment.

Issue of Labour Flexibility

Shorn of its frills to pay homage to inclusive growth, the 11th Plan Approach Paper is a new avatar of the Report of the Task Force Report headed by Ahluwalia in 2001. The Approach Paper mentions, "It must be emphasized that labour flexibility does not mean "hire and fire". There are many aspects of labour laws where greater flexibility is needed and would be in the interest of labour as a whole in the sense that it would actually generate large volumes of employment in the organized sector by encouraging employers to expand employment. This flexibility is especially needed if we want to exploit the enormous opportunities offered by export markets . . . we should evolve a consensus on the scope of reforming key labour laws including especially the Industrial Disputes Act and the Contract Labour (Regularization and abolition) Act."[18] The statement very admirably clothes the hidden agenda of the Planning Commission. This is due to the developments taking place in the organized sector in recent years. The Textile Minister wants (i) raising of working hours from 48 to 60 per week, (ii) allowing women to work in night shifts, (iii) permitting contract labour, (iv) easy exit norms and (v) treating export industry as a public utility for the purpose of Industrial Disputes Act. To add to it, Commerce and Industry Minister Kamal Nath wants Special Economic Zones to be exempted from labour laws. Obviously, the direction in which the UPA government intends to push labour laws is amply clear, however, it may camouflage its policy in the 11th Plan by soft words.

The Planning Commission has set the goal of inclusive growth. It notes the fact that despite sharp increase in productivity, real wages of labour have declined. ILO report on *Labour and social Trends in Asia and the Pacific (2006)* brings out the hard reality that between 1990 and 2002, there was a decline in real wages in manufacturing in India by 22 percent, despite an increase in manufacturing labour productivity of over 84 percent over the same period. Obviously this implies that the fruits of economic reforms are pocketed by the corporate sector, while labour is denied its due. Ironically, the salaries of managerial and technical personnel have been increasing at the rate of 15% per annum. The Planning Commission's 'inclusive growth' fails to provide any strategy for improving the share of labour in the surplus generated by faster growth. Critics have serious doubts about the sincerity with which the equity objective is sought to be achieved by the 11th Plan. The determination of wages by market forces and taking away even the modicum of protection by labour laws will give the organized sector business magnates unbridled power to freely exploit and pauperize labour.

Accelerating the Growth of Agriculture

The most important issue relating to the success of the 11th Plan is to accelerate the growth rate in agriculture to 4% per annum, as against the present level of less than 2%. A number of measures have been suggested such as remunerative prices for farmers for their crops, shift from productivity of individual crops to farm income security by diversifying agriculture, stepping up public investment in irrigation, watershed development, rural electrification and rural infrastructure, etc. and improving access to credit so as to help farmers not to fall into the clutches of moneylenders who charge high rates of interest. Prof. S. Mullainathan of Harvard University in this connection states: "Credit is the most important resource which the rural populace lacks... Despite priority sector lending of PSU banks, farmers are still borrowing from local moneylenders at high rates."[19] (*Business Line*, 12th September 2006). For this purpose, the Government must assert through the agency of PSBs and willing private sector banks that they should give top priority to priority sector lending. This would require opening more branches to increase access to credit which should be done forthwith. Emphasizing the immediacy of the problem, Prof. Mullainathan says: "A lot of soul-searching needs to be done by banks and the RBI about why this segment of population is not being served by the financial sector. How do we go about it? I suspect the outcome of this process will determine the shape of the economy. If the key players make the correct calls, we can see a huge transformation in Rural India. The PSU banks, the RBI and the private banks such as ICICI Bank recognize the credit problem, but there is an immediacy of action that is needed on the issue."[20] The Approach Paper lacks the need for "immediate action". This requires the determination shown by Prime Minister Indira Gandhi to push the availability of priority sector lending and provide benefits to a large number of people, mostly belonging to the weaker sections.

Rural Infrastructure Excludes Social Infrastructure

The Approach Paper focuses on Bharat Nirman as the principal mechanism to provide rural infrastructure in the form of irrigation, rural roads, rural housing, rural water supply, electrification and telephony. The focus on economic infrastructure development is welcome, but what about social infrastructure in the form of investment in education and health.

National Common Minimum Programme pledged to raise public expenditure on education to at least 6% of GDP and on health to 2-3% of GDP. There is no mention in the Approach Paper about the present state of knowledge and health deficit in the economy. Mr. A K Bagchi et.al. in this connection charge the Approach Paper of complete neglect on this front. They state: "The AP Projects a massive programme of rural infrastructure but curiously enough that does not include the building of hundreds, if not thousands of schools with toilet and drinking water facilities which practically all major states need. It does not also put forward any programme for building PHCs or hospitals."[21] There is ample evidence to show that development of human resources along with physical capital can significantly accelerate growth.

Sharp Expansion of Secondary Education

Despite the fact that the Approach Paper quotes a study by Pratham, an NGO (2005) which "found that 38% of children who completed four years of schooling cannot read a small paragraph with short sentences meant to be read by a student of class 2. About 55% of such children cannot divide a three digit number by a one digit number", it talks of moving towards rapid-expansion of secondary education, without completing the universalisation of primary education. For this purpose, it is necessary to improve the infrastructure and quality of education in fully public funded schools. It may be noted the teachers in state run schools are paid higher emoluments when compared with teachers in unaided private schools, but it is lack of accountability and absence of a proper school environment which are responsible for the sorry state of affairs. The need for better funding of infrastructure of rural schools and establishing an accountability system can improve performance, in the case of first generation learners and/or whose parents possess very low level of schooling, though they are classified as literates

Projecting current account deficit to 2.8 percent

The Approach Paper intends to use higher level of current account deficit as a means for arranging the component of increase foreign savings along with increased domestic savings. The Approach Paper outlining its policy mentions: "The higher level of investment has to be financed by some combination of increased domestic savings and increased foreign savings as reflected in the larger current account deficit. (CAD) there are limits to the extent to which the CAD can be widened but it is reasonalble to assume that the CAD could be allowed to increase form 1.3% of GDP in 2005-06 to 3%, provided it is financed mostly from foreign direct investment (FDI) and long term borrowings than short-term borrowings or portfolio flows."

TABLE 14.2
Foreign Investment Flows

(*US $ billion*)

	2004-05	*2005-06*
Foreign Direct Investment	6.05 (39.3)	7.72 (38.2)
Portfolio Investment	9.32 (60.7)	12.49 (61.8)
Total	15.37 (100.0)	20.21 (100.0)

Source : *Reserve Bank of India Bulletin*, (March 2007).

It would be of interest to examine the ground reality in this regard. The share of FDI in total foreign investment of the order of $ 15.37 billion during

2004-05 was $ 6.05 billion (39.3%). This share declined to 38.2% in 2005-06. Obviously, the share of portfolio investment has been over 61 percent which is not a healthy trend.

Anther point which deserves attention is that the entire net FDI is not available for greenfield investment, but takes the form of acquisition of Indian companies and as a consequence, a very small proportion is available for technological upgradation.

The upshot of the above analysis that the policy of raising CAD deficit to a level of 2.8 percent of GDP has very questionable validity. The country has to follow a policy of having a positive balance of trade or at least permit a trade deficit which can be completely compensated by invisibles surplus. The situation has been continuously deteriorating during the last 4 years. But over-enthusiastic about our achievements on the export front, we have been neglecting the warnings to apply brakes on the import front.

It may be noted that our trade deficit which was of the order of $10.69 billion in 2003-04 has shot up to $51.84 billion in 2005-06—nearly five times in a matter of barely three years. There is no doubt that the large surplus on invisibles of the order of $17.04 billion in 2002-03 not only wiped out the trade deficit but created a favourable CAD of the order of $6.34 billion in 2002-03. This surplus improved to $14.08 billion in 2003-04, but turned into a CAD deficit in 2004-05 and further the CAD deficit nearly doubled to $9.2 billion in 2005-06. The Approach Paper did not take note of this stark reality. It may be noted in this connection that the off-quoted China had a trade surplus in 1997 and it has continued thereafter. The Approach Paper should have heeded the warning signals.

Financial Pattern Issue Sidelined

The proposed financial pattern for financing the 11th Plan is conspicuous by its absence. Experience of financing the public sector plan during the first four years of the 10th Plan reveals that as against an expectation of 1.3 percent from current revenues, the performance indicates a negative balance of the order of 23.8 percent. Against an expectation of 37.6 percent from public sector enterprises, actual realization was of the order of 14.4 percent. There was practically a negligible net inflow from abroad of the order of just 1.7 percent. In this scenario, market borrowings provided 107.4 percent of total financial resources. The emerging pattern of financing only underlines the stark reality that the only and major source of plan financing is market borrowing. As a result of heavy dose of market borrowing, the liabilities of the government in terms of interest and repayment of principal would mount enormously. The Eleventh Plan financial pattern has not been outlined in the Approach Paper. Would it be another fictitious exercise by the Planning Commission, has not been spelled out.

SUMMING UP

The Approach Paper set the correct goal in the form of moving 'Towards Faster and More Inclusive Growth', but it intends to chart out a course which is basically anti-labour and pro-corporate sector. This is precisely in conflict with the goal of providing a secure income and employment security for 'aam admi' (common man). The best way to achieve this is to promote small and medium enterprises and small peasant agriculture. But there is no clear policy of promoting SMEs. It also side-tracks the issue of pushing up small peasant agriculture. The recommendations of the National Commission on Farmers (NCF) headed by eminent agricultural scientist Dr M S Swaminathan regarding the setting up a fund for farmers affected by crop losses on the lines of a calamity fund, reducing interest on farm loans to 4% and not charging compound interest, and imposing quantitative restrictions on import of agricultural products, have not been included in the Approach Paper.

Giving its reaction to the Government on the Approach Paper, the CPM expressed concern about the Plan panel's "silence" on some issues like food security, strengthening of price support system, creation of price stabilization fund for agricultural commodities, universalizing crop insurance, protection to peasantry from subsidized imports of agricultural commodities and land reform. The CPM opposed "unbridled entry of corporate players and promotion of contract farming and sought greater intervention to protect the interests of farmers.

Beside, its policy of raising current account deficit is very questionable. There is complete absence of the financial pattern to be developed in the 11th Plan.

Whereas its emphasis on development of physical infrastructure is welcome, it has not paid adequate attention to the development of social infrastructure in the form of education and health and the resources which would be deployed for the purpose.

To what extent the high growth of GDP of the order of 9% will help the removal of poverty and unemployment, the Planning Commission has not been able to develop a road map to this effect.

REFERENCES

1. Planning Commission (2006), *An Approach to the 11th Five Year Plan,* (December 2006) p. 1.
2. *Ibid.*, p. 1.
3. *Ibid.*, p. 97.
4. *Ibid.*, p. 57.
5. *Ibid.*, p. 58.
6. *Ibid.*, p. 29.
7. *Ibid.*, p. 30 and 31.
8. *Ibid.*, p. 32.
9. *Ibid.*, p. 31.
10. *Ibid.*, p. 40.

11. *Ibid.*, p. 71.
12. *Ibid.*, p. 72.
13. *Ibid.*, p. 72.
14. *Ibid.*, p. 73.
15. *Ibid.*, p. 82.
16. *Ibid.*, p. 63.
17. Guruswamy, Mohan and Abraham, Ronald, (2006), *Redefining Poverty—A New Poverty Line for a New India*, p. 2.
18. Planning Commission, *An Approach to the 11th Five Year Plan*, p. 61.
19. Mullianathan S, For farmers: The real issue is access to credit, *Business Line*, September 12, 2006.
20. *Ibid*
21. Bagchi, Amiya Kumar, Banerjee, Devdas and Chakraborty, Achin, A Critique of the Approach Paper to Eleventh Plan, *Economic and Political Weekly*, August 5, 2006.

Select References

Planning Commission, (2006), *An Approach to the 11th Five Year Plan (December 2006).*

Guruswamy, Mohan and Abraham Ronald (2006), *Redifining Poverty—A New Poverty Line for a New India.*

Bagchi, Amiya Kumar, Banerjee, Devadas and Chakraborty, Achin A Critique of the Approach Paper to Eleventh Plan, *Economic and Political Weekly*, August 5, 2006.

PART II

SOCIAL ISSUES

CHAPTER

15

Census Data on Religions—The Essential Message Lost

I. SALIENT FEATURES OF CENSUS DATA ON RELIGIONS

Census Commissioner J.K. Banthia committed a serious mistake while announcing the growth rate of Muslim population during 1991-2001 decade by comparing the figures of 1991 with those of 2001. Since the figures of Jammu & Kashmir were not a part of the census 1991, the comparison was obviously faulty. Since no census was held in Assam in 1981, the census all-India total did not include the population of Assam. The Census Commissioner was attacked by several critics and the Government for inflating the Muslim Population growth figures. The Census Commissioner compounded the earlier mistake by excluding the figures of Assam and Jammu & Kashmir from all censuses from 1961 to 2001 and the "adjusted" figures indicated a growth rate of Muslims by 29.3 per cent during 1991-2001—6.7 per cent lower than the initial figure. This was achieved by excluding Assam and Jammu & Kashmir knowing full well that both these states have a high proportion of Muslim population—in case of Jammu & Kashmir, out of a total population of 10.1 million, about 6.8 million (67 per cent) are Muslims and in case of Assam, out of a total population of 26.7 million, about 8.2 million (30.9 per cent) are Muslims in 2001. The Census Commissioner was charged by secular forces of exaggerating Muslim population growth rate in unadjusted figures and by communal forces in under-estimating Muslim growth rate in the adjusted figures. In the brief analysis of Census Data on Religions, the Census Report mentions: "No effort has been made to interpolate the religions data for Assam in 1981 and Jammu & Kashmir in 1991, although this could have been another way for making comparisons. *The data users, therefore, should adopt caution before drawing any conclusions in respect of trends in the proportions and growths at All India level.*"[1]

Since these two states, viz. Assam and Jammu & Kashmir, account for about 37 million people, their share in total population of India in 2001 was only 3.6 per cent and even if the interpolated figures lead to revision of the total population of India, the growth rates of population in the decade 1981-91 and 1991-2001 would be only marginally affected. Keeping this in mind, the exercise of interpolation was undertaken by the author. The population of Jammu & Kashmir was estimated at 7.78 million in 1991 and of Assam was estimated at 18.10 million for 1981. Consequently, the total population of India was revised at 683.4 million for 1981 and 846.4 million for 1991.

After making these adjustments for various religious communities, the results indicated that as against the overall growth rate of population for the 1991-2001 decade to be of the order of 21.5 per cent, the Hindu population growth was 19.9 per cent, while that of Muslims was of the order of 29.5 per cent. It was noted that the growth rate of Hindu population declined

TABLE 15.1

Total Population of Various Religious Communities

(Million)

	1961	*1971*	*1981*	*1991*	*2001*
All Communities	439.2 (100.0)	547.9 (100.0)	665.3 (100.0)	838.6 (100.0)	1028.6 (100.0)
Hindus	366.5 (83.4)	453.3 (82.7)	549.8 (82.6)	687.6 (82.0)	827.6 (80.5)
Muslims	46.9 (10.7)	61.4 (11.2)	75.5 (11.4)	101.6 (12.1)	138.2 (13.4)
Christians	10.7 (1.8)	14.2 (1.9)	16.2 (2.0)	19.6 (1.9)	24.1 (1.9)
Sikhs	7.8 (1.8)	10.4 (1.9)	13.1 (2.0)	16.3 (1.9)	19.2 (1.9)
Buddhists	3.2 (0.7)	3.8 (0.7)	4.7 (0.7)	6.4 (0.8)	7.9 (0.8)
Jains	2 (0.5)	2.6 (0.5)	3.2 (0.5)	3.4 (0.4)	4.2 (0.4)
Others	1.5 (0.3)	2.2 (0.4)	2.8 (0.4)	3.3 (0.4)	6.6 (0.6)

Notes : 1. No census was conducted in Assam in 1981 and Jammu & Kashmir in 1991. The figures for 1981 do not include these states. These are unadjusted figures.

2. Figures in brackets indicate percentage of total population in the respective column.

Source : Census of India (2001), *The First Report on Religions Data*, September 2004.

TABLE 15.2

Decadal Growth Rates of Population in India (%)

	Unadjusted[1]				Adjusted as per Census[2]			
	1961-71	1971-81	1981-91	1991-01	1961-71	1971-81	1981-91	1991-2000
(1)	(2)	(3)	(4)	(5)	(6)	(7)	(8)	(9)
All Religious Communities	24.8	21.4	26.0	22.7	24.8	24.8	23.8	21.5
Hindus	23.7	21.3	25.1	20.3	23.4	24.2	22.8	20.0
Muslims	30.8	22.9	34.5	36.0	31.2	30.8	32.9	29.3
Christians	32.6	13.7	21.5	22.6	36.0	19.2	17.0	22.1
Sikhs	32.3	26.0	24.3	18.2	32.0	26.2	25.5	16.9
Buddhists	17.1	23.8	35.3	24.5	17.0	25.4	36.0	23.2
Jains	28.5	23.1	4.6	26.0	28.5	23.7	4.0	26.0
Others	45.7	26.6	18.2	103.1	97.7	26.6	13.2	111.3
					As per Datt's Estimate[3]			
					1961-71	1971-81	1981-1991	1991-01
All Religious Communities					24.8	24.8	23.8	21.5
Hindus					23.8	24.1	22.7	19.9
Muslims					30.8	30.7	32.8	29.5
Christians					32.5	17.2	17.8	22.5
Sikhs					32.2	26.1	25.5	17.0
Buddhists					28.1	23.8	4.0	26.0
Others					16.4	20.3	10.5	103.1

Note : For 1 and 2, Census of India 2001—*The First Report on Religions Data.*
For 3, as per estimate prepared by Ruddar Datt after interpolation of population for Assam in 1981 and for Jammu & Kashmir in 1991.

from 22.7 per cent during 1981-91 to 19.9 per cent in 1991-2001. Similarly, growth rate of Muslim population also declined from 32.8 per cent to 29.5 per cent during the two decades under consideration. As against this decline, the population growth rate of Jains increased from 4 per cent during 1981-91 to 26.0 per cent during 1991-2001. This may be due to the fact the there appears to be an insistence on the part of Jains to be recorded as a separate religious category in 2001. The growth rate of Christian population has also shown an increase from 17.8 per cent during 1981-91 to 22.5 per cent during 1991-2001. This may be the result of conversions from lower caste Hindus to Christian community along with the natural growth of Christian population. (Refer Tables 15.1 and 15.2)

Growth Rate of Population Religion-wise

From the adjusted population data, it was revealed that in absolute terms, during 1961 to 2001—a span of 40 years, the Hindu population increased from 366 million to 827 million—a net addition of 461 million, the

TABLE 15.3

Adjusted Population of Various Religious Communities

(Million)

	1961	*1971*	*1981*	*1991*	*2001*
All Religious Communities	439.23 (100.0)	547.95 (100.0)	683.39 (100.0)	846.37 (100.0)	1,028.61 (100.0)
Hindus	366.53 (83.4)	453.29 (82.8)	562.42 (82.3)	690.05 (81.5)	827.58 (80.4)
Muslims	46.94 (10.7)	61.42 (11.2)	80.31 (11.9)	106.71 (12.6)	138.19 (13.4)
Christians	10.73 (2.4)	14.22 (2.6)	16.68 (2.4)	19.65 (2.3)	24.08 (2.3)
Sikhs	7.85 (1.8)	10.38 (1.9)	13.09 (1.9)	16.43 (1.9)	19.22 (1.9)
Buddhists	3.26 (0.7)	3.81 (0.7)	4.76 (0.7)	6.48 (0.8)	7.96 (0.8)
Jains	2.03 (0.5)	2.6 (0.5)	3.22 (0.5)	3.35 (0.4)	4.22 (0.4)
Others	1.5 (0.3)	2.46 (0.4)	2.96 (0.4)	3.27 (0.4)	6.64 (0.6)

Notes : 1. Totals may not tally upto 100 due to rounding off.

2. Absolute totals may not tally due to rounding off to the second decimal. This is also slightly due to religion not stated.
3. Adjusted population figures for Assam and Jammu & Kashmir for 1981 and 1991 respectively were interpolated and added to total population figures.

Source : Prepared by Ruddar Datt after interpolating the data for Assam for 1981 and Jammu & Kashmir for 1991.

Muslim population from 47 million to 138 million—a net addition of 91 million, Christian population from 11 million to 24 million—a net addition of 13 million, Sikh population from 8 million to 19 million—a net addition of 11 million, Buddhist population from 3 million to 8 million—a net addition of 5 million, Jain population from 2 million to 4 million—a net addition of 2 million. The point that has attracted attention is: whereas the share of Hindu population in total population has declined from 83.4 per cent in 1961 to 80.4 per cent in 2001—a fall by 3.0 per cent, the share of Muslim population has increased from 10.7 per cent in 1961 to 13.4 per cent in 2001—an increase by 2.7 per cent. The relative share of Christians, Sikhs, Buddhists, Jains—have remained more or less constant during 1961-2001.

Sex Ratio

The Census data on religions has also indicated other variables which are associated with population growth. Sex ratio indicated that as against the all-communities average of 933, the sex ratio of Hindus was slightly lower at 931, but that of Muslims was slightly above the national average at 936. Sex ratio was the highest among Christians at 1,009, followed by Buddhists at 953 and Jains at 940. But, the sex ratio among the Sikhs was abysmally low at 893. (Refer Table 15.4)

Among the States, highest sex ratio (1,058) has been reported among the Hindu population of Kerala, followed by Chhattisgarh (990). Among the Muslims, Kerala is again at the top rank (1,082) followed by Tamil Nadu (1,020).

Sex Ratio in 0-6 Age Group

Another indicator is the child sex ratio in the age group 0-6. The national child sex ratio was 927 and this was a shade lower in the Hindu community (925), but was significantly higher among Muslims (950), Christians (964) and Buddhists (942). Sikh population recorded the lowest child sex ratio of 786 in 2001 census, while the Jain population was also significantly lower at 870 as against the national average of 927.

A review of the child sex ratio in the various states of India reveals that "sex ratio in age group 0-6 is very depressed in northern states for all religions barring a few exceptions . . . the child sex ratio patterns among the major religious communities in some of the states such as Punjab, Haryana and Gujarat depict similar but pronounced bias against the girl child irrespective of their religions affiliations."[2]

Child Population (0-6) Proxy for Fertility Index

The proportion of child population in the age group 0-6 to total population provides a proxy of relative position of fertility among various

TABLE 15.4

Census of India—Some Characteristic Socio-Economic Indicators (2001)

	All Com.	*Hindus*	*Muslims*	*Christians*	*Sikhs*	*Buddhists*	*Jains*
(1)	*(2)*	*(3)*	*(4)*	*(5)*	*(6)*	*(7)*	*(8)*
Total Population (In million)	1028.6	827.6	138.2	24.1	19.2	7.9	4.2
% of Total Population	100	80.4	13.4	2.3	1.9	0.8	0.4
Growth Rate (1991-2001)	21.5	19.9	29.5	22.5	17	22.8	26
Sex Ratio	933	931	936	1,009	893	953	940
Sex Ratio (0-6 age)	927	925	950	964	786	942	870
Population (0-6 age)	15.9	15.6	18.7	13.5	12.8	14.4	10.6
Literacy rate	64.8	65.1	59.1	80.3	69.4	72.7	94.1
(a) Male	75.3	76.2	67.6	84.4	75.2	83.1	97.4
(b) Female	53.7	53.2	50.1	76.2	63.1	61.7	90.6
Male-Female Literacy Gap	21.6	23	17.5	8.2	12.1	21.4	6.8
Work Participation Rate	39.1	40.4	31.3	39.7	37.7	40.6	32.9
WPR (Male)	51.7	52.4	47.5	50.7	53.3	49.2	55.2
WPR (Female)	25.6	27.5	14.1	28.7	20.2	31.7	9.2
WPR (M-F Gap)	26.1	24.9	33.4	22	33.1	17.5	46

Source : Compiled and computed from the data provided in Census of India (2001), *The First Report on Religion Data* (September 2004).

religious communities. Muslims record the highest proportion in age group 0-6 at 18.7 per cent, while the national average stands at 15.9 per cent, Hindus record slightly lower than the national average at 15.6 per cent, followed by Buddhists (14.4%), Christians (13.5%), Sikhs (12.8%) and Jains (10.6%).

It is believed that in developing countries, high female literacy rate results in lowering fertility. Obviously, there is a negative relation between female literacy (a minimum educational level) and fertility. The Census Report after plotting the data of female literacy and proportion of child population reaches the following conclusion: "The level of proportion of child population age 0-6 is not the same for each of the religious groups for corresponding female literacy but is definitely showing a positive sign and shows that irrespective of religious affiliations, investments, creation of background environment and facilities leading to improving female literacy would prove to be beneficial in lowering fertility."[3]

Literacy

Census Report on Religions has provided data on male and female literacy by religions. The literacy rate for all communities in 2001 is 64.8 per cent, while male literacy is 75.3 per cent and female literacy is 53.7 per cent. The gap between male and female literacy is 21.6 per cent. Among the Hindus, the male literacy is 76.2 per cent and female literacy is 53.2 per cent and the male-female literacy gap is 23.0 per cent. But among the Muslims, the male literacy rate is 67.6 per cent, and female literacy is 50.1 per cent. Thus, the male-female literacy gap is 17.5 per cent. The point to note is that the literacy rate among Muslims is improving and it is improving at a relatively higher pace among Muslim females. Consequently, the male-female gap in literacy among Muslims is less than that among Hindus. This is a heartening development and if this trend is strengthened, Muslim-female literacy may in the next decade catch up with Hindu-female literacy and this is bound to impact on fertility among the Muslims. So far as other communities are concerned, female-literacy is 61.7 per cent among Buddhists, 63.1 per cent among Sikhs, 76.2 per cent among Christians, and 90.6 per cent among Jains who are at the top. It is also very welcome to find that the male-female literacy gap is only 6.8 per cent among Jains and 8.2 per cent among Christians, 12.1 per cent among Sikhs, but is quite high among Buddhists (21.4 per cent). Since Hindus and Muslims comprise 94 per cent of total populations, the literacy campaign has to concentrate on these two communities, especially the Scheduled Castes and Scheduled Tribes segment among the Hindus. The Census Report on Religion draws the right conclusion: "The past-legacy of low female Muslim literacy, which is to some extent true even for segments of the Hindu population such as the Scheduled Castes and Scheduled Tribes among them, has had possibly a (negative) role to play in not accelerating the pace of fertility decline. It is, therefore, imperative that governments invest in improving female literacy, particularly for the Muslims and sections of Hindu society and these communities in turn need to respond positively and faster than ever before and remove if there exists any female bias in educating their women—girls and adolescents both. This is one definite pro-active step to improve the status of women in India by empowering them across the religious group in the long run."[4]

The Census Report has highlighted the secular fertility pattern in Tamil Nadu, though Kerala is often mentioned as an outstanding case. It states : "Among the major states, Tamil Nadu has a distinct and secular fertility pattern as none of the religious communities are having more than 13 per cent population in the age group 0-6 and the range varies from the lowest 10.4 per cent among Sikhs to 12.9 per cent in Muslims. Thus, the message and practice of fertility limitation is widely dispersed and proportion of child has permeated to all religious communities."[5]

The Census Report has also studied the pattern of overall literacy rate among various religious communities. It is true that the overall literacy rate among Muslims is the lowest (59.1 per cent) as against that of Hindus (65.1 per cent), yet the State scenario shows that all religions communities show better or worse performance irrespective of the religions, but depending upon the social ethos and the level of development of a state. The Census Report observes: "It may be interesting to point out that Kerala, Lakshadweep and Pondicherry have very high literacy rate for all religious communities (above 80 per cent) while in Andaman & Nicobar Islands and Tamil Nadu also literacy is above 70 per cent for all religious communities. In Bihar, Jharkhand and Uttar Pradesh the literacy rates are rather depressed and below 60 per cent for Hindus, Muslims and others. Thus, there are regions in the country where all religions have a high literacy rate or low literacy rate. It appears that the religion effect may be weak in several parts of the country and the overall regional milieu and state of low or high development may be contributing to improvement or stagnancy in literacy rate."[6]

Work Participation Rate

Work Participation Rate (WPR) or percentage of workers to total population is 39.1 per cent in 2001 Census. For male population, it is 51.7 per cent and for female population, it is 25.6 per cent. Thus, the Male-Female gap in overall WPR is 26.1 per cent. A careful perusal of the male and female WPR among different religious communities reveals that the gap in male WPR among various religions is small (7.7 per cent)—highest for Jains (55.2 per cent) to lowest for Muslims (47.5 per cent). But as against it, the gap in female WPR among various communities is very large (19.5 per cent). It is the highest for Buddhists (31.7 per cent) followed by Christians (28.7 per cent) and Hindus (27.5 per cent). The female WPR is very highly depressed in the case of Muslims (14.1 per cent) and even much lower in Jains (barely 9.2 per cent). Thus, the female WPR has a dominant influence

TABLE 15.5

Growth of Hindus and Muslims in Major States of India (1991-2001) with a Population of over 10 million

(Million)

State	Hindus				Muslims				Total Population			
	1991	*2001*	*Increase in 2001*		*1991*	*2001*	*Increase*		*1991*	*2001*	*Increase*	
(1)	*(2)*	*(3)*	*(4)*		*(5)*	*(6)*	*(7)*		*(8)*	*(9)*	*(10)*	
1. Uttar Pradesh	107.6	134.0	26.4	(24.5)	23.4	30.7	7.3	(31.2)	132.1	166.2	34.1	(25.8)
2. Maharashtra	64.0	77.9	13.9	(21.7)	7.6	10.3	2.7	(35.5)	78.9	96.9	18.0	(22.8)
3. Bihar	54.3	69.1	14.8	(27.2)	10.1	13.7	3.6	(35.6)	64.5	83.0	18.5	(28.7)
4. Andhra Pradesh	59.3	67.8	8.5	(14.3)	4.5	5.9	1.4	(31.1)	66.5	76.2	9.7	(14.6)
5. West Bengal	50.9	58.1	7.2	(14.1)	16.1	20.2	4.1	(25.5)	68.1	80.2	17.9	(26.3)
6. Madhya Pradesh	44.6	55.0	10.4	(23.3)	3.0	3.8	0.8	(26.7)	48.6	60.3	11.7	(24.1)
7. Tamil Nadu	49.5	55.0	5.5	(11.1)	3.1	3.5	0.4	(12.9)	55.9	62.4	6.5	(11.6)
8. Rajasthan	39.2	50.1	10.9	(27.8)	3.5	4.8	1.3	(37.1)	44.0	56.5	12.5	(28.4)
9. Gujarat	37.0	45.1	8.1	(21.9)	3.6	4.6	1.0	(27.8)	41.3	50.7	9.4	(22.7)
10. Karnataka	38.4	44.3	5.9	(15.3)	5.2	6.5	1.3	(25.0)	45.0	52.8	7.8	(17.3)
11. Orissa	30.0	34.7	4.7	(15.7)	0.6	0.8	0.2	(33.3)	31.7	36.8	5.1	(16.1)
12. Chhattisgarh	16.8	19.7	2.9	(17.2)	0.3	0.4	0.1	(33.3)	17.6	20.8	3.2	(18.2)
13. Haryana	14.7	18.7	4.0	(27.2)	0.8	1.2	0.4	(50.0)	16.4	21.1	4.7	(28.6)
14. Jharkhand	16.8	18.5	1.7	(10.1)	2.7	3.7	1.0	(37.0)	21.8	26.9	5.1	(23.4)
15. Kerala	16.7	17.9	1.2	(7.2)	6.8	7.9	1.1	(16.2)	29.1	31.8	2.7	(9.3)
16. Assam	15.0	17.3	2.3	(15.3)	6.4	8.2	1.8	(28.1)	22.4	26.7	4.3	(19.2)
17. Delhi	7.9	11.4	3.5	(44.3)	0.9	1.6	0.7	(77.8)	9.4	13.8	4.4	(46.8)
18. Punjab	7.0	9.0	2.0	(28.5)	0.2	0.3	0.1	(50.0)	20.3	24.4	4.1	(20.2
19. Jammu & Kashmir	2.4	3.0	0.6	(25.0)	5.1	6.8	1.7	(33.3)	7.8	10.1	2.3	(29.5)
Total (for all States)	**690.0**	**827.6**	**137.6**	**(19.9)**	**106.7**	**138.2**	**31.5**	**(29.5)**	**846.4**	**1,028.6**	**182.2**	**(21.5)**

Notes : 1. States have been arranged in descending order of Hindu population in 2001.
2. Figures in brackets indicate percent increase during the decade (1991-2001).

in determining the overall WPR, since the variation in male WPR is rather small.

2. POLITICAL REACTIONS IGNORED THE ESSENTIAL MESSAGE

Following the release of demographic data on religions, apprehensions were expressed by the Hindu leaders that if the rapid increase in Muslim population was not checked by promoting family planning, in a century, Muslims may outnumber Hindus. On the other hand, the Muslim leaders and prominent among them, the President of the Muslim Personal Law Board and Shahi Imam of Jama Masjid expressed that Islam did not permit family planning. Both the groups were taking confrontationist positions. The leaders of majority community took a static view that the population growth rate among Muslims will not decline without family planning. On the other hand, the Muslim leaders tried to suppress the rational view of the vice-president of the Muslim Personal Law Board that the need for family planning would be considered by the Board in its next meeting. It is really heartening to find that some prominent and progressive Muslim intellectuals took pains to present the issue in a proper perspective. Dr. Rafiq Zakaria, in his highly documented and researched article (*Hindustan Times*, 19 September 2004) quoted the Prophet himself who stated: "More children add to poverty, while less numbers ease it."[7] On the basis of evidence provided by Operations Research Group (ORG), he clearly showed: Muslims do not lag far behind Hindus in the acceptance of the various methods of birth control. He nailed the untruth propagated by some leaders that Islam did not permit family planning. He candidly stated: "Most Muslim countries have, since long, been practising family planning; some of them like Bangladesh and Indonesia achieving remarkable success. Egypt and Pakistan are struggling hard to control their population. It is wrong to propagate that it is contrary to the teachings of Islam."[8] Writer and poet Javed Akhtar responding to the views of the All India Muslim Personal Law Board, which frowns on family planning said: "All they have done is damage the image of Indian Muslims."

The Government, to appease the fundamentalist lobbies among the Muslims, has declared that it proposes to conduct an enquiry into the conduct of Registrar General and Census Commissioner. Instead of explaining the essential message of the Census Report on Religions to the people of India, the Government was in a hurry to prove its secular credentials. But what was the message that the Registrar General intended to convey:

1. Population growth rate depends upon the social milieu and level of development of a state, irrespective of religious composition of its population.

2. Irrespective of religious affiliation, improvement in female literacy will prove beneficial to lowering fertility.
3. Male-Female literacy gap has to be reduced among all religious communities, more especially among Muslims and Scheduled Castes and Scheduled Tribes among the Hindus.
4. Sex ratio in the age group 0-6 is very depressed in northern states for all religious communities and in some of the states like Panjab, Haryana and Gujarat, it depicts a pronounced bias against the girl child irrespective of their religious affiliations.
5. In some states, such as Kerala, Pondicherry, Tamil Nadu, literacy rate for all religious communities is above 70 per cent (and even 80 per cent), but in Bihar, Jharkhand and Uttar Pradesh it is below 60 per cent for Hindus, Muslims and others.

It is really distressing that in the competitive politics of demography between the ruling dispensation and the opposition, the essential message of a basically secular, rational and well-researched approach is lost.

References

1. *Census of India (2001), The First Report on Religion Data,* p. xvii, September 2004.
2. *Ibid.,* pp. xviii and xix.
3. *Ibid.,* p. xix.
4. *Ibid.*
5. *Ibid.,* p. xx.
6. *Ibid.,* pp. xxi-xxii.
7. Zakaria, Rafique (2004), *The Hindustan Times,* 19th September.
8. *Ibid.*

CHAPTER

16

Sachar Committee Report (Objective Analysis, Need for Correct Interpretation)

Sachar Committee was appointed in March 2005 to prepare a report on the social, economic and educational status of the Muslim Community in India. The Committee submitted its report in November 2006. Credit must be given to the Committee for collecting information on a wide range of issues, analyzing latest information and studying trends over nearly 50 years of post-independence period and making a large number of recommendations to improve the status of the Muslim community. It would be relevant to examine the findings of the Committee as also the nature of its recommendations, since the Report has both its strong advocates and critics.

At the outset, the Committee mentions that the population of Muslims, according to 2001 Census was 138 million or 13.4 percent of the total population. On the basis of NSS data of 55th Round (1999-00) and 61st Round (2004-05), the Committee records that the proportion of OBCs among Muslims has increased from 31.7 percent of total Muslim population in 1999-2000 to 40.7 percent in 2004-05. The factors accounting for the sharp increase in OBC population have not been given. Is it due to the inclusion of more castes or is it due to natural increase of population, has not been made clear. But as common sense impels us to argue that an increase of 10 percent due to natural increase in population within a short span of 5 years is unthinkable, it is more inclusion of Muslim castes in OBCs that have resulted in this sharp increase.

TABLE 16.1

Distribution of Population According to SRCs All-India 1999-2000 and 2004-05

Region	Population 2001 (millions)	Population 2001 (%)	Hindus							Muslims					Others Population (2001) (%)
			% SC/STs		% OBCs		% General		Population 2001 (%)	% OBCs*		% General			
			1999-2000	2004-05	1999-2000	2004-05	1999-2000	2004-05		1999-2000	2004-05	1999-2000	2004-05		
(1)	(2)	(3)	(4)	(5)	(6)	(7)	(8)	(9)	(10)	(11)	(12)	(13)	(14)		(15)
All India	1028.6	80.5	31.3	31.2	38.3	43.0	30.5	25.9	13.4	31.7	40.7	68.3	59.3		6.1
Urban	286.1	75.6	20.6	20.5	33.0	36.9	46.5	42.6	17.3	32.6	40.2	67.4	59.8		7.1
Rural	742.5	82.3	34.6	34.5	39.9	44.9	25.5	20.6	12.0	31.2	40.9	68.8	59.1		5.7

* A small percentage of SCs and STs included in this category.

Source : NSSO 55th Round and 61st Round data.

TABLE 16.2
Distribution of Population of each Religion by Caste Categories

Religion/Caste	*SCs*	*STs*	*OBCs*	*Others*	*All*
Hindus	22.2	9.1	42.8	26.0	100
Muslims	0.8	0.5	39.2	59.5	100
Christians	9.0	32.8	24.8	33.3	100
Sikhs	30.7	0.9	22.4	46.1	100
Jains	0.0	2.6	3.0	94.3	100
Buddhists	89.5	7.4	0.4	2.7	100
Zoroastrians	0.0	15.9	13.7	70.4	100
Others	2.6	82.5	6.2	8.7	100
Total	19.7	8.5	41.1	30.8	100

Source : Distribution obtained from merged sample of Schedule 1 and 10 of NSSO 61st Round Survey.

The Committee also underlined the fact that "only 0.8% Muslims reported themselves as SCs; the share of Muslims reporting themselves as STs was even lower."

I. PERCEPTION OF MUSLIMS

Giving a broad view about the perceptions of Muslims, the Committee has highlighted the following on the basis of meetings with Muslim representatives:

1. Muslims "carry a double burden of being labeled as "anti-national" and as being "appeased" at the same time. . . . Muslims complained that they are constantly looked upon with a great degree of suspicion not only by certain sections of society but also by public institutions and government structures. (p. 11)
2. Markers of Muslim identity—*the burqa,* the *purdah,* the bread and the *topi.*

   Women complained "how in corporate offices *hijab* wearing Muslim women were finding it increasingly difficult to find jobs." (p. 12)

   Muslim identity comes in the way of owners to rent/sell property to Muslims.

   Muslim identity also comes in the way of admitting their children to good educational institutions.

   However, "a large majority of Muslims would apparently prefer to send their children to 'regular mainstream' schools. It was argued that while setting up of denominational institutions is a right of minorities under the Constitution, it was not meant to become their only option." (p. 12)

3. *Ghettoisation and Shrinking Spaces*—Muslims live together in concentrated pockets. Increasing ghettoisation of the community implies a shrinking space in the public sphere; an unhealthy trend that is gaining ground.

4. *Equity-related issues:*
   (a) The popular perception that religious conservatism among Muslims is a major factor for not accessing education is incorrect.
   (b) Madarsas and denominational institutions for improving the educational status of Muslims were also seen by some as violating the spirit of the Constitution.
   (c) Incidence of child labour was much higher among Muslims as compared to other socio-religious categories
   (d) Schools beyond the primary level are few in Muslim localities.
   (e) Labelling of Madarsas as dens for terrorists is extremely worrisome for the Muslim Community.
   (f) Modernising Madarasas by the Government has been a contentious issue with many differing view points. Some felt the need for modernization of Madarsas so that the teaching of science, mathematics and English can be imparted to Muslims.
   (g) Urdu medium schools are in a dismal state. School board examinations results of urdu medium schools bear this out.
   (h) It was argued that contrary to the popular perception that "religious conservatism among Muslims somehow militates against educating girls, current research indicates that poverty and financial constraints are the major causes that prevent Muslim girls from accessing 'modern'/'secular' education." (p. 20)

5. Economic Liberalisation and effect on Muslims.

The following points were highlighted:

(a) Lack of Muslims in Public employment—in the bureaucracy, police and the judiciary and so on.
(b) Private sector recruitment policy worked on sheer market forces. For instance, in the Business Process Outsourcing (BPO) sector, proficiency in English was the only criterion.
(c) The emergence of the ready-made garment industry has thrown a lot of tailors, mostly Muslims, out of business.

Most of the Muslims are engaged in the unorganized sector.

There is absence of proper civic amenities and infrastructural facilities in Muslim concentration areas.

The health of Muslims, especially women, is directly linked to poverty and the absence of basic services like clean drinking water and sanitation—leading to malnutrition, anaemia, a variety of diseases and poor life expectancy.

Non-availability of SC Quota for Muslim converts from SCs while it was available to Mazhabi Sikhs and neo-Buddhists.

There was a widespread demand for affirmative action, especially in the form of reservations or a separate quota for Muslims.

The Report after listing the problems faced and demands made by Muslim representatives concludes:

"Many of the problems enumerated are not specific to Muslims; all the disadvantaged socio-religious categories (SRCs) face them." (Emphasis added) (p. 25).

The basic question which begs an answer is: If most of the problems related to education, skill development, poverty and employment are common to all socio-religious categories, then instead of having a Committee on the social, economic and educational status of Muslims, would it not have been better to appoint a Committee on the social, economic and educational status of weaker sections of the society so as not to face the charge of 'minority appeasement'? Unfortunately, the UPA government did not think over the issue adequately, and appointed the Sachar Committee with very limited terms of reference.

It would be of interest to review the major findings of the Committee and thus, assess properly whether Muslims have benefited from the growth process initiated in India since 1950-51.

2. POPULATION SIZE, DISTRIBUTION AND HEALTH CONDITIONS OF MUSLIMS

The 2001census enumerates India's Muslim population at 138 million and by 2006, Muslim population would be 150 million—the largest Muslim population in the world next only to Indonesia.

The Committee notes: "In India, populations of all major religions have experienced large growth in the recent past, but the growth among Muslims has been higher than average. Over the 40 year period, 1961 to 2001, Muslim population increased rapidly from 47 million to 138 million, an increase by 194 percent, as against the average increase of 134%. Several reasons have been given for this in the Report:

(a) Infant mortality rate (IMR) under age 5, is lower for Muslims than for Hindus and hence also lower than the all-India average.
(b) Crude birth rate for Muslims was 30.8 in 2001, but it was 24.9 for Hindus and 25.9 for the total population.

(c) Total fertility rate (TFR) among the Muslims was highest at 3.6, whereas the national average for 2004-05 was 2.9, TFR for Hindus was 2.8, followed by Christians 2.4 and Sikhs 2.3.
(d) Family planning, especially sterilization, was less popular among Muslims as compared to other socio-religious categories.

The Report after taking note of these factors opines: As the level of education rises, the Muslim-non-Muslim differences will narrow down.

Urbanization

Share of urban population in India in 1961 was 18%, it rose to 27.8% in 2001. As against this, the share of Muslims in urban population rose from 27.1% in 1961 to 35.7% in 2001. Obviously, while Muslim population is also predominantly rural, yet the level of urbanization among them has been higher than the population of India as a whole.

Muslims and Malnutrition

On the question of malnutrition, children under 5 who are under-weight or stunted, the Report mentions: "Muslims are worse of than most other groups in terms of child under-nutrition. For instance, Muslims suffer from the highest rates of stunting and the second-highest rates of under-weight children among all social groups. *In general, though the differences across the social groups are not overly large, indicating that child malnutrition and low birth-weight are pervasive across all SRCs in India.*" (Emphasis added, p. 43).

Life Expectancy of Muslims

The Report on the basis of data provided by National Health Survey-2 for 2004-05, reaches the conclusion: "Life expectancy for Muslims is higher than the average by about one year. Besides estimates of maternal mortality also show lower than average maternal mortality among Muslims. Broadly, it could be said that the Muslims do have a slim advantage over the average in survival." (p. 38)

The survey of population growth and health of Muslims reveals that the population growth rate during the decade 1991-2001 of Muslims was 2.58% as against the national average of 1.95% and 1.82% for Hindus.

By 2101, the Muslim population may reach around 320-340 million in total population of 1,700-1,800 million. The Muslim share should be between 18 and 19 percent in total population of 2101.

•

TABLE 16.3
Annual Average Growth Rates of Population by Religion

	1961-71	*1971-81*	*1981-91*	*1991-2000*	*1961-2000*
All	2.21	2.21	2.14	1.95	2.13
Hindu	2.12	2.16	2.05	1.82	2.04
Muslim	2.69	2.68	2.85	2.58	2.70
Christian	2.82	1.60	1.63	2.03	2.02
Sikh	2.80	2.32	2.27	1.57	2.24
Buddhist	1.58	2.22	3.08	2.06	2.23
Jain	2.51	2.13	0.40	2.31	1.84

Source : Government of India (2006). *Report on Social and Educational Status of the Muslim Community of India*, p. 271.

The Committee's conclusion that "Muslim population growth has slowed down, as fertility has declined substantially clearly showing that Muslims are well into demographic transition" (p. 47), is to say the least biased and not even borne out by the facts given in its own report. Average decadal growth of Muslim population which was 2.69% during 1961-71 has marginally come down to 2.58% of during 1991-2001. Unless systematic efforts are made to encourage family planning, more especially sterilization after reaching a family size, there is yet no hope to reach replacement level of population in the next 50 years. The community leaders should help to shed conservatism in this regard so that total fertility rate declines.

In mortality, child malnutrition and life expectancy, the Muslim population is not at any serious disadvantage as compared with other socio-religious groups. Thus, it calls for measures relating to all socio-religious groups than for Muslims as a special category.

3. EDUCATIONAL CONDITION OF MUSLIMS

The Report mentions: "Muslims are at a double disadvantage with low levels of education combined with low quality of education; their deprivation increases manifold as the level of education rises." (p. 50)

It would be worthwhile to examine the situation at the ground level by a close examination of data.

Level of Literacy

The literacy rate among Muslims in 2001 was 59.1% as against the national average of 64.8%. The literacy rate among SC/STs was the lowest at 52.5%. The average for all Hindus is 65.1%, slightly above the national average. The gap between the national average and that of Muslims was

5.9%, while the gap in the case of SC/STs was 12.3%—more than double the gap of Muslims.

Another important point that emerges from an examination of state level data of literacy is that "in 10 out of 21 states, literacy levels among Muslims are higher than the state average." These include Jharkhand, Karnataka, Maharashtra, Andhra Pradesh, Gujarat, Madhya Pradesh, Tamil Nadu, Chhattisgarh. The states lagging behind are West Bengal, Uttar Pradesh, Bihar, Assam, Jammu & Kashmir and Rajasthan. These states, except West Bengal, are also laggards in overall literacy achievement. In Kerala, Muslim literacy rate is 89.4%, nearly equal to the State average of 90.9%.

TABLE 16.4
State-wise Literacy Levels—2001

	Total				
State	*All*	*Hindus*	*SC/STs*	*Muslims*	*All others*
India (13.4)	64.8	65.1	52.2	59.1	70.8
West Bengal (25.2)	68.6	72.4	56.1	57.5	81.6
Kerala (24.7)	90.9	90.2	80.8	89.4	93.1
Uttar Pradesh (18.5)	56.3	58.0	46.2	47.8	62.2
Bihar (16.5)	47.0	47.9	28.5	42.0	52.6
Assam (30.9)	63.3	70.0	64.0	48.4	71.3
Jammu & Kashmir (67.0)	55.5	71.2	46.5	47.3	100.0
Jharkhand (13.8)	53.6	54.6	39.7	55.6	63.7
Karnataka (12.2)	66.6	65.6	51.5	70.1	71.1
Uttaranchal (11.9)	11.6	74.1	63.4	51.1	77.4
Delhi (11.7)	81.7	82.8	70.8	66.6	86.5
Maharashtra (10.6)	76.9	76.2	64.3	78.1	80.0
Andhra Pradesh (9.2)	60.5	59.4	48.9	68.0	63.3
Gujarat (9.1)	69.1	68.3	55.3	73.5	72.8
Rajasthan (8.5)	60.4	60.2	49.1	56.6	66.1
Madhya Pradesh (6.4)	63.7	62.8	48.7	70.3	71.7
Haryana (5.8)	67.9	69.4	55.4	40.0	72.9
Tamil Nadu (5.6)	73.5	72.0	62.1	82.9	75.8
Orissa (2.1)	63.1	63.3	45.2	71.3	74.0
Himachal Pradesh (2.0)	76.5	76.8	69.6	57.5	79.8
Chhattisgarh (2.0)	64.7	63.9	55.3	82.5	71.3
Punjab (1.6)	69.7	74.6	56.2	51.2	75.4

Source : Estimated from Census of India (2001) Tables C9, C8-SCs and C8-STs. Figures within parenthesis are % share of the Muslim Population. •

The upshot of the analysis is that in an overall sense, Muslim literacy rate is improving. It is really the SC/STs who are at the lowest rung of the literacy ladder, especially the rural female SCs/STs. They deserve special attention.

TABLE 16.5
Literacy Rate in India by Religion (2001)

	All	*Hindus*	*SC/STs.*	*Muslims*	*All others*
Overall	64.8	65.1	52.2	59.1	70.8
Urban	80	81	68	70	85
(a) Urban Male	86	88	78	76	90
(b) Urban Female	73	74	58	63	78
Rural	59	59	49	53	64
(a) Rural Male	71	72	61	62	77
(b) Rural Female	46	46	36	43	52

Source : Sachar Committee Report, pp. 287-89.

Muslims literacy is brought down sharply due to low level of rural literacy at 53% and Muslim rural female literacy to an abysmally low level of 43%.

The Report mentions: "Muslims have not been able to respond to the challenge of improving their educational status." (p. 54) As a result, their gap with the group labeled as "All Others" has increased further, particularly since the 1980s.

Differentials in Education Attainment: School Education

Comparing the educational attainment level of Muslims during the last 50 years, it can be said that all the socio-religious groups were operating at very low levels. For instance, in 1948, percentage of those of age 12 years and above who completed primary education was 18.2% in the case of Muslims, barely 8.8% in case of SCs/STs and 27.8% in case of 'all others'. In 2001, Muslim percentage improved to 60.9%—a gain of 42.7% and in the case of all others, it improved to 79.3%—a gain of 51.5%. Whereas, the gap between SC/STs which was 19.0% in 1948 has reduced slightly to 17.9% in 2001, this gap in the case of Muslims has widened from 9.6% in 1948 to 18.4%. The main cause of this differential is the better performance of SC/STs in the case of female population as well as the overall rural population—both male and female. There is a need to study the factors responsible for this widening of gap in the case of Muslims. The Report only emphasizes the exogenous factors like non-availability of schools in backward districts, relative levels of poverty, but does not take into account endogenous cultural factors like attitude to women and their education. It is quite possible that SCs/STs have developed more progressive attitudes towards female education than Muslims. The availability of educational facilities cannot be a decisive factor. The question which the Muslim community must introspect is the use of available facilities. It is really gratifying to note that all communities have shown distinct upward trends, though in varying degrees.

Moreover, a state level analysis shows that Muslims have performed exceedingly well with a primary completion rate in Kerala to 97%, in Maharashtra to 80.4%, Andhra Pradesh to 74.7%, Gujarat 74.9%, Tamil Nadu 81.9% and in Madhya Pradesh 70.9%. The performance of Muslims depends also upon the attitude of state governments in providing resources for primary education in terms of finance, teachers and school environment. In UP and Bihar, the overall performance is rather much less than the national average. In UP, SCs/STs have improved their position *vis-a-vis* Muslims, but in Bihar, Muslims are ahead of SCs/STs, though both have shown low level of achievement.

Middle Level Education

Percentage of persons of age 15 years and above who completed 8 years of education was 8.6% in 1948 in case of Muslims, it improved to 40.5% 2001—a gain of 31.9 percentage points. In the case of SC/ST, this percentage improved during the period from 3.8% to 41.3%—a gain of 37.5 percentage points and in case of 'all others', it improved from 15.7% to 62.7%—a gain of 47 percentage points. The data reveal that though Muslims did gain sufficiently, but the gain was less than that of SCs/STs and relatively much less than that of 'all others'.

Matriculation Level of Education

Persons of age 17 years or above who completed 10 years of schooling, the percentage of Muslims improved from 5.4% in 1953 to 23.9% in 2001—a gain of 18.5 percentage points, in case of SC/ST, this percentage improved from 2.1% to 21.1%—a gain of 19.0 percentage points and in case of 'all others', it improved from 11.0% to 42.5%—a gain of 31.5 percentage points during the same period. The attainment of Muslims was slightly better than that of SCs/STs, but was much less than that of 'all others'.

Sachar Committee Report after presenting a detailed analysis of educational attainments states: "The first striking feature is that the probability of completing different levels of school education (primary, middle, secondary, etc.) has increased for all communities during 1983-2000. The sharpest rise has been in the probability of completing middle school

TABLE 16.6

Percentage of those who Completed Primary, Middle and Matriculation (2001)—All India

Socio-Religious Category	Primary				Middle				Matriculation			
	1948	1971	1991	2001	1948	1971	1991	2001	1953	1976	1991	2001
(1)	(2)	(3)	(4)	(5)	(6)	(7)	(8)	(9)	(10)	(11)	(12)	(13)
Total												
Muslims	18.2	33.6	47.3	60.9	8.6	19.3	30.5	40.5	5.4	12.5	16.1	23.9
SC/STs	8.8	23.1	40.2	61.4	3.8	13.2	27.1	41.3	2.1	7.9	12.9	21.1
All Others	27.8	50.4	64.7	79.3	15.7	35.0	50.0	62.7	11.0	25.5	32.5	42.5
Male (Urban)												
Muslims	43.4	58.8	68.2	71.3	25.5	39.8	49.4	49.6	18.3	28.7	31.9	36.1
SC/STs	33.4	57.6	71.9	80.2	19.2	40.9	55.7	59.8	12.8	28.6	35.0	42.1
All Others	66.7	80.3	85.5	89.6	50.3	67.2	74.3	76.7	41.0	55.5	59.0	63.0
Female (Urban)												
Muslims	13.9	35.0	54.0	70.9	5.2	18.5	34.8	51.1	3.2	12.3	18.8	32.2
SC/STs	7.5	27.4	49.6	74.8	3.3	15.9	34.8	56.3	1.8	9.8	17.3	31.8
All Others	34.1	61.5	74.6	88.1	18.8	45.2	61.4	76.7	12.4	34.6	44.4	57.9
Male (Rural)												
Muslims	21.8	36.1	49.5	58.9	9.4	20.6	32.1	37.3	5.0	12.2	16.5	22.0
SC/STs	13.5	29.6	50.5	66.1	5.1	16.4	34.6	43.7	2.6	9.3	16.5	24.5
All Others	31.6	54.3	70.3	80.8	15.2	35.7	54.0	62.0	9.3	23.7	32.8	41.8
Female (Rural)												
Muslims	4.0	13.5	28.3	47.8	0.9	4.9	14.8	29.4	0.4	2.1	4.8	11.2
SC/STs	1.6	7.7	21.7	47.0	0.5	3.2	12.4	29.3	0.2	1.5	3.9	10.2
All Others	7.4	23.9	43.2	67.6	2.2	11.2	27.6	49.0	1.0	6.1	12.4	23.8

Source : Compiled from the data provided in the *Report on Social, Economic and Educational Status of the Muslim Community of India* (2006).

for all communities, including Muslims. But differences still exist and the Muslims and SCs/STs are behind others. . . . Interestingly, in the transition from secondary to college education, Muslims perform somewhat better than SCs and STs; while only 23% of the SC/STs students who complete secondary education are likely to complete college education, this percentage is 26% for Muslims and 34% for other groups. Given these estimates, while disparities exist at every level, completion of primary education seems to be the major hurdle for school education." (pp. 62-64)

Graduate Attainment Rates (GARs)

Comparing the GARs, the Report states: "GARs for Muslims are somewhat higher than for SC/STs but lower than for all other SRCs. . . . However, among poor households the gap between GARs of Muslims and SC/STs and those of other SRCs is much lower than among non-poor households." (p. 73)

The basic question which needs an answer is: What are the causes for lower educational attainments of Muslims and SC/STs as against 'all others'? Firstly, there is a methodological fallacy in these comparisons. While in case of Muslims, the poor and non-poor households have been grouped together, in case of Hindus, a big chunk of SCs/STs have been excluded and as a result the disparities among Muslims and 'all others' get magnified. Including, Sikhs, Christians, Jains, Buddhists who are also among the better educated socio-religious categories in 'all others' further exaggerates these disparities.

Poverty is one principal factor in the determination of educational attainments, but this does not provide complete explanation of the phenomenon. Social attitude towards females is also the other important variable. The gap between male and female educational attainment among Muslims, more especially among rural females, explains to a large extent the lower educational attainment of Muslims.

Advantage of an early start in shedding conservatism among the Hindu-upper castes, Sikhs, Christians, Jains, etc. led to their relatively faster educational attainment at all levels.

It would be very unfair to lay the entire blame of disparities in educational attainment at the door of the Government policy of discrimination towards Muslims. The first Education Minister in the Central Government was Maulana Abul Kalam Azad who shaped the educational policy of India during the first two decades after independence. His secular credentials are beyond any doubt. Moreover, the Congress Government has been in power for over 50 years since independence which depended heavily for its survival on Muslim votes. As a consequence, the charge of discrimination against the Muslims is not warranted.

Former Professor Mahendra K. Premi of Jawaharlal Nehru University has, therefore, questioned the findings of the Sachar Committee by saying, "things aren't as bad for Muslims as the Committee makes them out to be". In support of his contention, he marshalled the following facts:

1. Muslims are far better than majority Hindus in 8 states though overall literacy rate among Muslims is the lowest in India.
2. Muslim literacy is above 80% in Kerala, Chhattisgarh, Tamil Nadu, Maharashtra, Gujarat. In Chhattisgarh, it is 91% for Muslims as against 77% for Hindus.
3. In Gujarat, Muslim men (83%) fare better than their Hindu counterparts (79%).
4. For Muslim women, the highest literacy rate of 70% was recorded in Kerala, Tamil Nadu, Maharashtra and Chhatisgarh.

Professor M.K. Premi, therefore, concludes:

"The level of economic and social development of the state is not the only factor in Muslim literacy rates, it is the tradition of sending children to school or not."

Failure of Muslims to cross the principal hurdle of primary education results in disparities at middle, matriculation, higher secondary and even college/university level. Muslim leaders should, therefore, campaign for persuading the Muslim community to send their children, especially girls, to primary schools. This campaign should be directed more in rural areas where the performance of Muslim is very disappointing. Once the demand for primary education increases, the state will be forced to fulfil its constitutional commitment to provide free and compulsory education. Merely creating educational infrastructure would not stimulate demand. For it is said, you can take a horse to drinking water, but it will no drink if it is not thirsty. The example of Jammu & Kashmir, a predominantly Muslim populated state where 67% of the population is Muslim shows that literacy rate among Muslims was only 47.3 % in 2001 as against 71.2% among Hindus. Muslim community should ponder over this question.

4. POVERTY LEVELS AMONG SOCIO-RELIGIOUS CATEGORIES

The Report mentions that in early 1970s, two decades after independence, the proportion of population below the poverty line or Head Count Ratio (HCR), was hovering around 55% at the all-India level. Thereafter, poverty has continued to decline, with the most recent estimate placing all-India poverty head count at 22.7 percent based on 365 days recall period and 28.5 percent based on 30 days recall period for 2004-05.

There is a consensus among economists that figures of HCR of poverty based on 30-day recall period are more reliable than those based on 365-days recall period, but Sachar Committee, for reasons best known to it, uses

Table 16.7
Poverty Incidence Compared Over time 1987-88 to 2004-05, Urban

States Urban	Total			All Hindus			Hindus SC/STs		
	2004-05	1993-94	1987-88	2004-05	1993-94	1987-88	2004-05	1993-94	1987-88
(1)	(2)	(3)	(4)	(5)	(6)	(7)	(8)	(9)	(10)
All India	**29**	**33**	**38**	**27**	**31**	**36**	**46**	**51**	**55**
West Bengal	24	23	33	21	20	29	41	37	48
Kerala	23	24	45	24	25	44	41	32	61
Uttar Pradesh	32	35	40	27	31	33	46	57	49
Bihar	42	34	53	38	31	52	70	52	62
Assam	7	8	17	5	6	17	7	14	22
Jammu & Kashmir	10	5	13	9	5	14	16	7	35
Jharkhand	22	—	—	20	—	—	51	—	—
Karnataka	33	40	49	30	35	46	54	61	65
Uttaranchal	17	—	—	16	—	—	31	—	—
Delhi	21	16	16	21	15	16	46	47	44
Maharashtra	33	35	35	28	32	33	43	57	61
Andhra Pradesh	34	38	45	32	37	42	48	47	55
Gujarat	18	28	40	16	25	37	21	42	57
Rajasthan	27	31	36	26	23	35	48	47	50
Madhya Pradesh	48	48	43	45	47	42	69	65	67
Haryana	21	16	18	21	15	19	40	25	38
Tamil Nadu	28	40	42	29	40	43	50	57	65
Orissa	50	41	43	49	40	42	74	57	62
• Himachal Pradesh	4	9	7	4	10	7	6	21	15
Chhattisgarh	46	—	—	47	—	—	50	—	—
Punjab	10	11	13	11	11	14	19	24	25
All other States	10	13	19	11	14	21	21	15	38

Source : *Op. cit.*, p. 367.

(*Contd.*)

TABLE 16.7 (Contd.)

States Urban	Other Hindus			Muslims			All Others		
	2004-05	1993-94	1987-88	2004-05	1993-94	1987-88	2004-05	1993-94	1987-88
(1)	(11)	(12)	(13)	(14)	(15)	(16)	(17)	(18)	(19)
All India	**22**	**26**	**32**	**44**	**47**	**53**	**16**	**23**	**27**
West Bengal	14	15	25	44	41	57	21	27	16
Kerala	21	24	42	31	27	56	12	21	39
Uttar Pradesh	22	25	30	43	46	58	5	7	31
Bihar	33	26	49	57	46	57	4	29	36
Assam	5	5	16	13	22	21	4	0	13
Jammu & Kashmir	7	5	10	11	23	13	5	0	8
Jharkhand	12	—	—	44	—	—	28	—	—
Karnataka	24	30	42	49	58	64	16	23	35
Uttaranchal	12	—	—	27	—	—	0	—	—
Delhi	10	5	8	29	30	21	2	6	5
Maharashtra	24	28	28	55	50	48	30	32	34
Andhra Pradesh	27	35	40	49	49	57	22	26	40
Gujarat	15	22	32	34	47	54	2	23	27
Rajasthan	18	23	29	39	56	47	7	14	21
Madhya Pradesh	37	40	35	70	60	52	7	31	39
Haryana	16	14	14	46	40	0	1	23	10
Tamil Nadu	25	36	40	24	46	44	21	34	30
Orissa	42	35	37	51	68	69	51	24	37
Himachal Pradesh	3	7	3	1	0	0	0	0	9
Chhattisgarh	45	—	—	62	—	—	11	—	—
Punjab	8	7	11	21	23	33	6	11	10
All other States	9	14	19	19	15	24	4	9	11

Source : *Op. cit.*, p. 367.

TABLE 16.8

Poverty Incidence Compared Over time 1987-88 to 2004-05, Rural

States Rural	Total			All Hindus			Hindus SC/STs		
	2004-05	1993-94	1987-88	2004-05	1993-94	1987-88	2004-05	1993-94	1987-88
(1)	(2)	(3)	(4)	(5)	(6)	(7)	(8)	(9)	(10)
All India	**28**	**37**	**39**	**28**	**36**	**40**	**41**	**50**	**54**
West Bengal	28	41	46	24	38	45	31	49	55
Kerala	13	25	25	13	24	24	24	37	36
Uttar Pradesh	34	42	45	33	43	45	45	59	60
Bihar	42	58	58	41	56	57	64	71	71
Assam	23	45	35	16	40	32	18	42	36
Jammu & Kashmir	3	18	26	3	16	26	4	20	38
Jharkhand	43	—	—	41	—	—	52	—	—
Karnataka	24	30	31	25	30	31	36	43	48
Uttaranchal	15	—	—	15	—	—	20	—	—
Delhi	7	2	1	7	2	2	0	12	8
Maharashtra	32	38	45	31	36	44	54	51	58
Andhra Pradesh	11	16	21	11	16	21	21	27	33
Gujarat	20	22	28	21	22	29	32	31	41
Rajasthan	18	26	31	18	26	32	29	42	44
Madhya Pradesh	37	41	46	37	41	46	52	53	62
Haryana	13	28	15	12	26	15	26	45	30
Tamil Nadu	24	33	42	24	33	42	32	44	58
Orissa	47	50	55	47	50	54	65	62	73
Himachal Pradesh	8	30	16	8	31	16	15	42	20
Chhattisgarh	43	—	—	43	—	—	51	—	—
Punjab	9	12	13	7	12	20	8	17	29
All other States	15	21	21	23	20	20	36	32	32

(Contd.)

TABLE 16.8 (Contd.)

States Rural	Other Hindus			Muslims			All Others		
	2004-05	1993-94	1987-88	2004-05	1993-94	1987-88	2004-05	1993-94	1987-88
(1)	(11)	(12)	(13)	(14)	(15)	(16)	(17)	(18)	(19)
All India	21	29	33	33	45	43	18	27	25
West Bengal	16	26	35	36	48	47	36	58	46
Kerala	10	22	21	17	32	37	7	21	14
Uttar Pradesh	28	36	39	37	43	47	49	6	29
Bihar	32	49	52	52	67	62	33	66	60
Assam	14	39	30	38	55	41	23	63	52
Jammu & Kashmir	2	14	20	3	47	27	11	5	9
Jharkhand	33	—	—	44	—	—	51	—	—
Karnataka	20	24	26	27	34	31	1	24	30
Uttaranchal	12	—	—	20	—	—	21	—	—
Delhi	8	0	0	0	0	0	0	0	0
Maharashtra	24	31	39	28	43	42	47	51	57
Andhra Pradesh	7	11	17	10	12	27	10	24	22
Gujarat	15	17	23	13	16	20	19	37	23
Rajasthan	11	17	24	14	32	27	13	15	4
Madhya Pradesh	24	30	33	35	28	41	2	24	42
Haryana	7	18	9	26	53	31	9	33	7
Tamil Nadu	21	28	36	10	25	37	22	41	47
Orissa	33	40	43	26	41	34	75	68	79
Himachal Pradesh	5	26	15	4	36	4	9	12	6
Chhattisgarh	36	—	—	42	—	—	34	—	—
Punjab	6	7	0	4	21	31	9	11	10
All other States	15	15	16	28	28	22	5	21	23

Source : *Op. cit.*, p. 368.

the data based on 365-day recall period to present the economic condition of SRCs. However, it does provide the data on the basis of 30-day recall both for urban and rural areas in Appendix Tables 8.5 and 8.6. Although the Sachar Committee mentions: "The estimate of poor continues to hover around 320 million when a 30-day recall period is used. On the other hand, if a 365-day recall period is used, there is a sharp fall in the number of poor to 251 million in 2004-05," (p.151). It appears that Sachar Committee did not want to confront the Government with the hard reality that whereas the growth rate of GDP was around 7 percent in 2004-05, the level of poverty in India on 30-day recall has gone up to 28.5% as against 26.1% in 1999-00. However, we shall base our analysis on 30-day recall period basis of poverty.

Since the data presents change in poverty over 17-year period (1987-88 to 2004-05), it indicates trends of decline in poverty among various socio-religious categories (SRCs). In urban areas, all-India poverty ratio declined from 38 percent in 1987-88 to 29% in 2004-05—a decline of 9 percentage points in 17-year period. Highest HCR of poverty was observed among SC/STs at 55% in 1987-88 declining to 46% in 2004-05. The next highest HCR was that pertaining to Muslims which declined from 53% in 1987-88 to 44% in 2004-05—a fall of 9 percentage points. However, the HCR for 'all Hindus' declined from 36% to 27% during the period—a reduction of 9% in poverty ratio. Obviously, HCR among Muslims residing in urban areas in 2004-05 was 44%, but that for SC/STs was 46% and all Hindus was 27%.

The situation in rural areas was more or less similar to that of urban areas. HCR of rural poverty declined for all-India from 39% in 1987-88 to 28% in 2004-05. in case of SCs/STs, it declined from 54% to 41% during the 17-year period—a fall by 13 percentage points. However, the situation among the Muslims was better as compared to SC/STs, and HCR of rural poverty among Muslims declined form 43% to 33%—fall of 10 percentage points. Among 'all Hindus', poverty reduction during the 17-year period was 12 percentage points, i.e. from 40% in 1987-88 to 28% in 2004-05.

Sachar Committee concludes: "A point to note is that the fall in HCR for Muslims has been only modest during the decade 1993-94 to 2004-05 in urban areas, whereas the decline in rural areas has been substantial." (p. 159). Since rural population accounted for about 72% of total population in India in 2001, the 'substantial decline' in the poverty of Muslims in rural areas should be a matter of satisfaction for the Muslim community. Poverty decline among all SRCs has been more of less modest during the last 17 years.

Sachar Committee draws the following conclusion: "The analysis of differentials in poverty across SRCs shows that Muslims face fairly high levels of poverty. Their conditions on the whole are only slightly better than those of SC/STs. As compared to rural areas, Muslims face much higher relative deprivation in urban areas. Over time changes in poverty levels also show that the economic conditions of Muslims in urban areas have not improved as much as the other SRCs. No systematic patterns emerge when over time changes in poverty levels of various SRCs are analyzed." (p. 161)

5. X-RAYING THE NUMBER OF POOR AMONG SRCS

An attempt has been made to find the total number of poor in different SRCs. The Census data on Religions for 2001 has been used. Poverty rates for rural and urban areas as revealed by 61st Round of NSS for 2004-05 have been used to calculate the absolute number of poor in rural and urban areas. The exercise reveals very interesting facts:

- The total number of poor works out to be 291.3 million in 2001, i.e. 28.3% of the total population was below the poverty line.
- The over-all Head Count Ratio (HCR) for poverty was 27.7% for Hindus, 36.3% for Muslims and 17.0% for others. This indicates that the proportion of poverty among Muslims was the highest.
- Within Hindus, SC/ST accounted for 258.2 million, out of which 41% lived below the poverty line. This implies that nearly 106 million SCs/STs were poor. Among the SRCs, the SCs/STs were the most deprived. Next in the deprivation order were the Muslims, followed by 'other Hindus' and other minorities.
- Out of the total number of poor reckoned at 291 million, 230 million were Hindus, 51 million Muslims and 11 million 'other religious minorities'.
- As a percentage share of the total poor, Hindus accounted for 78.8%, Muslims 17.5% and other minorities 3.7%. Among the Hindus, out of total percentage of 78.8%, SCs/STs accounted for 36.4%.

The upshot of the entire analysis is that the conclusions drawn by the Sachar Committee need further scrutiny. The question is not to eradicate poverty only among the Muslims, but among all socio-religious groups. The magnitude of poverty among Hindus in absolute terms is over 4 times than that of Muslims. The SC/STs account for more than double the number of total poor Muslims.

In a secular country like India, the Government must abide by its commitment to remove poverty among all SRCs and not only among Muslims. Even on relative basis of deprivation, SCs/STs deserve priority treatment, followed by Muslims, and in that order 'other Hindus' and 'other minorities'. This implies that separate budgeting for Muslims would be neither Constitutionally permissible nor socially justifiable. Obviously, the country should have a Committee for the uplift of all weaker sections of society and in this, the use of SRC data can be made an input, but not the sole criterion of determination of religion-wise grants. In this sense, a re-interpretation of the Sachar Committee Report has to be made.

TABLE 16.9
Break-up of Total Population (2001)

	Million			Poverty Ratio		
	Total	*Rural*	*Urban*	*Rural*	*Urban*	*Total*
Total	1028.6	742.5	286.1	28	29	28.3
Hindus	827.6	611.3	216.3	28	27	27.7
Muslims	138.2	88.8	49.4	33	44	36.3
Others*	62.8	41.9	20.2	18	16	17.0
SC/STs	258.2	n.a.	n.a.	41	41	41.0

Socio-Religious Categories	*Total Poor persons (million)*			*Share % of total Poor*
	Urban	*Rural*	*Total*	
Hindus	58.4	171.2	229.0	78.8
Muslims	21.7	29.3	51.0	17.5
Others	3.2	7.5	10.7	3.7
Total	83.3	208.0	291.3	100.0
SC/STs	n.a.	n.a.	105.9	36.4

* Others include Christians, Sikhs, Jains, Buddhists, etc.

Sources: Estimated on the basis of : (a) *Census of India* (2001), *First Report on Religion Data. (b) Report on Social, Economic and Educational Status of Muslims in India* (2006).

6. GOVERNMENT EMPLOYMENT AND SHARE OF MUSLIMS

Reviewing the employment situation, the Report observed that over 387 million people were employed in different sectors of the Indian economy. According to the Economic Survey (2005-06), about 27 million persons were employed in the organized sector. Of these, about 18.6 million persons were employed by government departments and public sector undertakings (PSUs), a share of 70%, while the remaining workers were employed in organized private sector.

Participation of Muslims in Government Employment

The Committee received data pertaining to 88 lakh employees. Table below gives the share of Muslims employees.

Data reveal that Government Departments, agencies and institutions employed only 4.4 lakh Muslim out of a total employment of 88 lakh employees, i.e. about 5% of total. Information about 1.4 million PSU workers shows that Muslims constituted only 3.3% of Central PSUs and 10.8% of state PSUs.

TABLE 16.10

Muslim Employees in Government Sector Employment

Department/ Institution Reporting	*Reported Number of employees*	*Reported number of Muslim employees*	*Muslims as percentage of reported employees*
State-Level Departments	44,52,851	2,78,385	6.3
Railways	14,18,747	64,066	4.5
Banks and RBI	6,80,833	15,030	2.2
Security Agencies*	18,79,134	60,517	3.2
Postal Service	2,75,841	13,759	5.0
Universities**	1,37,263	6,416	4.7
All Reported Government Employment (Excluding PSUs)	**88,44,669**	**4,38,173**	**4.9**
Central PSUs***	6,87,512	22,387	3.3
State PSUs	7,45,271	80,661	10.8
All PSUs	**14,32,783**	**1,03,048**	**7.2**

* CRPF, CISF, BSF, SSB and other agencies, ** 129 Universities (Central and State) and 84 Colleges *** Data from 154 PSUs.

Source : *Report of the Sachar Committee* (2006), p. 165.

The Committee further analyses employment in civil services and found that the presence of Muslims was only 3% in IAS, 1.8% in IFS and 4% in IPS.

UPSC Recruitment during 2003 and 2004

Table 16.11 gives an analysis of candidates who appeared for civil service examination, candidates selected for interview and recommended for employment.

TABLE 16.11

Analysis of UPSC Civil Services Examination (2003 and 2004)

Category	*Total*	*Muslim Candidates*	*Percentage of Muslim Candidates*
1. Appeared for the Main Examination	11,537	283	4.9
2. Selected for interviews	2,342	56	4.8
3. Selected as % of total appeared	20.2	19.8	—
4. Recommended candidates	835	20	—
5. Recommended candidates as % of Selected for interviews	35.7	35.7	—

Source : Compiled from the data given in Table 9.3 of the Report, p. 166.

Sachar Committee Report draws the conclusion: "Overall, Muslims constituted only 4.9% candidates who appeared in the written examination of Civil Services in the years 2003 and 2004; this is far below the 13.4% share of Muslims in the population. However, the success rate of Muslims is about the same as other candidates."

A review of the participation of Muslims in Government employment and that of PSUs shows that their share is relatively less as compared to their share of 13.4% in total population. Similarly, the share of Muslims in IAS, IFS and IPS is also very low. But data pertaining to UPSC civil service examination shows that only 4.9% participated in the written examination, but those selected for interview were about 20%, the percentage is nearly equal for other SRCs. Similarly, out of the Muslims who appeared for interview 36% were recommended for employment. This percentage is the same for other SRCs. The upshot of this analysis is that there is a need for enlargement of competencies, because the data does not show any problems with selection. The same is true for recruitment to IAS, IFS and IPS. Muslim community should, therefore, consider ways and means of developing competencies of its educated manpower, rather than wailing over their low participation rates in Government services. It is the enlargement of the competitive strength among the Muslim educated youth that will determine their degree of participation. The state should initiate affirmative action in this regard.

7. MUSLIM OBCS AND AFFIRMATIVE ACTION

Sachar Report has made a case for inclusion of Muslim OBCs within the ambit of Reservation extended to Hindu OBCs. The Report discussed three Models operative in some states of India where Muslims have been included in the category of OBCs.

1. Kerala and Karnataka Model

Karnataka Model classified Backward Classes into three categories: (a) Most backward; (b) More backward, and (c) Backward. All Muslims whose income is less than Rs. 2 lakh per annum have been declared as Backward and placed exclusively in one of the sub-categories of 'More backwards' with 4 percent of seats set aside for them.

Kerala operates at present the following reservation system: Backward classes 40% (Ezhavas 14%, Muslims 12%; Latin Catholics 4%; Nadars 2%; Christian converts from SC 1%; Dheevars 1%; other backward classes 3%; Viswakarmas 3%) and SCs and STs 10%.

2. Tamil Nadu Model

The state government has done away with reservation on the ground of religion, yet nearly 95% of the Muslims have been included in the fold of reservations. The quantum of reservation is currently 69%; far beyond the Supreme Court limit of 50%.

3. Bihar Model

The Karpoori Thakur Government in 1978 introduced the bifurcation of the backward classes into other Backward Classes (OBCs) and Most Backward Classes (MBCs). For purposes of recruitment to jobs, 8% was set aside for OBCs, 12% for MBCs and 14% for SCs, 10% for STs, 3% for women and another and 3% for the economically backward. Muslim Caste groups, depending on their level of backwardness have been included in the OBC or the MBC list.

From a discussion of the various models of reservations followed by different states, the following principles emerge:

(a) All persons belonging to different religions and caste groups which suffer from deprivation should be considered eligible for reservation.
(b) Religion cannot be made the basis of reservation as the Constitution prohibits its use for reservation in a secular society.
(c) Backwards should be further bifurcated into OBCs and MBCs; and MBCs should be provided a higher percentage of reservation as compared to OBCs.
(d) All state governments depending on the structure of their population should allocate the 50% reservation among the various competing groups in a following preferential order: (a) SCs and STs; (b) Most Backward classes; and (c) Other Backward Classes.

Rationalizing the Centre and State Lists

Sachar Report mentions that there are a few groups among Muslims which have found place in the Central list of OBCs, but are yet to be included in the State lists. But he Report hastens to add: "This is a general complaint and not confined to Muslims alone. There are many OBC groups, irrespective of their religion, that are present in the State List but missing in the Central list." (p. 200) A joint committee of the representatives of the Central and State Governments should carefully examine the anomalies and remove them.

SC Status for Muslim Groups

The Arzals Muslims are those who are the lowest comprising of those having similar traditional occupations as their Hindu counterparts in the list of Schedule Castes. The Report frankly admits: "It is widely believed that these communities are converts from the 'untouchables' among the Hindus.

Change in religion did not bring any change in their social or economic status." (Emphasis added, p. 201).

Rationality demands that converts of 'untouchables' from the Hindu religion into Islam, Christianity or Sikhism, if they continue to suffer the same deprivation in their social or economic status, should be eligible for the benefit of reservation in the SC category.

8. MAJOR RECOMMENDATIONS OF SACHAR COMMITTEE

The Committee observes that while there is considerable variation in the condition of Muslims across states, the Community exhibits deficits and deprivation in practically all dimensions of development. In fact, by and large, Muslims rank somewhat above SCs/STs but below Hindu-OBCs, other minorities and Hindu General (mostly upper castes) in almost all indicators considered.

Further, it states: the need for equity and inclusion in a pluralistic society can never be over emphasized. But the mechanisms to ensure equity should be such that the perception of discrimination is eliminated.

Policy Initiatives

The Committee recommends the creation a National Data Bank where all relevant data for various SRCs are maintained.

The Committee makes a very important observation: "It is wrong to assume that there is an inevitable conflict between the interests of majority and minority communities in the country. This is flawed reasoning and assumption. Deprivation, poverty and discrimination may exist among all SRCs although in different proportions." (p. 240) Flowing from this, the Committee recommends that an Equal Opportunity Commission (EOC) should be constituted by the Government to look into the grievances of the deprived groups.

To increase Muslim participation in Parliament and State assemblies, the Committee recommends that a more rational delimitation procedure that does not reserve constituencies with high minority population shares for SCs will improve the opportunity for the minorities, especially the Muslims, to contest and get elected to the Indian Parliament and the State Assemblies.

Specific Policy Initiatives

Criticality of Education: Access to education is critical for benefiting from emerging opportunities that are accompanied with economic growth. Sachar Committee Report brings out that the educational deprivation has been experienced by Muslims from the lowest to higher levels of education. The Report mentions: "And the problem is more acute for girls/women.

Reasons for this are varied—ranging from poverty to perceived discrimination resulting in alienating school environment. While the overall situation remains bad, the enrolment rates of Muslims have picked up in recent years and the policies should help sustain the momentum that can get created through this change. . . . Once the "hurdle" of school education is crossed, the differences across most SRCs in the likelihood of completing graduate studies narrow down and are at times not very significant. Therefore, a sharper focus on school education is desirable." (p. 243)

The Report makes the following recommendation: "Free and compulsory education up to age 14 is the responsibility of the State. And the fulfilment of this obligation is critical for the improvement in the educational conditions of Muslims, in fact, of all socio-economically deprived children." (p. 243)

Initiatives for School Education

Two important recommendations are made:

- High quality Government schools should be set-up in all areas of Muslim concentration.
- Exclusive schools for girls should be set-up for the 9-12 standards. This would facilitate higher participation of Muslim girls in school education. In co-educational schools, more women teachers need to be appointed.

Initiatives for Higher Education

- The University Grants Commission (UGC) should evolve a system where part of the allocation to colleges and universities is linked to diversity of student population.
- Low fees combined with merit-*cum*-means scholarships (partly funded from the additional grants) would enhance participation of poor among minorities.
- Sachar Committee suggests the following criteria to facilitate admission of "Most Backward" amongst all SRCs to colleges and universities.

Total Points	100
1. Assessment of merit to the maximum of	60
2. Assessment of Backwardness to the maximum of	40
Backwardness to be defined as the sum of the following (each with about one-third weight)	
(a) Household income (income criteria to be revised periodically)	13
(b) Backward district	13
(c) Backward class (assessed on the basis of a combination of family occupation and caste.	14

Need for the Urdu Language

Given the Commitment to provide primary education in the child's mother tongue, the state is required to run Urdu medium schools.

Three language Formula should be corrected, in order to accommodate Urdu in the Schools of the Hindi region.

Madarsas and Mainstream Education

Sachar Committee has underlined the fact that less than 4 percent of the Muslim children in the school going age attend the full-time regular Madarsas.

Madarsas should be linked to mainstream education so that children after having passed from Madarsas are able to move to higher levels of education.

There is a need to modernize Madarsas by introducing modern subjects along with traditional subjects.

Enhancing Access to Credit and Government Programmes

The Committee recommends promoting and enhancing access to Muslims in Priority Sector advances.

The Committee recommends that SIDBI should set aside a fund for training for minorities under its Entrepreneurial Development Programme.

The Committee recommends that participation of Muslims in Self-Help Groups (SHGs) and other micro-credit programmes be enhanced.

The Committee recommends that 58 districts with more than 25% Muslim population should be brought under Prime Minister's 15-point programme.

The Central Government should introduce a few schemes with large outlays for welfare of minorities with an equitable provision for Muslims.

Improving Employment Opportunities and Conditions

There is a need to provide financial and other support initiatives around occupations where Muslims are concentrated and that have growth potential.

Given the precarious conditions of self-employed persons in the informal sector, especially the home-based workers, it is desirable to have a mandated social security system for such workers. An early implementation of such a system would benefit a large section of Muslims along with the large segment of the informal sector workforce.

•

Enhancing the Efficacy of Infrastructure

Lack of access to crucial infrastructural facilities is another area of concern for all citizens to avail of schools, health care, sanitation facilities, potable water and means of daily transportation. It is the responsibility of the State to provide them for all of its citizens. The Committee notes: "As far as infrastructural facilities go there seems to be not much of an argument in building a case for Muslims alone." (p. 253).

9. SACHAR COMMITTEE REPORT—UNBALANCED AND ONE-SIDED

Sachar Committee Report on the Social, Economic and Educational Status of Muslims Community in India is a very assiduously prepared document within the short span of one and half years. The Committee makes an objective analysis not only of Muslim community, but also presents authentic information about the condition of SCs/STs, other Hindus (Upper caste Hindus), Sikhs, Christians, Jains, Buddhists. From the objective analysis, the following conclusions emerge:

1. Even 60 years after independence, SC/STs continue to remain the most disadvantaged groups of Indian society.
2. Muslims, though better than SC/STs, stand at the second place in order of disadvantage.
3. Upper Caste Hindus (other Hindus) have benefited much more than SCs/STs and the Muslims in all spheres—educational as well as economic, i.e. poverty reduction, economic opportunities in terms of better employment and vertical mobility.
4. Other minorities (Sikhs, Jains, Christians and Buddhists) were the most advantaged groups in social and economic hierarchy.
5. SC/STs who embraced Islam or Christianity or Sikhism or any other religion, continued to suffer the same deprivation in their social and economic status and thus remained "untouchables."
6. At various places, the Committee accepts that the problems of ghettoisation, poverty, unemployment, lack of opportunities of development, poor access to economic and social infrastructure, etc. are not specific to Muslims; all disadvantaged socio-religious categories (SRCs) face them.
7. So far as malnutrition is concerned, "the differences across the social groups are not overly large, indicating that child malnutrition and low birth-weight are pervasive across all SRCs in India."
8. Although overall literacy rate among Muslims is only 59%, as against the national average of 65%, in 10 out of 21 states, the

literacy level among Muslims is higher than the state average. These include Jharkhand, Karnataka, Maharashtra, Andhra Pradesh, Gujarat, Madhya Pradesh, Tamil Nadu, Chhattisgarh. Muslim literacy rate in Kerala is 89.4%, nearly equal to the state average.

9. Muslims have benefited considerably in primary, middle and secondary level education, though upper caste Hindus who had an initial advantage benefited more than Muslims, but the SCs/STs are still lagging behind all SRCs.
10. Among the poor households, the gap between Graduate Attainment Rates (GARs) between Muslims and SCs/STs and other SRCs is much lower than among the non-poor, implying the poor in all SRCs remained the most deprived.
11. Fall in Head Count Ratio (HCR) of poverty during 1993-94 to 2004-05 decade for Muslims was modest in urban areas, though this decline was substantial in rural areas. Since rural population accounts for 72% of total population, the substantial reduction in poverty of Muslims should be a matter of satisfaction for Muslims.
12. Out of the total number of poor estimated at 291 million for India as a whole in 2001, the poor among the Hindus accounted for 229 million (78.8%), among Muslims 51 million (17.5%) and among 'others' about 12 million (3.7%). The total number of poor SCs/STs number 106 million which were more than double the number of poor Muslims.
13. The share of Muslims in salaried government employment was considerably less at about 5% and in all PSUs at about 7% as compared to their population share of 13.4%.
14. Though a very small number of Muslim candidates (5%) appeared for civil service examination, the success rate of Muslims is about the same as that of other candidates.
15. The Report has clarified that only 4% of the School going age children attended full-time regular Madarsas. It has emphasized the need for linking Madarsas to Mainstream education.

The unique feature of the Report is that it does not recommend reservations for Muslim and emphasize affirmative action to improve the educational and economic status of the Muslims. Secondly, to facilitate the admission of the "Most Backward Classes" (MBCs) among all SRCs, the Report recommends criteria which combine merit with backwardness. Merit is to be assigned a weight of 60% and backwardness 40%. Backwardness has been defined to include: (a) household income, (b) backward district, and (c) backward class on the basis of family occupation and caste. The point which needs to be underlined is that Sachar Report recommends this formula for all SRCs and not for Muslims alone. It excludes the creamy layer.

Another unique recommendation of the Report is: "Deprivation, poverty and discrimination may exist among all SRCs although in different proportions." Based on this premise, the Report recommends that an Equal Opportunity Commission (EOC) be constituted by the Government to look into the grievances of the deprived groups. This is a very secular recommendation which needs to welcomed by all.

A Critique of the Report

Whereas the Congress and the Left saw the findings of the Report as vindication of their stand that Muslims need affirmative action, the BJP felt that the Report paved the way for communal divisiveness. Both these views can be described as extreme positions of the political class. It would be worthwhile to critically examine the Report.

An effort has been made in the Report to emphasize the point that Muslims have suffered due to discrimination. This charge has not been proved by facts. Rather the realities at the ground level reveal that Muslims have gained in all spheres, though not to the extent to which upper caste Hindus have benefited, due to better initial start. Muslims have also to introspect whether they have suffered due to the fact that they have continued to be prisoners of conservative forces and the progressive elements have failed to openly launch a crusade against conservatism. For instance, the attitude of Muslims toward the education of women, more especially in rural areas; needs greater transformation. A complaint mentioned in the Report that *burqa* clad Muslim women are not employed by the corporate sector. Corporate sector is guided by competition, efficiency and profitability. In this country, thousands of Muslim girls have discontinued *burqa* and have risen to higher positions in Universities, government and corporate sector. The Report should have suggested to the Muslim community to bring about a change in the attitudes and free themselves from the medieval chains in which majority of the Muslim households have bound themselves. This is not to suggest that among Hindus, the progressive forces have achieved all that they wanted. There are still conservative elements, but the degree of conservatism is less than that among Muslims.

It was heartening to find that the Report acknowledges the fact that enrolment rates for Muslims have picked up in recent years. The need of the hour is to strengthen and accelerate this trend.

The Report has recommended delimitation of constituencies with high concentration of Muslim population, rather than reserve them for SCs. This recommendation is highly uncalled for. The country after independence shifted to a system of joint electorates in place of separate electorates introduced by the British which led to the partition of the country. This recommendation, if accepted, would be the first step towards separate electorates. Muslim members of the Parliament and state assemblies should not be seen as representing a particular community. Rather they should appear as the representatives for the entire Indian society and for this, they must rise above religious parochialism.

The Report is worried about finding a place for Muslims in organized public and private sectors, while the fact of the matter is that 93 percent of employment is generated in the unorganized sector. In case of Muslims, this percentage would be even higher. The Report should have emphasized policies that strengthen the unorganized sector so that the enterprises in the small and medium sector graduate to the organized sector. This path would ensure poverty removal among all SRCs, including Muslims.

The bane of our so-called secular parties is that after the publication of the Sachar Committee Report, they are harping on reservations for Muslims in educational institutions and employment, knowing full well that the Supreme Court has already rejected religion-based reservations and thus such a policy militates against the secular spirit of our Constitution. Moreover, the Cap of 50% reservations is another limitation. But the so-called progressive elements of several political parties do not want to accommodate Muslims in the OBC quota of 27%. They have shamelessly forced the Congress-led UPA government not to exclude the creamy layer. A much better course would be to accept the Karnataka Model or the Kerala Model to include Muslim backwards among OBCs and give them a share and jettison the creamy layer to accommodate MBCs among Muslims.

To conclude: Certain grievances of Muslims pertaining to Urdu language, linking Madarsas to mainstream education, etc. should be immediately taken care of. The recommendation of the Sachar Committee to constitute an Equal Opportunities Commission needs urgent attention so that weaker sections among all socio-religious groups are taken care of and disparities among different communities are narrowed down. High quality Government schools are needed by the poor in all communities, because the richer classes are able to send their children to unaided high cost private schools, which operate under the pseudo-name of public schools. The weaker sections of the Indian society, belonging to Hindu, Muslim, Sikh, Jain or Buddhist cry for help and ways and means should be found so that their social and economic status is improved, rather than exclusively budgeting for Muslim community. A re-interpretation of the Sachar Committee Report is called for. Since the terms of reference of the Committee were restricted to the Muslims, the recommendations of the Committee were focussed on the Muslim community. But credit has to be given to the Committee that they have provided considerable leeway to work for the uplift of the weaker sections in all SRCs. It is, therefore, essential to sift the grain from the chaff of the Sachar Committee Report. In a secular democracy, the thinking in terms of Muslims, Hindus, Sikhs and Christians should give way to a better approach of thinking as Indians. This is what the national leaders during the struggle for independence and even after independence taught us and practiced. But the unfortunate aspect of the present polity is the rise of regional parties which are the main drivers of the ruling party. Principled politics has, therefore, been replaced by narrow political interests. We may describe it as the compulsion of coalition government. Such policies followed towards the upliftment of Muslims will bring about the charge of "Appeasement". Rather it would be better to work for the uplift of the weaker sections of our society, irrespective of religion to which they belong.

CHAPTER

17

Reservations and Social Justice

The announcement by HRD Minister Mr. Arjun Singh that the Ministry proposes to introduce reservations for 'Other Backward Classes' (OBCs), the controversy about reservations was revived. Various groups of people and institutions reacted according to their own interests. While the supporters of reservations from OBC ranks welcomed it as a historic decision which intended to correct a historic injustice to the OBCs by the higher castes, the students and faculty in medical institutions, engineering colleges and business schools considered it as an onslaught on their freedom and put forth the argument of dilution of merit and a serious set-back to their efforts to promote quality education to compete at the international level.

Before going into the arguments, it will be of interest to have a look at the factual scenario in this regards.

I. DATA SHEET ABOUT OBC, ST, SC AND OTHER CLASSES

The Mandal Commission (1980) basing its analysis on the proportion of population in different caste categories used figures of 1931 census and thus arrived at a figure of 52% as the size of the OBC in total population. The then government found that the data base of the Commission was faulty and thus shelved the report.

The data base of the Mandal Commission has been challenged by independent analysts as well. Mr. R. Vaidyanathan in his article "Reservations: Let down by weak data" in *Business Line* dated May 18, 2006 mentions: "the assumption made by Mandal Commission based on 1931 census and other parameters that more than 50 percent of population belong to OBC (Other Backward Caste) may not have been correct. But on that assumption the figure of 27 percent of reservation for OBC was arrived at. The National Sample Survey 2003 Round suggests that the non-Muslim OBC number may be around 32 percent and not 50 percent. Muslim OBCs are around 4 percent."

If we insert the Mandal OBC population in 2001 figures, the picture emerges as under:

TABLE 17.1
Census of India 2001

	Total Population
SC	16.2
ST	8.2
OBC	52.0*
Muslims	13.4
Christians	2.3
Sub-total	92.1
Others	7.9
Total	100.0

Note : *For OBC, the Mandal Commission figure has been inserted.

Using 52 percent OBC figure in 2001 census data reveals that SC, ST, OBC, Muslims and Christians account for 92.1 percent of the total population. Besides this, Sikhs, Buddhists, Jains constitute 3.1 percent (1.9 percent + 0.8 percent + 0.4 percent). This implies that 'others' implying higher castes are less than 5 percent which is a gross under-estimate. Obviously, Mandal Commission figure of 52 percent for OBC is unreliable as it is an over-estimate.

The National Family Health Statistics (NFHS) Survey of 1998 suggests that the population of OBCs (non-Muslims) is around 30 percent which is close to NSS figure.

Since NSS 55th Round for 1999-2000 has provided more recent data and this is considered as more reliable, it would not be useful to parrotwise repeat the 52 percent figure for OBC which the political class in India is doing even to this day. The NSS further reveals that OBC population in rural areas is 37.4 percent and in urban areas 31.4 percent and the overall figure is 35.7 percent for the country as a whole. It also suggests that others (mainly upper castes) are 30.7 percent in rural areas and 50.2 percent in urban areas and the overall figure is 36.2 percent for the country as a whole.

TABLE 17.2
Percent Distribution of Persons in NSS 55th Round by Social Group

All India

	Rural	*Urban*	*Total*
ST	10.6	3.9	8.7
SC	21.3	14.6	19.4
OBC	37.4	31.4	35.7
Other	30.7	50.2	36.2
Total	100.0	100.0	100.0

Note : Figures in Column 3 have been derived by applying a weightage of 72.2 percent for rural population and 27.8 percent for urban population as per Census 2001.

Source : *NSS Report No. 469* : (1999-2000).

NSS Data on the Proportion of SCs/STs, OBCs and Others

Critics have questioned the 52% figure of OBC population as arrived by the Mandal Commission based on data collected by 1931 Census. There is a strong element of exaggeration in Mandal Commission. More recently, NSS 55th Round for 1999-00 and NSS 61st Round for 2004-05 have estimated the proportion of SCs/STs, OBCs and General category among Hindus and Muslims. Since the data provide proportion of OBCs within the Hindu community and Muslim community, an effort has been made by using the Census Data on religions to determine the share of OBC population by using the proportions provided by the NSS Rounds. This provides us a broad estimate of the percentage population in various socio-religious categories.

The exercise reveals that at the All-India level in 1999-2000, percentage of OBCs among Hindus was 30.8% of the total population. If we add 4.2% of the Muslim OBC population, then the total OBC population is 35% of the total population.

But for 2004-05, OBC population among Hindus is reckoned at 34.6% of total population. If we add 5.5% of the Muslim OBC population, then the total OBC population would be 40.1% of total population. (Refer Table 17.3)

Table 17.4 provides the break-up in rural and urban areas. For 1999-00, in urban areas the OBC population (Hindus plus Muslims) was 24.9+5.6=30.5% of total urban population. However, the figure of OBC population in 2004-05 was 27.9+7.0=34.9% of total urban population.

Similarly, for rural areas, in 1999-00, Hindu OBCs accounted for 32.8% of total rural population. If we add 3.7% Muslim OBCs, the total OBC population in rural areas is (32.8+3.7) = 36.5% of total rural population (Refer Table 17.4). For 2004-05, the total OBC population is 36.9% among

TABLE 17.3

Distribution of Population According to Socio-Religions Categories—All-India

	*Proportion of Population in Religious group as per NSS**		*Percentage of Total population using 2001 Census percentages*		*Total Population Distribution using Census 2001 figures (million)*	
	1999-2000	*2004-05*	*1999-2000†*	*2004-05†*	*1999-2000*	*2004-05*
(1)	*(2)*	*(3)*	*(4)*	*(5)*	*(6)*	*(7)*
Hindus						
(a) SC/STs	31.3	31.2	25.2	25.2	259.0	259.0
(b) OBCs	38.3	43.0	20.8	34.6	316.0	355.8
(c) General	30.4	25.8	24.5	20.7	251.8	212.8
A: Sub-total	**100.0**	**100.0**	**80.5**	**80.5**	**827.6**	**827.6**
Muslims						
(d) OBCs**	31.7	40.7	4.2	5.5	43.2	56.7
(e) General	68.3	59.3	9.2	7.9	94.6	81.5
B: Sub-total	**100.0**	**100.0**	**13.4**	**13.4**	**138.2**	**138.2**
C: Others			**6.1**	**6.1**	**62.8**	**62.8**
Total Population (A+B+C)			100.0	100.0	1028.6	1028.6

* For 1999-2000, the proportion of SC/STs, OBCs and General Category are based on 55th Round of NSS and for 2004-05, are based on 61st Round of NSS as given in the Report on *Social, Economic and Educational Status of Muslim Community in India (2006).*

** Muslim SC/STs are included in OBCs since they form a very small percentage.

† Figures in columns 3 and 4 have been worked out by applying the NSS proportion within a socio-religious group to the population distribution by religions as given in Census 2001.

TABLE 17.4

Distribution of Population According to Socio-Religious Categories

	Proportion of Population in Religious group as per NSS (%)		*Percentage of Total population using 2001 Census percentages*		*Total Population Distribution using Census 2001 figures (millions)*	
	1999-2000	*2004-05*	*1999-2000*	*2004-05*	*1999-2000*	*2004-05*
(1)	*(2)*	*(3)*	*(4)*	*(5)*	*(6)*	*(7)*
			URBAN			
Hindus						
(a) SC/STs	20.6	20.5	15.6	15.5		
(b) OBCs	33.0	36.9	24.9	27.9		
(c) General	46.5	42.6	35.1	32.2		
A: Sub-total	**100.0**	**100.0**	**75.6**	**75.6**	**216.3**	
Muslims						
(d) OBCs	32.6	40.2	5.6	7.0		
(e) General	67.4	59.8	11.7	10.3		
B: Sub-total	**100.0**	**100.0**	**17.3**	**17.3**	**49.5**	
C: Others			**7.1**	**7.1**	**20.3**	
Total Population			100.0	100.0	286.1	

		RURAL			
Hindus					
(a) SC/STs	34.6	34.5	28.5	28.4	
(b) OBCs	39.9	44.9	32.8	36.9	
(c) General	**25.5**	**20.6**	**21.0**	**17.0**	
A: Sub-total	100.0	100.0	82.3	82.3	611.1
Muslims					
(d) OBCs	31.2	40.9	3.7	4.9	
(e) General	68.8	59.1	8.3	7.1	
B: Sub-total	100.0	100.0	12.0	12.0	89.1
C: Others			**5.7**	**5.2**	**42.3**
Total Population (A+B+C)			100.0	100.0	742.5

Hindus and 4.9% among Muslims. Adding together, the total OBC population is rural areas is (36.9+4.9) = 41.8% of total rural population.

A close perusal of the data given in Tables 17.3 and 17.4 reveals that whereas the SC/ST population during 1999-2000 and 2004-05, remains unaltered at 25.2%, the OBC population at the All-India level increases from 35% in 1999-2000 to 40.1% in 2004-05—5% increase.

Similarly, SC/ST population in urban areas for 1999-2000 as well as 2004-05 was 15.5%, but the OBC population increased from 30.5% in 1999-2000 to 34.9% in 2004-05—4.4% increase.

Likewise, SC/ST population in rural areas for 1999-00 as well as 2004-05 was 28.4%, but the OBC population increased from 36.5% in 1999-00 to 41.8% in 2004-05—5.3% increase.

The question arises: SC/ST population does not indicate any change in its percentage share of 1999-00 as well as 2004-05, but OBC population (Hindus and Muslims combined) increases from about 35% in 1999-00 to 40% in 2004-05. Why is it that OBC population indicates a 5% increase during the 5-year period? Since SC/STs are the poorest and the least educated socio-religious groups, the growth rate of population would be higher for SC/STs as compared with OBCs. Obviously, population growth rates do not explain the growth in the percentage share of OBCs. The probable explanation lies in the inclusion of more castes in the OBC category.

Despite all this, the OBC population according to NSS estimates works out be 35% in 1999-00 and 40.1% in 2004-05. Obviously, it is much lower than the Mandal Commission estimate of 52%.

2. THE DEBATE ABOUT OBC RESERVATIONS

Those who oppose reservations for OBCs argue that the Scheduled Castes faced special disadvantages arising out of 'untouchability'. Similarly, the Scheduled Tribes, who were living mostly in forest areas were physically separated from mainstream Hindu society, suffered from undisputed extreme poverty. The OBC faced no such discrimination and thus the 'caste argument' advanced in favour of OBC reservations is fallacious. If the logic of this assertion is accepted, then the OBCs can claim reservations on the basis of economic criteria at par with the poor and underprivileged classes among other castes, Muslims and other minorities. It is also a fact the upper OBCs have become economically powerful in many states and thus they do not qualify on the basis of economic criteria. But among them, the MBCs (Most Backward Classes) deserve the benefit of reservations. Mr. Chandra Bhan Prasad, Dalit Intellectual and Commentator in his article 'Quota for OBCs in Higher Education (*Economic Times*, April 12, 2006) states: "L.R. Naik, the only Dalit member of the Mandal Commission, had refused to sign the Mandal Commission recommendations. Naik held that the OBCS are made up of two larger occupational blocks—the intermediate backward classes or the Most Backward Castes (MBCs) who have been deprived and excluded by the system. He argued for splitting the Mandal quota into two, in order to safeguard the interests of the MBCs, who have been deprived and excluded by the system." B.P. Mandal, a Yadav zamindar himself rejected Naik's suggestions. Consequently, Mandal Report became the mouthpiece of the dominant upper OBCs.

By August 1991, the Mandal Report became the rallying point of all upper backward castes who occupied powerful positions among the ruling classes. Even when Mr. V.P. Singh used the Mandal Report to counter the Mandir Card of the BJP, he did not bother to pay any heed to Naik's suggestion, but became the messiah of the OBCs, a symbol for the downtrodden castes, though in fact he was blackmailed by the upper OBCs. The sum and substance of this historical development is that caste politics became votebank politics.

It may be mentioned that on August 8, 2006, the Supreme Court set aside an order of the Jharkhand High Court that upheld a state government notification amalgamating upper backward classes and most backward classes for the purpose of reservation. To quote:

> "The amalgamation of two classes of people for reservation would be unreasonable as two different classes are treated similarly, which is in violation of Article 14 of the Constitution of India, which is to treat similar similarly and to treat different differently," a Bench of Justices A.R. Lakshmanan and Lokeshwar Panta said. The Supreme Court pointed out that "there is no constitutional bar to a state categorizing the backward classes as backward and more backward."

The Supreme Court Judgment is a vindication of the view held by Mr. L.R. Naik, the Dalit Member of the Mandal Commission.

Class *versus* Caste and the Change in the Attitude of Political Parties

As mentioned earlier, after centuries of oppression which the SC and ST students suffered, it was logical that reservations should be used as an instrument to improve the lot of this category of students, but to equate OBCs with SCs and STs is unreasonable. This spirit guided the affairs of the Indian State for over four decades after independence. Jawaharlal Nehru, the first and most respected Prime Minister of India wrote in a letter to Chief Ministers dated 27th June 1961: "I dislike any kind of reservations . . . if we go in for reservations on communal or caste basis we (will) swamp the bright and able people and remain second-rate or third rate . . . this way lies not only folly but disaster."

It is really regrettable that under the sheer political pressure of upper OBCs who have become powerful votebanks, the political parties, the Congress and the CPM have changed their attitudes. Whereas earlier they conducted their social analysis in terms of Classes, they are now replacing class with caste.

The Congress Party which spearheaded the freedom and whose leaders used to proclaim that they will usher in free India a classless and casteless society have shifted their stand. In the Manifesto of the Congress Party, there was mention of reservations for OBCs and Muslims. In fact, the Congress Government in Andhra Pradesh enacted a law to provide 5% reservations in jobs to Muslims which was struck down by the Court as 'unconstitutional'. But the Congress is forging ahead its OBC agenda in case of reservations in institutions of higher education. In a very angry comment Mr. Chandra Bhan Prasad mentions: "The UPA government by proposing to announce quotas for OBCs in educational institutions, a quarter century after the Mandal Commission came into being, has now buried the very notion of social justice. The Mandal Commission recommendations are, in essence, meant for he MBCs, but the UPA government has betrayed them. . . . Instead of fighting the upper OBCs onslaught on democracy, the government has decided to facilitate their onslaught on democracy. . . . In the process, the Congress has abandoned Dalits, Adivasis and MBCs, who are the real social proletariat of the nation."

The left parties have also allowed themselves to be steamrollered by the high pressure of upper OBCs. They have abandoned their Marxian class analysis and succumbed to caste as the main determinant of social justice. Prof. Niraja Gopal Jayal of the Centre for the Study of Law and Governance, of JNU writes: "Even the Left parties, which recognized caste inequality only after prolonged internal debate, seem to have capitulated to the idea that there is only one form of inequality in India, and that is caste. Sadly, the secular project of addressing material inequalities appears not to be owned by any political party today." (*Economic Times*, May 2, 2006).

It is really strange that the BJP while endorsing 27 percent reservations for OBCs has put forward the case of the "poor and the deprived" even among the upper castes. This passes one's comprehension that the position which the Left parties should have taken on reservations, is being taken by the BJP to use the criterion of class in place of caste. Even the BJP approach is half-hearted because BJP has also endorsed OBCs as a single category and not pleaded for MBCs as the real group which needs to be lifted by the policy of reservations.

Professor Dipankar Gupta of JNU in a very strong indictment of Mandal Commission approach mentions: "The Big lie is that backward castes have been persecuted and marginalized through history by the upper castes and treated akin to untouchables. The Mandal Commission has leveraged this lie to its advantage to benefit precisely those castes that are economically and socially among the prosperous in rural India." (*Hindustan Times*, Milking Backwardness, August 28, 2006). Rather the upper backward castes like Yadavs and Kurmis, Jats, Thevars, the Goundas, the Okkaligas and the Gujars are notorious for exploiting the most backward castes and were considered as the worst perpetrators of caste atrocities in rural India. These castes were economically well-off. But the Mandal Commission Report totally ignored economic criteria and emphasized only social criteria.

Thus, the Mandal Commission purposefully tried to advance the interests of the band of castes which were economically and socially more advanced.

Another argument put forth against reservations is the quantity *vrs.* quality argument. The Knowledge Commission appointed by the UPA government under the chairmanship of Sam Pitroda rejected Arjun Singh's quota proposal for OBCs in higher educational institutions. He mentioned that we are not against reservations *per se,* but it should not be at the cost of meritocracy. The Commission rejected the HRD minister's proposal voting 6:2 against it. A better way to achieve social justice would be to expand the capacity right form the primary school to higher educational and professional institutions.

125 professors of IIT, Kanpur in their memorandum to the President of India stated that there is a need to reconsider the move to force OBC reservations on all Institutions of higher and professional education. The professors maintained: "It is clear for all to see that other factors like poverty, region and gender have greater adverse impact on the chances of a person becoming an engineer or a doctor."

Similarly, the strike by the doctors at All-India Institute of Medical Sciences (AIIMS) was another stiff opposition to OBC quotas. The Supreme Court intervened and asked the government to furnish details of the data on the basis of which the decision of 27 percent reservations has been taken.

3. CREAMY LAYER ISSUE

Another issue is that of the creamy layer. *Creamy layer refers to people belonging to Other Backward Castes (OBCs) who are financially well-off.* More recently, the upper OBCs who form the creamy layer are pressurizing the Government to abandon the idea of exclusion of persons or groups who would be affected by the implementation of the 27 percent reservations for OBCs. While the CPM leaders made statements that the creamy layer should not get the benefit of reservation, but ironically, at the UPA-Left Co-ordination Committee deciding on the reservations, CPM never raised the issue. Though UPA-Left have swept the creamy layer issue below the carpet, but the Judgment of the Supreme Court on the issue in 1992 would force the government to implement it.

The Supreme Court while hearing a petition challenging former PM V.P. Singh's implementation of the recommendations of the Mandal Commission suggested 27 percent job reservations for OBCs in 1992, observed that while it upheld the quota, it directed that socially advanced persons/sections from among the OBCs be excluded. The Government was, therefore, forced to appoint a panel to evolve the criteria for identification of the creamy layer among the OBCs. The Government accepted the recommendations of the panel in 1993.

Criteria Laid Down for the Creamy Layer

Broadly, children of people holding high posts in government, armed forces, judiciary, public sector undertakings, banks, insurance organizations and universities are part of the creamy layer. Officers holding equivalent comparable posts in the private sector too fall under this bracket. The monetary criterion: Gross annual income of Rs. 2.50 lakh or possession of wealth above the exemption limit as prescribed in the Wealth Tax Act for a period of three consecutive years.

The Government has released the list of persons/sections covered under Creamy Layer on July 19, 2006. This comprises of the following:

1. Children of the President, Vice-president and Judges of the Supreme Court and High Courts fall under the "Creamy Layer" among OBCs under the criteria fixed for exclusion from reservations in Civil posts and services.
2. Children of the members of the UPSC and State public Service Commission, Chief Election Commissioner, Comptroller and Auditor General of India and persons holding constitutional positions of this nature also fall under the creamy layer category.
3. Under the criteria, persons with gross annual income of Rs. 2.5 Lakh or above or possessing wealth above the exemption limit as prescribed in the Wealth Tax Act for a period of three consecutive years are also excluded.
4. The creamy layer covers Group A/Class 1 officers of the All India Central and State Services.

The Supreme Court in its judgment on October 19, 2006 has said that the purpose of the affirmative action is to transcend the caste system and not to perpetuate it.

"Reservation is necessary for transcending caste and not for perpetuating it. Reservation has to be used in a limited sense otherwise it will perpetuate casteism in the country."

The 5-Judge bench headed by Chief Justice Y.K. Sabharwal said it was important "to find a stable equilibrium between justice to the backwards, equity for the forwards and efficiency for the entire system."

For the first time, the Supreme Court introduced the concept of creamy layer in the quota of for Scheduled Castes and Scheduled Tribes to keep the better-offs among them out of the purview of reservations. While upholding the quota system in promotions, the Supreme Court ruled: "Backwardness has to be based on objective factors whereas inadequacy has to be factually examined. The fact that considerable number of members of backward class have been appointed/promoted against general seats in the State services may be a relevant factor for the State Governments to review the question of continuing reservations for the said class."

The Supreme Court further observed: "if the extent of reservations goes beyond cut-off point, then it results in reverse discrimination." It ordered a 50 percent ceiling on quota saying, "a numerical bench mark is the surest immunity against charges of discrimination."

In a consultation held with State Governments in October 2006, the States demanded the exclusion of the creamy layer of OBC from the purview of reservations. Instead, they wanted priority to be given to those OBC members who were both economically and socially backward. The creamy layer would be considered only if there was any vacancy in the reservation quota.

4. 93RD AMENDMENT TO THE CONSTITUTION AND RESERVATIONS

Following certain judgments of the Supreme Court that stated that the policy of reservations can only be limited to state-run educational institutions, the Parliament discussed the issue in all its aspects. There was unanimity round the view that reservations be extended to aided as well as unaided privately-run educational institutions. This led to the passage of the 93rd Amendment to the Constitution in January 2006, by insertion of a new Clause in Article 15(5). The amendment stated:

> All educational institutions—private and government—will implement the reservation policy as enacted by Parliament except those considered minority institutions as defined by Article 30 of the Constitution.

It may be noted that during 2005-06, the total intake in private unaided professional institutions (excluding medical colleges) was 5,14,356. If reservations of 50 percent seats is ensured for SCs, STs and OBCs, this will ensure over 2.0 lakh seats for the deprived sections. Private medical colleges account for a little over 20,000 students. Nearly 10,000 seats will be earmarked for the deprived sections.

5. THE ARGUMENTS IN FAVOUR OF RESERVATIONS

Mr. Udit Raj, Chairman, All-India Confederation of SC/ST Organizations put forth the following arguments in favour of reservations:

In quite a large number of professional institutions, there is a quota for Non-Resident Indians (NRIs) and also quite a big share for 'payment seats' which go by auction by way of payment of capitation fees. Obviously, merit is not the basis of admission so far as NRI and Capitation Fee quota is concerned. This is nothing but reservation by the rich. To that extent, the merit argument appears to be fallacious. Merit should not, therefore, become an issue when the deprived sections (SC, ST and OBC) are provided access to these institutions. This is downright rational.

Secondly, reservation is not a phenomenon exclusive to our country. The American MNC, IBM, voluntarily introduced reservations for Blacks in 1930. Similarly, there are reservations for depressed and weaker sections in Brazil, South Africa, Japan, Netherlands and Ireland. There is 50 percent reservation for Blacks and women in the medical faculty of Harvard University.

Thirdly, Tamil Nadu had as much as 69 percent reservations. The state has also fared better than many other states in Health and Human Development Index.

Fourthly, the meritorious, though trained in India seek jobs in foreign countries. Nearly 70 percent AIIMS doctors seek appointments abroad. Over 80 percent of he engineers graduating from Roorkee are exported. SC/ST/OBCs, if admitted in larger number, will help the process of economic and social development in India.

Lastly, merit, as it is being presently understood, does not include honesty, hard work and patriotism. The doctors who come out of medical colleges after paying capitation fees in their life as professionals treat the medical profession as a milch cow to recover payments made to meet the cost of medical education and thus, establish nursing homes to serve the rich and affluent sections. The 'service motive' is completely overpowered by the spirit of self-aggrandizement. This is also true of engineering and management professionals.

Moreover, most of the products of public schools who are admitted to professional colleges on the basis of marks secured incur 50 to 100 times expenditure on their education in public schools besides tuitions in their areas of deficiency as compared to their underprivileged counterparts in corporation/Government schools.

Udit Raj concludes: "Reservation is only a concession given to socially and educationally backward people so that they may integrate with the mainstream. We have no objection if the poor among the upper caste people too, are given the benefit of reservation. But the problem is that here, there is the danger of the rich among them taking advantage of this policy."

It is really strange that Udit Raj does not talk about the creamy layer benefiting under the label of 'socially and educationally backward' people. Secondly, OBCs are not a homogeneous category and thus a decision has to be taken to exclude upper OBCs and extend the benefit to MBCs.

6. ISSUE OF MINORITY INSTITUTIONS

93rd Constitutional Amendment has incorporated a provision to exempt minority institutions as defined by Article 30 of the Constitution. The questions arises: Is this exemption justified or is it pandering to votebank politics of the UPA-Left Co-ordination Committee? Mr. Ravi Shankar Prasad, BJP spokesperson charged the UPA Government: "This is the worst form of minority appeasement by the Manmohan Singh Government. The hard fact remains that majority of he educational institutions in south India are run by the minorities. The quota regime, however, will not extend to them . . . . The UPA government has traded everything for votes."

Though this sharp criticism has come form the BJP, but this has an important bearing for the policy of reservations. It defies logic as to why minority institutions should be exempted from participating in the noble effort for uplifting SC/ST/OBCs. Moreover, there is a catch-22 situation. There is a demand by the Muslim community that since they account for 9.1% of the total backward population, they should be provided the benefit of reservations, but if their own institutions are exempted for the purpose, with what logic Muslim community would be able to demand the benefit of reservations from institutions run by the majority community! The Government should, therefore, reconsider the issue.

In the consultation held with state governments in October 2006, Left-ruled Kerala, joining forces with the BJP-ruled states, demanded the inclusion of minority institutions in the proposed bill.

7. REAL ISSUES RELATED TO RESERVATIONS

1. Reservations for SCs/ STs have been in existence right from the beginning of the Constitution, since they pertain to a special category which suffered for centuries the humiliation perpetrated on them by the upper castes and there is no voice of dissidence on this issue. The comparison with the Blacks is also synonymous of the discrimination on the basis of the colour of the skin which was totally unjustified in USA and other countries.
2. There is a fit case for reservation for the OBCs so that they become the beneficiaries of the growth process, but they should be split into upper OBCs and Most Backward Castes (MBCs). The MBCs really deserve the benefit of Mandal Commission recommendations.
3. The creamy layer in all cases (SCs, STs and OBCs) should by law be excluded from the benefit of reservations.
4. There should be strict adherence to a time-frame by which reservations should be withdrawn for all sections of the society. The 'temporary reservations' continue to be extended and they become 'permanent' in nature. This has got to be avoided. Even Dr. Ambedkar when he was asked why he has provided only a period of 10 years for reservations for SCs and STs is reported to have stated: I do not want my community to walk on crutches for ever.
5. There is a need to balance quantity, quality and equity. To achieve this, the country will have to strengthen primary, middle and secondary level institutions and target at narrowing the differences between the drop-out rates of the upper middle and affluent classes and the SC/ST/OBC categories.

6. There is a need to provide an extensive system of scholarships and educational loans so that any poor (OBC or non-OBC or Minority community) student who on the basis of merit is able to secure admission in a professional or higher education institution, is not handicapped for want of funds.
7. Reservations should be used as a means in the short period to end reservations in the long period and there is a need to set the goal for the purpose. "It is true" to quote Udit Raj, "that reservation is not a permanent solution to the vexed problem of our society. As and when equal and compulsory education is introduced in the country, Dalits and OBCs will not stake their claim to reservation."

8. MANDAL REPORT RECOMMENDATIONS THAT POLITICIANS OVERLOOKED

V.P. Singh earlier and now the UPA government, in their pre-occupation with reservations, completely overlooked other far-reaching and basic recommendations of the Mandal Commission.

Mandal Commission debated at length caste, merit and reservations in all their aspects. It recommended structural changes in our social system that would make reservations for OBCs work properly. But our myopic politicians only picked up those parts of the Mandal Commission Report that suited their party agenda. The Report made some path-breaking recommendations:

Firstly, Mandal Commission clearly stated that reservations would have only a palliative effect unless backwardness is tackled at the roots. So educational reforms come first and be given highest priority.

Secondly, the Report emphasized two-pronged approach towards education of OBCs. First, it recommended adult education programmes of OBC parents, so that they can motivate their children to acquire education. Second, the setting up of residential schools for OBC children. There are places where they would have an environment to study. The Government should pay their boarding, lodging and tuition fees. The students would also be given vocational training.

Thirdly, to check the fall of educational standards as a result of admission of less meritorious students into higher quality institutions, the Report warned: "The concerned authorities should appreciate that their job is not finished once candidates on the reserved quotas have been admitted to various institutions. In fact, the real task starts only after that. Unless follow-up action is taken to give special coaching assistance to these students, not only will these young people feel frustrated and humiliated but the country will also be loaded with ill-equipped and sub-standard engineers, doctors and other professionals."

Fourthly, the Government should set-up financial institutions to provide loans on easier terms to OBCs, and help them to set-up small businesses.

Lastly, all state governments should be directed to implement progressive land reforms to effect structural changes along the production chain in the rural areas.

Mandal was conscious of the "heartburns" that would be caused between OBCs and non-OBCs whenever reservations are introduced. A chorus of alarm will be raised by the ruling elite and thus, his purpose was to reduce the area of conflict. It is distressing that Mandal Commission Report was not studied in its entirety, but only selective portions were used by politicians and for over two decades and a half. All important structural reforms did not form an essential part of the national agenda.

9. EXPERIENCE OF RESERVATION IN INDIA

Reservations in educational institutions have been in force in India for over five decades for SCs and STs. It would be useful to understand whether we have achieved the avowed goal of promoting social upliftment.

TABLE 17.5

Percentage of Total Enrolment at the Primary Stage

	1980	*2000*
SCs	15.1	18.0
STs	6.4	9.4

Drop-out Rates at Various Stages (%)

	Primary	*Middle*	*Secondary*
SCs	49.4	67.8	77.7
STs	62.5	82.2	85.0

Source : Government of India, Ministry of HRD, *Selected Educational Statistics.*

Data provided in Table 17.5 reveals that enrolment of Scheduled Castes went up tardily from 15.1 percent in 1980 to only 18.0 percent in 2000—a very small increase of about 3 percent in 20 years. Similarly, enrolment of scheduled tribes which was barely 6.4 percent in 1980 improved to only 9.4 percent in 2000—a very small rise of 3 percent in 20 years. All this shows that mere reservations would not be able to improve the lot of SCs and STs in the absence of supporting measures mentioned in the Mandal Commission Report. This is also corroborated by high drop-out rates prevailing to the extent of about 78 percent up to secondary stage in case of SCs and 85 percent in case of STs. With these high drop-out rates, a very small proportion of SC and ST students are available for enrolment in higher education. This underlines the need for taking effective policy measures at the school stage—primary, middle and secondary—so that there is a higher turnout of SC and ST completers at the higher secondary level.

Tamil Nadu has the longer experience of reservations. With 69 percent of the admissions and jobs reserved, it can be described as the most intensive reservations drive to improve the lot of SCs, STs and OBCs. Reviewing the Tamil Nadu experience Mr. P.V. Indiresan, former Director, IIT Madras writes: "The Tamil Nadu experience can be described both as a success and as a failure. It is a success because backward castes have wrested leadership—both in the academic and administrative spheres—apart from acquiring total command of the political space. Not only have the backward castes taken command, they have also made Tamil Nadu one of the most successful states."

"Reservations in Tamil Nadu can also be described as a failure on two counts; even after three quarters of a century, the backward castes are unwilling to compete openly. There are third, or even fourth generation beneficiaries of reservations who are unable to get over their dependence on the handicaps reservation provides for them. It appears, reservation is a crutch, not a remedy."

The real test of reservations and its success lies in the fact that after a time-frame (say of 20 to 30 years), the oppressed and backward classes do not need reservations for their protection any longer. But the experience of reservation in India for nearly six decades reveals that *'temporary'* has become *'permanent'* and there appears to be no chance of their abolition even during the next 20 or 30 years, given the kind of votebank politics in the era of coalition governments.

Although the Government under Article 15(4) stipulates 22.5 percent reservation for SC & STs (15% for SC and 7.5% for ST), the ground reality is that there is gross under-utilization of these quotas fixed by the Government.

The National Commission on Scheduled Castes and Scheduled Tribes in their sixth report for the period 1999-2000 and 2000-01 revealed that in Graduate, Post-graduate and Research level taken together, only 8.2 percent seats were filled for SCs and a merely 2 percent for STs.

TABLE 17.6
Seats filled in Higher Education in India

Courses	*Total Seats*	*Filled by SC (%)*	*Filled by ST (%)*
Graduate	68,09,100	8.37	3.00
Post-graduate	7,58,000	8.00	1.40
Research	68,369	2.77	1.00
Total	**76,35,469**	**8.18**	**2.0**

Source : National Commission for Scheduled Castes and Scheduled Tribes, *Sixth Report*, 1999-2000 and 2000-01.

Figures given in Table 17.6 reveal that the situation deteriorates as we move from graduates to post-graduates and research. The share of STs in the seats filled in Research is barely 1.0 percent and that of SCs only 2.8 percent. Obviously, the quota remains unfilled for a variety of reasons.

The situation in IITs and Business Schools is no better. In 1992, a study by two IIT-B professors revealed that only 10.5 percent of the total seats available in 2001 were filled by SC/ST students as against the quota of 22.5 percent—that is, less than half the prescribed quota.

Although voices are being raised to allow job reservations in the private sector, the performance of the Government and Public Sector Enterprises to fill up vacancies from SC/ST/OBC categories is not satisfactory. In 2005, the combined representation of SC/ST/OBC in 211 PSEs was 43.9 percent as against the mandatory quota of 49.5 percent. Even these figures are exaggerated because the departments fill more seats in Class D services to hike the average.

In 2002, reserved posts for SC/ST indicated a short fall of 7.44 percent in Group A services and 4.24 percent in Group B services.

The upshot of this analysis is that low enrolment rates and high drop-out rates among SC/STs in basic education lead to unequal access in higher education. This failure gets further reflected in failure to recruit SC/STs in employment.

The lackadaisical manner in which the quota seats are filled and quite a large number are left unfilled is due to lack of follow-up action, absence of regular monitoring by some statutory authority. If the government itself cannot fulfil its constitutional obligation, how can it expect the private sector to enforce reservations in jobs faithfully? Although the idea of job reservation in private sector was moved, but the Government has yet to take a decision in the matter because the Industry Associations (FICCI, CII and ASSOCHAM) are strongly opposed to it and have brought out a policy of affirmative action, including voluntary effort to fill vacancies from SC/ST/OBC categories.

10. EMPOWERMENT THROUGH ENTREPRENEURSHIP

According to the Economic Census (1998) conducted by the CSO covering 30.35 million enterprises revealed that 50.2 percent of rural and 37.2 percent of urban enterprises were owned by SC/ST/OBCs.

TABLE 17.7
Enterprises Owned by Social Group

(*percent*)

	Rural	*Urban*	*Combined*
SC	9.0	5.8	7.7
ST	5.2	2.3	4.0
OBC	36.0	29.1	33.1
Total of above	50.2	37.2	44.8

Source: CSO, *Economic Census* (1998) Table 2(b).

These enterprises include manufacturing, construction, trade, hotels, restaurants, transport, finance and business and other services. The survey also reveals that out of 30.25 million enterprises, 24.39 million are self-financing. This implies that the size of their operations remains very limited. The situation is specially depressing in the case of SCs/STs, more especially in the urban areas compared to the rural areas. However, OBCs share a big proportion both in the rural and urban areas. This appears to be due to upper caste OBCs who wield more economic and social power in the society. But the social status of SC/ST/OBCs can be further enhanced if credit delivery system, specially directed towards lower castes is extended in the society. This can become a major instrument of empowerment. Prof. R. Vaidyanathan of IIM, Bangalore stated in this regard: "The dramatic change in the status of Nadar community of Tamil Nadu in the last five decades indicates the power of business and entrepreneurship. The corporate sector and government can play a major role by encouraging weaker sections to become suppliers, vendors, dealers, distributors, outsourcing agents and so on."

11. NINTH SCHEDULE—USE AND MISUSE

The Supreme Court in a very historic Judgment on January 11, 2007 upheld in a petition by Chennai's Senior Advocate K.M. Vijayan regarding the fact whether any law placed under the Ninth Schedule could be reviewed by the Supreme Court, the impugned law was "Tamil Nadu Backward classes, scheduled castes and scheduled tribes (Reservation of Seats in Educational Institutions and appointment or posts) which prescribed 69 percent reservation for OBC, SC/STs, that was much higher than the ceiling prescribed by the Supreme Court at 50%. A nine judge bench headed by Chief Justice Y.K. Sabharwal said: "Justification for conferring protection, not blanket protection, on the laws included in the Ninth Schedule by Constitutional Amendment shall be a matter of adjudication by examining the nature and extent of infraction of a "fundamental right." Any law placed in the Ninth Schedule after April 24, 1973 will be open for judicial review by the Supreme Court. It was on this day that the Supreme Court propounded the basic structure doctrine in the Keshavananda Bharti's case mentioned: Laws already upheld by the Supreme Court cannot be challenged.

The Court, however, upheld the validity of Article 31-B of the Constitution, which empowers the parliament to place laws in the Ninth Schedule. But it said that even if an act is included in the Ninth Schedule, its provisions would to open to attack "on the ground that they destroy the basic structure of the constitution, if the fundamental rights are taken away or abrogated pertaining to the basic structure."

The Supreme Court for the first time held: That Articles 15 and 16 of the Constitution on reservations in educational institutions and governmental jobs respectively were part of the basic structure.

Nature of Laws in the Ninth Schedule

It would be relevant to examine the nature of laws which have been included in the Ninth Schedule. In all, there are presently 284 laws in the Ninth Schedule. Out of them, over 240 laws pertain to land reform, ceiling on agricultural holdings and tenancy acts passed by various state governments. Since most of these laws were passed before April 23, 1973, the Supreme Court judgment does not permit that they are open for judicial scrutiny.

The other acts in the Ninth Schedule relate to Insurance Act, Railway Companies (Emergency Provisions) Act, 1951, Industries Development and Regulation Act, 1957, Monopolies and Restrictive Trade Practice Act, 1969, Foreign Exchange Regulation Act (1973), Sick Textiles Undertakings (Nationalization) Act (1974), The Essential Commodities Act (1955), Private Forests (Act), Coking Coal Mines (Nationalization) Act (1972), Tamil Nadu Backward Classes, scheduled castes and scheduled tribes (Reservation of Seats in Educational Institutions and of appointments or posts in the services under the State) Act, 1993, etc.

Initially, when under the leadership of Prime Minister Jawaharlal Nehru, Article 31-B was adopted, it was guided by the noble intention of implementation of land reform. Even then, Nehru made it clear that intention is not to usurp the powers of the judiciary, but only to curb vested interests which forestall land reform legislation on the plea of justiceable compensation. Extensive litigation was resorted by the landlords and zamindars to nullify the legislative effort towards redistribution of land ownership.

Even later, the Government placed certain other Acts such as MRTP Act, Coal Mines Nationalization Act, Sick Textiles Undertaking (Nationalization) Act in the Ninth Schedule, but the Supreme Court did not confront the powers of the legislature.

Opposition to SC Judgement

The recent decision of the Supreme Court asserting its right to examine laws under the Ninth Schedule has been vehemently opposed by several political leaders. The most vociferous was the DMK who felt that the verdict was shocking and pleaded for re-writing the Constitution to establish the supremacy of the legislature over the judiciary. DMK ally PMK also joined in raising its voice against the Supreme Court verdict. Lok Jan Shakti leader Ram Vilas Paswan, however, was ambivalent when he said: "If it is a matter that tempers with the basic structure of the Constitution, then it must not be put in the Ninth Schedule. But the 69% quota fixed by Tamil Nadu must not be subject to review since the Constitution does not draw up a limit on reservations." Paswan pleaded that the Judgement should be reviewed by 13-member bench of the SC. The CPI also voiced its dissent in the following manner: "the 9th Schedule is a safeguard for pushing forward the cause of social justice and economic reforms according to the needs of the time and society. This is a matter which only the legislature, which represents the people's will, can decide." President of the JD (U) Mr. Sharad Pawar stated his stand very categorically and forcefully: "With this judgement the Apex Court has struck down a Constitutional provision made by the makers of our Constitution. This is a policy issue and the Supreme Court is not empowered to decide on it. The responsibility to run the government lies with the executive. The Judiciary has no business running the government." (*Hindustan Times*, February 4, 2007)

Support for Supreme Court Verdict

However, the Supreme Court verdict got support from the main opposition party the BJP and legal experts. For instance, BJP spokesperson Ravi Shankar Prasad said: "This is a welcome judgement. It will act as a sober restraint on the government, Parliament and the polity in placing laws that are unconstitutional under the Ninth Schedule." Former Law Minister and BJP General Secretary Arun Jaitley said: "The verdict would serve to function as important safeguard to Indian democracy."

The Congress party did not feel the necessity of challenging this judgment and asking for a review by a 13-member bench of SC as suggested by its ally Ram Vilas Paswan. It also played cool to the outburst of Karunanidhi to have an other constituent assembly to rewrite the Constitution. Law Minister H.R. Bhardwaj clarified: "The judgement will have no adverse impact on the functioning of the Executive. I think that the judgemnet only means that if some thing happens against the basic features of the Constitution or the Fundamental Rights, then the Supreme Court can strike it down." In a similar vein, Mr Abhishek M. Singhvi, Congress spokesperson and eminent lawyer said: "The judgment reflected the expanded frontiers of judicial review and reiterated the established wisdom that the basic structure of the Indian Constitution is supreme." Likewise, Senior Congress leader and former additional Solicitor General Devendra Dwivedi welcomed the verdict saying, the Ninth Schedule could not function as a "parliamentary locker."

The basic question is: Is the Judiciary overactive to establish its supremacy over the Executive or the Legislature, or is the purpose of the judgement to restrain the executive and the legislature to pass laws irrespective of the tenets of social justice propelled by group interests? To understand the issue, it would be appropriate to examine the actions of the various actors in the political drama on the issue of reservations. Firstly, P.V. Narashima Rao government placed the Tamil Nadu Act granting 69 percent reservations to OBCs and SC/STs in the Ninth Schedule knowing full well that this Act violates the limit of 50% reservations decided by the Supreme Court and already accepted by the Central Government. This was an act of impropriety of the Executive pandering to a political lobby which wanted to provide 50% reservations only to the OBCs and 19% to SC/STs.

Secondly, as far back as 1993, the Supreme Court had adjudicated that creamy layer should not be provided the benefit of reservations. It defined the criteria for determining the creamy layer. Prime Minister Manmohan Singh is on record that creamy layer should not be included in reservation. But the RJD Chief Lalu Prasad Yadav, Mr Karunanidhi of DMK, Mr Ramdoss of PMK and Mr. Paswan of LJP forced the Congress-led UPA government to include the creamy layer while extending the benefit of reservations in admission to institutions of higher education. The so-called defenders of social justice for the poor and dalits, approved a framework which would in practice jettison out the MBCs and enable the upper OBCs to grab the major portion of reservations for their kith and kin. The question is: Social justice for whom!!

Thirdly, what is special about Tamil Nadu that despite the fact that several generations of OBCs have come up and improved their lot and are occupying seats of power and privilege, now a stage has come when the benefit of reservations should be allowed to percolate to MBCs. At present, out of 50% reservations provided to OBCs alone in Tamil Nadu, 30% go to upper OBCs and 20% to MBCs. The tenets of justice and fairplay would require 30% for MBCs and only 20% of OBCs and the creamy layer out of basket of reservations. The Karpoori Thakur government of Bihar made the distinction between upper OBCs and MBCs and granted a bigger share of reservations to MBCs. Rather than following the real social justice model based on poverty and deprivation, Tamil Nadu uses reservation as an instrument of votebank politics in its favour.

Fourthly, the legislature in Andhra Pradesh, passed a law granting 5% reservations to Muslims. Since this was violative of the Constitution as religion could not be the basis of reservation, the law was struck down by the Court.

Legislature versus Supreme Court Supremacy

It is futile to debate the question of supremacy of the Legislature over the judiciary. The Supreme Court has not questioned the Supremacy of the Legislature to frame laws in consonance with the aspirations of the people. It has upheld the right of the Legislature to frame laws under Article 16 of the Constitution pertaining to reservations. The basic issue is that the Legislature should abide by the tenets of social justice as provided in the basic structure of the Constitution. In a democratic society, laws framed by the legislature are challenged in the Court. The Supreme Court interprets the laws on the touchstone of the provisions of the Constitution. The Supreme Court and the Legislature instead of confronting each other should work in harmony. If the Supreme Court has fixed the upper limit of Reservation at 50%, it is based on certain basic considerations of reconciling merit and social justice. Similarly, the principle of excluding the creamy layer is based on sound grounds of social justice. The very fact that the major political party, the Congress in the UPA government does not intend to challenge the

Supreme Court verdict on the Ninth Schedule, and major opposition party—the BJP considers that the verdict is a 'sober restraint' on the government that will strengthen Indian democracy, this only underlines the fact that the Government respects the Supreme Court and the Supreme Court respects the jurisdiction of the Government.

12. UPA GOVERNMENT'S DILEMMA AND POLICY MEASURES

UPA Government has made up its mind to introduce 27 percent reservations for OBCs in higher education institutions, in government-run and aided as well as unaided and run by the private sector. However, there is a dilemma faced by the Government. As a consequence of the initiative taken by HRD Minister Arjun Singh, it has to implement 27 percent quota for OBCs. Simultaneously, it does not want to reduce the General Category seats available to upper castes at present so that the upper caste students can also acquire higher and professional education. In other words, it wants to reconcile the two objectives of merit and equity. It, therefore, devised the strategy for increasing seats in all higher education and professional institutions by 54 percent and simultaneously provide a quota for OBCs to the extent of 27 percent. The clearest expression to this was provided in the Independence Message speech given by Prime Minister Manmohan Singh on 15th August 2006.

The Prime Minister stated in a very forth right manner: "As we expand educational opportunities, we must ensure that these opportunities are accessible to all marginalized and weaker sections of our society. Our government is committed to providing reservations in educational institutions for students from the socially backward sections of our society."

"We will do so, while expanding opportunities for all youth. This is our solemn commitment. In this manner, we will recognize and reward merit and hardwork while working for an inclusive society." (As reported by *Economic Times*, August 16, 2006).

The Prime Minister's statement needs to be studied carefully, because it has been very carefully worded so as to meet the concerns of both OBCs and upper castes.

For instance, the use of the phrase "all marginalized and weaker sections of our society" covers besides OBCs, the poor among the upper castes, Muslims and other minorities. In fact, it also leaves enough scope for excluding the 'creamy layer' from all sections of our society. Besides this, Prime Minister is firmly of the view that to develop an inclusive society, we have to expand seats in educational institutions so that merit and social justice can be effectively reconciled. Dr. Manmohan Singh, therefore, does not provide a backseat to merit but the guidelines in his speech are a balancing act with quota and merit.

Supreme Court Judgment (2006) and the Creamy Layer Issue

The judgment of the Supreme Court on 19th October 2006, while upholding the quota system in promotions for SCs and STs has ruled the exclusion of persons belonging to these castes who are a part of the creamy layer. The Supreme Court verdict cited a Judgment of a Constitution Bench in 1993 in the Indira Sawhney case, counts the concept of creamy layer in reservations as one of the Constitutional requirements without which the structure of equality in opportunity in public employment will collapse. Since the basic concept of equality of opportunity is enshrined in Article 16(1) and (2) of the Constitution, the inclusion of creamy layer in the Central Educational Institutions (Reservations in Admission) Bill, 2006 will violate Article 16(1) and (2). The concept of the creamy layer was introduced by the Supreme Court to strike a balance between accepting caste as a determinant of backwardness and the principle of secularism that was a basic feature of the Constitution. Obviously, Reservation in Admission Bill (2006) now has to incorporate the concept of creamy layer for OBCs as well. The Government will have to reckon the concept of the creamy layer among all reserved groups so that the Bill can stand the test of judicial scrutiny.

But who forms the creamy layer? Children of backward sections of society who hold high posts in government, armed forces, judiciary, public sector banks, insurance organizations and universities are part of the creamy layer. Officers holding equivalent or comparable posts in the private sector too fall in the category of creamy layer. This list includes professionals such as doctors, lawyers, chartered accountants and income tax consultants.

The Supreme Court in its Judgment of October 19, 2006 has also emphasized: "If the extent of reservations goes beyond a cut-off point (50% laid down by the SC), then it results in reverse discrimination. Therefore, a numerical bench-mark is the surest immunity against charges of discrimination."

This has resulted in protests from Lok Janshakti Party (LJP), JD(U) and DMK who now demand that the Government should bring a constitutional amendment and place the Reservation in Admission Bill in the Ninth Schedule of the Constitution so that it is outside the purview of the Supreme Court. JD(U) President, Sharad Yadav also demanded the formation of a protective cordon around all such laws. Tamil Nadu Chief Minister M. Karunanidhi attacked the Supreme Court judgment by asserting that the Supreme Court judgment has "pulled down the ladder for scheduled castes and backward classes." According to Karnunanidhi, the ruling that 50 percent reservation limit cannot be breached and creamy layer cannot be obliterated "runs against the spirit of the Constitution. The Constitution contemplates reservations for only socially and backward classes, not for economically backward classes."

Since the Supreme Court has already set-up a Bench to decide about the nature of laws which can be placed under the Ninth Schedule, the ruling

Congress party does not deem it desirable to have a confrontation with the judiciary.

The BJP has also not yet made up its mind on the issue. Although the BJP insists that the minority institutions should not be exempt from the law on reservations, the Party does not favour a confrontation with the judiciary. It appears that both the Congress and the BJP may ultimately decide to work within the bounds of the Constitution. It may be noted that the Supreme Court said while extending the policy of reservations, Article 335 has to be read with Article 46 which provides that the State should promote with special care the educational and economic interests of the weaker sections of the people, and in particular of the SCs & STs and protect them from social injustice.

The position taken by the Supreme Court in its judgment is eminently sensible. If the principal purpose is to help SCs, STs and other weaker sections, then both social and economic criteria become relevant. The Centre for Management Development, Thiruvananthapuram, conducted a study which showed if the creamy layer is excluded, it helped the poor students from the weaker sections to get admission. This study has been quoted by the Oversight Committee headed by Moily. But unfortunately, Moily could not get a unanimous recommendations from the Committee on the issue and, thus, argued that the creamy layer issue be left to the Government for a final decision.

13. FLEXIBILITY IN IMPLEMENTATION OF RESERVATIONS

Table 17.8 provides information regarding SCs, STs, OBCs and other social groups. The NSS Report (1999-00) has given data on rural and urban basis. Since for reservations, state has been taken as the unit of administration, an effort has been made to present data State/UT-wise. The data reveals startling differences among states on the percentage distribution of OBCs. The figures varies from 72% in Pondicherry, 66 percent in Tamil Nadu, 53% in Kerala, about 50% in Bihar which are much above the All-India figure of 34.4%. On the other extreme are West Bengal 5.8%, Assam 15%, Jammu and Kashmir 8%, Himachal Pradesh 10.1. Similarly, tribal states have very high percentage of STs: Nagaland 90%, Mizoram 96%, Lakshdweep 98%, Meghalaya 87%.

The basic issue which needs to be raised is: Should states be given flexibility in determining the relative percentage within ST, ST and OBC categories or should all of them be forced to adopt a uniform policy? However, two riders be attached: (a) the concept of exclusion of creamy layer will be applied in all categories, SC, ST, OBC and others. Secondly, states which have a share in SC, ST and OBC population higher than the limit prescribed in reservations, i.e. 15%, 7.5% and 27% respectively should be provided flexibility in determining the relative shares of different categories within the overall ceiling of 50% prescribed for reservations by

Table 17.8
Percent Distribution of Households and Persons in NSS 55th Round by Social Group

(*Total = Rural + Urban*)

State/UT	*ST*	*SC*	*OBC*	*Other*
Pondicherry	1.7	18.9	72.0	7.4
Tamil Nadu	1.3	21.6	66.1	11.0
Kerala	1.5	8.6	53.2	36.7
Bihar	6.8	16.5	49.6	27.1
Andhra Pradesh	5.3	18.5	43.5	32.7
Uttar Pradesh	1.2	20.1	39.0	39.7
Manipur	25.3	3.4	38.6	32.7
Madhya Pradesh	19.5	14.9	37.3	28.3
Karnataka	7.4	16.1	35.4	41.1
All-India	**7.3**	**17.9**	**34.4**	**40.4**
Sikkim	26.6	9.8	30.5	33.1
Delhi	2.9	13.6	30.4	53.1
Orissa	18.8	18.2	29.0	34.0
Gujarat	12.6	12.6	27.7	47.1
Haryana	1.3	21.3	24.8	52.6
Maharashtra	10.7	13.6	23.9	51.8
Tripura	7.2	22.3	20.1	50.4
Daman & Diu	24.7	6.5	19.0	49.8
Chandigarh	0.7	20.3	15.9	63.1
Assam	10.6	12.4	15.3	61.7
Punjab	1.2	37.4	13.8	47.6
Himachal Pradesh	2.6	19.5	10.1	67.8
Jammu & Kashmir	0.6	10.7	8.1	80.6
Dadra & Nagar Haveli	51.6	3.1	6.9	38.4
West Bengal	3.7	24.2	5.8	66.3
Goa	1.3	2.5	4.2	92.0
A & N Islands	13.2	3.9	2.5	80.4
Nagaland	89.7	3.0	2.5	4.8
Arunachal Pradesh	59.6	2.5	2.5	35.4
Mizoram	96.0	0.9	0.9	2.2
Lakshdweep	97.6	0.0	0.8	1.6
Meghalaya	86.6	1.5	0.8	11.1

Note : States have been arranged in the descending order on the basis of OBC share.

Source : Derived from *NSS Report No. 473, Literacy and Levels of Education in India*, 1999-2000.

•

the Supreme Court. In our view, this flexibility will bring about greater rationality in implementing reservations.

14. MODALITIES OF IMPLEMENTATION

The moot question is: How can the nation increase 54 percent seats in higher educational institutions? This requires enlargement of not only physical infrastructure in the form of additional rooms and laboratories, but also human infrastructure in the form of additional teachers and other supporting staff. A rough estimate made by the Moily Committee indicated an investment of the order of Rs. 18,200 crores, though it appears to be a gross underestimate, keeping in mind the high cost of education per student at the graduate, post-graduate and research levels. These costs are even higher for IIT and IIM, Engineering and Medical institutions. Apprehensions were expressed by the professors and directors of IITs and IIMs that it would not be possible to increase 54 percent seats in one year. Dr. Deepak Pental, Vice-Chancellor, Delhi University openly expressed that it would not be possible for Delhi University to expand seats by 54 percent in the short span of one year.

On the other hand, PMK, DMK and even JD(U)—a constituent of NDA were putting pressure on the government to implement quota in one go. DMK Chief K. Karunanidhi went to the extent of writing a strong letter to the Prime Minister that a staggered approach will not be acceptable to his party.

To assuage the strong feelings of alliance partners, the Government appointed on *Oversight Committee* with Mr. Veerappa Moily, former Karnataka Chief Minister as its Chairman with the twin tasks of working out the modalities for bringing the OBCs under a wider quota net in higher educational institutions, while providing a cushion for upper castes.

The committee, in its report, came out in favour of a staggered implementation of the quota regime in existing IITs, IIMs, other engineering and medical institutes, medical colleges, agricultural and Central Universities.

There is a strong feeling in many quarters that instead of rushing in the quota policy for OBCs, it would be better to have staggered implementation, thus providing time and resources to higher educational institution to do preparatory work and put the necessary infrastructure in place so that a smooth transition becomes possible.

15. ALTERNATIVE INCLUSIVE MODELS

Social thinkers believe that equality of opportunity is more important for the entire population rather than laying exclusive emphasis on caste as a factor of social disadvantage. There are multiple disadvantages faced by various groups. It is, therefore, necessary that we incorporate in the inclusive model the various dimensions of disadvantages. They are:

1. Gender disadvantage.
2. Class disadvantage (based on economic criteria).
3. Rural *versus* urban disadvantage.
4. Source of schooling (a government/municipal corporation run school, an aided institution or an unaided English medium public school).
5. Caste as a factor and within a caste, there can be different layers, e.g. upper OBCs and Most Backward OBCs, Hindu and Sikh upper castes and Hindu and Sikh OBCs, etc.

Four Models have been suggested to incorporate multiple disadvantages and merit so that both quality and equity can be accommodated. The models do not ensure a block or quota and thus solidify caste identities, but follows a holistic approach in combining merit with social justice.

JNU Model

Jawaharlal Nehru University (JNU) provides 10 deprivation points on the basis of caste, gender and region. These deprivation points are added to the merit score in the following manner:

- 5 points for OBCs (10 points for OBC women).
- 5 points for most backward region (three for less backward region).
- 5 points for other groups (Kashmiri migrants and dependants of armed forces personnel killed in action).

To the merit score of the candidate out of 100 marks, the deprivation points allotted to a candidate are added to arrive at the final score for rating for admission list. However, it may be noted that SC and ST students are provided 22.5 percent reservations as per stipulation by government.

Purushottam Agrawal's Model

Purushottam Agrawal of JNU feels that only giving a maximum of 10 deprivation points does not do full justice to the various deprivations. He has, therefore, suggested a modified version of the JNU model, allotting 30 points on the basis of deprivation/disadvantages.

Marks for entrance test/interview and academic performance will account for 70 points. The remaining 30 points will be under the following heads:

Caste/Tribe: (5 points) All SC/ST candidates get 5 points; MBCs 4 points and OBCs 2 points

Gender: (5 points) for women irrespective of scores on any other index

Economic Status: (6 points) No points for yearly family income above Rs. 2,50,000; 3 points for income from Rs. 1,00,001 to Rs. 2,50,000; and 5

points for income up to Rs. 1,00,000 and 6 points for the beneficiaries of poverty alleviation schemes/ employment provision schemes of Central/ State govts.

Region: (5 points) No points for candidates from metros and large cities; 3 points for non-metros; 3 points for all towns, and also cities in conflict regions; and 5 points for those from villages and tribal areas.

Schooling: (5 points) No points for students from public, boarding and premier schools; 2 points to students from Central government schools; 3 points for students from vernacular schools and 5 points for students from village/panchayat or municipal schools.

(No backward region points for candidates studying in a public, boarding or premier school)

First generation learner: (4 points) No points for a candidate whose both parents are graduates; 1 point if one parent is graduate and the other is matriculate; 3 points if one parent is non-matriculate and 4 points and if both parents are non-matriculate.

Example: An SC/ST candidate from Delhi public school with graduate parents and annual family income above Rs. 2,50,000, gets 5 caste points but his sister gets 10. A BPL MBC from panchayat school in a backward region with illiterate parents gets 23 points. A forward caste candidate with same background gets 20 points.

Deshpande and Yadav Model

Satish Deshpande and Yogendra Yadav of the Centre for the Study of Developing Societies (CSDS) have developed another inclusive model. It is claimed that such an approach promotes affirmative action without "appeasement" and tends to cut across caste and religious identities.

Combine 'merit points' with 'disadvantage points'. Convert marks in the qualifying/entrance exam to a maximum of 80 points. The remaining 20 points (maximum) would be 'disadvantage points.'

Disadvantage points (maximum 12 points) can have sub-components based on social groups, gender, schooling and family background. The backward castes can be divided into 'upper' and 'lower' OBCs' (or MBC) depending on the regions they come from.

Example: 10 points for a male MBCs from most backward region, 6 points for a male OBC from less backward region and 2 points for a male OBC from a developed region. (Women in each category get +2 points)

Schooling points: (maximum 5 points) 5 points for Class XII from a rural government school; 3 points for a corporation run school in metro; 2 points for small town private (non-English medium) school and no points for English medium private school in metros or for residential public schools.

Family background points: (maximum 3 points) 3 points if none of the parents is in organized sector jobs or runs tax paying business, 2 points if one of them is a clerk or equivalent and 1 point if both of them are in low salaried jobs. No points if any one of the parents is a professional, officer or Income tax payer.

The points for schooling and family background would apply to all non-SC/ST categories, including forward caste students from poorer families. There is no need for a separate OBC quota. The disadvantage points also take care of the 'creamy layer.'

The three models presented above assign different weights to different disadvantages. The problem with the JNU model is that it assigns only 10 points for various deprivations and combines them to arrive at the final score by adding them to merit score, and thus it predominantly protects merit.

Purushottam Agrawal's model assigns 30 points and Deshpande & Yadav model assigns 20 points for deprivations—a middle course between JNU and Purushottam Agrawal's model.

Sachar Committee Model

Sachar Committee on Social, Economic and Educational Status of the Muslim Community in India (2006) suggests the following criteria to facilitate admission of "Most Backward" among all socio-religious categories to colleges and universities:

1.	Total Points	100
2.	Assessment of Backwardness to the maximum of Backwardness to be defined as the sum of the following (each with about one-third weight).	40
	a. Household income (income criteria to be revised periodically)	13
	b. Backward District	13
	c. Backward class (assessed on the basis of a combination of family occupation and caste)	14

The point to be noted is that Sachar Committee provides 40 percent weight to backwardness and excludes the creamy layer.

An assessment of the Sachar Committee Model reveals certain serious shortcomings. First, the formula is too broad and needs to fine-tuned so that sub-categories within the criteria are also defined and assigned different weights. Secondly, it does not recognize gender as a serious disadvantage. Thirdly, it does not make a distinction between rural *versus* urban disadvantage. Lastly, it does not recognize the source of schooling (a government/municipal corporation run school), an aided institution or an unaided English medium public school).

However, the merit of the model is that its assigns 40 points to backwardness and give substantial weight to backwardness to ensure equity.

Our Model

The models given earlier provide disadvantage points ranging from 10% to 30%. We, however, believe that the weightage of even 30 points is not enough if the intention is to bring the most-backward classes to benefit from higher education without following the path of reservation. It would, therefore, be proper to provide 50 points weightage to disadvantage so as to enable the MBCs to make up the grade. The model suggests the following:

> The basic purpose behind our approach is to completely do away with reservation and inculcate a spirit of enterprise and competition within all socio-economic groups. Simultaneously, to support the socially and economically backward, the points of backwardness be added to merit score to determine the place of a candidate in total score. This is an

Our Model

Total Marks	150
Merit Points	100
Backwardness Weighted to the maximum of	50
Caste/Tribe (Maximum 10 points) 10 points for SC/STs, 7 points for MBCs and 4 points for OBCs.	10
Gender (Maximum 5 points) Irrespective of score on any other criterion for girls but no points for those in the creamy layer.	5

Economic status (Maximum 10 points)

1. No points for family income above Rs. 2.5 lakhs per annum
2. 5 points for income ranging from Rs. 1 lakh to Rs. 2.5 lakhs
3. 7 points for income ranging Rs. 50,000 and Rs. 1,00,000
4. 10 points for those below the poverty line.

Schooling (Maximum 10 points)

No points for students from unaided English Medium Public Schools; 5 points for students from vernacular schools; and, 7 points from village/panchayat or municipal schools.

First Generation Learners (Maximum 10 points)

1. 10 points if both parents are below matric
2. 5 points if one parent is a matriculate and the other a graduate
3. No point if both the parents are graduates.

Region (Maximum 5 points)

1. No point for candidate from Metros and large cities
2. 3 points for non-Metros or all towns and cities in conflict regions
3. 5 points for those from villages or tribal areas or slums.

inclusive model for all socio-economic groups. Even the poor among the upper castes will earn some points on the basis of their economic backwardness and schooling. However, SC/STs, OBCs and MBCs will get disadvantage points on the basis of their social as well as economic backwardness. Girls from poor families would get additional 5 points while this benefit will not be available to girls belonging to the creamy layer category of family income levels above Rs. 2.5 lakhs per annum. The procedure to be followed is as under:

For rating candidates for admission, marks out of 100 be taken as marks on the basis of merit. To these are added the marks based on backwardness to determine the total score for ranking purposes.

Example:

	Marks out of 100 on the basis of examination (merit) (100)	*Marks for Backwardness (50)*	*Total score for ranking*
A	70	10	80 (4)
B	61	30	90 (1)
C	50	35	85 (3)
D	89	—	89 (2)

The basic issue pertains to the acceptability of the alternative inclusive models in place of reservations. For this purpose, firstly, at the academic level, there is need for acceptability so that some model after discussion is accepted for experimentation. Secondly, there is need for convincing the politicians and policy-makers that this path of inclusive model is better than the path of reservation. In case, a break-through is achieved, then it would be possible to take further steps regarding implementation. This will mean developing a good machinery of implementation. Along with this, the awareness level of the people has to be increased so that the inclusive model is accepted by the society as a better long-term instrument, which while taking care of backwardness produces less heartburn or opposition from the better-off classes who were monopolizing higher education.

16. CENTRAL EDUCATIONAL INSTITUTIONS (RESERVATION IN ADMISSION BILL), 2006

After a long debate, the UPA Government, on the 25th August 2006 introduced the Central Educational Institutions (Reservation in Admission Bill), 2006 in the Lok Sabha.

The Bill provides for 27 percent reservation for OBCs, 15 percent for SCs and 7.5 percent for STs—a total of 49.5 percent—in Central higher education institutes like IITs, IIMs and AIIMS and all Central Universities.

Only those Central Institutions will be included in its purview which received Central Government grants directly or indirectly.

According to the Bill, "OBC means the class or classes of citizens who are socially and educationally backward, and are so determined by the Centre."

The provisions of the bill will not apply to minority institutions established and administered under clause (1) of Article 30 of the Constitution.

Besides, the provisions of reservations will not apply to Central educational institutions in tribal areas and institutions of excellence.

The bill will also not apply to "any course or programme at higher levels of specialization, including at the post-doctoral level, within any branch of study or faculty, which the Central government may, in consultation with the appropriate authority, specify."

Alongside, the Bill provides that every Central educational institution should, with the prior approval of the appropriate authority, increase the number of seats in a branch of study or faculty over and above its annual permitted strength so that the number seats, excluding the reserved seats available for the persons belonging to SCs, STs and OBCs, is not less than the number of such seats available for the academic session immediately preceding the date of the coming into force of this Act. The Bill has been passed by the Parliament.

The Act will come into force from academic year 2007-08 and provides for a staggered implementation over a period of three years. 5 percent in the first year, 10 percent in the second year and 12 percent in the third year.

The implication of the Act is that educational institutions shall have to increase the seats by 54 percent in order to keep the General Category seats at the level of the preceding year. The following example clarifies it:

Total seats in 2006-07	=	**100**
SC Seats	=	15
ST Seats	=	7.5
General Category Seats	=	77.5
Total seats in 2007-08	=	**154**
SC Seats @ 15%	=	23
ST Seats @ 7.5%	=	12
OBC Seats @ 27%	=	42
General Category Seats Remaining	=	77

Critique of the Bill

The original draft prepared for the consideration of the Cabinet included a clause for creamy layer, but strong opposition form DMK and

PMK leaders, besides Lalu Prasad Yadav of RJD, Ram Vilas Paswan of Lok Janashakti and A.R. Antulay of the Congress forced the government to drop the following clause from the draft bill excluding the creamy layer:

> "but excluding such advanced members thereof, as may, from time to time, be notified by the Central Government in the official gazette, having regard to the factors such as the persons holding constitutional offices or particular services, practising professions, or having particular income level or particular holding of property so as to distinguish children of socially advanced members from children of other class or classes of citizens who are socially and educationally backward."

It may be noted that Law Minister H.R. Bhardwaj argued in the cabinet meeting that unless creamy layer was exempted, the new quota proposal would not stand the test scrutiny by the Supreme Court. The apex court had introduced the concept of creamy layer while upholding the job reservations in 1993 and the Government had accepted the concept of exclusion of creamy layer in reservation of jobs. The UPA Government, however, did not pay adequate attention to the legal advice.

Left parties which had not raised the issue of creamy layer at the Congress-Left Co-ordination Committee earlier are now critical of the Government on two counts: CPM Politburo member Sitaram Yechury said they would insist on extending reservations to unaided institutions as well. The CPM will oppose the "creamy layer" among the OBCs as this must be weeded out and the affluent among the OBCs should not benefit from the proposed bill.

Another issue which has been raised by the critics is the exemption of minority institutions form reservation. The BJP is already on record that it is illogical and smack of "gross appeasement" of the minorities. Even Mr. V. Radha Krishanan of the CPM said: "the exemption created a problem in Kerala where 95 percent of higher education institutions are run by minority communities."

The Bill has been referred to the Standing Committee of the parliament for further deliberations and will come up for the consideration of the Parliament.

The UPA Government may be feeling that they have resolved the reservation issue for OBCs, but the drama may unfold itself if some of leaders of MBCs challenge it in the Supreme Court. Moreover, opposition to exclusion of minority institutions is likely to be pushed further both by the BJP and CPM, though for different reasons. Shall the Left parties succeed in building sufficient pressure on UPA government to exclude the creamy layer? The final act will be seen only when the drama unfolds itself and the various actors play their part. In view of the Supreme Court Judgment dated October 19, 2006 the government has to introduce the creamy layer concept in the Bill.

17. SOME RECENT DEVELOPMENTS ON RESERVATION ISSUE

In view of the petition filed by the Anti-quota activists, the Supreme Court on March 23, 2007 granted a stay against the implementation of the Central Educational Institutions (Reservation in Admission), Act 2006. Meanwhile, the Supreme Court directed the Central Government to place before the Court the data on the basis of which the Central Government determined 27 percent reservations for OBCs. The anti-quota petitioners had alleged that the Central government took the figure of OBC population on the basis 1931 Census which has become irrelevant and that the basis of reservation should be such information as is obtained in recent years. Secondly, the Supreme Court did not accept the plea of the Central Government that the 'creamy layer' concept was relevant only in case of quota in jobs and does not apply to reservations in educational institutions. Thirdly, the Supreme Court also wanted the Government to file an affidavit that the Centre has obtained the approval of the competent authorities for the increase in seats proposed by the Government.

Hearing the petition on August, 7, 2007 Chief Justice K.G. Balakrishnan said that the Act cannot be implemented since the necessary permission of the Medical Council of India has not been obtained for the increase in seats as envisaged under OBC quota law.

Pleading for the vacations of stay, Solicitor General G.E. Vahanvati conceded if the stay was vacated, this year the OBC quota would be implemented only in those institutions where the approval for the increase in seats has already been obtained from the competent authorities. The Supreme Court noted that so far the necessary permission for the proposed increase in seats has not been obtained from the Medical Council of India.

The Solicitor-general also conceded: "If the Court feels that the creamy layer be excluded, the Centre will obey."

There is, therefore, a decisive shift in the attitude of the Central Government. Earlier, under pressure from coalition partners, it had argued that for reservation in educational institutions, the creamy layer concept was not relevant and it was only relevant in reservations for jobs. Sensing the mood of the Supreme Court, Centre has now conceded that the 'creamy layer' concept is valid for admissions to higher educational institutions as well. The Government is now willing to obey the Supreme Court and exclude the creamy layer among the OBCs.

Ceiling on Quotas

The Government of Orissa had pleaded the enhancement of reservations ceiling from 50% to 66.75% in Government posts on the plea that Orissa be treated as a far-flung and remote area and people or Orissa were out of the mainstream of national life. The Orissa High Court rejected the plea of the Orissa Government to raise the ceiling of reservations in government from 50% to 66.75%, because it did not find justification in the plea of the Orissa Government. The Supreme Court also did not agree with the contention of the State government that it was competent to provide quota beyond 50% in the extraordinary situation. The arguments of the State Government were not found sustainable by the apex court.

Reservations for the Economically Weaker Sections among the Upper Castes

The UP Government under the stewardship of Chief Minister Mayavati decided to introduce voluntary reservations to the extent of 30% jobs in private sector. It was decided that industrial units, infrastructure projects, educational institutes, service sector and disinvestments units shall have to sign a contract with the state government to provide 30% reservation in jobs in case they are provided land, grants or tax concessions from the state government. Out of 30% reservations in jobs, 10% would be reserved for Scheduled Castes and Scheduled Tribes (SCs/STs), 10% for OBCs and religious minorities, and 10% for economically weaker sections from the upper castes. Ms. Mayavati had earlier asked the Prime Minister to amend the Constitution for earmarking quotas for the poor among the upper castes.

The UP Government has added a new dimension to reservation in jobs by using the economic criterion in the case of upper castes who also suffer an economic disadvantage. The Central Government should also give serious consideration to the proposal to amend the Constitution so that the poor among the upper castes are also provided reservations in jobs within the 50% ceiling fixed by Supreme Court for this purpose.

18. BEYOND THE LIMITS OF RESERVATIONS

West Bengal Chief Minister Budhadev Bhattacharya has suggested that country should look beyond reservations so as to enlarge the area of socio-economic reforms. Instead of promoting divisive tendencies by enforcing the process of reservation among the various social groups as also within the same social group by fixing quotas in jobs or seats in institutions of higher education, it would be far better to take a holistic view of socio-economic reforms so as to effectively tackle the problems of poverty and deprivation. In other words, it would be far better to pursue a policy of inclusive growth.

In fact, the political parties contemplate only short-term goals, by either enhancing the interests of certain groups of the Indian society so as to develop blocks of vote banks, either within the dalits, or OBCs or upper caste Hindus or promoting interests of the minority community, especially the Muslimas so as to wean away a big chunk of the minority votes in their favour. This short-sighted approach is only a continuation of the British policy of 'divide and rule' in independent India. This is the misfortune that has engulfed Indian politics after the exit of leaders of all-India stature like

Jawaharlal Nehru, Sardar Vallabh Bhai Patel, Jagjivan Ram and Indira Gandhi and their replacement by leadership which is restricted to one or two states like Lalu Prasad Yadav, Mulayam Singh, Ram Villas Paswan, M. Karunanidhi, Jai Lalitha, Chandrababu Naidu, etc.

Mr. Budhadev Bhattacharya's suggestion does not imply a criticism of the policy of reservations in jobs in the organized sector or seats in centres of higher education, but the need to realize that the scope of this policy is very limited. For instance, only 8 percent of the workforce is engaged in the organized sector (both public and private sector) and 92 percent is engaged in the unorganised sector which is outside the ambit of job reservations. Even out of the 8 percent in the organized sector, the share of the public sector is 5.5 percent and that of the private sector is hardly 2.5 percent. Similar is the case of participants in higher education. In 2000-01, the total enrolment in all educational institutions was of the order of 192.6 million, out of which only 8.4 million were in colleges/university, i.e. 4.4 percent of total enrolment and 184.2 million (i.e. 95.6%) were in various stages in schools upto the higher secondary level (10+2). Obviously, reservations are aimed at this miniscule portion of the total student population which is able to reach higher education level. From this, it follows that our socio economic policies should strengthen the unorganised sector so as to enable it to graduate into the organized sector. Similarly, there is a need to strengthen primary and secondary education so that dropout rates at various levels decline and more and more students enrolled at the primary level complete their education and we are enabled to redeem our pledge given in the Constitution for providing primary education to all in the 6-14 age group. This will expand the base further and force the state to strengthen the secondary and higher education. The education pyramid which is of a tapering variety has to be broadened. This way lies hope for all.

19. SUMMING UP

In conclusion, it may be stated that reservations based on caste divide societies and if our ultimate goal is to develop a casteless and classless society, then it would be more desirable to develop models of social justice which take into account gender, caste, class, schooling, region (Rural/ Urban) and not limit reservations only on the basis of OBCs or non-OBCs. There may be political consensus on caste-based reservations due to the compulsions of vote-bank politics, but there is no social consensus. From the point of view of social justice treated in a wider sense, it would be necessary to develop a multi-dimensional model.

However, there is a caveat. All efforts at building superstructure without strengthening the base of school education will not succeed in the long-run. It is, therefore, necessary to expand school education as well as to work out measures by which the drop-out rates are reduced among the disadvantage classes. Merely administering 'pain killer' of reservations may alleviate the pain in the short-term, but will not cure the malady unless the roots are strengthened. For this purpose, the country has to launch a social movement.

References

Deshpande, Satish and Yadav, Yogendra, Redesigning Affirmative Action (*Economic and Political Weekly*, June 17, 2006).

Gupta, Dipankar, Milking Backwardness, *Hindustan Times*, August 28, 2006.

Indiresan, P.V., The Price of Reservation (*Business Line*, May 15, 2006).

_____, Quota debate and the Orwellian Doublespeak (*Business Line*, May 29, 2006).

Jayal, Niraja Gopal, Is Affirmative Action Limited to Quotas? (*Economic Times*, May 2, 2006).

National Sample Survey 55th Round, 1999-2000 and *61st Round*, 2004-05.

Prasad, Ravi Shankar (*Economic Times*, August 14, 2006).

Report of the First Backward Classes Commission (1955).

Report of the Second Backward Classes Commission (1980).

Thapar, Karan, the Mandal Muddle, (*Hindustan Times*, May 21, 2006).

Udit Raj, Some Merit to quotas (*Hindustan Times*, June 6, 2006).

Vaidyanathan, R., Reservations: Let down by weak data (*Business Line*, May 18, 2006).

_____, Empowering through Entrepreneurship (*Business Line*, May 1, 2006).

Yadav, Sharad, Fitting into Ninth Schedule, *Hindustan Times*, February 4, 2007.

Yechury, Sitaram, Brand Equity (*Hindustan Times*, May 18, 2006).

_____, Nothing to lose but chains (*Hindustan Times*, June 29, 2006).

Appendix

RESERVATIONS FOR ADMISSION IN HIGHER EDUCATION INSTITUTIONS

Those who have been Included

IITs, IIMs, the 20 Central Universities (like JNU and DU), NITs and Central-government Managed professional institutions like the six Central medical colleges, including AIIMS, National Law School, and Indian Institute of Mass Communication

Those who have been Excluded

1. Minority institutions.
2. Homi Bhabha National Institute, Mumbai, and its constituent units.
    - Bhabha Atomic Research Centre, Trombay.
    - Indira Gandhi Centre for Atomic Research, Kalpakkam.
    - Raja Ramanna Centre for Advanced Technology, Indore.
    - Institute of Plasma Research, Gandhinagar.
    - Variable Energy Cyclotron Centre, Kolkata.
    - Saha Institute of Nuclear Physics, Kolkata.
    - Institute of Physics, Bhubaneshwar.
    - Institute of Mathematical Sciences, Chennai.
    - Harish-Chandra Research Institute, Allahabad.
    - Tata Memorial Centre, Mumbai.
3. Tata Institute of Fundamental Research, Mumbai.
4. North-Eastern Institute of Health and Medical Science, Shillong.
5. National Brain Research Centre, Manesar, Gurgaon.
6. Jawaharlal Nehru Centre for Advanced Scientific Research, Bangalore.
7. Physical Research Laboratory, Ahmedabad.
8. Space Physics Laboratory, Thiruvananthapuram.
9. Indian Institute of Remote Sensing, Dehradun.

TABLE 1

Per 1000 Distribution of Persons Aged 7 and above by Level of Education, Separately by Sex and Social Group

Social group	*not literate*	*litereate*	*literate below primary*	*Primary*	*Middle*	*Secondary*	*Higher Secondary*	*Graduate & above*	*All*	*No of sample persons*
(1)	*(2)*	*(3)*	*(4)*	*(5)*	*(6)*	*(7)*	*(8)*	*(9)*	*(10)*	*(11)*
All India				**Rural**						
										Male
Scheduled Tribe	462	538	220	134	108	44	20	12	1000	22129
Scheduled Caste	412	588	227	144	124	56	25	13	1000	26695
Other Backward Class	322	678	227	157	157	78	37	21	1000	55653
Others	219	781	210	163	182	124	58	44	1000	55750
Not recorded	349	651	163	188	172	87	10	31	1000	277
All	**322**	**678**	**221**	**154**	**153**	**85**	**40**	**26**	**1000**	**16050**
										Female
Scheduled Tribe	699	301	139	78	56	18	7	2	1000	20866
Scheduled Caste	664	336	156	91	58	22	6	3	1000	24944
Other Backward Class	589	411	160	110	86	36	13	6	1000	52991
Others	433	567	186	146	126	68	27	14	1000	52040
Not recorded	615	385	196	78	105	3	2	1	1000	257
All	**566**	**434**	**165**	**114**	**90**	**41**	**15**	**8**	**1000**	**151098**
										Person
Scheduled Tribe	578	422	181	106	83	32	14	7	1000	42995
Scheduled Caste	534	466	192	119	92	39	16	8	1000	51639
Other Backward Class	452	548	194	134	123	58	25	14	1000	108644
Others	323	677	198	155	155	97	43	30	1000	107790
Not recorded	481	519	179	134	139	45	6	16	1000	534
All	**440**	**560**	**194**	**135**	**123**	**64**	**28**	**17**	**1000**	**311602**

All India — **Urban**

										Male
Scheduled Tribe	219	781	201	137	170	1[illegible]1	82	91	1000	6496
Scheduled Caste	240	760	214	174	171	1[illegible]2	57	41	1000	12399
Other Backward Class	165	835	181	168	195	1[illegible]4	76	71	1000	28384
Others	86	914	139	133	168	1[illegible]1	120	182	1000	54653
Not recorded	136	864	203	96	176	1[illegible]1	136	102	1000	193
All	**135**	**865**	**164**	**149**	**177**	**1[illegible]1**	**97**	**127**	**1000**	**102125**
										Female
Scheduled Tribe	388	612	176	127	135	[illegible]8	49	47	1000	6290
Scheduled Caste	443	557	175	139	131	[illegible]8	34	20	1000	11308
Other Backward Class	336	664	168	155	151	[illegible]1	53	37	1000	26340
Others	190	810	145	139	161	[illegible]5	93	127	1000	49248
Not recorded	343	657	170	78	118	[illegible]3	43	55	1000	173
All	**277**	**723**	**157**	**143**	**153**	**[illegible]7**	**71**	**82**	**1000**	**93359**
										Persons
Scheduled Tribe	300	700	189	133	153	[illegible]0	66	70	1000	12786
Scheduled Caste	338	662	195	157	152	[illegible]1	46	31	1000	23707
Other Backward Class	247	753	175	162	174	1[illegible]3	65	55	1000	54724
Others	135	865	142	136	165	1[illegible]9	107	156	1000	103901
Not recorded	236	764	187	87	148	1[illegible]2	91	79	1000	366
All	**202**	**798**	**161**	**147**	**165**	**1[illegible]5**	**85**	**105**	**1000**	**195484**

Source : NSS Report No. 473, *Literacy and Levels of Education In India, 1999-2000.*

TABLE 2
Percent Distribution of Household and Persons in NSS 55th Round by Social Group

Rural

State/U.T.	*ST*	*SC*	*OBC*	*Other*
(1)	*(2)*	*(3)*	*(4)*	*(5)*
Pondicherry	1.6	25.2	70.5	27.0
Tamil Nadu	1.4	31.6	63.0	4.0
Bihar	7.1	20.7	52.1	20.1
Kerala	1.9	10.9	51.2	35.9
Andhra Pradesh	7.7	22.7	47.7	21.9
Delhi	4.3	10.4	46.3	39.1
Uttar Pradesh	1.2	25.3	43.3	30.2
Madhya Pradesh	28.4	16.6	42.2	12.8
Sikkim	26.6	8.6	38.4	26.3
Karnataka	9.2	21.1	38.1	31.6
All India	**10.6**	**21.3**	**37.4**	**30.7**
Gujarat	20.7	13.4	29.9	36.0
Haryana	1.1	22.9	29.7	46.3
Orissa	26.4	21.1	29.3	23.2
Maharashtra	17.2	14.2	28.4	40.2
Tripura	8.3	23.3	24.8	43.7
Chandigarh	0.0	22.5	21.0	56.5
Assam	16.9	10.1	19.8	53.2
Manipur	44.9	6.2	19.2	29.7
Punjab	0.9	42.8	12.8	43.4
Jammu & Kashmir	0.8	12.7	12.6	73.9
Himachal Pradesh	3.1	22.0	11.4	63.5
Daman & Diu	42.2	6.3	10.0	41.5
Goa	2.2	4.0	7.2	86.7
West Bengal	5.8	28.6	6.4	59.1
Dadra & N. Haveli	82.6	2.6	5.5	9.4
A & N Islands	18.2	7.2	4.4	70.3
Nagaland	94.9	0.4	3.0	1.7
Arunachal Pradesh	74.8	1.0	2.9	22.2
Mizoram	95.3	0.4	1.2	3.0
Lakshadweep	97.7	0.0	0.5	1.9
Meghalaya	95.1	0.0	0.4	4.5

Note : States have been arranged in the descending order on the basis of Column (4).
Source : Derived from *NSS Report No. 473, Literacy and Levels of Education in India, 1999-2000.*

TABLE 3
Percent Distribution of Household and Persons in NSS 55th Round by Social Group

Urban

State/U.T.	*ST*	*SC*	*OBC*	*Other*
(1)	*(2)*	*(3)*	*(4)*	*(5)*
Pondicherry	1.7	12.7	73.5	12.1
Tamil Nadu	1.1	11.7	69.2	18.0
Manipur	5.7	0.6	57.9	35.8
Kerala	1.0	6.3	55.2	37.4
Bihar	6.4	12.3	47.2	34.1
Andhra Pradesh	2.9	14.3	39.3	43.6
Uttar Pradesh	1.1	14.9	34.8	49.2
Karnataka	5.6	11.1	32.7	50.6
Madhya Pradesh	10.5	13.3	32.4	43.7
All India	**3.9**	**14.6**	**31.4**	**50.2**
Orissa	11.1	15.4	28.8	44.0
Daman & Diu	7.1	6.7	28.1	58.0
Gujarat	4.4	11.9	25.4	58.3
Rajasthan	4.0	21.2	24.1	50.8
Sikkim	26.6	11.0	22.5	39.9
Haryana	1.5	19.7	19.8	59.0
Maharashtra	4.1	13.0	19.5	63.4
Tripura	6.1	21.2	15.5	57.1
Punjab	1.4	32.0	14.9	51.8
Delhi	1.5	16.9	14.5	67.1
Chandigarh	1.3	18.2	10.9	69.7
Assam	4.3	14.7	10.8	70.3
Himachal Pradesh	2.0	17.1	8.8	72.1
Dadra & N. Haveli	20.7	3.6.	8.3	67.4
West Bengal	1.5	19.9	5.2	73.4
Jammu & Kashmir	0.3	8.8	3.6	87.2
Arunachal Pradesh	44.3	4.9	2.1	48.6
Nagaland	84.5	5.6	1.9	8.0
Meghalaya	78.1	0.3	1.3	17.6
Goa	0.4	1.0	1.1	97.5
Lakshadweep	97.5	0.1	1.0	1.4
Mizoram	96.7	1.3	0.6	1.4
A & N Islands	8.2	0.7	0.5	90.6

Note : States have been arranged in the descending order on the basis of Column (4).
Source : Derived from *NSS Report No. 473, Literacy and Levels of Education in India, 1999-2000.*

TABLE 4

System of Reservations for Different Groups in Different Sectors

	Existing Status of Reservation Benefits in			
	Share in Population	*Lok/Vidhan Sabha*	*Central/State Govt. jobs*	*Higher Education*
(1)	*(2)*	*(3)*	*(4)*	*(5)*
Dalit/Scheduled Castes	16.2% (as per Census 2001)	Yes, in proportion to population (not applicabe to Rajya Sabha)	Yes, 15% at Centre, as per population in the states	Yes, 15% at Centre, as per population in the states
Adivasi/ Scheduled Tribes	8.2% (as per Census 2001)	Initially proposed for 10 years	Yes, 7.5% at Centre, as per population in the states	Yes, 7.5% at Centre, as per population in the states
Other Backward Classes	43% (Mandal Commission estimate was 52%)	No (some states grant it for Panchayat)	27% after Mandal I at the Centre (minus creamy layer); different status in different states	27% proposed by Central Government some states have had it

TABLE 5

Percent of Post-graduates and Professional Degree Holders by Caste/Community, Class and Gender : Data from the National Election Study, 2004

		All classes	Rich	Middle	Lower-Middle	Poor	Very Poor	N
(1)	(2)	(3)	(4)	(5)	(6)	(7)	(8)	(9)
All caste communities	All	2.5	8.1	6.8	1.6	0.8	0.6	26829
	Men	3.4	9.8	9.7	2.2	1.2	1.0	14345
	Women	1.4	5.8	3.9	0.8	0.4	0.1	12484
Hindu dwija upper caste	All	5.6	13.6	8.8	2.7	1.8	0.5	4148
	Men	7.4	17.8	10.3	3.9	2.7	1.0	2230
	Women	3.5	8.3	7.3	1.4	0.3	0.0	1918
Hindu and Sikh intermediary caste (non-dwija, non-OBC)	All	2.8	6.2	4.6	0.7	1.2	0.8	2521
	Men	3.5	7.3	5.8	1.2	0.9	1.7	1361
	Women	2.0	4.8	3.4	0.0	2.2	0.0	1160
OBC (Hindu and Sikh)	All	1.8	5.8	6.6	1.1	0.7	0.7	9505
	Men	2.7	6.2	10.1	1.6	1.3	1.3	5020
	Women	0.8	5.2	1.9	0.4	0.1	0,1	44811
SC (any religion)	All	1.4	4.2	8.0	1.6	0.5	0.4	4278
	Men	2.1	2.3	11.7	2.8	0.7	0.8	2287
	Women	0.6	5.0	2.5	0.2	0.2	0.1	1991
	All	0.9	1.9	6.1	1.4	0.6	0.4	2181

(*Contd.*)

TABLE 5 (Contd.)

(1)	(2)	(3)	(4)	(5)	(6)	(7)	(8)	(9)
ST (any religion)	Men	1.3	3.3	10.0	1.6	0.3	0.7	1185
	Women	0.5	0.0	1.8	1.1	0.5	0.2	996
	All	1.8	7.1	4.0	1.5	0.3	0.0	2963
Muslims	Men	2.5	10.1	6.0	1.2	0.5	0.0	1638
	Women	0.9	1.7	1.6	2.0	0.0	0.0	1327
	All	3.3	13.2	7.8	1.8	0.8	0.0	630
Christian 302	Men	3.0	(11.1)	5.7		3.3	1.5	0.0
	Women	3.7	15.0	9.5	0.0	0.0	0.0	328

Note : All figures are for percent of respondents belonging to a category who report having a Post-graduate or professional degree. Figures based on less than 50 cases have been put within parentheses. Class categories are based on a combination of self-reported data on income and observed data on possession of assets.

Source : National Election Study, 2004, CSDS Data Unit. Data is weighted by state population.

TABLE 6
Evidence on Social Profile in National Media

Castelcommunity group	*Share in Indias*	*Share in key media*
Twice born' Hindus (Brahmin, Kshatriya, Vaishya, others)	16%	85%
Intermediary Hindu castes (Jat, Reddy, Maratha, Patel, etc.)	8%	3%
Hindu OBC	34%	4%
Muslim	13%	4%
Christian	2%	3%
Sikhs	2%	1%
SC	16%	0%
ST	8%	0%

Note : Figures for population share are based on Census of India, 2001 and estimates generated by National Election Study, 2001 of CSDS. Share of key media personnel based on a study of social profile of top ten decision-makers in 37 organisations (315 decision-makers in all) by Anil Chamaria, Jitendra Kumar and Yogendra Yadav.

Index